PRINCIPLES OF INDIAN BANKING

PRINCIPLES OF INDIAN BANKING

By

DR. JASBIR SINGH
MA(Economics), MA(Rural Development),
MBA(IBM), M Phil, PhD
Associate Proffessor
Department of Business Administration
Maharaja Surajmal Institute, New Delhi
(Affiliated to GGSIP University)

DR. RUCHIKA GAHLOT
MBA(IB), PhD
Assistant Proffessor
Department of Business Administration
Maharaja Surajmal Institute, New Delhi
(Affiliated to GGSIP University)

TRIUNITY PRESS
(An Imprint of Laxmi Publications Pvt. Ltd.)
An ISO 9001:2015 Company
BENGALURU • CHENNAI • GUWAHATI • HYDERABAD
KOCHI • KOLKATA • LUCKNOW • RANCHI
NEW DELHI

PRINCIPLES OF INDIAN BANKING

Printed and bound in India
Typeset at Kalyani Computer Services, Delhi
First Edition : 2017, Second Edition : 2024
ISBN 978-93-85750-83-0

Branches

✆	Bengaluru	080-26 75 69 30
✆	Chennai	044-24 34 47 26
✆	Guwahati	0361-254 36 69
✆	Hyderabad	040-27 55 53 83
✆	Kochi	0484-405 13 03
✆	Kolkata	033-40 04 77 79
✆	Lucknow	0522-430 36 13
✆	Ranchi	0651-224 24 64

PUBLISHED IN INDIA BY

TRIUNITY PRESS
(An Imprint of Laxmi Publications Pvt. Ltd.)

An ISO 9001:2015 Company
113, GOLDEN HOUSE, GURUDWARA ROAD, DARYAGANJ,
NEW DELHI - 110002, INDIA
Telephone : 91-11-4353 2500, 4353 2501
www.laxmipublications.com
info@laxmipublications.com

C—00310/024/01
Printed at : Sagar Color Scan, Delhi

Preface

The banking system plays a very significant role in the economy of a country. Banking, the world over, has been changing at a spectacular pace. This change is due to multifarious factors like the need to be efficient in functions, the thirst for becoming finance superpowers rather than mere banks, the growing importance of private banking, the rise in the high net worth of individuals, etc. With the ongoing financial depression, the position of banks has become all the more important in the workings of the money market and hence the economy of a nation. The banking sector, which forms a portion of the financial sector, primarily works as a financial intermediary, generating money supply. From the different macroeconomic models, banks have been found to be a part of the supply side of the economy. However, over time, banks have transformed from merely money-generating organisations to multi-tasking entities.

This book is an attempt to provide an understanding of the banking sector to graduate students to make them ready as per the demands of the banking industry. It is comprehensive study material that integrates conceptual knowledge with business knowledge. This book covers various theories and functions of money, the evolution of the banking sector and its system, types of banks and their regulation, the Indian money market and capital market, Indian monetary policy and system, regulation and supervision of the banking system, the Banking Ombudsman Scheme, development of banking and financial institutions, and various developments in the banking sector. This book will enable students to equip themselves with all the basics of the banking sector before entering the corporate world.

We are thankful to publishers for their encouragement and cooperation in bringing out this edition.

We sincerely request comments and inputs from readers to improve the content of this book further in its future editions.

—Author

Syllabus

B.B.A. (B & I)

G.G.S. INDRAPRASTHA UNIVERSITY

B.B.A (B & I): 18105 Principles of Banking

L-4 T/P-0 Credits-4

Instructions to Paper Setters **Maximum Marks: 75**

- Question no. 1 should be compulsory and cover the entire syllabus. The question should have objective or short answer type questions. It should be of 15 marks.
- Every unit should have two questions. Students may be asked to attempt only 1 question from each unit. Each question should be of 15 marks.

Note: Students are expected to have elementary knowledge of the topics specified in the syllabus

Objective

The course aims to acquaint the student with a basic and elementary knowledge of the business and corporate laws.

Course Contents

Unit I **No. of Hrs: 14**

Money and Banking- Nature, Origin and Functions of Money, Evolution of Banking-Types of Banks, Systems of Banking- Mixed Branch, Unit, Group, and Chain.

Unit II **No. of Hrs: 14**

Reserve Bank of India- Establishment, organization, Functions, Methods of Credit Control, Clean Note Policy of RBI, RBI Policy on detection and impounding of Counterfeit Notes.

Unit III **No. of Hrs: 14**

Commercial Banking- Meaning & Functions, Deposits-Banker- Customer Relationship, KYC Guidelines, Credit- Principles of Lending, Different Methods of Charging.

Structure and Characteristics of Financial & Banking system in India; Indian Money Market; Indian Capital Market; Indian Monetary Policy & System.

Unit IV **No. of Hrs: 14**

Emerging Trends in Banking: Universal Banking, Venture Capital, Project Financing, Merchant Banking, Anti Money Laundering, Electronic Fund Transfer System (ECS, NEFT, RTGS, SIPS), MICR

Contents

Nature and Origin of Money

1

1.1 THE CONCEPT OF BARTER SYSTEM

Money is something that is generally accepted as a medium of exchange. It is one of mankind's most fundamental and drastic inventions. Before money came into existence, the barter system was used to exchange goods and services. Barter is a direct exchange. For example, corn may be exchanged for cloth, houses for horses and bananas for oranges and so on.

Barter is usually a bilateral trade of goods and services, but it may be multilateral and usually exists in parallel with monetary systems in most developed countries, though to a very limited extent. Barter system usually replaces money as the method of exchange in times of monetary crisis, when the currency may be either unstable (e.g., hyperinflation or deflationary situation) or simply unavailable for conducting trade and commerce. In ancient times, when money was not invented, trade as a whole was based on a barter system. This was possible only in a simple economy but after the development of the economy, the direct exchange of goods without the use of money was not possible without defects. In other words, it may be possible only in a closed economy which does not involve in inter-country trade.

A trade or barter exchange is a commercial organisation that provides a trading foundation and accounting program for its associates or customers. The participants engage in the exchange of goods and services with each other using internal Forex known as barter or business dollars. Contemporary barter system and business have progressed significantly to become an effective method of improving sales, preserving cash, going stock and making use of unwanted development potential for companies around the world. Businesses in barter generate business breaks that are placed into their account. The exchange is considered as an important part because they provide the record-keeping, brokering skills and per month claims to each participant. Business barter concentrates on bigger dealings, which are different from a conventional, store, focussed barter exchange. Business barter deals generally use press and promotion as power for their bigger dealings. It requires the utilization of a Forex tool referred to as 'trade-credit'. This trade-credit should not only be recognized and guaranteed but also held in high regard, equivalent to the value of advertising and promotion that would have been acquired if the 'client' had procured it independently.

1.1.1 Advantages of the Barter System

The barter system has certain advantages:

1. **Increase in Production:** It helps to increase the production of goods and services whose demand is very high in the market.
2. **Gain in the Exchange of Goods:** All people will gain from this system. All will get good things.
3. **Independent Work:** In this system, people work independently. Nobody interferes in these activities.
4. **Absence of Payment Risk:** In this system, people don't need to make payment reducing risk.
5. **Popular in Rural Areas:** This system is beneficial in rural areas as it suffers from a deficiency of money.
6. **Full Employment:** Full employment implies no question of over or under-production (or of unemployment or over-full employment). Under the barter system, goods are produced only to meet the needs of society.
7. **Useful in a Closed Economy:** It is helpful for a closed economy that doesn't involve inter-country trade.

1.1.2 Disadvantages of the Barter System

The following are the limitations of Barter system:

1. **Wants that Coincide:** Exchange can occur between two people only if each possesses the goods which the other wants and has a surplus of these goods, for example, if a weaver requires shoes and he has extra cloth to offer in exchange, he should not only find a cobbler who makes shoes but find such a cobbler who has excess of cloth and is willing to give shoes in exchange for clothes. In this case, it was very difficult to find such a person.
2. **Absence of Standard Value:** Under the barter system, there was no measure of the standard value of goods. Even if, two people meet who want to exchange goods but cannot find a satisfactory equilibrium price due to the standard value of goods, it will lead to loss to either person.
3. **Lack of a Value Store:** Wealth cannot be easily stored for future use in the form of commodities because they perish in the long run. But in the present monetary system, we can store our surplus products in terms of money. In the modern economy, the barter system cannot succeed. Money is indispensable for large scale production.

4. **Difficulty of Deferred Payments:** Deferred payment means payment of a debt in the future. The barter system does not provide a satisfactory unit in terms of deferred (future) payments. In an exchange economy, many contracts relate to future activities and future payments. Under a barter system, future payments are written in terms of specific goods. That was not possible to pay the same quantity of the same goods in the future. It creates a lot of problems like:
   - It may create a controversy regarding the quality of goods or services to be repaid in the future.
   - The two parties may be unable to agree on the specific good to be used for repayment.
   - Both parties run the risk that the goods to be repaid may increase or decrease in value over the period of contract.
5. **Problem of Transportation:** Another difficulty of barter system is that goods and services cannot be transported conveniently from one place to another. For example, an individual cannot take their house to a distant place to exchange them for other goods. With the use of money, such type of inconveniences of transportation is removed.
6. **Lack of Divisibility:** Another difficulty of barter system relates to the fact that all goods cannot be divided and subdivided. In the absence of a common medium of exchange, a problem arises, when a big indivisible commodity is to be exchanged for a smaller commodity. For example, if the price of a horse is equal to 10 shirts, then a person having one shirt, he cannot exchange it for the horse because it is not possible to divide the horse into small pieces without destroying its utility. Exchange can take place between two individuals only if each offers the products which the other wants, e.g., if a weaver needs footwear and he has a surplus towel to offer in exchange, he should not only discover a cobbler who makes footwear but also discover such cobbler who needs towel and is ready to give footwear in exchange for it. In this case, it was very difficult to discover such type of individual. It was challenging to split an investment without loss in its value. Barter needs a twice chance of wants. If an individual for insistence has whole grain and wants to exchange it with natural cotton, he has to discover an individual owning natural cotton and demanding whole grain. It was possible only when people resided in small areas and their wants were too restricted. Another great drawback of the barter system was the lack of divisibility.

   Now it is clear that the functions of money have removed those difficulties which were present in the barter system.

1.2 EVOLUTION OF MONEY

1.2.1 Invention of Money

The increase in difficulties and inconveniences of the barter system led to the – Invention of money. As society developed, the division of labour and specialisation increased and as a result, the volume of production and trade expanded. In such conditions, the barter system or direct exchange between various goods and services creates difficulties, such as the problem of double coincidence of wants, the problem of common measure of value, etc. To overcome these difficulties, money was invented. According to Crowther, "Money is one of the most fundamental of all inventions. Every branch of knowledge has its fundamental discovery. In mechanics, it is the wheel in science, fire in politics the vote. Similarly, in Economics, in the whole commercial side of man's social existence, money is the most essential invention on which all the rest are based."

Money was an invention in the sense that "it needed the conscious reasoning power of man to make the step from simple barter to money-accounting". Money was first used as a unit of account or as a numeric in terms of which all other things were to be measured and compared. The introduction of money as a unit of account was simple but a significant invention. It allowed the process of goods to be expressed in terms of a common unit of account; made the non-comparable goods comparable; and extended the scope of the division of labour and specialisation. But, even after the introduction of a common unit of account, trading was still a simple exchange of goods and services for goods and services. Prices were fixed in terms of money or one standard commodity (e.g., goat).

The only use of money as a unit or account did not remove all the difficulties of the barter system. This difficulty was removed when the money, the unit of account, also became a medium of exchange. The use of money as the medium of exchange saved time and effort made multilateral trade possible. Another important use of money is act as a store of value. With the invention of money, it is stored because money has the general purchasing power through which we can purchase anything at any time. In this way, the three basic functions, i.e., unit of account, medium of exchange and store of value, performed by a commodity (called money) together constitute the invention of money.

1.2.2 Development of Money

The origin of money is not known because of its non-availability or recorded information. It is deep-rooted in antiquity. No doubt, the evolution of money has been a secular process and shall continue to remain so, but the development of money in the present form can be historically traced as it has passed through different stages following the growth of human civilisation.

These stages are discussed below:

1. **Animal Money:** In primitive agricultural communities, domestic animals were used as money. Cattle were considered a common instrument of exchange. Different things were valued in terms of the number of cattle they could command, in exchange.
2. **Commodity Money:** In many countries, primitive money took the form of commodity money. Many commodities like bows, arrows, animal skins, shells, precious stones, rice, tea, etc., were used as money. The selection of a commodity to serve as money depends on the factors, like, the location or the community; climate or the region; cultural and economic development of the society, etc. Animal and commodity money had many serious disadvantages:
    - It lacks uniformity and standardization; all cows and goats were not identical.
    - Animals and commodities are an inefficient store of value; there was always a possibility of a loss of value over a period of time; moreover, the cost of storing animals and commodity money was very high.
    - Animals and commodities were not easily transferable because of portability issues.
    - The problem of indivisibility .
    - The supply of animals and commodities was not easily and quickly changed.
3. **Metallic Money:** With the growth of society from pastoral to the commercial stage, the composition of money also changed from animal money, commodity money to metallic money. Gold and silver were the metals mostly used for metallic money. Due to their scarcity, usefulness and attractiveness, gold and silver were used as natural money. The use of metals as money ultimately led to the development of the coinage system. Metallic money (uncoined metals and coins) overcame most of the difficulties of animal and commodity money. But it had its own disadvantages:
    - Quick transactions were not possible through coins.
    - On account of its weight, large quantities of coins were not easily portable.
    - Metallic money can be easily lost and stolen.
    - Short-weighing and adulteration problems made the transaction costs of uncoined metallic money higher. Every time the quantity and quality of the metal were to be tested.
4. **Paper Money:** Paper Money formed the next stage in the evolution of money. It was introduced in the 17th and 18th centuries and has now become the most popular form of money. Initially, due to the safety problem of carrying costlier metals, like gold and silver, from one place to another, the merchants used to carry paper receipts against metallic money. With the passage of time, the scarcity of

metals led the state authorities to introduce convertible paper currency; paper money was convertible into metals. In the later stages, however, paper money developed into flat money or inconvertible legal tender; in the present era paper money is non-convertible into metals.

Merits of Paper Money

- It is economical because the paper is much cheaper than any other metal.
- It economises the use of valuable metals, like gold and silver.
- There is no depreciation of metals in paper money.
- Paper money is convenient to carry from one place to another.
- It is easy to store in large amounts.
- It can be easily replaced.
- Changes in the supply of money can be easily made according to the requirements of the economy.

Demerits of Paper Money

There is always a danger of over-issue of currency notes because the changes in the money supply can be made according to government requirements. Over-issue of paper currency may be a result of the inflationary situation in the country.

- Paper money lacks public confidence because most paper money is not backed by metallic reserves.
- Paper money is less durable than metallic money.
- Paper currency is exclusively valid for transactions within the domestic economy and cannot be used for foreign exchange transactions.
- Since the supply of paper money is liable to quick changes, there is a lack of stability in its value.
- Fluctuations in the value of paper money generate an atmosphere of uncertainty in the economy which promotes speculative activities.
- Paper money has no intrinsic value of its own. Thus, when paper money is demonetised, its value falls to zero.

The merits of paper money are more than its demerits. In reality, all countries used paper money extensively. Its so-called demerits arise mainly due to ineffective management by the monetary authority. Proper and effective control of paper money is conducive to economic prosperity in the country.

5. **Credit Money:** Along with the paper money, credit money or bank money also emerged due to the development of banking institutions and their credit creation activities. Credit money (i.e., cheques issued against demand deposits) is not money; it only performs the functions of money. Credit money is, therefore, regarded as near-money.

- The credit money is becoming more and more popular because of the following advantages: Bank money is not as liable to loss or theft as other types of money.
- It can be transported very cheaply, no matter how large is the amount of payment and how great is the distance from payer to the payee,
- Cheques can be issued for precise amounts, eliminating the need for providing change or counting bills and coins.
- When endorsed by the payee, cheques serve as a convenient receipt for payment.

6. **Electronic Banking Stage:** Instead of using cash or cheques, people can make deposits and purchases simply by electronic signals like online, phone, ATM, credit and debit cards, smart card, etc. Electronic banking does not mean the death of money. It only means that the method of transferring money is changing. Electronic banking is only one step on a long path in the evolution of money and if history is any guide, it will not be the last step.

In short, during the long process of evolution, the character of money has undergone a drastic change. In modern times, coins, paper currency, and credit money are the popular forms of money and that used anyone everywhere. Animal and commodity money due to their drawbacks has been obsolete and is rarely in existence in the present world. But, in spite of the great progress of the monetary system in the present era, nowhere in the world has the present monetary system become perfect. It has been under evolution since ages; it is still evolving, and shall ever remain so. In other words, the evolution of money has been one secular process and shall continue to be so.

1.2.3 Classification of Money

Broadly speaking, three main types of money exist in the modern economy:

(*a*) Metallic money

(*b*) Paper money

(*c*) Credit money

Economists, however, further classify them into many other forms. Important classifications of money are explained below:

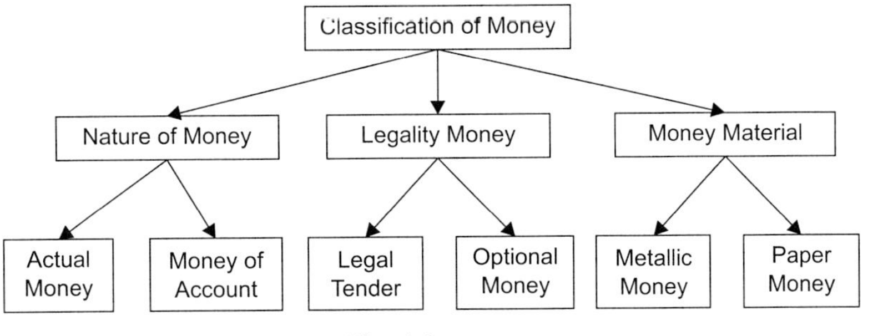

Fig. 1.1

On the basis of the **nature of money**:

(*i*) Actual Money: Money proper or actual money is the money that is in circulation in a country. It is the medium of exchange and a means of payment. In India, for example, the Rupee note and all coins are the actual money because different types of transactions and payments can be made through them. Actual Money is further classified into two types:

- *Commodity Money*: Commodity money is made of metal and its face value may or may not be equal to its intrinsic value. It serves not only as a medium of exchange but also as a store of value or purchasing power. Full-bodied money is money whose face value and internal value both are the same.
- *Representative Money*: The money that is in circulation and whose face value and internal value are different, is called representative money. It is money whose value is materially greater than the actual value. Paper currency' notes are an example of representative money. Representative money may be convertible or inconvertible. It is convertible if the issuing authority has the obligation to convert it into commodity money like gold or silver. It is inconvertible if the issuing authority has no obligation to convert it into commodity money.

(*ii*) Money of Account: Money of account is that in which accounts are maintained. The money of account is that in which debt and general purchasing power are expressed. The term 'money of account' refers to the unit of currency we use to set prices for goods and services, measure purchasing power, and quantify debts. Typically, the money of account is the same as the physical currency we use in everyday transactions.

On the basis of **legality of money**:

- **Legal Tender money:** Legal tender money is currency that is backed and enforced by law. No one can refuse to accept it as a means of payment. Legal tender money may be of two types: (*a*) limited legal tender and (*b*) unlimited legal tender. Limited legal tender money is accepted as legal tender only up to a certain limit. For example, in India, the small coins of 1, 2, 5, 10, 25, and 50 paise are legal tender and they can be accepted only up to a sum of ₹25. That means up to ₹25 a person cannot refuse a payment through these small coins and beyond ₹25 he is free to refuse these coins. Unlimited legal tender is the money that has to be accepted as a medium of payment up to an unlimited amount. For example, in India, all rupee coins and all currency note denominations are unlimited legal tender.
- **Optional Money:** Optional money is money that may or may not be accepted as a means of payment; it has no legal sanction. Different credit instruments, like, Cheques, Bank drafts, and so on are examples of optional money. No one can be forced to accept them.

On the basis of **money material**:

Metallic Money: Money made of metal is called metallic money. It refers to coins made of certain metals, e.g., gold, silver, copper, nickel, etc. A coin is a piece of metal of a specific size, shape, weight and fitness whose value is certified by the government. The minting of coins is the monopoly of the government. Metallic money is of two types:

- **Standard Money:** Any money whose face value (i.e., the exchange value of the coin as fixed by the issuing authority and embossed on it) is equal to its intrinsic value (i.e., the worth of the metallic content of money) is called standard money or full-bodied money. Full-bodied money requires two conditions:

  (*i*) Money can be shifted from monetary to non-monetary uses without any cost.

  (*ii*) The metal can be coined into money without limit and cost. Standard coins are generally made of gold and silver and the monetary systems using these standards are known as gold standard and silver standards. Main characteristics of standard money are given below:

  ✓ The face value of standard money is equal to its intrinsic value.

  ✓ There is free coinage of standard money and the mint is open to the public.

  ✓ Standard money is unlimited legal tender, i.e., all big payments can be made in terms of standard money to an unlimited extent.

  ✓ Standard money is the principle money of the country, i.e., it is the country's medium of exchange and money of account.

  ✓ The purchasing power of standard money may change in terms of other commodities.

  The standard money has various advantages and disadvantages. The main advantages of using standard money are:

  (*a*) Since standard money is full-bodied money, it inspires public confidence,

  (*b*) Standard money serves as a better means of storing purchasing power,

  (*c*) Standard money is easily acceptable in foreign payments.

  (*d*) There is no danger of over-issuing of standard money since the metals of which the standard money is made of short supply.

  The disadvantages of issuing standard money are:

  (*a*) Standard money is uneconomical because it is composed of the most valuable metals and thus involves national wastage.

  (*b*) The supply of standard money is not elastic, i.e., it cannot be increased according to the country's demand requirements.

1. **Token Money:** Money with a face value greater than its intrinsic value is called token money. Token coins are generally made of cheaper metals, like, copper, nickel, etc. and mostly represent lower denominations. For example in India 10, 20, 25, 50 paisa is called token money.

   The main characteristics of token money are:

   (*a*) The face value of token money is greater than its intrinsic value.

   (*b*) Token money is minted by the government and there is no free coinage.

   (*c*) Token money is limited legal tender, i.e., it can be used for making payments only to a limited extent.

   (*d*) Token money is a subsidiary of standard money and is generally used for making payments in smaller transactions.

   Merits of token money are:

   (*a*) It is more economical than the standard money because it does not use valuable metals,

   (*b*) The supply of token money is more elastic because it can be easily adjusted to its changing demand.

   Demerits of token money:

   (*a*) Token money inspires less public confidence because it is not full body money.

   (*b*) It is not a desirable means of storing purchasing power.

   (*c*) There is always a danger of over-issue of token money.

   (*d*) Token money is accepted only within the boundaries of a country, it cannot be used for international payments.

   (*e*) Token money is used only in smaller transactions.

2. **Paper Money**: The money made of paper is called paper money. It consists of currency notes issued by the government or the Central Bank of a country. In India, one rupee notes are issued by the Ministry of Finance of the Government of India and all other currency notes are issued by the Reserve Bank of India.

   Paper money is of four types:

   (*a*) Representative Paper Money (*b*) Convertible Paper Money

   (*c*) Inconvertible Paper Money and (*d*) Fiat Money

   (*a*) *Representative Paper Money:* Representative paper money is fully backed by gold and silver reserves. Under the monetary system of representative money, gold and silver equal to the value of paper currency issued are kept in the reserves by the central bank/ monetary authority. The main advantages of representative paper money are:

   (*i*) It economices the use of precious metals. These metals are kept in the reserves.

(*ii*) There is no fear of over-issue of representative money since paper money is fully backed by metallic reserves.

(*iii*) It inspires public confidence because the public can get the paper money converted into gold when needed.

Disadvantages of paper money:

(*i*) Since gold and silver reserves are to be maintained, these metals cannot be put to other uses.

(*ii*) Representative paper money system lacks elasticity because under this system money supply cannot be increased unless the equivalent amount of metallic reserves are kept.

(*iii*) It is not suitable for the poor nations which have a deficiency of gold and silver.

(*b*) *Convertible Paper Money:* The paper money which is convertible into standard coins and in gold and silver is called *convertible paper money*. It may be fully convertible or partially convertible.

The main characteristics of convertible paper money are:

(*i*) The individuals can convert their paper money into cash or gold/silver.

(*ii*) The paper money is backed by gold and silver reserves. But on the assumption that all the currency notes are not simultaneously presented by the public for encashment, the value of metallic reserves is less than the value of the notes issued.

(*iii*) The reserves comprise of (i) metallic portion containing gold, silver, and standard coins, and (ii) Fiduciary portion containing approved securities.

(*iv*) The public can get gold and silver for making foreign payments.

The main advantages of the convertible paper money are:

(*i*) It economies the use of valuable metals.

(*ii*) It is flexible because the money supply can be increased without maintaining cent percent metallic reserves.

(*iii*) It inspires public confidence because paper money is convertible into standard coins or gold/silver.

(*iv*) It facilitates foreign trade because paper money is converted into gold and silver to make foreign payments.

The disadvantages of the convertible paper money are:

(*i*) Since the paper money system doesn't hold cent percent backed by gold and silver, there is a fear of over-issue of money supply and the resultant there may be danger of inflation, (*ii*) The convertible paper money does not inspire as much public confidence as the representative paper money.

(*c*) *Inconvertible Paper Money:* The paper money which is not convertible into standard coins or valuable metals is called *inconvertible paper money.* Under the system of inconvertible paper money, the monetary authority maintains no metallic reserves against issuing the paper currency. It also gives no guarantee to convert the paper currency into gold and silver. The merits of inconvertible paper money are:

(*i*) Such a paper currency system economies can use valuable metals,

(*ii*) It is also elastic in the sense that the monetary authority can change the money supply according to the needs of the economy without keeping proportionate metallic reserves.

The inconvertible paper money also has the following demerits:

(*i*) The danger of paper currency is leading to inflation that always exists in this system.

(*ii*) It inspires less public confidence than a system of representative paper money.

(*d*) *Fiat Money:* Fiat money is only a variety of inconvertible paper money. Fiat money is backed neither by the metallic nor the fiduciary reserves. In other words, the monetary authority gives no guarantee to convert fiat money into valuable metals. According to Keynes, "Fiat money is Representative (or, Token) Money (i.e., something the intrinsic value of the material substance of which is divorced from its monetary face value) now generally made of paper except in the case of small denominations – which is created and issued by the State, but is not convertible by law into anything other than itself and has no fixed value in terms of an objective standard."

The main characteristics of fiat money are:

(*i*) It has significantly less intrinsic value than its face value.

(*ii*) It is not convertible into any valuable asset.

(*iii*) It is accepted in transactions at face value because it is unlimited legal tender.

Initially, fiat money was used during the period of war or emergency. But, now, it has become a common phenomenon in most of the countries of the world. Fiat money is partially largely useful for underdeveloped countries which generally lack financial resources for economic development. Fiat money removes this deficiency and promotes economic development by providing sufficient resources to the government. However, fiat money also has certain demerits:

(*i*) The danger of over-issue of fiat money (or inflation).

(*ii*) It lacks public confidence due to not backed by metallic reserves.

(*iii*) Foreign exchange rates are liable to wide fluctuations under fiat money because fiat money is not linked with other country's money through gold.

1.2.4 Money and Near-Money

Money

Money consists of (*a*) legal tender money, i.e., coins and currency notes, and (*b*) bank money (i.e., demand deposits). Money is the perfect liquid asset and can be directly used for making purchases of goods and services. But, the coins and currency are used only for small transactions. In the case of big transactions where large payments are involved (for example, purchasing a car or a house), bank money in the form of bank cheques or bank drafts are used. In modern monetary economy, people mostly use bank money in their transactions and thus bank money forms a major proportion of money supply. In this way, bank money is considered as liquid as the legal tender money.

Near-Money

There are other assets also which cannot be technically regarded as money, but are claimed to be money and they do perform some functions of money. Such assets are called *near-money*. Near-money refers to all those assets which possess many of the characteristics of money, have a high degree of liquidity, and can inexpensively be converted into money. Near-money cannot be directly used for making transactions. First, it will be converted into money proper before spending. In this way, near-money assets measure potential and not actual, transactions in near-money assets can be easily converted into money without loss of nominal value; capital gains and losses of near-money assets are very small. Near-money assets are highly liquid but are not as liquid 'money'. They are close substitutes for money, but not the perfect substitutes. Some examples of near-money are bills of exchange, bonds, debentures, shares, etc.

'Nearness' of near-money depends on the degree of liquidity of the near-money assets. Liquidity refers to the ease with which the asset can be converted into money (i.e., sold or discounted on short notice and with minimum cost). Greater the liquidity, the more near an asset is to money and vice versa. Overall liquidity of an economy depends upon the composition of the total stock of financial assets because different assets carry different degrees of liquidity. For instance (*a*) Coins, currency notes and demand deposits represent first-grade liquidity; (*b*) Time deposits, treasury bills, government securities, saving bonds, etc. represent second-grade liquidity; and (*c*) other assets, like deposits of building societies, financial claims of hire-purchase companies, etc. represent third-grade liquidity. It is not clear where the line of demarcation is to be drawn between money and near-money assets: it is always arbitrary. In other words, any asset which earns interest rate is not money and thus is near money. On the other hand, an asset which does not earn interest rate is called *money*.

Types of Near-Money

The following assets can be considered as near-money.

1. *Bill of Exchange*: Bill of exchange is a promise to pay a specified sum of money on a specified date, generally after 15 days to 364 days but most popular are months or 90 days. Bills of exchange may be treasury bills or commercial bills or financial bills:
   (*a*) Commercial bills are drawn in connection with commercial transactions.
   (*b*) Finance bills are drawn when a person lends money to another person,
   (*c*) Treasury bills are the finance bills through which the government raises short-period funds.
2. *Bond*: Bond is an instrument of borrowing for long periods. It promises to pay a fixed sum of money by way of interest annually for a specified number of years and to repay the capital sum borrowed at the end of the period. This method of borrowing is adopted by the government and the industrial units. Bonds issued by the firms are known as debentures. Bonds issued by the government without a maturity date but with interest payable for the indefinite period are called irredeemable bonds or consoles or perpetuities.
3. *Equity Shares*: Equity shares offer their owners a claim to a share in the profits of the firm declared as dividend. They are marketable in the stock exchange. Bonds and debentures also are transacted in the stock exchange, but the bills of exchange operate in the money market.
4. *Other Near-Money Assets*: Besides bills of exchange, bonds, equity shares, there are a large number of financial assets that can be considered as near-money. They are time deposits and saving deposits with commercial banks and other banks; bankers' acceptances; cash surrender values of life insurance policies; re-purchasable shares in savings and loan associations; deposits of building societies; travelers' cheques; postal saving deposits; savings in units of Unit Trust; etc.

Significance of Near-Money

Following are the main significance of near-money:

1. *Broader Definition of Money*: The existence of near-money has broadened the definition of money. In the liquidity approach, the definition of money includes: (*a*) legal tender money (*b*) bank money and (*c*) near-money, i.e., all those financial assets which can be easily and with minimum cost converted into money proper within a short period of time.
2. *Increase in Velocity of Money*: Near-money influences the velocity of money. A person's ability to spend does not depend only on the amount of money that he has with him and he holds in the bank (i.e., legal money and bank money), but also on his ability to raise additional funds by selling his near-money assets. Thus, the existence of near-money increases the velocity of money (V) and hence

aggregate demand (MV) in the economy by activating idle demand deposits and currency.

3. *Policy Implications*: Near-money has important policy implications for the monetary authorities. The prevalence of near-money assets significantly increases the overall level of liquidity and hence the level of aggregate expenditure. The monetary authority which aims at influencing the level of aggregate expenditure by controlling the money supply alone will fail to achieve its objective. In other words, it must influence not only the money supply alone but the overall level of liquidity. Since the central bank does not have much control over the-rending activities of non-bank financial institutions, the growth of near-money assets may create problems in the effective implementation of the monetary' policy.

Similarities between Money and Near-Money

There are some similarities between money and near-money:

(*i*) *Both money and near-money are claims.* Coins and currency are a claim over the government and the central bank. Bank money is a claim over the bank in which the deposits are held. Near-money assets are claims over their respective parties or institutions. For example, a government bond is a claim over the government which has issued it; a bill of exchange is a claim on the party which has agreed to pay the amount mentioned in the bill.

(*ii*) *Money is not qualitatively different from near-money.* Liquidity is the common attribute of both money and near-money. They differ only in terms of the degree of liquidity.

(*iii*) *Both money and near-money act as a store of value.* But, near-money assets are preferred because they yield income along with being a store of value.

Distinction between Money and Near-Money

Near-money can be distinguished from Money on the following grounds:

1. *Definition*: Money consists of coins, currency notes, and demand deposits of the banks. But Near-money includes financial assets, like time-deposits, bills of exchange, bond, shares, etc.
2. *Liquidity*: Money possesses 100% liquidity; i.e., it is perfectly liquid or can be readily accepted as a means of payment. Near-money lacks 100 percent liquidity, i.e., it involves time or cost for its conversion into money.
3. *Function*: Money serves as a unit of account or a common measure of value and all prices are expressed in terms of money. Near-money does not perform such functions faster; its own value is expressed in terms of money.
4. *Use in Transactions*: Money is directly used for making transactions. Near-money, on the other hand, is an indirect medium of exchange; it has to be first converted into ready money and then used for transactions.
5. *Income-Yielding Quality*: Money is not an income-yielding asset. On the contrary, near-money assets are income yielding assets.

1.2.5 Qualities of Good Money Material

To make able to perform the functions of money well, the money material may possess the following qualities:

1. *General Acceptability*: The material of which money is made should be acceptable to all people without any hesitation and without any force. In this connection, gold and silver are considered good money material because they are acceptable to the general public.
2. *Portability*: Money should be easily carried or transferred from one place to another. In other words, the money material must have easy to carry.
3. *Durability*: Money material must survive for a long time without losing its value. It should durable for long life.
4. *Divisibility*: Money material must be easily sub-divided into smaller units of the commodities. For example, a cow cannot function as good money because a cow cannot be divided into parts without losing its value; and a fraction of cow is quite different entity than a whole cow.
5. *Homogeneity*: Money should be homogeneous. It's all units that should be identical and they should be equal in quality and quantity.
6. *Recognisability*: Money should be easily recognized. If it is not easily recognizable, it would be difficult for the individuals to determine whether they are dealing with money or in some other inferior asset.
7. *Stability*: The value of money should remain stable and should not change for a long period of time. If the value of money is not stable, it will not be able to function as a measure of money, as a store of value and as a standard of deferred payment.
8. *Malleability*: The money material should be capable to melt and put it in different forms as Gold, silver, copper, etc.

1.3 MONETARY ECONOMY

Monetary economy refers to the economic system in which money is used as a medium of exchange. In other words, the value of all goods and services can measure in terms of money. It is a monetised economy in which goods are exchanged indirectly through money, money purchases goods, and goods purchase money. The monetary economy is the opposite of the barter economy. In the barter economy, no money is employed and the exchange takes place directly between goods to goods. In short, the use of money converts a barter economy into a monetary economy.

1.3.1 Features of Monetary Economy

A monetary economy, as distinguished from a barter economy has the following characteristics:

1. *Use of Money*: In the barter economy no money exists and a monetary economy employees money to perform the following function:
   (*a*) Money is generally accepted as a medium of exchange, without any force.
   (*b*) All payments are made in terms of money,
   (*c*) Money serves as a unit of account, a store of value, or a measure of value,
   (*d*) Money functions as a standard of deferred payments,
   (*e*) Money facilitates the transfer of value from one place to another place.
2. *Money as an Asset*: In a monetary economy, individuals can use money as an asset. Like other assets, wealth can be stored in the form of money. In other words, it is a claim against all goods and services which individual desires to have. In a Barter economy, wealth is stored only in the form of physical goods, which is not so easy to store.
3. *Greater Liquidity*: Monetary economy has greater liquidity than the barter economy. Money is the most liquid form of asset. It linked between the present and the future in any monetary economy. But such a facility is absent in a barter economy.
4. *Existence of Financial Institutions*: In the barter system there is no existence of the financial institutions, while various financial institutions, such as a central bank, commercial banks, and other financial institutions exist in a monetary economy. These institutions deal with a variety of non-cash financial assets or near-money assets such as bills of exchange, bonds, shares, etc. There exists a money market that dealing in short-term credit and a capital market which deals in long-term credit. Thus, in a monetary economy, besides money (i.e., currency and coins), a number of near-money assets are also created and widely used.
5. *Efficient Exchange System*: As compared to the barter system, exchange activities are performed more efficiently and more conveniently in a monetary economy where the money is used as a medium of exchange. All the difficulties and inconveniences of the barter system, such as the problem of double coincidence of wants, the problem of divisibility, the problem of storing wealth, the problem of common measure, the problem of deferred payments, the problem of transportation, etc., are eliminated in a monetary economy.
6. *Price Mechanism*: As against the barter system, price mechanism operates in a monetary economy due to the use of money. In price mechanism, the market forces as like demand and supply determents the prices. Thus, the use of money is essential for the full and effective working of the price mechanism. But there was an absence of price mechanism in a barter system.
7. *Interaction between Monetary and Real Factors*: As opposed to the barter economy, there is a circular flow of money, corresponding to the circular flow of real transactions in a monetary economy. In the circular flow of real transactions,

the flow of factor services will from households to the firms and goods and services flow will from firms to households.

8. *Stage of Economic Development*: Monetary economy is a relatively advanced economy as compared to the barter economy. In the barter economy, economic activities (product, money, and trade) will be at a low and subsistence level and there will be economic backwardness. But in a monetary economy division of labour takes place, technology developed, production increases, and trade expands and there is all-round economic development.

   In short, money plays an important and dynamic role in a monetary economy. It acts as a great wheel of circulation and a big instrument of exchange. The use of money makes it possible to carry specialization to its fullest extent, thereby, resulting in economic progress. The basic difference between a monetary and a barter economy is the use and non-use of money.

REVIEW QUESTIONS

1. What is barter exchange? How does it help in case of monetary crisis?
2. What are limitations of a barter system in terms of modern business transactions? How do these impact the efficiency of trade and what solutions have been developed to address these challenges?
3. Trace the historical development of money from barter and commodity money to modern fiat currency system. Discuss the factors that led to the evolution of money. How has the evolution of money impacted the contemporary financial systems?
4. Explain the functions of Central Banks in modern economy and how does this impact the economic stability?
5. What is price mechanism?

Functions of Money (Demand for Money)

2

2.1 INTRODUCTION

The demand for money occurs from two significant roles of money. The prime factor is that money performs as a medium of exchange and the next it is a store of value. Therefore, individuals and businesses wish to keep money in a portion of cash and in the form of assets. There are two outlooks on this matter. The first is the scale outlook which is associated to the contact of the earnings or affluence level upon the demand for money. The demand for money is straight associated to the earnings level. The higher the earnings level, there will be higher demand for money. The second is the substitution outlook which is associated to relative attractiveness of assets that can be substituted for money.

In the early stages of civilization, different people used different things as money. Cattle, tobacco, shells, wheat, tea, salt, knives, leather, animals such as sheep, horses and oxen, and metals like iron, lead, tin, and copper have been used as money. Gradually, precious metals such as gold and silver replaced other metals such as iron, copper, and bronze as money. Now paper is used as money. Almost all countries in the world today have paper money. We may describe one more form of money; that is, bank deposits that goes from person to person by means of cheques.

Money is one of the most fundamental inventions of mankind. Every branch of knowledge has its fundamental discovery. In mechanics, it is the wheel; in science fire; in politics the vote. Similarly, in economics, in the whole commercial side of man's social existence, money is the essential invention on which all the rest is based. Money is indispensable in an economy, whether it is capitalistic or socialistic. Price mechanism plays a vital role in capitalism. Production, distribution, and consumption are influenced to a great extent by prices, and prices are measured in money. Even a socialist economy, where the price system does not play so important a role as under capitalism, cannot do without money. For a while, the socialists talked of ending money, i.e., abolishing money itself, because they considered money as an invention of the capitalists to suppress the working class. But later on they found that even under a system of planning, economic accounting would be impossible without the help of money.

2.1.1 Factors Influencing Currency Money

The monetary authority while determining the supply of currency and coins must be guided by the general requirement of the economy. The currency component of the money supply, i.e., coins and notes is influenced by a number of factors as discussed below:

(i) **Volume of Transactions:** The supply of currency must vary in accordance with the changes in the physical volume of trade and transactions of the economy. If the issue of the currency is more than what is required, it creates inflationary pressures. On the other hand, if the money supply is less than the requirements, it leads to deflationary trends.

(ii) **Nature of Trade:** the nature of trade, whether wholesale or retail, determines the proportion of currency of different denominations. For the wholesale trade, the notes of higher denominations are required while the retail trade requires larger proportion of notes and coins of lower denominations.

(iii) **Methods of Payment:** The method of payment being used in the economy also determines the currency component of the money supply. If most of the payments are made in cash, greater proportion of currency to money supply is needed. If the payments are generally made through cheques, the proportion of currency to money supply will be lowered.

(iv) **The Price Level:** Price level also affects the requirements of currency considerably. Higher the price level, larger the amount of currency required and lower the price level, smaller the amount of currency required to carry out the given volume of transactions.

(v) **Banking Habits:** If the public has confidence in the bank money and has banking habits, the currency requirements will be less. But if the people have less banking habits, the transactions will be conducted with currency and more currency is required.

(vi) **Distribution of Income:** Distribution of income also influences the currency requirements. If the distribution of income is in favour of the rich, greater proportion of currency of higher denominations is required. On the other hand, if the distribution is in favour of the poor, a larger proportion of currency should be low denominations.

(vii) **Bank Money:** The demand deposits held by the public in commercial banks also constitute the total money supply of the economy. The demand deposits are transferable by cheque for the settlement of debts. The creation of bank money depends upon the credit creation activities of the banks. Credit creation is based on the volume of cash, i.e., the high-powered money, held by the banks. The money created by the banks is known as secondary money. Thus, the total money supply in an economy is composed of (*a*) the primary or high-powered money and (*b*) the secondary or bank money.

The relative proportions of the two constituents of money supply, i.e., currency money and bank money depend upon the degree of monetisation of the economy, the development of the banking system and the banking habits of the people. In the economically advanced/ developed countries chequable demand deposits held the major proportion of the total money supply. In such countries over 90 percent of the payments are made through cheques.

(*viii*) Other Factors: Other factors, like the volume of demand deposits with the banks, the taxation policy of the government, the extent of public loans, the volume of deficit financing, etc., also influence the amount of currency required in the economy significantly.

2.2 FUNCTIONS OF MONEY ACCORDING TO CLASSICAL APPROACH

2.2.1 The Classical Approach

The classical economists did not unambiguously devise demand for money thesis but their outlooks are intrinsic in the volume of thesis of money. They highlighted the transactions demand for money of exchange and smooth the progress of the exchange of goods and services. In Fisher's Equation of Exchange,

$$MV = PT$$

where M is the total supply of money, V is the velocity of money, P is the general price level and T is the total transaction (aggregate amount) of goods and services which is exchanged for money.

The right hand side of this equation (PT) represents the demand for money which actually based on the value of the transactions. MV represents the supply of money which is specified and in symmetrical parities the demand for money. Thus the equation becomes

$$MV = PT$$

This transaction demand for money, in turn is ascertained by the level of full employment earnings. This is due to the classical economists that assumed in Say's Law whereby supply creates its own demand, presuming the full employment level of earnings. Thus, the demand for money in Fisher's approach is invariable proportion of the level of transactions which in turn abides an invariable association to the level of national earnings. Moreover, the demand for money is connected to the quantity of business going on in a fiscal system at any point of time. Therefore, its underlying hypothesis is that people keep money to buy goods.

However, people also keep money for other causes such as to earn interest and to provide against unanticipated proceedings. It is therefore, not feasible to say that V will remain constant where, M is variable. The most significant thing about money in Fisher's equation is shiftable. However, it does not describe fully, why people possess money. It does not elucidate whether to add as money such items as time deposits or savings deposits that are not right away accessible to pay debts without first being rehabilitated into currency.

Cambridge Demand Equation for money is as follows:

$$M_d = kPY$$

Where M_d is the demand for money which should parity the supply of money ($M_d = M_s$) in symmetry in the fiscal system. k is the proportion of the actual money earnings (PY) which people wish to keep in cash and demand deposits or the ratio of money stock to earnings, P is the generalprice level and Y is the aggregate actual earnings. This equation tells us that other things remaining the same demand for money in normal condition depends on the supply of money.

Functions of Money

All the difficulties of barter were overcome with the introduction of money. Crowther had defined money as "anything that is generally acceptable as a means of exchange (i.e., as a means of settling debts) and that at the same time acts as a measure and as a store of value." An important point about this definition is that it regards anything that is generally acceptable as money. Thus, money includes coins, currency notes, cheques, Bills of Exchange and so on. It is not always easy to define money. That is why Prof. Walker has said that money is that which money does. By this, he refers to the functions of money. Money performs many functions in a modern economy. The most important functions are given in the form of a couplet quoted below. "Money is a matter of functions four a medium, a measure, a standard, a store."

Thus, money is a medium of exchange, a measure of value, a store of value, and a standard of deferred payments.

1. **Medium of Exchange:** The most important function of money is that it acts as a medium of exchange. Money is accepted freely in exchange for all other goods. Barter system is very inconvenient. So the introduction of money has got over the difficulty of barter.
2. **Measure of Value:** Money acts as a common measure of value. It is a unit of account and a standard of measurement. Whenever, we buy a good in the market, we pay a price for it in money. Price is nothing but value expressed in terms of money. So we can measure the value of a good by the money we pay for it. Just as we use yards and meters for measuring length, and pounds for measuring weights, we use money for measuring the value of goods. It makes economic calculations easy.
3. **Store of Value:** A man who wants to store his wealth in some convenient form will find money admirably suitable for the purpose. It acts as a store of value. Suppose the wealth of a man consists of a thousand cattle. He cannot preserve his wealth in the form of cattle. But if there is money, he can sell his cattle, get money for that and can store his wealth in the form of money.

4. **Standard of Deferred Payments:** Money is used as a standard for future (deferred) payments. It forms the basis for credit transactions. Business in modern times is based on credit to a large extent. This is facilitated by the existence of money. In credit, since payment is made at a future date, there must be some medium which will have as far as possible the same exchange power in the future as at present. If credit transactions were to be carried on the basis of commodities, there would be a lot of difficulties and it will affect trade.
5. **Unit of Account.** Money also functions as a unit of account, providing a common measure of the value of goods and services being exchanged. Knowing the value or price of a good, in terms of money, enables both the supplier and the purchaser of the good to make decisions about how much of the good to supply and how much of the good to purchase.

2.2.2 The Keynesian Approach

The modern concept of demand for money is associated with the Keynesian analysis of the demand for money. In his book "General Theory of Employment, Interest and Money (1936)", written by J.M. Keynes expounded his theory of demand for money.

Essentially, Keynes' theory of demand for money is an extension of the Cambridge cash-balances approach and stresses the asset role (i.e., the store of value function) of money. Keynes, demand for money does not mean the actual money balances held by the people, but what amount of money balances they want to hold. Keynes states that the demand for money means demand of money to hold the cash balances. Money is not just meant for spending. It can be held as a form of wealth or asset which commands in other forms of wealth in exchange, for all the time.

Thus, money being the most liquid asset, can serve as an efficient store of value; so it is demanded for its own sake. In this sense, the demand for money is the inverse of the velocity of circulation. In short, the Keynesian approach to the demand for money stresses the public's need for cash or money balances as a store of value at a particular point of time.

Keynes distinguished three such motives which induce people to hold money. These are:

(1) The Transactions Motive;

(2) The Precautionary Motive, and

(3) The Speculative Motive.

Corresponding to these motives, thus, Keynesian separated the demand for money into three parts: (*i*) the transactions demand, (*ii*) the precautionary demand, and (*iii*) the speculative demand for money. He further holds that, the total demand for money implies total cash balances. Analytically, total cash balances may be classified into two parts:

(A) Active Cash Balances; and (B) Idle Cash Balances.

A. Active Cash Balances

Active cash balances relate to the demand for money held under transactions and precautionary motives. In other words, transactions demand for money and precautionary demand for money together constitute active cash balances held by the people.

(*i*) Demand of Money for Transactions Motive ($L_t = f(Y)$):

Money being a medium of exchange, the primary demand for money balances arises directly out of its use for carrying on ordinary trade and business affairs of the economy. People have to do daily transaction to fulfil their requirement. Demand for transaction motive is the function of income. If there is high level of income in any economy there will be high demand of money for transaction motive. The transactions-prompted demand for money arises on account of the lack of synchronisation between receipts and payments. Individuals, in general, do not receive money income as frequently as they make payments. Thus, when income is received at discrete intervals of time, but is paid out more or less continuously against the exchange of goods and services, it is inevitable that people should need a certain stock of money all the time in order to carry out their transactions.

(*ii*) Demand of Money for Precautionary Motive ($L_p = f(Y)$):

Our future is totally uncertain; to remove the uncertainty people held some money. This demand of money called the precautionary demand for money. It is the function of money. In other words it depends on the income level of any economy. High level of income implies high demand of money for precautionary motive. Apart from transactions purposes, people generally desire to hold some additional money balances against unforeseen contingencies. Thus, the second reason for holding money balances is the precautionary motive. The money balances which people hold under the precautionary motive will be devoted to fulfilling the function of a store of value. The precautionary demand for money depends largely on the uncertainty of future receipts and expenditures. This demand is very sensitive to the anticipation of the level of income.

Naturally the precautionary demand for money varies with the type of emergency envisaged. The increased desire for liquidity, related to the precautionary motive, is described by Keynes as "the desire for security as to the future cash equivalent of a certain proportion of total resources." Thus, the precautionary demand for money is income-determined and is relatively stable. Obviously, the larger the income of the individual, the larger the cash balance set aside for future contingencies.

Moreover, the estimate of future contingencies is normal under normal circumstances, which do not fluctuate suddenly. Thus, the precautionary demand will be relatively stable. Though money is held under the precautionary demand as a store of value, it is not affected by the interest rates.

Therefore, the precautionary demand for money is also interest-inelastic, and is income-determined, but, by and large, it changes in response to the changes of uncertainties. In symbolic terms, by denoting the precautionary demand for money as Lp, we can represent the money- demand function as follows:

$$L_p = f(Y)$$

In practice, however, it is difficult to bifurcating the transactions demand and the precautionary demand for money. And, it must be remembered that both are income-determined. The combined sum of money balances, held under the transactions and precautionary motives, is however, and referred to as "active balances" by Keynes. In symbolic terms, the demand for active balances may be stated as:

$$L_1 = L_t + L_p.$$

Since $L_t = f(Y)$, and $L_p = f(Y)$, it follows that $L_1 = f(Y)$, it is to say that the demand for active balances is a function of income.

Factor affecting the Demand of Money for Transactions Motive:

Keynesian defines transactions motive for holding money as "the need of cash for the current transactions of personal and business expenditure." Thus, both households and firms hold money balances under the transactions motive. Their respective transactions motives may be referred to as income motive and business motive. Following are the factors which affect demand of money for transaction motive:

1. National Income: This refers to the transaction motive of the households, i.e., consumers' class. Consumers hold money balances to facilitate their day-to-day purchases of consumption goods. By keeping cash-balances, they tend to bridge the gap of time interval between receipt of incomes and its disbursement. The consumer's/individual's demand for money, thus, depends upon:

(*a*) **The level of income:** Usually, the amount of consumption oriented transactions increases with the rise in an individual's income. Thus, a rich man tends to hold more money balances for transactions purposes than a poor man does.

(*b*) **The price level:** With the rising prices, more money is required to buy a given quantity of goods. During inflation, thus, the consumers' transactions demand for money tends to rise, corresponding to the rising price level and vice versa.

(*c*) **The spending habits:** People's tendency to spend on consumption depends on their habits. A spendthrift obviously needs more transactions demand for money than a saver does.

(*d*) **The time-interval:** The time gap involved between the receipts of successive income flows and the corresponding expenditure is very important in determining an individual's transactions demand for money. The longer the time-interval involved, the larger will be the money balances required to be held for transactions purposes and vice versa. In other words, the transactions demand for money tends to be high when there is lesser frequency of income receipts over a period of time, and it will tend to be low in case of more frequent income receipts.

Assuming, given the habit of spending, the price level, and the length of time interval between the flow of incomes and outlays, the consumer's/individual's transactions demand for money is an increasing function of his level of income. It is to say that money for transactions motive rises with the increase in income and vice versa.

2. Business Activity: This refers to the transactions motive of the entrepreneur class or business community. Businessmen require money balances in order to meet business expenses like payment for new materials and transport, payment of wages and salaries, and allied current expenditure. Thus, money held by producers for these purposes is said to be held to satisfy the business motive. Money balances held under this motive will depend on the turnover of the firm. The larger the turnover, the larger will be the demand for money. It follows, therefore, that the amount of money balances held under the transactions motive will depend: (i) on the time and size of firms, incomes, and (ii) on the turnover of business. As income rises and the business becomes more prosperous, the amount of money demanded for the transactions motive will rise and vice versa.

B. Idle Cash Balances (The Speculative Demand for Money)

Keynesian theory pointed out that a section of people in the community hold cash balances for speculative purposes. This demand for money held under the speculative motive is referred to as the demand for "idle balances". The speculative motive for holding cash balances arises from uncertainty about the future rates of interest. More precisely, the speculative demand for money represents the demand for cash for being invested rapidly, as and when attractive opportunities for monetary investments appear.

The speculative motive, in fact, confines itself to the store of value as a property of money. Money held under the speculative motive constitutes a store of value, a liquid asset, which the holder intends to use for gambling or to make a speculative gain, e.g., investment in securities for profit motive. According to Keynes theory, people make capital gains by speculating in securities or bonds hoping to gain from knowing better than others in the market what the future holds in store for them. Thus, the speculative motive concerns an increase in the demand for money balances as a means to realising a gain, possibly, in anticipation of likely changes in the value of bonds (a form of security asset), but also, most generally, in expected changes in the value of a variety of assets.

(Demand of money for speculative motive ($L_s = f(r)$)):

Speculation is a situation of business when businessmen want to maximise their profit. In other words, when businessmen make predications regarding future prices and he thinks that prices will be fall or rise then he take the decision regarding to investment. So, he has to sacrifice some amount that he can earn as an interest. This demand depends on the rate of interest in the market. There is inverse relationship between rate of interest and demand of money for speculative motive. If there is high rate of interest there will be low demand for speculative motive and vice versa. The desire to keep extra money in case an unforeseen situation requires a capital outlay. For example, one may wish to save extra money to pay for medical bills in case of an accident. According to John Maynard Keynes, people keep savings accounts, as well as some stocks and commodities, with a precautionary motive in order to cover unexpected events.

3. Neutrality of Money: Money is said to be neutral if changes in the stock of money change only absolute prices and leave relative prices unaltered. On the contrary, money is non-neutral when changes in the stock of money influence relative prices. In other words, when money supply changes affect only monetary phenomenon and do not at all affect real phenomena, money is neutral. Neutrality of money means that changes in money stock has no influence on the level of real income, the real rate of interest, the rate of capital formation, and the volume of employment. The only influence of a change in the money stock is to alter the general level of prices. The policy of maintaining neutrality of money is called the policy of neutrality of money. This policy seeks to do away with the disturbing effects of changes in the quantity of money on important economic variables like income, output, employment and prices. According to this policy, money supply should be controlled in such a way that money should be neutral in its effects. The notion of neutrality of money has been viewed differently by different economists. Broadly, there are three different views as presented by the classical economists, the keynesians and the monetarists.

Advantages of Demand Theory of Money

Following are the advantages of Demand theory:

Lowered Nominal Interest Rates: Keynesian theory advocates lowering the nominal interest rate helpful to increase investment. Commercial banks pay the nominal interest rates when they borrowing from the central bank. When the rate is lowered, commercial banks borrow more money to lend to investors. Likewise, investors are more willing to borrow from commercial banks when the cost of investment, represented by the interest rate, is lowered. Investors use the borrowed funds to start new businesses, expand existing businesses or finance personal spending. It is believed that the resulting spending by borrowers directly contributes to the renewed growth of the economy.

Improved Infrastructure: Government spending on infrastructure is a hallmark of demand-side of economic policies. Infrastructure improvements provide to the nation with updated bridges, expanded highways and repaired roads. During the Great Depression of the 1930s, government spending on infrastructure provided new public works, such as Hoover Dam. Improved and expanded infrastructure paves the way for new businesses and expansion of existing business for the anticipated economic rebound.

Disadvantages of Demand Theory of Money

Following are the disadvantages of Demand theory of Money:

1. Inflation: Inflation is the leading disadvantage of demand-side economics. The demand-side perspective argues that the market economy, left to its own devices, will not ensure sufficient adequate demand, which means that society will not utilize its full production capacity. The demand-side, or Keynesian, remedy is for government to ensure sufficient adequate demand and full employment through fiscal policy. Opponents of the Keynesian approach, including many conservative economists, have argued that higher government spending provides excessive stimulus to the economy, raising prices for consumers and businesses. These forces central banks, such as the Federal Reserve, to boost interest rates, are making it more difficult for consumers to obtain credit for large purchases, as well as hampering the ability of companies to borrow money. This is known as the "crowding out effect," when increased government spending hampers private investment by causing interest rates to rise.

2. Budget Deficits: During a recession or other economic slowdown, output declines as a result of reduced economics activity. Higher government spending to compensate for the decline in aggregate demand is generally financed by borrowing, which increases government deficits and raises the national debt. As government debt grows, an increasing share of the government budget must be allocated to interest payments on the debt, leaving less funding for more productive government activities such as education and infrastructure.

3. Policy Lags: Demand-side economics requires government action to ensure stable aggregate demand. Because excessive demand causes inflation to rise and insufficient demand leads to higher unemployment, demand-side economics often requires regular government action such as reduced spending in a healthy economy and higher spending in weaker times. The problem is the lag between recognition of the need for government action and the actual implementation of appropriate policy measures. Often, the policy-making process itself is responsible for the delay in the adoption and implementation of policy measures. Further, there is an additional lag between the policy itself and the effects resulting from it. Often, many months may elapse between a change in government economic policy and the policy's effect on the economy.

4. Importance to Money: Today, money supply figures pervade the financial press. Every Friday, investors breathlessly watch for the latest money figures, and Dlal Street often reacts at the opening on the following Monday. If the money supply has gone up sharply, interest rates may or may not move upward. The press is filled with ominous forecasts of RBI actions, or of regulations of banks and other financial institutions. This close attention to the money supply is rather new. Until the 1970s, over the many decades of the Keynesian Era, talk of money and bank credit had dropped out of the financial pages. Rather, they emphasized the GNP and government's fiscal policy, expenditures, revenues, and deficits. Banks and the money supply were generally ignored. Yet after decades of chronic and accelerating inflation which the Keynesians could not begin to cure and after many bouts of "inflationary recession," it became obvious to all even to Keynesians that something was wary. The money supply therefore became a major object of concern.

2.2.3 Modern function of Money (Friedman's Modern Theory of Money)

During 1950's. Milton Friedman took over the reins of the Chicago School and led to the development of the modern quantity theory of the money and the monetarist school. Milton Friedman presented his most elegant and sophisticated version of the quantity theory of money in his paper. *The Quantity Theory of Money - A Restatement*, published in 1956, which he regards as an attempt, "to convey the flavor of the oral tradition" of the Chicago School. Friedman also admits his indebtedness to Keynes and owes a great debt to the Cambridge cash-balance approach in the development of his theory of money.

Basic Features of Friedman's Theory

The basic features of Friedman's quantity theory of money are summarized below:

1. Wealth Theory of Demand for Money: Friedman's quantity theory of money is wealth theory of demand for money and not a theory of the price level, money income, or output. In his view, money is "a durable consumer good held for the services it renders, and yielding a flow of services proportional to the stock." Money is no longer a 'veil' without any permanent influence on the real sector. It is a type of capital goods which is held for the services it provides. Thus, money is demanded as an asset or capital and the theory of demand for money is a part of the capital or wealth theory.

2. Broader Concept of Money: Friedman analyses the demand for money as a whole instead of examining it in terms of specific motives. He include all those things those effects the wealth and quantity of money. It does not distinguish between active and idle balances.

3. General Demand Analysis: In this theory Friedman assumes that the tastes and preferences of money-holders are constant. He also assumes that money is subject to the law of diminishing marginal rate of substitution, i.e., With the increase in the stock of money held, its marginal utility of money will be diminishing relative to the yield of other assets.

4. Forms of Wealth: Friedman uses a broader concept of wealth in his analysis of demand for money. It includes physical wealth or assets and human assets. Friedman distinguishes five forms of assets in which wealth can be held.

(*i*) **Money:** Money is returns in the form of convenience, security or money itself. In other words money defined as claims to commodity units that are generally accepted in payment of debts at a fixed nominal value. The real yield on money depends on the changes in price level. When general price level falls, the value of money appreciates. During inflationary situation value of money falls due to raise in general price level and vice versa.

(*ii*) **Bonds:** Bonds are financial assets promising a perpetual fixed income. In other words bonds defined as a claim to a time stream of payments that are fixed in nominal units. The real income from bonds may change due to fluctuations in price level or changes in the rate of interest on bonds.

(*iii*) **Equities:** Equity defined as a claim to a time stream of payments that are fixed in real units. It will affected by the change in the price level and their capital value. Expected rate of return on equities include expected change in their prices also.

(*iv*) **Physical Goods:** Physical Goods promise an income in kind that cannot be measured in terms of rate of interest. But their nominal rate of return affected by the rate change in the price level.

(*v*) **Total Wealth:** Total wealth includes human wealth as well as non human wealth. One can buy physical assets by using their current income or can finance education and acquire skill by selling one's non-human assets.

Expected rate of return on real assets measured by expected rate of return on real assets and variable other than income affecting the tastes and preferences of individuals are additional determinants of money.

5. Determinants of Demand for money: Broadly speaking, the demand for money is depend on three major factors:

(*a*) Total wealth to be held in various forms of assets

(*b*) Relative price and return on wealth as compared to the other forms of money; and

(*c*) tastes and preferences of the wealth holder.

Cost of holding cash balances is influenced by (*a*) the rate of interest and (*b*) the expected rate of change in the price level. An increase in the rate of interest or the price level causes a decline in the cash balances and vice versa.

Friedman's Demand-for-Money Function

The demand function for money formulated by Friedman is given below:

$$M/P = f(r_m, Y, w, P^*, r_b, r_e, r_c, u)$$

where, M/P = aggregate demand for money.

Y = Total income.

w = Fraction of wealth in non-human wealth.

P = General Price level.

P^* = Expected rate of change of prices.

r_m = Expected rate of return on money.

r_b = Expected rate of return on bond.

r_e = Expected rate of return on equity.

r_c = Expected rate of return on physical goods.

u = Variable affecting utility attached to services of money and tastes and preferences.

Friedman thus maintains that a change in the stock of money leads to a change in the price level, or income or in both the variables in the same direction. The modern quantity theory of money states that as long as the demand for money is stable, a change in money supply causes a change in the price level; money supply also affects the real value of national income and economic activity but in the short run only. For Friedman, stability in the demand for money is a behavioural fact proved by evidence. As long as the demand for money is stable, it is possible to predict the effects of changes in money supply on total expenditure and income.

Friedman leads the monetarist school which maintains that if there is less-than-full employment, an increase in money supply will lead to a rise in output and employment because of a rise in expenditure. But this will happen only in the short run; soon the economy will return to the less-than-full employment level caused by other real factors. The monetarists believe that changes in money supply cannot affect real variables in the long run. At full employment level, an increase in money supply will raise prices.

Before full employment, income (Y) rises with a rise in money supply (M) and expenditure. This rise in income crucially depends upon the ratio of income to money supply (i. e. Y/M or velocity). Income will continue to rise until it has reached a limit where it achieves its previous ratio to money supply (Y/M) because at that point, output cannot be increased further. People will raise their demand for money rather than spend it and the demand for and supply of money will once again become equal.

M_s represents money supply and is perfectly inelastic with respect to changes in income. Demand for money M_d varies with income but this relationship is proportional since $M_d = kY$ (i.e., people always hold a given proportion k of their income). The equilibrium income will be there $M_d = M_s$. If M, rises, the M_s will increase and income also will rises $M_s > M_d$ and spending rises until $M_s = M_d$ at a higher level of income (Y).

Significance of Friedman's Modern Quantity Theory of Money

Important implications of the modern quantity theory of money as propounded by Friedman are presented below:

1. Stable Demand Function: According to Friedman, a stable function does not mean a constant velocity, but that the function is stable in terms of the variables which determine its value. Thus, an increase in velocity during inflation is consistent with functional stability.

2. Key Roll of Price Level: Price level, which is the reciprocal of the value of money, plays an important role in bringing the demand and supply of money into balance.

3. Explanation of Changes in Income Velocity: During prosperity, the demand for money rises proportionately with permanent income but less than proportionately with a rise in current income because permanent income rises less than current income in business expansion. This implies that income velocity rises in prosperity because income velocity is defined as a current income concept. Similarly, during depression, permanent income and the demand for money fall proportionately in relation to each other but less than proportionately in relation to current income and income velocity falls.

4. Importance of Expected Inflation: Expected rate of inflation is another important variable affecting the demand for money (inversely) in cases of rapid inflation.

5. Low Interest Elasticity of Demand for Money: Friedman and the monetarists regard the rate of interest as having very little influence on the demand for money.

6. Role of Monetary Policy: According to the monetarists, effective monetary policy maintains the stability in the demand for money, and control the money supply. The stabilization policy should concentrate on monetary policy. According to Keynesians theory only fiscal policies can change the level of income by changing aggregate demand. The monetarist argument assumes interest-inelastic demand for money, whereas the Keynesians assume a very low interest elasticity of the investment function.

7. Factors Affecting Supply of Money: The quantity theorists maintain that there are important factors affecting the supply of money and they do not affect the demand for money. The view that the supply of money expands or contracts according to the needs of trade is rejected by the quantity theorists.

To Sum Up.

(*a*) Friedman can be viewed as being in the Cambridge tradition and as a formulator of a capital theory of demand for money,

(*b*) The difference between Friedman and the Keynesians regarding the demand for money shrinks considerably when we view the results of empirical studies. The studies have found permanent income and the actual rate of interest and not the rate of change in the price level, as explaining most of the variations in the demand for money,

(*c*) However, basic differences between the monetarists and the Keynesians. Such as regarding the neutrality of money and the mechanism though which money affects the real variables still remains.

REVIEW QUESTIONS

1. Discuss the factors which influence currency money.
2. According to the Classical Approach discuss the functions of money.
3. What is the Keynesian approach to demand for money?
4. List the advantages and disadvantages of demand theory of money?
5. What do you mean by budget deficits?

Supply of Money

3

3.1 MONEY DEMAND

The demand for money is the desired holding of financial assets in the form of money: that may be in the form of cash or bank deposits. It can refer to the demand for money, that narrowly defined as M-1 (non-interest-bearing holdings), or in the broader sense demand of money defined as M-2, M-3 and M-4. Money in the sense of M1 is dominated as a store of value by interest-bearing assets. However, money is necessary to carry out transactions. In other words, it provides liquidity to the customer. This creates a trade-off between the liquidity advantage to holding money and the interest advantage to holding other assets. The demand for money is a result of this trade-off regarding the form in which a person's wealth should be held. In macroeconomics motivations for holding one's wealth in the form of money can roughly be divided into transaction motive and asset holding motive. Further these can be subdivided into micro economically founded motivations for holding of money. Generally, the nominal demand for money increases with the level of nominal output (price level, times and real output) and decreases with the nominal interest rate. The real demand for money is defined as the nominal amount of money demanded, divided by the price level. The magnitude of the volatility of money demand has crucial implications for the optimal way in which a central bank should carry out monetary policy and its choice of a nominal anchor.

3.1.1 Factors Affecting Money Demand

Following are the factors which affect money demand:

1. Interest Rates: Two of the more important stores of wealth are bonds and money. These two items are substitutes, as money is used to purchase bonds and bonds are redeemed for money. The two differ in a few key ways. Money generally pays very little interest (and in the case of paper currency, none at all) but it can be used to purchase goods and services. Bonds do pay interest, but cannot be used to make purchases, as the bonds must first be converted into money. If bonds paid the same interest rate as money, nobody would purchase bonds as they are less convenient than money. Since bonds pay interest, people will use some of their money to purchase bonds. The higher the interest rate, the more attractive bonds become. So a rise in the interest rate causes the demand for bonds to rise and the demand for money to fall since money is being exchanged for bonds. So a fall in interest rates causes the demand for money to rise.

2. Consumer Spending: During periods of higher consumer spending, such as the month before Christmas, people often cash in other forms of wealth like stocks and bonds, and exchange them for money. They want money in order to purchase goods and services, like Christmas presents. So, if the demand for consumer spending increases, the demand for money will also increase.

3. Precautionary Motives: If people think that they will suddenly need to buy things in the immediate future (say it's 1999 and they're worried about Y2K), they will sell bonds and stocks and hold onto money, so the demand for money will go up. If people think that there will be an opportunity to purchase an asset in the immediate future at a very low cost, they will also prefer to hold money.

4. Transaction Costs for Stocks and Bonds: If it becomes difficult or expensive to quickly buy and sell stocks and bonds, they will be less desirable. People will want to hold more of their wealth in the form of money, so the demand for money will rise.

5. Change in the General Level of Prices: If we have inflation, goods become more expensive, so the demand for money rises. Interestingly enough, the level of money holdings tends to rise at the same rate as prices. So while the nominal demand for money rises, the real demand stays precisely the same.

6. International Factors: Usually when we discuss the demand for money, we're implicitly talking about the demand for a particularly nation's money. Since Canadian money is a substitute for American money, international factors will influence the demand for money. The following factors can cause the demand for a currency to rise:

- An increase in the demand of that country's goods abroad.
- An increase in the demand for domestic investment by foreigners.
- The belief that the value of the currency will rise in the future.
- A central banking wanting to increase its holdings of that currency.

3.2 MONEY SUPPLY

Money may be regarded as something which is generally used as a means of payment and accepted for the settlement of debts. The term 'supply of money' means the total stock of money held by the public in spendable form. The term 'public' refers to the individuals and the business firms in the economy, excluding the central government, the central bank and the commercial banks. Thus the cash balances held by the central government, the central bank and the commercial banks do not form money supply because they are not in actual circulation.

Money supply is a stock as well as a flow concept. When money supply is viewed at a point of time, it is stock, and when viewed over a period of time, it is flow. Money supply at a particular moment of time is the stock of money held by public at a moment of time. It refers to the total currency notes, coins and demand deposits with the banks held by the public. Over a period of time, money supply becomes a flow concept. It may be spent several times during a period of time. The average number of times a unit of money passing from one hand to another during a given period is called the velocity of circulation of money. Thus the flow of money supply over the period of time can be known by multiplying a given stock of money held by the public by the velocity of circulation of money.

3.2.1 Constituents of Money Supply

Monetary economists hold different views regarding the constituents of money supply. Broadly, there are two views: the traditional views and the modern view.

Traditional View: According to the traditional view, money supply is composed of (*a*) currency money and legal tender, i.e. coins and currency notes, and (*b*) bank money, i.e. chequable demand deposits with the commercial banks.

Modern View: According to the modern view, the phenomenon of money supply refers to the whole spectrum of liquidity in the asset portfolio of the individual. Thus in the modern approach, money supply is wider concept which includes (*a*) coins (*b*) currency notes (*c*) demand deposits with the banks (*d*) time deposits with the banks (*e*) financial assets, such as deposits with the non-banking financial intermediaries, like the post office saving banks, building societies, etc. (*f*) treasury and exchange bills, (*g*) bonds and equities.

(*a*) **Currency Money:** Currency money is a legal tender money and thus is called high-powered money. It includes the currency notes and coins issued by the central bank of a country. Generally, the central bank possesses the monopoly of notes issue. But, in certain countries, the treasury or the ministry of finance also issues notes or coins along with the central bank. In India one rupee note and the coins are issued and managed by the Finance Ministry of the government of India. All other notes are issued and managed by the RBI.

The supply of notes and coins in a country are regulated by the system of note issue adopted in the country. According to the RBI Act, 1934, not less than 40 percent of the total assets of the issue department should consist of gold coins, bullion and foreign securities with the provision that gold coins and bullion were not at anytime to be less than ₹ 40 crores. This requirement was changed by the RBI Act, 1956, which provides for the substitution of the proportional reserve system by minimum reserve system. According RBI Act, in 1957 the provision was made that the total value of gold coins, gold bullion and foreign securities, held in the issue department at anytime should not be less than ₹ 200 crores and gold value should not be less than ₹ 115 crores. Thus in India, the minimum reserve method is the governing principle of note issue.

Factors Influencing Currency Money

The monetary authority while determining the supply of currency and coins must be guided by the general requirement of the economy. The currency component of the money supply, i.e. coins and notes is influenced by a number of factors as discussed below:

1. **Volume of Transactions:** The supply of currency must very in accordance with the changes in the physical volume of trade and transactions of the economy. If the issue of the currency is more than what is required, it creates inflationary pressures. On the other hand, if the money supply is less than the requirements, it leads to deflationary trends.
2. **Nature of Trade:** The nature of trade, whether wholesale or retail, determines the proportion of currency of different denominations. For the wholesale trade, the notes of higher denominations are required while the retail trade requires larger proportion of notes and coins of lower denominations.
3. **Methods of Payment:** The method of payment being used in the economy also determines the currency component of the money supply. If most of the payments are made in cash, greater proportion of currency to money supply is needed. If the payments are generally made through cheques, the proportion of currency to money supply will be lowered.
4. **The Price Level:** Price level also affects the requirements of currency considerably. Higher the price level, larger the amount of currency required and lower the price level, smaller the amount of currency required to carry out the given volume of transactions.
5. **Banking Habits:** If the public has confidence in the bank money and has banking habits, the currency requirements will be less. But if the people have less banking habits, the transactions will be conducted with currency and more currency is required.
6. **Distribution of Income:** Distribution of income also influences the currency requirements. If the distribution of income is in favour of the rich, greater proportion of currency of higher denominations is required. On the other hand, if the distribution is in favor of the poor, a larger proportion of currency should be low denominations.
7. **Other Factors:** Other factors, like the volume of demand deposits with the banks, the taxation policy of the government, the extent of public loans, the volume of deficit financing, etc., also influence the amount of currency required in the economy significantly.

(*b*) **Bank Money:** The demand deposits held by the public in commercial banks also constitute the total money supply of the economy. The demand deposits are transferable by cheque for the settlement of debts. The creation of bank money depends upon the credit creation activities of the banks. Credit creation is based on the volume of cash, i.e., the high-powered money, held by the banks. The money created by the banks is known as secondary money. Thus, the total money supply in an economy is composed of (a) the primary or high-powered money and (b) the secondary or bank money.

The relative proportions of the two constituents of money supply, i.e., currency money and bank money depend upon the degree of monetisation of the economy, the development of the banking system and the banking habits of the people. In the economically advanced/ developed countries chequable demand deposits held the major proportion of the total money supply. In such countries over 90 percent of the payments are made through cheques.

In the less-development/ under developed countries, like India, on the contrary, the proportion of currency money to the total money supply with the public is much higher. It is because in these countries, banking habits of the people have not yet fully developed and majority of the transactions are conducted through cash payments. In India currency constitutes about $2/3^{rd}$ of the total money supply, while the demand deposits are only $1/3^{rd}$.

3.2.2 Approaches to the Definition of Money Supply

Economists are not in agreement on the question of definition of money supply. There are four broad approaches of money supply. They are as follows:

1. Traditional Approach: The traditional approach focuses on the medium of exchange function of money. According to this approach, money supply is defined as currency with public and demand deposits with commercial banks. Demand deposits are the current accounts of depositors in the commercial bank. The traditional approach is analytically superior because it provides the most liquid and exact measure of money supply. The Central Bank can have better control over the money supply if it includes currency and demand deposits of banks alone. But this approach limits money supply to a very narrow area.

2. Monetarist Approach: Milton Friedman includes in money supply currency plus demand deposits plus time deposits. Time deposits are the fixed deposits of the banks which earn a fixed rate of interest depending upon the period for which the amount is deposited. Money can act as a temporary abode of purchasing power if it is kept in the form of cash, demand deposits or any other asset which is close to currency, i.e., time deposits. This approach focuses/emphasis on the store of value functions of money and provides a broader measure of money.

3. Gurely and Shaw Approach: Gurely and Shaw further widened the scope of money supply by including in its constituents currency plus demand and time deposits of banks plus the liabilities of non-banking intermediaries. The liabilities of non-banking intermediaries cover saving bank deposits, shares, bonds, etc. and are close substitutes to money.

4. Redcliffe Committee Approach: Redcliffe Committee approach or liquidity approach provides much wider view of the concept of money supply. In this approach the concept of money supply is viewed in terms of general liquidity of the economy. Money supply covers "the whole liquidity position that is relevant to appending decisions". The spending is not limited to the amount of money in existence. It is related to the amount of money people think they can get hold of whether by receipts of income, by disposal of assets or by borrowing. Thus, according to this approach, money supply includes cash, all kinds of bank deposits, deposits with other institutions, near-money assets and the borrowing facilities available to the people. The practical difficulty with this liquidity approach is that the money supply in this wider sense cannot be successfully measured because the degree of liquidity of different constituents of money supply varies considerably. Moreover most of the constituents remain outside the control of central bank and thus restrict the effective implementation of monetary policy.

3.2.3 Determinants of Money Supply

Various factors influencing the money supply are discussed below:

1. Monetary Base: Magnitude of the monetary base (B) is the significant determinant of the size of money supply. Money supply varies directly in relation to the changes in the monetary base. Monetary base refers to the supply of funds available for use either as cash or reserves of central bank. Monetary base changes due to the policy of the government and is also influenced by the value of money.

2. Money Multiplier: Money Multiplier (*m*) has positive influence upon the money supply. An increase in the size of m will increase the money supply and vice versa.

3. Reserve Ratio: Reserve ratio (*r*) is also an important determinant of money supply. The smaller cash-reserve ratio enables greater expansion in the credit by the banks and thus increases the money supply and vice versa. Reserve ratio is often broken down into its two component parts (*a*) excess reserve ratio which is the ratio of excess reserves to the total deposits of the banks (*b*) required reserve ratio which is the ratio of required reserves to the total deposits of the banks.

4. Currency Ratio: Currency ratio (*c*) is a behavioural ratio representing the ratio of currency demand to the demand deposits. The effect of the currency ratio on the money multiplier (*m*) can't be clearly recognised.

5. Confidence in Bank Money: General economic conditions affect the confidence of the public in bank money and thereby, influence the currency ratio (*c*) and the reserve ratio (*r*). During recession, confidence in bank money is low and as a result, *c* and *r* ratios rise. Conversely, during prosperity, *c* and *r* ratios tend to be low when confidence in banks is high.

6. Time Deposit Ratio: Time deposit ratio (*t*), which represents the ratio of time deposits to the demand deposits is a behavioural parameter having negative effect on the money multiplier (*m*) and thus on the money supply. A rise in *t* reduces *m* and thereby the supply of money decreases.

7. Value of Money: The value of money (1/P) in terms of other goods and services has positive influence on the monetary base (B) and hence on the money stock.

8. Real Income: Real Income (Y) has a positive influence on the money multiplier and hence on the money supply. A rise in real income will tend to increase the money multiplier and thus the money supply and vice versa.

9. Interest Rate: Interest rate has a positive effect on the money multiplier and hence on the money supply. A rise in the interest rate will reduce the reserve ratio (*r*), which raises the money multiplier (m) and hence increases the money supply and vice versa.

10. Monetary Policy: Monetary policy has positive or negative influence on the money multiplier and hence on the money supply, depending upon whether reserve requirements are lowered or raised. If reserve requirements are raised, the value of reserve ratio (r) will rise reducing the money multiplier and thus the money supply and vice versa.

11. Seasonal Factors: Seasonal factors have negative effect on the money multiplier, and hence on the money stock. During holiday periods the currency ratio (*r*) will tend to rise, thus reducing the money multiplier and thereby the money supply.

3.2.4 Money Supply in India

Till 1967-68, RBI used to adopt only the narrow measure of money supply (M) defined as the sum of currency and demand deposits, both held by public. From 1967-68 it started publishing additionally a broader measure of money supply, called Aggregate Monetary Resources (AMR). It was defined empirically as money narrowly defined plus the time deposits of banks held by public. From April 1977, the RBI has adopted four alternative definitions of money supply, labelled as M1, M2, M3, and M4.

M or M1 = C+ DD + OD

M2 = M1 + Savings deposits with post office saving banks.

AMR or M3 = M1 + Net time deposits of Banks.

M4 = M3+ Total deposits with the Post Office Savings Organisation (Excluding National Saving Certificates)

In the above definitions;

C = Currency held by public

DD = Net demand deposits of banks

OD = 'Other deposits' of the RBI which include demand deposits of quasi-government institutions (like the IDBI), foreign central banks and governments, the IMF and the World Bank etc.

High-Powered Money (H): In addition, the concept of 'high-powered money' (H) is also used in India which includes the currency held by the public (C) and the banks (R) and 'other deposits' of the RBI (OD).

$$H = C + R + OD$$

In short, for practical purposes, mainly two money supply concepts are used in India. (*i*) Narrow Money (M1), and (*ii*) Broad Money (M3) or aggregate monetary resources.

New Series: Since 1997-98, monetary data in India have been revised in line with the new accounting standards and consistent with the methodology suggested by the Work Group on "Money Supply: Analytics and Methodology of Compilation" (June 1998).

The new series of broad money (NM3) differs from the old series (M3) by a magnitude comprising, FCNR (B) deposits and RIBs, and banks' pension and provident funds.

(*a*) Reparable foreign currency fixed non-resident deposits with banks FCNR (B) and proceeds under the Resurgent India bonds (RIBs) do not directly constitute a part of the domestic demand for money and hence should be excluded from monetary aggregates.

(*b*) Similarly, pension and provident funds are essentially a portfolio of assets created to provide old age and retirement benefits, and differ from deposits redeemable for cash at face value plus accrued' interest. Thus they need to be excluded from monetary aggregates

Sources of Change in Money Supply in India

The RBI analyses the various sources of variation in money supply in India (M3) under the following:

1. **Net Bank Credit to Government:** It includes (*a*) RBI's net credit to government; and (*b*) other banks' credit to government.
2. **Bank Credit to Commercial Sectors:** It includes (*a*) RBI's credit to commercial sector and (*b*) other banks' credit to commercial sector. Other bank's credit further consists of (*i*) credit by commercial banks (*ii*) credit by cooperative banks; and (*iii*) investment by commercial and cooperative banks in other securities.
3. **Net Foreign Exchange Assets of the Banking Sector:** It includes (*a*) RBI's net foreign assets and (*b*) other banks' net foreign exchange assets.
4. **Government's Currency Liabilities** of the Public.
5. **Net Non-Monetary Liabilities of the Banking Sectors:** It includes (*a*) net non-monetary liabilities of RBI and (*b*) net non-monetary liabilities of other banks.

REVIEW QUESTIONS

1. What is Demand for money? How do international factors influence demand for money?
2. What do you mean by the term supply of money? What are the components of money supply in an economy?
3. What role does the Central Bank play to control the money supply? What are the tools and mechanisms which it employs to manage monetary policy?
4. What are the implications of an increase in the money supply on the economy? Describe the effects of an expansionary monetary policy on interest rates, inflation, and economic growth?
5. Explain the role of commercial banks in the creation of money through the process of fractional reserve banking. How does this process impact the overall money supply in an economy

Evolution of Banking in India

4

4.1 EVOLUTION OF BANKING IN INDIA

Modern Banking in India originated in the last decades of the 18th century. The first banks were – the Bank of Hindustan (1770–1829) and the General Bank of India, established in 1786 and has since defunct.

The largest bank and the oldest still in existence, is the State Bank of India, which originated at the Bank of Calcutta in June 1806, which almost immediately became the Bank of Bengal. This was one of the three presidency banks, the other two being the Bank of Bombay and the Bank of Madras, all three of which were established under charters from the British East India Company. The three banks merged in 1921 to form the Imperial Bank of India, which, upon India's independence, became the State Bank of India in 1955. For many years, the presidency banks served as quasi-central banks, as did their successors, until the Reserve Bank of India was established in 1935.

In 1969, the Indian government nationalised all the major banks that it did not already own and these have remained under government ownership. They are run under a structure known as 'profit-making public sector undertaking' (PSU) and are allowed to compete and operate as commercial banks. The Indian banking sector is made up of four types of banks, as well as the PSUs and the state banks; they have been joined since the 1990s by new private commercial banks and a number of foreign banks.

Banking in India was generally fairly mature in terms of supply, product range and reach – eventhough reach in rural India and to the poor still remains a challenge. The government has developed initiatives to address this through the State bank of India expanding its branch network and through the National Bank for Agriculture and Rural Development (NABARD) with things like micro-finance.

4.1.1 Post Independence Banking in India

The partition of India in 1947 adversely impacted the economies of Punjab and West Bengal, paralysing banking activities for months. India's independence marked the end of a regime of the laissez-faire for the Indian banking. The Government of India initiated measures to play an active role in the economic life of the nation, and the Industrial Policy Resolution adopted by the government in 1948 envisaged a mixed economy. This resulted into greater involvement of the state in different segments of the economy including banking and finance. The major steps to regulate banking included:

(*i*) The Reserve Bank of India, India's central banking authority, was established in April 1935, but was nationalised on 1 January, 1949, under the terms of the Reserve Bank of India (Transfer to Public Ownership) Act, 1948.

(*ii*) In 1949, the Banking Regulation Act was enacted which empowered the Reserve Bank of India (RBI) "to regulate, control, and inspect the banks in India".

(*iii*) The Banking Regulation Act also provided that no new bank or branch of an existing bank could be opened without a license from the RBI and no two banks could have common directors.

4.1.2 Nationalisation in the 1960s and 1980s

Despite the provisions, control and regulations of the Reserve Bank of India, banks in India except the State Bank of India or SBI, continued to be owned and operated by private persons. By the 1960s, the Indian banking industry had become an important tool to facilitate the development of the Indian economy. At the same time, it had emerged as a large employer, and a debate had ensued about the nationalisation of the banking industry. Indira Gandhi, the then Prime Minister of India, expressed the intention of the Government of India in the annual conference of the All India Congress Meeting in a paper entitled "Stray thoughts on Bank Nationalisation." The meeting received the paper with enthusiasm.

Thereafter, her move was swift and sudden. The Government of India issued an ordinance (Banking Companies 'Acquisition and Transfer of Undertakings' Ordinance, 1969) and nationalised the 14 largest commercial banks with effect from the midnight of 19 July 1969. These banks contained 85% of bank deposits in the country. Jayaprakash Narayan, a national leader of India, described the step as a 'masterstroke of political sagacity.' Within two weeks of the issue of the ordinance, the Parliament passed the Banking Companies 'Acquisition and Transfer of Undertaking' Bill, and it received the presidential approval on 9 August, 1969.

A second dose of nationalisation of six more commercial banks followed in 1980. The stated reason for the nationalisation was to give the government more control of credit delivery. With the second dose of nationalisation, the Government of India controlled around 91% of the banking business in India. Later on, in the year 1993, the government merged New Bank of India with Punjab National Bank. It was the only merger between nationalised banks and resulted in the reduction of the number of nationalised banks from 20 to 19. After this, until the 1990s, the nationalised banks grew at a pace of around 4%, closer to the average growth rate of the Indian economy.

4.1.3 Liberalisation in the 1990s

In the early 1990s, the then government embarked on a policy of liberalisation, licensing a small number of private banks. These came to be known as New Generation tech-savvy banks and included Global Trust Bank (the first of such new generation banks to be set up), which later amalgamated with Oriental Bank of Commerce, UTI Bank (since renamed Axis Bank), ICICI Bank and HDFC Bank. This move, along with the rapid growth in the economy of India, revitalised the banking sector in India, which has seen rapid growth with strong contribution from all the three sectors of banks, namely, government banks, private banks and foreign banks.

The next stage for the Indian banking has been set up with the proposed relaxation in the norms for Foreign Direct Investment (FDI), where all Foreign Investors in banks may be given voting rights which could exceed the present cap of 10%, at present it has gone up to 74% with some restrictions.

The new policy shook the Banking sector in India completely. Bankers, till this time, were used to the 4–6–4 method (Borrow at 4%; Lend at 6%; Go home at 4%) of functioning. The new wave ushered in a modern outlook and tech-savvy methods of working for traditional banks. All this led to the retail boom in India. People not only demanded more from their banks but also received more.

4.1.4 Current Period

By 2010, banking in India was generally fairly mature in terms of supply, product range and reach-even though reach in rural India still remains a challenge for the private sector and foreign banks. In terms of quality of assets and capital adequacy, Indian banks are considered to have clean, strong and transparent balance sheets relative to other banks in comparable economies in its region. The Reserve Bank of India is an autonomous body, with minimal pressure from the government.

With the growth in the Indian economy expected to be strong for quite some time, especially in its services sector – the demand for banking services, especially retail banking, mortgages and investment services are expected to be strong. One may also expect M&As, takeovers and asset sales.

In March 2006, the Reserve Bank of India allowed Warburg Pincus to increase its stake in Kotak Mahindra Bank (a private sector bank) to 10%. This is the first time an investor has been allowed to hold more than 5% in a private sector bank since the RBI announced norms in 2005 that any stake exceeding 5% in the private sector banks would need to be vetted by them.

In recent years critics have charged that the non-government owned banks are too aggressive in their loan recovery efforts in connation with housing, vehicle and personal loans. There are press reports that the banks' loan recovery efforts have driven defaulting borrowers to suicide.

4.1.5 Latest Developments in the Banking Sector

1. **Payment Bank:** Payment bank is a new model of banks conceptualised by the Reserve Bank of India (RBI). These banks can accept a restricted deposit, which is currently limited to ₹1 lakh per customer. These banks may not

issue loans or credit cards, but may offer both current and savings accounts. Payments banks may issue ATM, debit cards, offer net-banking and mobile-banking. The banks will be licensed as payments banks under Section 22 of the Banking Regulation Act, 1949 and will be registered as public limited company under the Companies Act, 2013.

There are six payments banks:

1. Airtel Payments Banks Ltd.
2. Fino Payments Bank Ltd.
3. India Post Payments Bank Ltd.
4. Jio Payments Bank Ltd.
5. NSDL Payments Bank Ltd.
6. PayTm Payments Bank Ltd.

2. **Small Finance Banks:** To achieve the objective of financial inclusion, the RBI granted approval in 2016 to ten entities to set up small finance banks. Since then, all ten have received the necessary licenses. A small finance bank is a niche type of bank to cater to the needs of people who traditionally have not used scheduled banks. Each of these banks is to open at least 25% of its branches in areas that do not have any other bank branches (unbanked regions). A small finance bank should hold 75% of its net credits in loans to firms in priority sector lending and 50% of the loans in its portfolio must be less than ₹25 lakh (US$38,000).

There are ten small finance banks:

1. AU Small Finance Bank Ltd.
2. Capital Small Finance Bank Ltd.
3. Equitas Small Finance Bank Ltd.
4. ESAF Small Finance Bank Ltd.
5. Fincare Small Finance Bank Ltd.
6. Jana Small Finance Bank Ltd.
7. North East Small Finance Bank Ltd.
8. Suryoday Small Finance Bank Ltd.
9. Ujjivan Small Finance Bank Ltd.
10. Utkarsh Small Finance Bank Ltd.

(*i*) **Banking Codes and Standards:** The Banking Codes and Standards Board of India is an independent and autonomous banking industry body that monitors banks in India. To improve the quality of banking services in India, S.S. Tarapore (former deputy governor of RBI), had the idea to form this committee.

(*ii*) **Adoption of Banking Technology:** The IT revolution has had a great impact on the Indian banking system. The use of computers has led to the introduction of online banking in India. The use of computers in the banking sector in India has increased many folds after the economic liberalisation of 1991 as the country's banking sector has been exposed to the world's market. Indian banks were finding it difficult to compete with the international banks in customer service, without the use of information technology. The RBI set up a number of committees to define and co-ordinate banking technology. These have included:

In 1984 the Committee on Mechanisation in the Banking Industry was formed whose chairman was Dr. C. Rangarajan, Deputy Governor, Reserve Bank of India. The major recommendations of this committee were introducing Magnetic Ink Character Recognition (MICR) technology in all the banks in the metropolises in India. This provided for the use of standardised cheque forms and encoders.

In 1988, the RBI set up the Committee on Computerisation in Banks (1988) headed by Dr. C. Rangarajan. It emphasised that settlement operation must be computerised in the clearing houses of RBI in Bhubaneshwar, Guwahati, Jaipur, Patna and Thiruvananthapuram. It further stated that there should be National Clearing of inter-city cheques at Kolkata, Mumbai, Delhi, Chennai and MICR should be made operational. It also focussed on computerisation of branches and increasing connectivity among branches through computers. It also suggested modalities for implementing on-line banking. The committee submitted its reports in 1989 and computerisation began from 1993 with the settlement between IBA and bank employees' associations.

In 1994, the Committee on Technology Issues relating to Payment systems, Cheque Clearing and Securities Settlement in the Banking Industry (1994) was set up under Chairman W.S. Saraf. It emphasised Electronic Funds Transfer (EFT) system, with the BANKNET communications network as its carrier. It also said that MICR clearing should be set up in all branches of all those banks with more than 100 branches.

In 1995, the Committee for proposing Legislation on Electronic Funds Transfer and other Electronic Payments (1995) again emphasised EFT system.

In July 2016, Deputy Governor Rama Gandhi of the Central Bank of India "urged banks to work to develop applications for digital currencies and distributed ledgers."

(*iii*) **Automatic Teller Machine Growth (ATM):** The total number of automated teller machines (ATMs) installed in India by various banks as of 2018 was 2,38,000. The new private sector banks in India have the most ATMs, followed by off-site. ATMs belonging to SBI and its subsidiaries and then by nationalised banks and foreign banks, while on-site is highest for the nationalised banks of India.

(*iv*) **Cheque Truncation Initiative:** In 2008 the Reserve Bank of India introduced a system to allow truncation the conversion of checks from physical form to electronic form when sending to the paying bank in India, the cheque truncation system as it was known, was first rolled out in the National Capital Region and then rolled out nationally.

(*v*) **Expansion of Banking Infrastructure:** Physical as well as virtual expansion of banking through mobile banking, internet banking, tele-banking, bio-metric and mobile ATMs, etc., is taking place since last decade and has gained momentum in last few years.

(*vi*) **Data Breaches:** A huge data breach on debit cards issued by various Indian banks was reported in October 2016. It was estimated 3.2 million debit cards were compromised. Major Indian banks – SBI, HDFC Bank, ICICI Bank, YES Bank and Axis Bank were among the worst hit. Many users reported unauthorised use of their cards in locations in China. This resulted in one of the India's biggest card replacement drive in banking history. The biggest Indian bank State Bank of India announced the blocking and replacement of almost 600,000 debit cards.

(*vii*) **Bank Merger:** The merger of banks started for the boosters for the economy, Finance Minister Niramala Sitharaman announced amalgamation of 10 public sector banks into four big banks. After this the total number of Public Sector Banks in the country will come down to 12 from 27 banks in 2017. Apart from this the government announced ₹55,250 crore upfront capital infusion in the public sector banks (PSBs). The consolidation of all SBI associated banks merged in that was start from 13 August 2008 to August 27, 2010. The remaining 27 nationalised banks were merged into 12 banks from 2017–19. The State Bank of Bikaner & Jaipur, State Bank of Hyderabad, State Bank of Mysore, State Bank of Patiala and State Bank of Travancore, and Bharatiya Mahila Bank were merged with State Bank of India with effect from 1 April 2017. Vijaya Bank and Dena Bank were merged into Bank of Baroda in 2018. IDBI Bank was categorised as a private bank with effect from January 2019.

On 30 August 2019, Finance Minister Nirmala Sitharaman announced the government's plan for further consolidation of public sector banks: Indian Bank is to be merged with Allahabad Bank (anchor bank – Indian Bank); PNB, OBC and United Bank are to be merged (anchor bank – PNB); Union Bank of India, Andhra Bank and Corporation Bank are to be merged (anchor bank – Union Bank of India); and Canara Bank and Syndicate Bank are to be merged (anchor bank – Canara Bank)

4.2 NATIONALISATION OF BANKS IN INDIA

After independence the Government of India (GOI) adopted planned economic development for the country (India). Accordingly, five-year plans came into existence since 1951. This economic planning basically aimed at social ownership of the means of production. However, commercial banks were in the private sector those days. In 1950–51 there were 430 commercial banks. The Government of India had some social objectives of planning. These commercial banks failed helping the government in attaining these objectives. Thus, the government decided to nationalise 14 major commercial banks on 19th July, 1969. All commercial banks with a deposit base over ₹50 crore were nationalised. It was considered that banks were controlled by business houses and thus failed in catering to the credit needs of poor sections such as cottage industry, village industry, farmers, craftsmen, etc. The second dose of nationalisation came in April 1980 when six banks were nationalised.

Nationalised banks dominate the banking system in India. The history of nationalised banks in India dates back to mid-20th century, when Imperial Bank of India was nationalised (under the SBI Act of 1955) and re-christened as State Bank of India (SBI) in July 1955. Then on 19th July 1960, its seven subsidiaries were also nationalised with deposits over 200 crores. These subsidiaries of SBI were State Bank of Bikaner and Jaipur (SBBJ), State Bank of Hyderabad (SBH), State Bank of Indore (SBIR), State Bank of Mysore (SBM), State Bank of Patiala (SBP), State Bank of Saurashtra (SBS), and State Bank of Travancore (SBT).

However, the major nationalisation of banks happened in 1969 by the then–Prime Minister Indira Gandhi. The major objective behind nationalisation was to spread banking infrastructure in rural areas and make cheap finance available to Indian farmers. The nationalised 14 major commercial banks were Allahabad Bank, Andhra Bank, Bank of Baroda, Bank of India, Bank of Maharashtra, Canara Bank, Central Bank of India, Corporation Bank, Dena Bank, Indian Bank, Indian Overseas Bank, Oriental Bank of Commerce (OBC), Punjab and Sind Bank, Punjab National Bank (PNB), Syndicate Bank, UCO Bank, Union Bank of India, United Bank of India. In the year 1980, the second phase of nationalisation of Indian banks took place, in which 6 more banks were nationalised with deposits over 200 crores. With this, the Government of India held a control over 91% of the banking industry in India. After the nationalisation of banks there was a huge jump in the deposits and advances with the banks. At present, the State Bank of India is the largest commercial bank of India and is ranked one of the top five banks worldwide. It serves 90 million customers through a network of 9,000 branches.

The first major step was Nationalisation of the Imperial Bank of India in 1955 via State Bank of India Act. State Bank of India was made to act as the 'principles' agent of RBI and handle banking transactions of the Union and State Governments. In a major process of nationalisation, 7 subsidiaries of the State Bank of India were nationalised by the Indira Gandhi regime. In 1969, 14 major private commercial banks were nationalised. These 14 banks Nationalised in 1969 are as follows:

1. Central Bank of India
2. Bank of Maharastra
3. Dena Bank
4. Punjab National Bank

5. Syndicate Bank
6. Canara Bank
7. Indian Bank
8. Indian Overseas Bank
9. Bank of Baroda
10. Union Bank
11. Allahabad Bank
12. Union Bank of India
13. UCO Bank
14. Bank of India.

The above was followed by a second phase of nationalisation in 1980, when Government of India acquired the ownership of 6 more banks, thus bringing the total number of Nationalised Banks to 20. The private banks at that time were allowed to function side by side with nationalised banks and the foreign banks were allowed to work under strict regulation. After the two major phases of nationalisation in India, the 80% of the banking sector came under the public sector/government ownership.

The following sequences of events during nationalisation are as follows:

(*a*) **Creation of Reserve Bank of India:** 1935 and Nationalisation of Reserve Bank of India: 1949 (January).

(*b*) **Enactment of Banking Regulation Act:** 1949 (March)

As per Section 5(*c*) of Banking Regulation Act, 1949 a 'Banking Company' means any company which transacts the business of banking in India.

Explanation: Any company which is engaged in the manufacture of goods or carries on any trade and which accepts the deposits of money from public merely for the purpose of financing its business as such manufacturer or trader shall not be deemed to transact the business of banking within the meaning of this clause."

As per Section 5(b) of Banking Regulation Act, 1949, banking means the accepting, for the purpose of lending or investment, of deposits of money from the public, repayable on demand or otherwise, and withdrawable by cheque, draft, and order or otherwise.

As per Section 5(d) of Banking Regulation Act, 1949, company means any company as defined in Section 3 of the Companies Act, 1956 and includes a foreign company within the meaning of Section 591 of that Act. As per section 51 of Banking Regulation Act, 1949, certain provisions of the Banking Regulation Act are also applicable to the State Bank of India, any corresponding new bank, a regional rural bank and any subsidiary bank. "Corresponding new bank" has been defined under clause (ee) of section 2 of the DICGC Act to mean a corresponding new bank constituted under the Banking Companies (Acquisition and Transfer of Undertakings) Acts of 1970 or 1980.

(*c*) **Nationalisation of State Bank of India, 1955:** The roots of the State Bank of India lie in the first decade of 19th century, when the Bank of Calcutta, later renamed the Bank of Bengal, was established on 2 June 1806. The

Bank of Bengal was one of three Presidency banks, the other two being the Bank of Bombay (incorporated on 15 April 1840) and the Bank of Madras (incorporated on 1 July 1843). All three Presidency banks were incorporated as joint stock companies and were the result of the royal charters. These three banks received the exclusive right to issue paper currency till 1861 when with the Paper Currency Act, the right was taken over by the Government of India. The Presidency banks amalgamated on 27 January 1921, and the re-organised banking entity took as its name Imperial Bank of India. The Imperial Bank of India remained a joint stock company but without Government participation. Pursuant to the provisions of the State Bank of India Act of 1955, the Reserve Bank of India, which is India's central bank, acquired a controlling interest in the Imperial Bank of India. On 1 July 1955, the Imperial Bank of India became the State Bank of India. In 2008 the government of India acquired the Reserve Bank of India's stake in SBI so as to remove any conflict of interest because the RBI is the country's banking regulatory authority. In 1959, the government passed the State Bank of India (Subsidiary Banks) Act, which made eight state banks associates of SBI. A process of consolidation began on 13 September 2008, when the State Bank of Saurashtra merged with SBI.

State Bank of India has acquired local banks in rescues. The first was the Bank of Behar (est. 1911), which SBI acquired in 1969, together with its 28 branches. The next year SBI acquired National Bank of Lahore (est. 1942), which had 24 branches. Five years later, in 1975, SBI acquired Krishnaram Baldeo Bank, which had been established in 1916 in Gwalior State, under the patronage of Maharaja Madho Rao Scindia. The bank had been the *Dukan Pichadi*, a small moneylender, owned by the Maharaja. The new banks first manager was Jall N. Broacha, a Parsi. In 1985, SBI acquired the Bank of Cochin in Kerala, which had 120 branches. SBI was the acquirer as its affiliate, the State Bank of Travancore, already had an extensive network in Kerala.

(*d*) **Nationalisation of SBI Subsidiaries, 1959:** State Bank of India is the largest government owned bank in India. SBI along with its subsidiaries has more than 25000 branches across India and more than 40000 ATMs. Given below are the subsidiaries of SBI –

1. State Bank of India
2. State Bank of Jaipur
3. State Bank of Hyderabad
4. State Bank of Mysore
5. State Bank of Patiala
6. State Bank of Travancore

7. State Bank of Indore – It was merged with SBI in the year 2010.
8. State Bank of Saurashtra – It was merged with SBI in the year 2008.

The government is planning to merge all other subsidiaries also with SBI in coming future.

(*e*) **Nationalisation of 14 Major Banks, 1969:** It would seem unreal now in the era of liberalisation and privatisation. But it is a fact that 14 private banks were nationalised in 1969 by the then Central Government head by Prime Minister Smt. Indira Gandhi. The date was 19th July 1969.

In 1955, State Bank of India was nationalised, SBI subsidiaries in 1959, 14 private banks in 1969 and another 6 private banks nationalised in 1980. The private banks nationalised in 1969 & 1980 are given below:

(*a*) Central Bank of India
(*b*) Bank of Baroda
(*c*) Union Bank
(*d*) Allahabad Bank
(*e*) United Bank of India
(*f*) UCO Bank
(*g*) Bank of India
(*h*) Indian Overseas Bank
(*i*) Bank of Maharashtra
(*j*) Dena Bank
(*k*) Punjab National Bank
(*l*) Syndicate Bank
(*m*) Canara Bank
(*n*) Indian Bank

The nationalisation of the private banks was done since these banks were not performing good and also as part of the focus on public sector growth. But now the policy of the government has changed to liberalisation, globalisation and privatisation. Accordingly, the government wants to marginalise the PSU banks and bring new private banks by giving licences to the corporates for starting new banks. The Bank workers and their unions are against this move and have strongly opposed it.

(*f*) **Creation of Credit Guarantee Corporation, 1971:** The 1960s and 1970s were a period of institution building. 1971 witnessed the establishment of another institution, the Credit Guarantee Corporation of India Ltd. (CGCI). While Deposit Insurance had been introduced in India out of concerns to protect depositors, ensure financial stability, instill confidence in the banking system and help mobilise deposits, the establishment of the Credit Guarantee Corporation was essentially in the realm of affirmative action to ensure that the credit needs of the hitherto neglected sectors and weaker sections were met. The essential concern was to persuade banks to make available credit to not so creditworthy clients.

(*g*) **Creation of Regional Rural Banks, 1975:** Regional Rural Banks were established under the provisions of an Ordinance passed on 26 September 1975 and the Regional Rural Bank (RRB) Act 1976 to provide sufficient banking and credit facility for agriculture and other rural sectors. These were set up on the recommendations of The Narasimham Working Group during the tenure of Indira Gandhi's government with a view to include rural areas into economic mainstream since that time about 70% of the Indian Population was of Rural Orientation. The development process of RRBs started on 2 October 1975 with forming the first RRB, the Prathama Bank. Also on 2 October 1976 five regional rural banks were set-up on with a total authorised capital of ₹100 crore ($ 10 Million) which later augmented to 500 crore ($ 50 Million). There were five commercial banks, Punjab National Bank, State Bank of India, Syndicate Bank, United Bank of India and United Commercial Bank, which sponsored the regional rural banks. Earlier Reserve Bank of India had laid down ceilings on the rate of interest to be charged by these RRBs. However, from August 1996 the RRBs have been granted freedom to fix rates of interest, which is usually in the range of 14–18% for advances.

(*h*) **Nationalisation of six more Banks with Deposits over ₹200 Crore, 1980:** In 1980, in order to provide government more power and command over credit delivery, six more commercial banks in India were nationalised. In 1993, New Bank of India merged with Punjab National Bank (PNB), which brought the number of nationalised banks in India to 19. It's also the only merger between two Indian nationalised banks. In the following years, the nationalised banks in India saw a growth rate of around 4%, which was close to average growth rate of country's economy. Here is the list:

1. Bank of India
2. Union Bank of India
3. Bank of Baroda
4. Bank of Maharashtra
5. Punjab National Bank
6. Indian Bank

4.2.1 Objectives behind Nationalisation of Banks in India

The nationalisation of commercial banks took place with an aim to achieve following major objectives:

(*i*) **Social Welfare:** It was the need of the hour to direct the funds for the needy and required sectors of the Indian economy. Sector such as agriculture, small and village industries were in need of funds for their expansion and further economic development.

(ii) **Controlling Private Monopolies:** Prior to nationalisation many banks were controlled by private business houses and corporate families. It was necessary to check these monopolies in order to ensure a smooth supply of credit to socially desirable sections.

(iii) **Expansion of Banking:** In a large country like India the numbers of banks existing those days were certainly inadequate. It was necessary to spread banking across the country. It could be done through expanding banking network (by opening new bank branches) in the un-banked areas.

(iv) **Reducing Regional Imbalance:** In a country like India where we have a urban-rural divide; it was necessary for banks to go in the rural areas where the banking facilities were not available. In order to reduce this regional imbalance nationalisation was justified.

(v) **Priority Sector Lending:** In India, the agriculture sector and its allied activities were the largest contributor to the national income. Thus, these were labelled as the priority sectors. But unfortunately they were deprived of their due share in the credit. Nationalisation was urgently needed for catering funds to them.

(vi) **Developing Banking Habits:** In India more than 70% population used to stay in rural areas. It was necessary to develop the banking habit among such a large population.

(vii) **Mobilise the Savings of People:** It means that people should trust the bank enough to deposit their savings into particular bank so that the saving should be mobilised towards such banks.

(viii) **Channelise the Small Saving:** To insulate the small saving among the people, especially among weaker section of society so that there is equality when it comes to the commercial bank and its function.

(ix) **To Develop a Financial Infrastructure:** Before nationalisation, a lot of banks were running in losses & the government had to maintain a financial infrastructure in the economy, nationalisation of the same helped them to develop the very required financial infrastructure.

(x) **Proper Operation of banking functions & the System**: Banks before nationalisation used to follow their way of operations as the decision making power was in the hands of bank itself but with nationalisation and government can change the functioning of it as per requirement of country's economy and people in the nation.

(xi) **To Meet the Credit Requirement of Agriculture and Weaker Section of Society**: There should be equality in credit facilities for the people and thus after nationalisation of private sector it made to achieve that bank should meet the credit requirement of both sectors.

Some Other Objectives:

- To meet the credit requirements of the industries—Large and Small.
- To ensure that productive activities of economy should go on.
- Unproductive activities should be stopped.
- To remove poverty as a whole.
- Stable lending rates.
- To support economic activities of the country.

4.2.2 Demerits of Nationalisation of Banks in India

Though the nationalisation of commercial banks was undertaken with all objectives, in many senses it failed in attaining them. In fact, it converted many of the banking institutions in the loss making entities. The reasons were obvious lethargic working, lack of accountability, lack of profit motive, political interference, etc. Under this backdrop it is necessary to have a critical look to the whole process of nationalisation in the period after bank nationalisation.

The major limitations of the bank nationalisation in India are:

(*i*) **Inadequate Banking Facilities:** Even though banks have spread across the country; still many parts of the country are unbanked. Especially in the backward states such as the Uttar Pradesh, Madhya Pradesh, Chhattisgarh and north-eastern states of India.

(*ii*) **Limited Resources Mobilised and Allocated:** The resources mobilised after the nationalisation is not sufficient if we consider the needs of the Indian economy. Sometimes the deposits mobilised are enough but the resource allocation is not as per the expansions.

(*iii*) **Lowered Efficiency and Profits:** After nationalisation banks went in the government sector. Many times political forces pressurized them. Banking was not done on professional and ethical grounds. It resulted into lower efficiency and poor profitability of banks.

(*iv*) **Increased Expenditure:** Due to huge expansion in a branch network, large staff administrative expenditure, trade union struggle, etc. banks expenditure increased to dangerous levels.

(*v*) **Political and Administrative Inference:** Many public sector banks badly suffered due to the political interference. It was seen in arranging loan meals. It ultimately resulted in huge non-performing assets (NPA) of these banks and inefficiency.

Apart from this there are certain other limitations as well, such as weak infrastructure, poor competitiveness, etc.

But after Economic Reform of 1991, the Indian banking industry has entered into the new horizons of competitiveness, efficiency and productivity. It has made Indian banks more vibrant and professional organisations, removing the bad days of bank nationalisation.

4.2.3 Arguments in Favour of Nationalisation of Banks

(*i*) **Preventing Concentration of Economic Power:** Initially, a few leading industrial and business houses had close association with commercial banks. The directors of these banks happened to be the same industrialists who established monopoly control on the bank finance. They exploited the bank resources in such a way that the new business units cannot enter in any line of business in competition with these business houses. Nationalisation of banks, thus, prevents the spread of the monopoly enterprise.

(*ii*) **Social Control was not Adequate:** The 'social control' measures of the government did not work well. Some banks did not follow the regulations given under social control. Thus, the nationalisation was necessitated by the failure of social control.

(*iii*) **Channel the Bank Finance to Plan – Priority Sectors:** Banks collect savings from the general public. If it is in the hand of private sector, the national interests may be neglected, besides, in Five-Year Plans, the government gives priority to some specified sectors like agriculture, small industries, etc. Thus, nationalisation of banks ensures the availability of resources to the plan-priority sectors.

(*iv*) **Greater Mobilisation of Deposits:** The public sector banks open branches in rural areas where the private sector has failed. Because of such rapid branch expansion there is possibility to mobilise rural savings.

(*v*) **Help to Agriculture:** If banks fail to assist the agriculture in many ways, agriculture cannot prosper, that too, a country like India where more than 70% of the population depends upon agriculture. Thus, for providing increased finance to agriculture banks have to be nationalised.

(*vi*) **Balanced Regional Development:** In a country, certain areas remained backward for lack of financial resource and credit facilities. Private Banks neglected the backward areas because of poor business potential and profit opportunities. Nationalisation helps to provide bank finance in such a way as to achieve balanced inter-regional development and remove regional disparities.

(*vii*) **Greater Control by the Reserve Bank:** In a developing country like India there is need for exercising strict control over credit created by banks. If banks are under the control of the government, it becomes easy for the

Central Bank to bring about co-ordinated credit control. This necessitated the nationalisation of banks.

(viii) **Small Stake of Shareholders:** The nationalised banks had deposits totalling ₹2742 crore at the end of December 1968. But the capital contributed by their shareholders was only ₹28.5 crore, which was just 1% of deposits. Even if we include the reserves, the amount comes to only 2.4% of the bank's deposits with such a small and insignificant stake, it is unjustifiable to allow the private shareholders to exercise control over such vital credit machinery with large resources.

(ix) **Greater Stability of Banking Structure:** Nationalised banks are sure to command more confidence with the customers about the safety of their deposits. Besides this, the planned development of nationalised banks will impart greater stability for the banking structure.

(x) **March Forward towards Socialism:** India aims at socialism. This requires the financial institutions to run under the government's control and only through nationalisation, this objective can be effectively achieved.

(xi) **Better Service Conditions to Staff:** Nationalisation ensures the staff of banks to enjoy greater job security and higher emoluments. It can provide other benefits as well. In this way the banks can motivate their staff and thereby the operational efficiency of banks will be increased.

(xii) **New Schemes:** Through nationalised banks, new schemes like village adoption scheme, Lead Bank Scheme can be formulated and implemented. Besides, different types of financial facilities can be extended to persons like doctors, engineers, self-employed persons like artisans, etc.

4.2.4 Arguments against Nationalisation of Banks

(i) **Political Purpose Rather than for Productive Purpose:** The government has acquired the strength of a giant and there is the danger of using the financial resources for political purposes rather than for productive purpose.

(ii) **Beginning of State Capitalism:** Such a drastic step of nationalisation of about 90% of the banking resources is wholly unnecessary, especially if we take into consideration the enormous powers vested in the Reserve Bank of India for controlling banks' resources. It is considered as the beginning of state capitalism and not socialism in India.

(iii) **Scope for Inefficiency:** Some are of the opinion that after nationalisation banks will degenerate to the level of agricultural co-operatives, which are known for their inefficiency and corrupt practices. Some fear that the officers who manage these big banks also have to bow down to the politicians in course of time.

(*iv*) **India's Prestige Abroad:** The political prestige of India in foreign countries was damaged by this act of nationalisation. Doubts are expressed especially in countries which are rendering large-scale financial assistance to India, about the assurances and promises given by the government with regard to freedom of foreign enterprise in India. This may adversely affect the foreign assistance which India was receiving then.

(*v*) **Less Attractive Customer's Service:** The nationalised banks are sure to join the banks of other public undertakings which are known for their working to losses. Inefficiency, indecision, corruption, and lack of responsibility are the evils with which the government undertakings are suffering. A government bank may not care to attach importance to the customer's service.

(*vi*) **Secrecy of Customer's Accounts:** In spite of the assurances given and provisions made in the Act, businessmen still fear about the maintenance of the secrecy of the customer's accounts. As such, they may be forced to withdraw their deposits and go to some bank in the private sector and foreign banks. Thus nationalisation of big Indian banks will diverts some of the deposits of Indian banks to the foreign banks which is not at all desirable.

(*vii*) **Promises May not Materialise:** Nationalisation cannot convert the commercial banks overnight into agricultural banks. Similarly, the hopes raised among the poor and middle class people about the bank loans may ultimately prove to be false.

(*viii*) **Industry and Trade May Suffer:** Diversion of large sums of finances from the industry and trade to agricultural product is sure to starve the large-sized industries and business for finance. We cannot ignore the fact that the big industries and businesses are providing employment to millions of people and largely contributing to the production of wealth. To starve them for finance simply because they are 'big' will be upsetting the job opportunities and production in these concerns.

(*ix*) **Branch Expansion:** To argue that nationalisation will help to facilitate branch expansion to rural areas much more rapidly than the private banks cannot be supported by facts. Whether it is private bank or nationalised bank; it has to go by business principles and satisfy itself that the new branch is economically viable. In other words, branch expansion can be achieved by private banks as well, without nationalisation.

(*x*) **Burden of Compensation:** Nationalisation leads to the payment of heavy compensation to the shareholders. This gives additional financial burden on the government. Moreover, it is also argued that nationalisation will not bring much income to the government.

4.2.5 Achievements of Nationalised Banks

Development of Banking Industry

(*i*) **Lead Bank Scheme:** The lead bank scheme was introduced by the reserve bank of India towards the end of 1969 with the objective of enabling the commercial banks to assume the role of leadership for the development of banking and credit facilities throughout the country on the basis of area approach. A lead bank is assigned the role of a catalytic agent of economic development through the expansion of bank branches and diversification of credit facilities in the district allotted to it.

(*ii*) **Branch Expansion:** There has been a spectacular expansion of bank branches after nationalisation of major commercial banks in 1969. The lead bank scheme has played an important role in the bank expansion programme. The number of branches of all scheduled commercial banks, which increased from 4151–8262 (i.e., about 100% increase) during the 18 years of pre-nationalised period (1951–69), has further gone up from 8262 to 53840 (i.e., 522% increase) during the 18 years of post-nationalisation period.

(*iii*) **Coverage of Rural Areas:** The main thrust of branch expansion policy in the post-nationalisation period has been on increasing the banking facilities in the rural areas. There has been a significant increase in the rural branches of banks since 1969.

(*iv*) **Reduction of Regional Imbalances:** Another highlight of the branch expansion policy since the nationalisation of banks has been extending banking facilities in the deficit and unbanked areas and to reduce the regional imbalances.

(*v*) **Expansion of Bank Deposits:** Since nationalisation of banks, there has been a significant increase in the deposits of commercial banks. During the 18 years of pre-nationalisation period, the deposits in the banks increased from ₹908 crore to ₹4646 crore. In post nationalisation period from ₹4646 crore to ₹107345 crore.

(*vi*) **Change in Composition of Deposits:** The relative proportions of demand and time deposits have also changed markedly after the nationalisation of banks. The proportion of time deposits has increased continuously from 50% in 1951 to 75% in 1969 and further to 85% in 2006.

(*vii*) **Credit Expansion:** The expansion of bank credit has also been more spectacular in the post bank nationalisation period.

(*viii*) **Investment in Government Securities:** The nationalised banks were also expected to provide finance for economic plans of the country through the purchase of government securities.

Financing of Priority Sectors

(*i*) **Lesser Importance to Big Industries:** The sectoral deployment of credit has undergone a great qualitative change after the nationalisation of banks. In the pre-nationalisation days, large and medium industries and wholesale trade account for about 78% of the total bank credit, while agriculture accounted for only 2.2% of the total bank credit.

(*ii*) **Advances to Priority Sectors:** One of the main objectives of nationalisation of banks was to extend credit facilities to the borrowers in these so far neglected sectors of the economy. To achieve this objective, the banks formulated various schemes to provide credit to the small borrowers in the priority sectors like agriculture, small scale industry, road and water transport, retail trade, and small business. Considering the necessity of meeting specific credit requirements of the weaker sections, consumption credit has been included in the priority sectors.

(*iii*) **Agricultural Finance**: After nationalisation, the commercial banks have been giving special attention to the financial needs of agriculturists and of rural areas.

(*iv*) **Bank Credit for Small Scale Industries**: Small scale industries sector has also been recognised by the government as an important productive sector of the economy which deserves special financial assistance by the commercial banks.

(*v*) **Banks and Export Promotion:** In a developing economy like India, there is a great need to promote exports in order to earn sufficient foreign exchange able to meet the country's large and growing foreign exchange obligations.

(*vi*) **Housing Finance:** Housing finance is another priority sector and the public sector banks play a crucial role in this area. The major issue in respect of housing finance is how to bridge the gap between the demand for housing finance and its supply from all sources put together.

(*vii*) **Credit to Weaker Sections:** In order to increase the flow of bank credit to the smaller and poorer borrowers the government has broadened the concept of weaker sections of the society. Now the weaker sections include small and marginal farmers, landless labourers, tenant farmers and share croppers, artisans, village and cottage industries, beneficiaries of integrated Rural Development Programme, scheduled castes and scheduled tribes, and beneficiaries of differential rate of interest scheme.

(*viii*) **Differential Rate of Interest Scheme:** With a view to provide bank credit to the weaker sections of the society at a concessional rate, the government introduced the differential rate of interest scheme from April 1972.

(*ix*) **Kisan Credit Card Scheme:** Kisan Credit Card was introduced in 1998–99 to provide better access to short-term institutional credit (i.e., from commercial banks and regional rural banks) to farmers.

4.2.6 Failures (Critical Appraisal) of Nationalisation of Banks

(*i*) **Criticism by Estimates Committee:** The Estimates Committee of Lok Sabha (1975) headed by R.K. Sinha has expressed dissatisfaction over the working of nationalisation banks.

(*ii*) **Insufficient help to Priority Sectors:** In spite of much increase in the loans advanced to the priority sectors, the total help is not sufficient for the large size of these sectors. The rate of increase in the advances to the priority sectors which was rapid in the initial years of post-nationalisation period has slowed down in the late years.

(*iii*) **Inadequate Facilities in Rural Areas:** No doubt, much progress has been made in expanding bank branches in respect of bank expansion, deposit mobilisation and credit expansion in rural areas. But, it is not adequate to meet the financial needs of the population living in the rural areas.

(*iv*) **Regional Imbalances:** Though the overall expansion in the bank branches has taken place in the country, their expansion is not equitably distributed among the different states. According to the reserve Bank's report, about half of the banking institutions concentrate in the two regions i.e., southern and western only.

(*v*) **Insufficient Deposit Mobilisation:** Despite good progress on the deposit mobilisation front, much remains to the done. Deposit mobilisation by the public sector banks has been about 16% to 17% per annum since nationalisation. On the other hand, it has been found that foreign banks and the smaller private banks have received much greater increase in deposits.

(*vi*) **Problem of Liberal Credit Policy:** Although liberal credit policy is necessary for providing financial support to the weaker sections of the rural community, but such a policy may prove harmful for stability of the banking system. The experience of the nationalised banks has shown that these banks were about 24% as compared to the deposit expansion about 17%.

(*vii*) **Low Profitability:** A major defect of banking after nationalisation is that the nationalised banks are either operating under losses or experiencing falling dividends.

(*viii*) **Political Pressure:** Political interference also disturbs the smooth working of the nationalised banks. Political pressure in the granting of loans to particular parties, the selection of personnel, opening branches, etc. creates difficulties for these banks.

4.3 MERGER OF 10 PUBLIC SECTOR BANKS

Ten Public Sector Undertaking (PSU) banks will be amalgamated into four banks, 1st April, 2020. In the biggest consolidation exercise in the banking space, the government in August 2019 had announced the merger of 10 public sector lenders into four bigger and stronger banks. With this, the number of public sector banks in India will come down to 12 from 27 in 2017. It was widely speculated that the government may defer the consolidation exercise for some time due to the novel coronavirus pandemic that has impacted our economy. Some mega merger of PSU banks, that will came into force from 1 April, 2020.

1. Oriental Bank of Commerce (OBC) and United Bank of India will be merged into Punjab National Bank (PNB). After the merger, these together will form the second-largest public sector bank in the country, after State Bank of India (SBI).
2. Syndicate Bank will be merged into Canara Bank, which will make it the fourth-largest public sector lender.
3. Indian Bank will be merged with Allahabad Bank.
4. Union Bank of India will be merged with Andhra Bank and Corporation Bank
5. Customers, including depositors of merging banks will be treated as customers of the banks in which these banks have been merged with effect from 1 April, 2020.
6. After the merger, there will be 12 PSUs – six merged banks and six independent public sector banks.

   Six merged banks – SBI, Bank of Baroda, Punjab National Bank, Canara Bank, Union Bank of India, Indian Bank – Six independent banks – Indian Overseas Bank, UCO Bank, Bank of Maharashtra, Punjab and Sind Bank, Bank of India, Central Bank of India.
7. The Oriental Bank of Commerce and United Bank of India will operate as the branches of the Punjab National Bank.
8. Syndicate Bank will function as the branch of Canara Bank.
9. Similarly, all Allahabad Bank branches will be treated as branches of the Indian Bank.
10. All branches of Andhra Bank and Corporation Bank will function as Union Bank of India branches.

Earlier this month the cabinet gave its approval for the mergers that will consolidate operations of 10 public sector banks (PSBs) into four 'mega banks'.

REVIEW QUESTIONS

1. Discuss the nationalisation of the banking industry from 1960s to 1980s.
2. What are small finance banks? Which are the 10 small finance banks?
3. Discuss the impact of the IT revolution on the banking industry.
4. What were the objectives behind the nationalization of banks in India?
5. Discuss the merger of the 10 Public Sector banks.

Banking Structure and System in India

5

5.1 INTRODUCTION

In the earlier societies functions of a bank were done by the corresponding institutions dealing with loans and advances. Britishers brought into India the modern concept of banking by the start of Bank of England in 1694. In 1708, the Bank of England was given the monopoly for the issue of currency notes by an Act. In nineteenth century various banks started operations, which primarily were receiving money on deposits, lending money, transferring money from one place to another and bill discounting.

History of Banking in India: Banking in India has a very old origin. It started in the Vedic period where literature shows the giving of loans to others on interest. The interest rates ranged from two to five per cent per month. The payment of debt was made pious obligation on the heir of the dead person.

Modern banking in India began with the rise of power of the British. To raise the resources for attaining the power, East India Company on 2nd June, 1806 promoted the Bank of Calcutta. In the mean while two other banks Bank of Bombay and Bank of Madras were started on 15th April 1840 and 1st July, 1843 respectively. In 1862 the right to issue the notes was taken away from the presidency banks. The government also withdrew the nominee directors from these banks. The Bank of Bombay collapsed in 1867 and was put under the voluntary liquidation in 1868 and was finally wound up in 1872. The bank was however able to meet the liability of public in full. A new bank called 'New Bank of Bombay' was started in 1867.

5.2 STRUCTURE OF BANKING IN INDIA

Indian banking system comprises of both organised and unorganised banks. Figure 5.1 represents the structure of banking structure. Unorganised banking includes indigenous bankers and village money-lenders. Organised banking includes the following:

1. Reserve Bank of India (Central Bank)
2. Commercial Banks (including Foreign Banks)
3. Development Banks

4. EXIM Bank
5. Cooperative Banks
6. Regional Rural Banks
7. National Banks for Agricultural and Rural Development (NABARD)
8. Land Development Banks

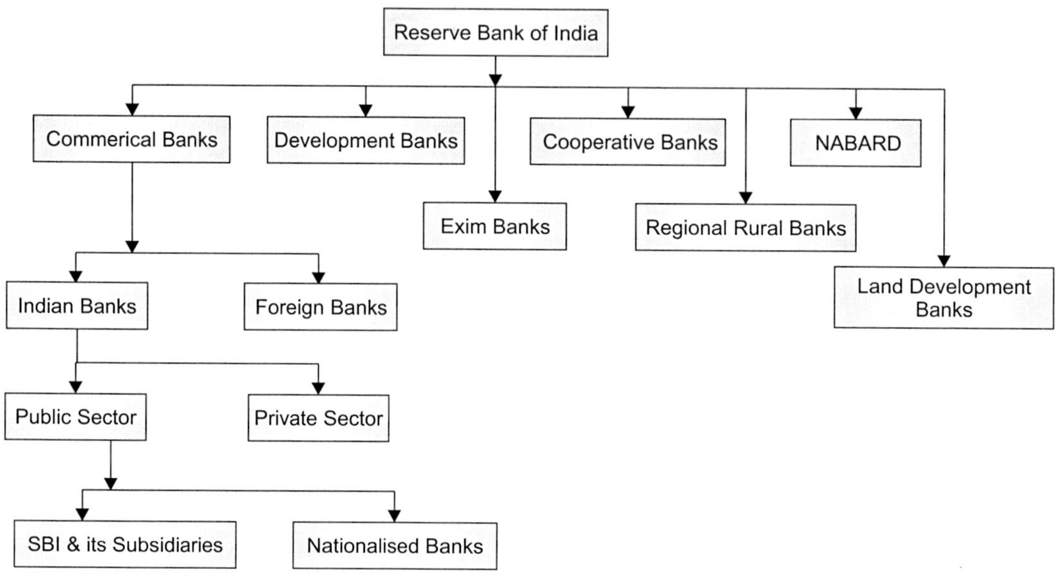

1. **Reserve Bank of India:** The Reserve Bank of India (RBI) is the Central Banks of our country. It came into being on April1, 1935 under the Reserve Bank of India Act, 1934. This acts as a leader of money market and the bank of the bankers. It supervises and regulates the activities of commercial banks and other financial institution. It frames and supervises various policies to bring and maintain monetary equilibrium in the economy. It also acts as the banks to the Central Government.

   Its functions are:

   (*a*) to issue paper money

   (*b*) to regulate control and supervise the commercial banks of the country

   (*c*) to control money market

   (*d*) to frame policies to regulate and control the loans and advances

   (*e*) to regulate and control the foreign exchange

   (*f*) to publish monetary and financial information

   (*g*) to regulate and control the value of Indian rupee in relation to different foreign currencies.

   (*h*) to frame policies for credit to priority sectors

2. **Commercial Banks:** It is a financial institution which accepts deposits against which cheques can be drawn, lends money to commerce and industry and renders a number of other useful services to the customers and the society. Commercial banks receive deposits in the form of fixed deposits, saving banks accounts and current accounts and advance money, generally for short periods, in the form of cash credits, overdrafts and loans.

   The functions of Commercial Banks are:

   (*a*) Receiving deposits from the public and the business firms

   (*b*) Lending money to various sections of the economy for productive activities.

   (*c*) Issue of demand drafts, traveler's cheques, banks card, for the smooth remittance of funds.

   (*d*) Provision of locker facility to the customers

   (*e*) Safe custody of documents, ornaments and other valuable of customers

   (*f*) Payments of telephone, electric bills on behalf of the customer

   (*g*) Collections of cheques of the customers

   (*h*) Acting as trustee and executor of wills

3. **Development Banks:** Development banks provide long-term funds to the industrial enterprises. They are also known as industrial banks or special financial institutions. They raise their funds by the issue of shares and debentures and mobilising long-term deposits from the public. Out of these funds, they are in a position to lend money for long period. Industrial banks specialise in financing large scale industrial units.

   The functions of Development Banks are:

   (*a*) Provision of long-term loans to industrial organisations requiring fixed capital for their expansion and modernisation programmes

   (*b*) Promotion of new industrial ventures. They invest in the shares and debentures of industrial organisation and also underwrite the issue of their shares and debentures.

   (*c*) Provision of technical guidance in project studies and the management of projects.

   (*d*) Controlling and guiding the affairs of the industrial undertaking by securing representation on their boards of directors.

4. **EXIM Bank:** The Export-Import Banks of India (EXIM bank) was set up in January, 1982 as a statutory corporation and it commenced operations on March1, 1982. The Bank, with its headquarters at Bombay, has an authorized capital of ₹200 crore, which may be increased to ₹500 crore by the Central Government. The EXIM Bank has a 17-member Board of Directors, with Chairman and Managing Director as the chief executive and full-time director.

The Board of Directors consists of the representative of the Government of India, RBI, IDBI, ECGC, commercial banks and the exporting community. Its recourses mainly comprises contributions from the government in the form of grants and loans, markets borrowing, deposits of long-terms duration from the public and the short-term and long-term funds from the Reserve Bank of India.

The functions of EXIM bank include:

(*a*) Planning, promoting and developing exports and imports;

(*b*) Providing technical, administrative and managerial assistance for promotion, management and expansion of exports; and

(*c*) Undertaking market and investment surveys and techno-economic studies related to development of exports of goods and services.

5. **Cooperative Banks:** Cooperative banks are formed on the principle of co-operative to extend credit facilities to farmers and small scale industrial concerns and promotes in general the habit of thrift and self-help among the low and middle income groups of the society. The distinguishing feature of a co-operative bank is the absence of profit motive. Cooperative banks are very helpful to meet the requirement of small farmers, artisan, In India; co-operative banks have been the pioneers in mobilising rural deposits.

   Co-operative banking has a three-tier structure. At the top there is State Co-operative Bank at the state level. At the intermediate level, there are Central Cooperative Banks. At the base of the pyramid there are Primary Credit Societies at the village level.

6. **Regional Rural Banks (RRBs):** Regional Rural Banks are local level banking organisations operating in different States of India. They have been created with a view to serve primarily the rural areas of India with basic banking and financial services. However, RRB's may have branches setup for urban operations and their area of operation may include urban areas too. The main purpose of RRB's is to mobilise financial resources from rural/semi-urban areas and grant loans and advances mostly to small and marginal farmers, agricultural labourers and rural artisans. The area of operation of RRBs is limited to the area as notified by Government of India covering one or more districts in the State. RRB's also perform a variety of different functions. RRB's perform various functions in following heads:

   (*a*) Providing banking facilities to rural and semi-urban areas.

   (*b*) Carrying out government operations like disbursement of wages of MGNREGA workers, distribution of pensions, etc.

   (*c*) Providing Para-Banking facilities like locker facilities, debit and credit cards.

7. **National Bank for Agriculture and Rural Development – NABARD (National Farm Bank):** The National Bank for Agricultural and Rural Development started its operations with effect from July 15,1982. It is an apex development bank with a mandate for providing credit flow for promotion and development of agriculture, small scale industries and all other allied economic activities in rural area. Its main function is to provide refinance to lending institutions in rural area.

   Other functions of NABARD include:

   (*a*) Prepare on annual basis, rural credit plans for all the districts in the country. These plans form base for annual credit plans of all rural financial institutions

   (*b*) Undertakes monitoring and evaluation of projects refinanced by it.

   (*c*) Promotes research in the fields of rural banking, agriculture and rural development.

   (*d*) Functions as a regulatory authority, supervising, monitoring and guiding co-operative banks and regional rural banks.

8. **Land Development Banks:** These banks provide long-term credit to agriculturalists against security of their land for purchasing tools and implements and for permanent improvements of land. In India, these banks were set up to provide loans to agriculturists on easy terms against mortgage of land for the purpose of repayment of loans to village money-lenders and indigenous bankers.

   They raise their recourses by issuing shares and debentures to the public. They also accept long-term deposits from the public. They grant loans to agriculturists which are repayable by instalments spread over a number of years ranging from twenty to thirty years.

9. **Indigenous Banks:** In many countries, there are businessmen doing banking business as side occupation. The merchant bankers of England and the indigenous bankers in India are the example of such bankers. The Indian central Banking Enquiry Committee defined an indigenous banker as an individual or private firms receiving deposits and dealing in hundis or lending money. These banks borrow by accepting deposits on current accounts as well as fixed deposits. The indigenous banks form an unorganised part of the banking structure because they do not follow the banking practices as others banks in the country. They do not publish their accounts and do not get them audited. They inherit their banking business from their great grandfather. The main drawback of indigenous bankers is that they are still following the conservative practices. They are not governed by RBI.

5.3 BANKING SYSTEM IN INDIA

Different countries adopt different banking systems. Various types of banking systems are:

1. Branch Banking
2. Unit Banking
3. Group Banking
4. Chain Banking, and
5. Mixed Banking.

1. Branch Banking: Branch banking centre or financial centre refers to a single bank which operates through various branches in a city or in different locations or out of the cities. This kind of banking system is common in India, *e.g.*, State bank of India. It offers a wide array of face to face service to its customers. Historically, branches were housed in imposing buildings, often in a neoclassical architecture style. Today, branches may also take the form of smaller offices within a larger complex, such as a shopping mall. Services provided by a branch include cash withdrawals and deposits from a demand account with a bank teller, financial advice through a specialist, safe deposit box rentals, bureau de change, insurance sales (where it is allowed by law), etc. Other financial institutions reduce their costs by having no branches and are sometimes known as virtual banks. In this type of banking system a big bank as a single owner ship operates through a network of branches spread all over the country. This type of banking system was initially developed in England. Later on it become popular in other countries like Canada, India and Australia, etc.

The advantages of Branch Banking:

(*a*) *Economies of Large Scale Operation:* Under branch banking system the bank with a number of branches posses' huge financial resources and enjoy the benefits of large scale operations. In this type of banking system highly trained and experienced staff is appointed which increases the efficiency of the management.

(*b*) *Spreading of Risk:* Another advantage of branch banking system is lesser risk and greater capacity to meet risks. Since there is a wide geographical spreading and diversification of risk is possible in this system. Further the possibilities of failures are very less.

(*c*) *Economy in Cash Reserve:* Under this system a particular branch can operate without keeping large amount of ideal resources. The funds can be easily transferred from one branch to another.

(*d*) *Cheap Remittance Facility:* In this type of banking system as branches are spread all over the country. So, it is easier and cheaper to transfer the funds.

(*e*) *Uniform Rate of Interest:* Under branch banking system mobility of capital increases as a result of equality in the rate of interests. The funds can be transferred from the excess branches to the shortage branches. Consequently, uniformity in the rate of interest prevails in the whole area.

The disadvantages of Branch Banking:

(a) *Problem of Management:* Under branch banking system a number of difficulties regarding management and supervision and control may arise. Banks get concentrated at the head office. The branch manager has to seek permission from the head office on each and every matter. This results in unnecessary delay in banking business.

(b) *Lack of Initiative:* In this type of banking system the branch manager generally lacks of initiatives on all the matters. He cannot take independent decisions on every matter. He has to wait for the clearance signal from head office.

(c) *Regional Imbalances:* Under this system the financial resources collected in the rural areas and backward regions are transferred to big industrial sectors. This encourages regional imbalance in the country.

(d) *Monopolistic Tendencies:* Branch banking encourages monopolistic tendencies in the banking system of a country. It may lead to the concentration of resources in few hands. A few banks may dominate the whole banking system in the country.

(e) *Inefficient Branches:* In this type of banking system weak and unprofitable branches continue to operate under the protection of large and profitable branches

2. Unit Banking: A unit bank operates with a single office or place of business. It has its own board of directors and stockholders; it usually has no branches and acts with a single office as a separate and independent unit. Unit banking grew in USA because of legislative enactments. As said earlier certain states allow only limited branch banking while some states prohibit branch banking. The areas of operation of a unit bank are localised and are far more limited as compared to branch banking.

The advantages of Unit Banking:

(a) *Local Development:* Unit banking is localised banking. It knows the local problem and serves the requirement of the local people in better way than branch banking.

(b) *Promotes Regional Balance:* Under this system there is no transfer of resources from rural/backward areas to urban/industrial areas. This helps to reduce to regional imbalance.

(c) *Easy Management:* Supervision and management of unit banking is very easy and more effective than branch banking system. There is less chances of fraud and irregularities in this system.

(d) *Quality Customers Service:* Unit banking system provides quality services to customers.

(*e*) *Initiatives in Banking Business:* In unit banking decisions can be taken very quickly. Due to full knowledge and greater involvement in the problem they are in a position to take initiatives to tackle these problems through financial help.

(*f*) *No Monopolistic Tendencies:* Unit banking is generally small in size, so that there is no possibility of monopolistic tendency in banking system.

(*g*) *No Inefficient Branches:* Under unit banking system, weak and inefficient branches will be shutdown. No protection is provided to such banks.

(*h*) *No Diseconomies of Large Scale Operations:* This system is free from diseconomies and problems of large scale operations which are generally experienced by branch banks.

The disadvantages of Unit Banking:

(*a*) *No Distribution of Risks:* Under this system the bank operations are highly localised. There is no possibility of distribution and diversification of risk between branch as well as areas.

(*b*) *Inability to Face Crisis:* Due to limited resources this system is unable to face the crisis. These banks are not in a position to stand a sudden rush of withdrawals.

(*c*) *No Banking Development in Backward/Rural Areas:* Due to their limited resources unit banking cannot afford to open uneconomic banking business in smaller towns, backward, remote and rural areas.

(*d*) *Lack of Specialisation:* Unit banks due to their small size are not capable to get advantages of division of labour and specialisation. Such banks cannot afford to employ highly trained and specialised staff.

(*e*) *Costly Remittance of Funds:* Due to lack of other branches it is very costly to transfer funds.

(*f*) *Disparity in Interest Rates:* Unit banking has different interest rates in every unit banking and different places.

(*g*) *Local Pressures:* Since unit banks are highly localised in their business, local pressures and interferences generally disrupt their normal functioning.

(*h*) *Undesirable Competition:* Unit banks are independently run by different managements. This results in undesirable competition among different unit banks.

(*i*) *High Cash Reserve:* Unit banks have to maintain high cash reserve ratio. As a result, the bank's capacity to create credit will be less.

3. Group Banking: Group Banking is the system in which two or more independently incorporated banks are brought under the control of a holding company. The holding company may or may not be a banking company. Under group banking, the individual banks may be unit banks, or banks operating branches or a combination of the two. Participating banks retain their own boards of directors which are responsible to the supervising and regulatory authority and depositors for the proper operation of the bank. That is, each bank in the group has got a separate entity. This system has developed in United States in 1900. It was popular and extensively developed in 1920's.

The following are the advantages of the Group Banking System:

(*a*) *Centralised Administration:* The participating banks enjoy the benefits of centralised administration. The group banking is generally working in the centralised administration and also works for the welfare of the centralised administration.

(*b*) *Enhancement of operational efficiency:* Because of group banking system, the operational efficiency of participant banks is enhanced through shared knowledge and experience. The group banking also providing the efficiency of the operational enhancement in the market

(*c*) *Broader market:* Group Banking offers broader market to the small banks for their excess resources. Thus, their earning capacity and network improved. It is broader market rather than the chain banking and unit banking.

(*d*) *Mobility and transfer of resources:* In the case of crisis, the funds are transferred among participating banks. This helps them to face the financial crisis if any, more effectively. The group banking helps their customer by providing mobility and transfer of resources.

(*e*) *Large scale operation:* Group banking paves the way for large scale operation. The member banks can get the economies of large scale operation. The group banking consists of large scale of operations in the markets.

The disadvantages of Group Banking are:

(*a*) *Lack of effective management and control:* Under Group banking system the control and management is not effective because the control is indirect and more flexible. It cannot offer specialised management.

(*b*) *Inefficiency of member banks protected:* The inefficiency of one participating bank affects the other participating banks. The group banking consists of inefficiency of members that protects the banks.

(*c*) *Fewer facilities:* This system cannot provide all the facilities offered by branch banking. The group banking providing the less facilities in compared to the branch banking and other banking in the market.

(*d*) *Can't mobilise funds:* Group banking does not have the capacity to mobilise funds as in the case with branch banking. Hence, it cannot offer the same economy of operations as are offered by branch banking.

4. Chain Banking: Chain banking is a situation in which three or more banks that are independently chartered are controlled by a small group of people. The mechanisms used to establish this type of arrangement normally involve securing enough stock between the individuals to have a controlling interest in each of the bank corporations involved. The arrangement can also be managed with the establishment of interlocking directorates or boards of directors that effectively create a network between the banks without the need for some type of central holding company. In years past, chain banking afforded several benefits for investors. The strategy made it possible to earn steady returns from several banks that operated in the same community, without any fears of a great deal of competition from other banks in the area. The network approach made it possible for investors to use their cumulative influence to keep bank services and their attendant fees similar from one enterprise to another, thus ensuring that returns remained consistent.

The advantages of Chain Banking are:

(*a*) *Optimum utilisation of resources:* The chain banking helps in optimum utilisation fully and do not waste the resources unnecessary. They used the resources fully.

(*b*) *High level of earnings:* The chain banking consists of high level of earnings by attracting more and more customers in the markets. If they consists more customer then they earn more profits.

(*c*) *Diversification of risks:* The chain banking consists of less risk as compared to the other banking systems use the risks is diversified in the chain banking.

(*d*) *Centralised control:* The chain banking is working under the central governments so that it consists of the centralised control.

(*e*) *Economy in administration and operation:* In the point the chain banking is working to increase their economy. If the economy increases then the administration of the banking also increases.

The disadvantages of Chain Banking are:

(*a*) *Lack of flexibility:* There is a lack of flexibility the chain banking does not change itself very quickly according to the various situations that are take place in the chain banking system.

(*b*) *Absence of efficient supervision:* The main disadvantage of the chain banking is that there is a absence of efficient supervision and without the efficient supervision the banking is incomplete.

(*c*) *Harm due to existence of speculation:* The chain banking is also affected due to the existence of the speculation. The chain banking gets harm due to existence of speculation.

(*d*) *Irregularities of work:* In the chain banking there is a irregularity of work. Due to the irregularity of the chain banking gets affected.

(*e*) *More cases of maladministration and fraud:* In the chain banking there are most of the cases are of maladministration and frauds. The chain banking is safer banking rather than other banking.

5. Mixed Banking System: The origin of mixed banking lies in the extension of the operations of the investment bank to the commercial in banking field. Mixed banking is defined as a system where banks make both short-term and long-term investments. For industrial development, the industries, trade and commerce need both short-term and long-term loans. Investment banking provides long-term loans while commercial banks provide short-term funds. So, mixed banking combines the principles of both investment banking and commercial banking. In brief, it is a system of banking under which commercial banks provide both short-and long-term loans for commerce and industries.

Factors leading to the Origin of Mixed Banking:

(*a*) Trade and industries requires both short-term and long-term loans. Under the mixed banking system the commercial banks meet the short- as well as long-term credit requirements of industries.

(*b*) The need for industrial revival is felt both by the government and the banks. Many industrial units to which the banks have supplied short-term loans, they are not in a position to repay their loan amount. So, the bank took a wise step to take debentures of such companies instead of writing off these short-term loans.

(*c*) The deposits of commercial banks were increasing very fast and thus it is advisable for the banks to advance loans for long periods.

(*d*) The growth of big industries led to a decrease in the dependence of bank finance as they built-up their own surplus funds to supplement their working capital. Thus, banks are deprived of their best customers. So, they are compelled to grant long-term loans to big industries and gradually start holding industrial securities.

(*e*) In many European countries the banks undertook the responsibility of supplying long-term finance to industries for speedy industrialisation.

The advantages of Mixed Banking System are:

(*a*) *Credit requirements are fulfilled:* It grants short-term loans for the purchase of raw materials and the payment of wages and salaries and also grants long term loans for the purchase of plant and machinery and other assets.

(*b*) *Banking resources are utilised for industrial development:* A commercial bank raises large funds from the public by way of deposits. Thus, if a commercial bank undertakes industrial banking; it will have large funds to provide substantial aid to industries.

(*c*) *Expert guidance and advice to Industries:* A mixed bank appoints experts to access the soundness of an industrial unit and to evaluate its securities. On the basis of the advice given by the experts it can subscribe to the shares and debentures of the companies and can appoint its nominees in their board of directors.

(*d*) *Investment guidance to general public:* Mixed bank provides valuable advice to its customers on investments in shares and debentures since it has a personal knowledge of the working of number of industrial organisations. Thus, mixed banking stimulates capital formation in the country.

(*e*) *Promote rapid industrial development through investment banking:* Mixed banking facilities industrialisation in developing countries. It does so by providing both short-term and long-term financial accommodations.

(*f*) *Risk sharing mechanism:* The banks can join together into groups to share the risk of industrial finance. The mixed banks have followed this practice and appointed their person in the board of directors of companies. This helps the banks to have personal knowledge of the working of the industrial enterprises.

The disadvantages Mixed Banking System are:

(*a*) *Liquidity of banks may be affected:* It reduces the liquidity of banks. A large part of the funds of the bank is raised from deposits, which are repayable either on demand or after a short period.

(*b*) *Possibility of engaging in speculative business:* There is a huge possibility to use their funds in the speculative business to maximise their profit.

(*c*) *Scope for over lending:* During the periods of boom, banks are tempted to over invest their funds in industries beyond their safe limits. The bank may indulge into speculation of shares in the hope of earning higher profits. This carries great results into huge losses.

(*d*) *Threat to Stability of Banks:* The stability of the bank may be affected if the prices of securities in which banks have invested depreciate.

REVIEW QUESTIONS

1. Discuss in brief the history of banking in India.
2. What is the structure of banking in India?
3. Write a brief note about the EXIM bank.
4. What are commercial banks? What is development bank?
5. Give a brief gist of the NABARD.

Reserve Bank of India

6

6.1 INTRODUCTION

The Reserve Bank of India (RBI) is India's central banking institution, which controls the monetary policy of the Indian economy. It was established on 1 April, 1935 during the British Raj in accordance with the provisions of the Reserve Bank of India Act, 1934. The share capital was divided into shares of ₹100 each and fully paid which was entirely owned by private shareholders in the beginning. Following India's independence in 1947, the RBI was nationalised in the year 1949.

The RBI plays an important role in the development strategy of the Government of India. It is a member bank of the Asian Clearing Union. The general superintendence and direction of the RBI is entrusted with the 21-member-strong Central Board of Directors; the Governor, four Deputy Governors, two Finance Ministry representatives, ten Government-nominated Directors to represent important elements from India's economy, and four Directors to represent Local Boards headquartered at Mumbai, Kolkata, Chennai and New Delhi. Each of these Local Boards consists of five members who represent regional interests, as well as the interests of co-operative and indigenous banks.

6.1.1 Organisation of RBI

The organisation of RBI consists of:

Central Board of Dirсctors: The Central Board of Directors is the main committee of the Central Bank. The Government of India appoints the directors for a four-year term. The Board consists of a governor, four deputy governors, fifteen directors to represent the regional boards, one from the Ministry of Finance and ten other directors from various fields.

Governors: RBI has one Governor. The RBI can extend the period of the Governor. There are four deputy governors.

Supportive Bodies: The Reserve Bank of India has ten regional representations: North in New Delhi, South in Chennai, East in Kolkata and West in Mumbai. The representations are formed by five members, appointed for four years by the central government and serve; beside the advice of the Central Board of Directors; as a forum for regional banks and to deal with delegated tasks from the central board. The institution has 19 regional offices.

The Board of Financial Supervision (BFS): It is formed in November 1994, serves as a CCBD committee to control the financial institutions. It has four members, appointed for two years, and takes measures to strength the role of statutory auditors in the financial sector, external monitoring and internal controlling systems.

The Tarapore Committee was set up by the Reserve Bank of India under the chairmanship of former RBI deputy governor S.S. Tarapore to 'lay the road map' to capital account convertibility. The five-member committee recommended a three-year time frame for complete convertibility by 1999–2000. On 1, July 2007, in an attempt to enhance the quality of customer service and strengthen the grievance redressal mechanism, the Reserve Bank of India created a new customer service department.

Offices and Branches: The Reserve Bank of India has four zonal offices. It has 19 regional offices at most state capitals and at a few major cities in India. Few of them are located in Ahmedabad, Bangalore, Bhopal, Bhubaneswar, Chandigarh, Chennai, Delhi, Guwahati, Hyderabad, Jaipur, Jammu, Kanpur, Kolkata, Lucknow, Mumbai, Nagpur, Patna and Thiruvanathapurm. Besides it has nine sub-offices at Agartala, Dehradun, Gangtok, Kochi, Panaji, Raipur, Ranchi, Shimla and Srinagar. The bank has also two training colleges for its officers, viz. Reserve Bank Staff College at Chennai and College of Agricultural Banking at Pune. There are also four Zonal Training Centres at Mumbai, Chennai, Kolkata and New Delhi.

Necessity of Central Bank/RBI: Since the First World War, the most important developmental in the field of monetary theory is the emergence of central banks with added prestige and power. Nowaday, the institution of central bank is considered indispensable in every country. Now, there is hardly a civilised country which does not possess a central bank. Central banks are necessary because of the following reasons:

Monetary system requires management. Money will not manage itself said Bagehot long ago. Even gold standard was not fully automatic. Now paper standard is in operation in every country, has to be directed by some central authority. Almost all modern economies main aim is achieving the twin objective of employment and price stability. Therefore, a sound monetary policy directed by a central bank is badly needed.

Banking system requires control and regulation, the banks of a country, being private institution, act by profit motive because they are comparative concerns, they cannot follow a common policy according to national requirements. The result is either creation to much credit sometimes or too little at the times. Therefore, a central co-ordinating authority, which will compel them to follow the policy appropriate under economic situation is necessary, hence, birth of an institution called the Central Bank in every country.

6.1.2 Objectives of RBI

Following are the main objectives of RBI:

1. *To Manage the Monetary and Credit System of the Country:* RBI is an apex institution which controls the credit policy through qualitative and quantitative methods. RBI is responsible for increase or decrease of credit in the market.

2. *To Stabilises Internal and External Value of Rupee:* As we know the value of rupee is declining as compared to foreign currency. Rupee value is declining on continuous basis. It is the duty of RBI to take care of value of rupee.

3. *To Make Balanced and Systematic Development of Banking in the Country:* Central bank is a banker of all banks. All banks have to deposit a sum of amount from their public deposits. It is according to cash reserve ratio. All banks are come under central bank and it is responsible for all banks.

4. *To Develop Organised Money Market in the Country:* There are many organised money market which provide the facility of credit and loans, etc. Central bank is responsible for the development of organised money market in Indian economy.

5. *To Make Proper Arrangement of Agriculture Finance:* RBI's main objective is to make new policies and open new institution to provide finance for agricultural sector. Hence he is working in continuous order and working for the betterment of agricultural sector.

6. *To Make Proper Arrangement of Industrial Finance:* RBI also concern for industrial sector. It also looks out for proper facilities of credit to the industrial sector also. RBI take care all other facilities for industrial sector.

7. *To Make Proper Management of Public Debts:* RBI works for the proper management of public debts. It is very concerned about the public debt and supply of money that gives more importance to public debts.

8. *To Establish Monetary Relations with other Countries of the World and International Financial Institutions:* RBI also works as foreign exchange bank. People can get another country's currency and can make foreign exchange transaction also. But it charges some money as a fee for the exchange.

9. *To Centralised Cash Reserves of Commercial Banks:* All banks submit some amount of their deposits to central bank as a cash reserve ratio, which central bank uses for the credit creation and he can lend money to commercial bank from these deposits.

10. *To Maintain Balance between the Demand and Supply of Currency:* Central bank can maintain the demand and supply of currency by using the quantitative methods and qualitative methods.

6.1.3 Functions of RBI

The function of RBI can be categorised into traditional function, developmental function and supervisory function which are discussed below:

1. **Traditional Functions:** Traditional functions are those functions which every central bank of each nation performs allover the world. Basically these functions are inline with the objectives which the bank is setup. It includes fundamental functions of the Central Bank. They comprise of the following tasks:
   (*i*) *Issue of Currency Notes:* The RBI has the sole right or authority or monopoly of issuing currency notes except one rupee note and coins of smaller denomination. These currency notes are legal tender issued by the RBI. Currently it is in denominations of ₹2, 5, 10, 20, 50, 100, 500 and 1,000. The RBI has not only powers to issue the currency notes and withdraw but even to exchange these currency notes for other denominations. It issues these notes against the security of gold bullion, foreign securities, rupee coins, exchange bills and promissory notes and government of India bonds.

   (*ii*) *Banker to Banks:* The RBI being an apex monitory institution has obligatory powers to guide, help and give direction to other commercial banks in the country. The RBI can control the volumes of banks reserves and allow other banks to create credit in that proportion. Every commercial bank has to maintain a part of their reserves with its parent's viz. the RBI. Similarly, in need or in urgency these banks approach the RBI for fund. Thus it is called as the *lender of the last resort.*

   (*iii*) *Banker of Government:* The RBI being the apex monitory body has to work as an agent of the central and state governments. It performs various banking functions such as to accept deposits, paid taxes and make payments on behalf of the government. It works as a representative of the government even at the international level. It maintains government accounts, provides financial advice to the government. It manages government public debts and maintains foreign exchange reserves on behalf of the government. It provides overdraft facility to the government when it faces financial crunch.

   (*iv*) *Exchange Rate Management:* It is an essential function of the RBI. In order to maintain stability in the external value of rupee, it has to prepare domestic policies in that direction. It also needs to prepare and implement the foreign exchange rate policy which will help in attaining the exchange rate stability. In order to maintain the exchange rate stability it has to bring demand and supply of the foreign currency (U.S Dollar) close to each other.

   (*v*) *Credit Control Function:* Commercial bank in the country creates credit according to the demand and supply in the economy. But if this credit creation is unchecked or unregulated then it leads the economy into inflationary cycles. On the other hand, credit creation is below the required limit then it harms the growth of the economy. As a central bank of the nation the RBI has to look for growth with price stability. Thus, it regulates the credit creation capacity of commercial banks by using various credit control tools.

(*vi*) *Supervisory Function:* The RBI has been endowed with vast powers for supervising the banking system in the country. It has powers to issue license for setting-up new banks, to open new branches, to decide minimum reserves, to inspect functioning of commercial banks in India and abroad, to guide and to give direction to commercial banks in India. It can have periodical inspections and audit of the commercial banks in India.

(*vii*) *Banker, Agent and Adviser of the Government:* Central bank advice to make the various types of policy. They play the role of adviser of the government especially in case of the financial policy as a banker and agent to the government, the central bank makes and receives payment on behalf of government.

(*viii*) *Lender of the Last Resort:* Central bank never refuses to accommodate any eligible commercial bank needing fund. By the lender of the last resort. It is implied that the central bank assumes the responsibility of meeting directly and indirectly all reasonable demands for accommodation by commercial banks in times of difficulties and crises.

(*ix*) *Cleaning Agent:* All types of cheques are cleared by the central bank of all types of bank.

(*x*) *Custodian of Foreign Exchange Reserve:* Central bank helps to solve the problem of foreign exchange. He has to maintain the rate of exchange fixed by the government and manage exchange control and other restriction imposed by the state.

(*xi*) *Controller of Credit:* Central bank control credit with the help of financial infrastructure. It controls credit operation of commercial banks.

2. **Developmental Functions:** The RBI has been performing as a promoter of the financial system since its inception. Some of the major development functions of the RBI are mentioned below:

(*i*) *Development of the Financial System:* The financial system comprises the financial institutions, financial markets and financial instruments. The sound and efficient financial system is a precondition of the rapid economic development of the nation. The RBI has encouraged establishment of main banking and non-banking institutions to cater to the credit requirements of diverse sectors of the economy.

(*ii*) *Development of Agriculture:* In an agrarian economy like India, the RBI has to provide special attention for the credit need of agriculture sector and allied activities. It has successfully rendered services in this direction by increasing the flow of credit to this sector. It has earlier the Agriculture Refinance and Development Corporation (ARDC) to look after the credit, National Bank for Agriculture and Rural Development (NABARD) and Regional Rural Banks (RRBs).

(*iii*) *Provision of Industrial Finance:* Rapid industrial growth is the key for faster economic development. In this regard, the adequate and timely availability of credit to small, medium and large industry is very significant. In this regard the RBI has always been instrumental in setting up special financial institutions such as ICICI Ltd. IDBI, SIDBI and EXIM Bank, etc.

(*iv*) *Provisions of Training:* The RBI has always tried to provide essential training to the staff of the banking industry. The RBI has setup the bankers' training colleges at several places. National Institute of Bank Management, i.e., NIBM, Bankers Staff College, i.e., BSC and College of Agriculture Banking, i.e., CAB is few to mention.

(*v*) *Collection of Data:* Being the apex monetary authority of the country, the RBI collects process and disseminates statistical data on several topics. It includes interest rate, inflation, savings and investments, etc. This data proves to be quite useful for researchers and policy makers.

(*vi*) *Publication of the Reports:* The Reserve Bank has its separate publication division. This division collects and publishes data on several sectors of the economy. The reports and bulletins are regularly published by the RBI. It includes RBI weekly reports, RBI Annual Report, Report on Trend and Progress of Commercial Banks in India, etc. This information is made available to the public also at cheaper rates.

(*vii*) *Promotion of Banking Habits:* As an apex organisation, the RBI always tries to promote the banking habits in the country. It institutionalises savings and takes measures for an expansion of the banking network. It has setup many institutions such as the Deposit Insurance Corporation-1962, UTI-1964, IDBI-1964, NABARD-1982, NHB-1988, etc. These organisations develop and promote banking habits among the people. During economic reforms it has taken many initiatives for encouraging and promoting banking habits in India.

(*viii*) *Promotion of Export through Refinance:* The RBI always tries to encourage the facilities for providing finance for foreign trade especially exports from India. The Export-Import Bank of India (EXIM Bank of India) and the Export Credit Guarantee Corporation of India (ECGC) are supported by refinancing their lending for export purpose.

3. **Supervisory Functions:** Following are the supervisory function of RBI:

(*i*) *Granting License to Banks:* The RBI grants license to banks for carrying its business. License is also given for opening extension counters, new branches, even to close down existing branches.

(*ii*) *Bank Inspection:* The RBI grants license to banks working as per the directives and in a prudent manner without undue risk. In addition to this it can ask for periodical information from banks on various components of assets and liabilities.

(*iii*) *Control over Non-Banking Financial Institutions (NBFIs):* The NBFIs are not influenced by the working of a monetary policy. However, RBI has a right to issue directives to the NBFIs from time to time regarding their functioning. Through periodic inspection, it can control the NBFIs.

(*iv*) *Implementation of the Deposit Insurance Scheme:* The RBI has set-up the Deposit Insurance Guarantee Corporation in order to protect the deposits of small depositors. All bank deposits below ₹1,00,000 are insured with this corporation. The RBI work to implement the Deposit Insurance Scheme in case of a bank failure.

(*v*) *Periodical Review of the Work of Commercial Banks:* The RBI checks the work of commercial bank on regular basis so that they can test the maintenance of commercial banks and can help out to solve the problems of commercial banks.

(*vi*) *Giving Directives to Commercial Banks:* The RBI provides directions to all the commercial banks so that they cannot face any problem during the working of banks. So, that RBI directions provide great help.

(*vii*) *Ensuring the Health of Financial System through on-site and off-site Verification:* The RBI helps in the maintenance of financial system through on-site and off-site verification.

Methods of Banking Supervision

- An effective banking supervisory system should consist of some form of both on-site and off-site supervision.
- Banking supervisors must have regular contact with bank management and thorough understanding of the institution's operations.
- Banking supervisors must have a means of collecting, reviewing and analysing prudential reports and statistical returns from banks on a solo and consolidated basis.
- Banking supervisors must have a means of independent validation of supervisory information either through on-site examinations or use of external auditors.
- An essential element of banking supervision is the ability of the supervisors to supervise the banking group on a consolidated basis.

6.2 MONETARY POLICY OF RBI

Monetary Policy: Monetary policy is concerned with the changes in the supply of money and credit. It refers to the policy measures undertaken by the government or the central bank to influence the availability, cost and use of money and credit with the help of monetary techniques to achieve specific objectives. Monetary policy aims at influencing the economic activity in the economy mainly through two major variables, i.e., (*a*) money or credit supply, and (*b*) the rate of interest.

6.2.1 Objectives of Monetary Policy

While the main objective of the monetary policy is economic growth as well as price and exchange rate stability, there are other aspects that it can help with as well. Following are the objectives of RBI:

(*i*) *Full Employment:* This is the principle objective of monetary policy in developed countries. Full employment refers to the situation wherein all competent persons who willing to work at the prevailing rate of wage, get work easily. To attain this situation it is necessary to increase production and demand. For this purpose, government adopts cheap monetary policy. Under cheap monetary policy rate of interest is lowered in order to expand credit. If central bank of country lowered the bank rate then all commercial bank also reduce their interest rates correspondingly, low interest rate reduces the cost of production.

(*ii*) *Globalisation and Liberalisation:* The process of globalisation and liberalisation has thus necessitated a widening of the mandate of central banks. At the same time, for their policies to be effective, monetary authorities have been required to modify the way in which they conduct monetary policy.

(*iii*) *Rapid Economic Growth:* It is the most important objective of a monetary policy. The monetary policy can influence economic growth by controlling real interest rate and its resultant impact on the investment. If the RBI opts for a cheap or easy credit policy by reducing interest rates, the investment level in the economy can be encouraged. This increased investment can speed up economic growth. Faster economic growth is possible if the monetary policy succeeds in maintaining income and price stability.

(*iv*) *Price Stability:* All the economy suffer from inflation and deflation. It can also be called as Price Instability. Both inflation and deflation are harmful to the economy. Thus, the monetary policy having an objective of price stability tries to keep the value of money stable. It helps in reducing the income and wealth inequalities. When the economy suffers from recession the monetary policy should be an 'easy money policy' but when there is inflationary situation there should be a 'dear money policy'.

(*v*) *Exchange Rate Stability:* Exchange rate is the price of a home currency expressed in terms of any foreign currency. If this exchange rate is very volatile leading to frequent ups and downs in the exchange rate, the international community might lose confidence in our economy. The monetary policy aims at maintaining the relative stability in the exchange rate. The RBI by altering the foreign exchange reserves tries to influence the demand for foreign exchange and tries to maintain the exchange rate stability.

(*vi*) *Balance of Payments (BOP) Equilibrium:* Many developing countries like India are suffering from the disequilibrium in the BOP. The Reserve Bank of India through its monetary policy tries to maintain an equilibrium in the balance of payments. The BOP has two aspects, i.e., the 'BOP Surplus' and the 'BOP Deficit'. The former reflects an excess money supply in the domestic economy, while the later stands for stringency of money. If the monetary policy succeeds in maintaining monetary equilibrium, then the BOP equilibrium can be achieved.

(vii) *Neutrality of Money:* Economist such as Wicksted, Robertson has always considered money as a passive factor. According to them, money should play only a role of medium of exchange and not more than that. Therefore, the monetary policy should regulate the supply of money. The change in money supply creates monetary disequilibrium. Thus, monetary policy has to regulate the supply of money and neutralise the effect of money expansion. However, this objective of a monetary policy is always criticised on the ground that if money supply is kept constant then it would be difficult to attain price stability.

(viii) *Equal Income Distribution:* Many economists used to justify the role of the fiscal policy are maintaining economic equality. However, in recent years economists have given the opinion that the monetary policy can help and play a supplementary role in attainting an economic equality. Monetary policy can make special provisions for the neglect supply such as agriculture, small-scale industries, village industries, etc. and provide them with cheaper credit for longer term. This can prove fruitful for these sectors to come up. Thus, in recent period, monetary policy can help in reducing economic inequalities among different sections of society.

(ix) *Financial Liberalisation:* The Reserve Bank adopted a three pronged strategy of financial liberalisation. Improvement in the allocation efficiency of the financial system entailed deregulation of financial prices, including the institution of a market determined exchange rate regime in March 1993. This was supported by the development of financial markets. In tune with the process of financial liberalisation, the Reserve Bank, like other central banks in most emerging market economies (EMEs), has shifted from direct to indirect instruments of monetary policy. The Reserve Bank has been able to develop an array of monetary levers that are designed to manage market liquidity in order to achieve the overall objectives of price stability and credit availability for growth and to ensure orderly conditions in the financial markets. As a result, monetary policy emerged as a key instrument of stabilisation in the economy.

(x) *Stability in Economy:* The main motive of the monetary policy is to save the economy from the business cycle. In other words, to save the economy from boom and recession situation.

(xi) *To Promote Efficiency:* It is another essential aspect where the central banks pay a lot of attention. It tries to increase the efficiency in the financial system and tries to incorporate structural changes such as deregulating interest rates, ease operational constraints in the credit delivery system, to introduce new money market instruments, etc.

(*xii*) *Controlled Expansion of Bank Credit:* One of the important functions of RBI is to control the expansion of bank credit and money supply with special attention to seasonal requirement for credit without affecting the output.

(*xiii*) *Promotion of Fixed Investment:* The aim here is to increase the productivity of investment by restraining non-essential fixed investment.

(*xiv*) *Restriction of Inventories:* Overfilling of stocks and products becoming outdated due to excess of stock and due to this reason a unit may be convert into sick unit. To avoid this problem the central monetary authority carries out this essential function of restricting the inventories. The main objective of this policy is to avoid over-stocking and providing idle money in the organisation

(*xv*) *Promotion of Exports and Food Procurement Operations:* Monetary policy pays special attention in order to boost exports and facilitate the trade. It is an independent objective of monetary policy.

(*xvi*) *Desired Distribution of Credit:* Monetary authority has control over the decisions regarding the allocation of credit to priority sector and small borrowers. This policy decides over the specified percentage of credit that is to be allocated to priority sector and small borrowers.

(*xvii*) *Equitable Distribution of Credit:* The policy of Reserve Bank's aims is to make equal distribution of income and wealth to all sectors of the economy and all social and economic class of people.

(*xviii*) *Reducing the Rigidity:* RBI tries to bring about the flexibilities in the operations which provide a considerable autonomy. It encourages more competitive environment and diversification. It maintains its control over financial system whenever and wherever necessary to maintain the discipline and prudence in operations of the financial system.

(*xix*) *Promotion of saving and Investment:* Since the monetary policy controls the rate of interest and inflation within the country, it can impact the savings and investment of the people. A higher rate of interest translates to a greater chance of investment and savings, thereby, maintaining a healthy cash flow within the economy.

(*xx*) *Controlling the Imports and Exports:* By helping industries secure a loan at a reduced rate of interest, monetary policy helps export-oriented units to substitute imports and increase exports. This, in turn, helps improve the condition of the balance of payments.

(*xxi*) *Managing Business Cycles:* The two main stages of a business cycle are boom and depression. The monetary policy is the greatest tool using which the boom and depression of business cycles can be controlled by managing the credit to control the supply of money. The inflation in the market can be controlled by reducing the supply of money. On the other hand, when the money supply increases, the demand in the economy will also witness a rise.

(xxii) *Regulation of Aggregate Demand:* Since the monetary policy can control the demand in an economy, it can be used by monetary authorities to maintain a balance between demand and supply of goods and services. When credit is expanded and the rate of interest is reduced, it allows more people to secure loans for the purchase of goods and services. This leads to the rise in demand. On the other hand, when the authorities wish to reduce demand, they can reduce credit and raise the interest rates.

(xxiii) *Generation of Employment:* As the monetary policy can reduce the interest rate, small and medium enterprises (SMEs) can easily secure a loan for business expansion. This can lead to greater employment opportunities.

(xxiv) *Helping with the Development of Infrastructure:* The monetary policy allows concessional funding for the development of infrastructure within the country.

(xxv) *Allocating More Credit for the Priority Segments:* Under the monetary policy, additional funds are allocated at lower rates of interest for the development of the priority sectors such as small-scale industries, agriculture, underdeveloped sections of the society, etc.

(xxvi) *Managing and Developing the Banking Sector:* The entire banking industry is managed by the Reserve Bank of India (RBI). While RBI aims to make banking facilities available far and wide across the nation, it also instructs other banks using the monetary policy to establish rural branches wherever necessary for agricultural development. Additionally, the government has also set up regional rural banks and cooperative banks to help farmers receive the financial aid they require in no time.

6.2.2 Instruments of Credit Control/Monetary Policy

Monetary system implies supply and demand of money in the market for the purpose of consumption, saving, investment, etc. Thus, measures which control credit and the money supply of an economy are termed as monetary policy. This policy aim is to make stability in the prices of commodities and services, stability of exchange rate, control over trade cycles that implies compromising high inflation or deflation, pushing the level of employment, etc. Government use to take number of measures to control money supply and credit. Following are the main measures used by RBI:

Open Market Operations: An open market operation is an instrument of monetary policy which involves buying or selling of government securities from the public and banks. This mechanism influences the reserve position of the banks, to yield on government securities and cost of bank credit. The RBI sells government securities to constrict the flow of credit and buys government securities to increase the credit flow. Open market operation make's bank rate policy effective and maintains stability in government securities market.

Cash Reserve Ratio: Cash Reserve Ratio is a certain percentage of bank deposits which banks are required to keep with RBI in the form of reserves or balances. Due to higher CRR with RBI there will be lower liquidity in the system and vice versa. RBI is empowered to vary CRR between 3–15%. But as per the suggestion by the Narasimham Committee Report the CRR was reduced from 15% in the 1990 to 5% in 2002. As on March 2014, the CRR was 4%. As on August 01, 2021, current CRR is 4%.

Variable Cash Reserve Ratio

In modern times the main function of a central bank is to control and regulate the monetary system of an economy. Monetary system implies supply and demand of money in the market for the purpose of consumption, saving, investment, etc. Thus, measures which control credit and the money supply of an economy are termed as monetary policies. These policies aim at stability of prices of commodities and services, stability of exchange rate, control over trade cycles that implies compromising high inflation or deflation, pushing the level of employment, etc.

De-merits of the Above Instruments

Quantitative instruments such as CRR, SLR, Bank Rate and Open Market Operations were not effective since these techniques prove useful only when marginal changes are required. Moreover, they were applicable only if the credit policies remain constant on the part of banks as well as customers and no requirements were instantaneous. Many of these instruments were prone to high inelasticity in many economies. Inflation and Deflation in the economy can also be controlled on the basis of policies framed by the government termed as fiscal policies. These policies take expenditure and revenue of the government into account.

Cash Reserve Ratio (CRR): The method of cash reserve ratio or changing minimum cash reserves to be kept with the central bank by the commercial banks relatively a new method of credit control used by the central bank. Cash Reserve Ratio is the ratio which scheduled banks maintain between their holdings of cash and deposit liabilities with the central bank. In simple terms, Cash Reserve Ratio is the minimum percentage of deposits to be kept with their respective central bank as a reserve fund. Bank has to keep a certain proportion of their assets in the form of liquid assets such as cash for meeting day-to-day expenses on deposits of the public. This fund is held in the form of 'cash in hand' and balances with the central bank that is the Reserve Bank of India.

Functions and Advantages

Change in CRR is a powerful method for influencing not only the volume of excess reserves but also the credit multiplier in the banking system. The two broad functions of CRR are:

- It changes level of excess reserves and;
- It changes credit multiplier

Cash Reserve Ratio is more effective in dealing with abnormal situations especially when banks have excessive reserves and they are creating too much credit leading to inflationary situation. It is a more direct method because it controls the volume of credit. Moreover, the effects of CRR are not marginal and are quite instantaneous as compared to other instruments. It can act as both alternative and supplement to other methods of monetary control undoubtedly.

Impact: Cash reserve ratio is often used by the central bank of an economy to drain excess liquidity or to release funds vital for the growth of the economy in the following manner:

To reduce credit (slow inflation rate), the central bank raises the ratio of CRR. As a result, the cash balances of banks fall which in turn reduce their capacity to create credit. Similarly, to create more credit (slow deflation rate) central banks reduce the ratio of cash reserves which it keeps with itself from banks. As a result, more money is available with banks for creation of credit. For example, commercial banks keep 10% of their cash reserves with central bank. This means ₹ 10 of reserves would be required to support ₹100 of deposits and the credit multiplier is 10. To check inflation, the central bank raises the CRR from 10–12%. As a result of the increase in the CRR, the commercial banks will have to maintain a greater cash reserve of ₹12 instead of ₹10 for every deposit of ₹100 and they will now decrease their lending to get the additional 2% cash. The credit multiplier will fall from 10–8. On the other hand, to check deflation the central bank may reduce the CRR from 10% to 8% and thus make available 2% excess cash reserves to the commercial banks which they utilise to expand credit. The credit multiplier will then rise from 10 to 12.

Impact on Stock Market: CRR has an indirect impact on the stock market. An increase in CRR rate is followed by an increase in market rate that is the rate of interest charged by banks to borrowers. Rising inter rate increases cost of payment of liabilities which changes the stock prices. However, the rate of investment is not affected in the long run.

Variable Cash Reserve Ratio in Underdeveloped Countries

CRR is popular in underdeveloped countries because of narrow market for government securities. In these economies a small sale of government securities will lead to a sharp fall in their prices.

In these economies commercial banks enjoy excess liquidity. As a result, instruments like Bank Rate and Open Market Operations will produce marginal changes. Keeping in consideration drastic effects of CRR, this instrument is used more as a stabilisation device rather than using it as a technique of credit control. Adverse effects can be avoided if reserve requirements are changed with due notice and by small degrees.

Limitations

Like any other instrument CRR is also not free from limitations.

- CRR is not effective when commercial banks keep very large reserves. In such a case even if CRR is raised, and banks have sufficient reserves remain after satisfying the minimum operations than it will be ineffective instrument to control the money and credit.
- This method is not effective when the commercial banks happen to possess large foreign funds. Thus, even if central bank increases CRR, those banks will continue to create credit on the basis of foreign funds.
- This instrument is appropriate only when incremental (large) changes in reserves are required. It is not suitable for marginal changes.
- CRR also depends on the general mood of the business community in the economy, for example a decrease in CRR may not be able to expand credit due to low expectations of investors.
- CRR is also discriminatory in nature meaning it only benefits banks having large reserves.
- The method may have effect on the securities market of an economy as high rate may force banks to sell securities in the market and this will in turn decrease their prices.
- Moreover, this method regulates only the banking sector of our economy and is of no effect to Non-Banking Financial Institutions (NBFI) as RBI has negligible control over these institutions.
- A frequent change in the CRR implies uncertainty.

CRR is the most direct and immediate method and therefore has to be used very carefully by the concerned authorities as a slight carelessness may be fatal for the functioning of the economy.

CRR and the Indian Economy

History and Legal Status:

- The method of variable CRR was first adopted in 1935 by the Federal Reserve System (FRS) in USA as a result of 'side affects' of other quantitative instruments that were injurious to the policy of credit expansion or contraction in the economy in many circumstances.
- In the Indian economy RBI had prescribed statutory returns as per Form A (for CRR and Statutory liquid ratio) under section 42 (2) of RBI Act, 1934.
- Under the law enacted in 1962, RBI was empowered to impose CRR anywhere between 3–15% of their net demand and time liabilities as a tool of money control. CRR was initially used by RBI in 1973.

- The RBI (Amendment) bill 2006 has been enacted with a gazette notification stating consequent to sub-section RBI can prescribe CRR for any scheduled bank without any floor or ceiling rate.

Role

RBI used the policy of CRR in 1973 when it raised the ratio from 3%–5% and 7% in September 1973. Since then there were subsequent changes in CRR. In 1991, the report given by Narasimham Committee was of the view that was crucially responsible for wiping out profits of various commercial banks. It was decided to reduce CRR over a 4-year period to a level below 10%. The current rate of CRR is 4.00 with effect from December13, 2019. It decreased from 4.25 that were continuing since October 13, 2012.

1. **Statutory Liquidity Ratio:** Every financial institution has to maintain a certain quantity of liquid assets with the RBI for time and demand liabilities. Government securities are the most liquid form of liquidity assets. These assets can be cash, precious metals, approved securities like bonds, etc. The ratio of the liquid assets to time and demand liabilities is termed as the statutory liquidity ratio. There was a reduction of SLR from 38.5% to 25% because of the suggestion by Narasimham Committee. The SLR was 23% on March 2014. As on July 31, 2021, current SLR is 18.00 per cent.

2. **Bank Rate Policy:** Bank rate is the rate of interest which charged by the RBI for providing funds or loans to the banking system. This banking system involves commercial and co-operative banks, Industrial Development Bank of India, IFC, EXIM Bank, and other approved financial institutes. Funds are provided either through lending directly or rediscounting or buying money market instruments like commercial bills and treasury bills. Increase in Bank Rate increases the cost of borrowing by commercial banks which results the reduction in credit volume to the banks and hence declines the supply of money. Increase in the bank rate is the symbol of tightening monetary policy by RBI monetary policy. Bank rate is also known as *Discount rate*. The Bank rate was 9% on March 2014. As on December 13, 2019, bank rate was 5.4%. As on July 31, 2021 bank rate was 4.25%. Various effects of the bank rate policy are discussed below:

(*a*) *Effect on Cost and Availability of Credit:* By changing the bank rate, the central bank affects the cost of credit by raising the bank rate, it raises the cost of credit and by lowering the bank rate, it lowers the cost of credit. By changing the rules of eligibility or the conditions under which commercial banks can secure loans, the central bank influences the availability of credit. Strict eligibility rules make it difficult for the commercial banks to acquire loans from the central bank while the presence of lenient eligibility rules makes the same process easy.

(*b*) *No Simultaneous Determination of Interest Rates and Money Supply:* The central bank is able to influence the interest rate and changes the money supply in the economy. Changes in the bank rate influence the interest rates in the money market. Changes in the amount that the central bank is willing to lend will influence the money supply. However, the central bank cannot set both interest rates as well as money supply. It must choose one goal or the other.

(c) *Effect on the Level of Economic Activity:* The bank rate policy affects the level and structure of interest rates and thereby the level of economic activity in an economy. Changes in the bank rate leads to corresponding changes in the market interest rates, thus making the credit dearer or cheaper. Changes in the market rates affect the borrowing and investing capacity of a businessman which, in turn, affects the level of economic activity in the economy.

(d) *The Announcement Effect:* The announcement effect of a change in bank rate influences the credit psychology in the economy. A rise in the bank rate is regarded as the official signal of the period of relatively dearer money and a fall in the bank rate is an indication for the onset of a cheaper money phase.

(e) *Bank Rate Policy during Inflation and Depression:* During inflation the central bank increases the bank rate, resulting in an increase in the market interest rates thereby raising the cost of bank credit. While during depression, the bank rate will reduce. This leads to a fall in the market interest rates, thus encouraging the businessmen to borrow, invest and push up the level of economic activity and the price level.

Effect on Balance of Payment: As the bank rate is raised, other interest rates in the money market go up. As a result, there will be movement of foreign capital into the country because of better returns and stoppage of capital going out of the country. Moreover, the demand for domestic currency will rise, raising its value and making the exchange rate more favourable.

Bank Rate Policy: Bank rate is the rate of interest which charged by the RBI for providing funds or loans to the banking system. This banking system involves commercial and co-operative banks, Industrial Development Bank of India, IFC, EXIM Bank, and other approved financial institutes. Funds are provided either through lending directly or rediscounting or buying money market instruments like commercial bills and treasury bills. Increase in Bank Rate increases the cost of borrowing by commercial banks which results into the reduction in credit volume to the banks and hence declines the supply of money. Increase in the bank rate is the symbol of tightening monetary policy by RBI monetary policy. Bank rate is also known as *Discount rate*. The current bank rate is 5.65% (as on Dec. 2019).

Bank Rate Policy

Definition: The bank rate or the discount rate is the rate at which the central bank is prepared to discount the first class bills of exchange of commercial banks. The bank rate is distinct from the market interest rate on the following basis:

- The bank rate is the rate of interest of the central bank while the market interest rate is the lending rate charged in the money market by the ordinary financial institutions.
- A change in the bank rate leads to a change in other interest rates prevailing in the market. However, any change in the existing market rates is not an incentive of the central bank to increase or decrease its bank rate.

Assumptions of Bank Rate Policy

The success of the bank rate policy is based on the following assumptions:

- The commercial banks possess sufficient quantities of eligible securities.
- Commercial banks are not against rediscounting their eligible securities with the central bank.
- Commercial banks keep only minimum cash reserves just sufficient enough to carryon their day-to-day operations. For additional cash requirements, they freely approach the central bank.
- There exists a close relationship between the bank rate and other interest rates.
- Borrowing and investing of the businessmen depends upon the prevailing interest rates of the commercial banks. A rise in the interest rates restricts borrowings and investment and vice versa.
- There exists an elastic economic structure. In other words, prices, costs, wages, employment and production are flexible enough to change according to the changes in borrowing and investment by businessmen.
- There exist no artificial barriers on the international flow of capital.

Effects of Bank Rate Policy

Various effects of the bank rate policy are discussed below:

1. *Effect on Cost and Availability of Credit:* By changing the bank rate, the central bank affects the cost of credit by raising the bank rate, it raises the cost of credit and by lowering the bank rate, it lowers the cost of credit. By changing the rules of eligibility or the conditions under which commercial banks can secure loans, the central bank influences the availability of credit. Strict eligibility rules make it difficult for the commercial banks to acquire loans from the central bank while the presence of lenient eligibility rules makes the same process easy.

2. *No Simultaneous Determination of Interest Rates and Money Supply:* The central bank through its bank rate policy is able to influence the interest rate changes and the money supply in the economy. Changes in the bank rate influence the interest rates in the money market. Changes in the amount that the central bank is willing to lend will influence the money supply. However, the central bank cannot set both interest rates as well as money supply. It must choose one goal or the other.

3. *Effect on the Level of Economic Activity:* The bank rate policy affects the level and structure of interest rates and thereby the level of economic activity in an economy. Changes in the bank rate leads to corresponding changes in the market interest rates, thus making the credit dearer or cheaper. Changes in the market rates affect the borrowing and investing capacity of a businessman which, in turn, affects the level of economic activity in the economy.

4. *The Announcement Effect:* The announcement effect of a change in bank rate influences the credit psychology in the economy. A rise in the bank rate is regarded as the official signal of the period of relatively dearer money and a fall in the bank rate is an indication for the onset of a cheaper money phase.

5. *Bank Rate Policy during Inflation and Depression:* During inflation the central bank increases the bank rate, resulting in an increase in the market interest rates thereby raising the cost of bank credit. While during depression, the bank rate will reduce. This leads to a fall in the market interest rates, thus encouraging the businessmen to borrow, invest and push-up the level of economic activity and the price level.

6. *Effect on Balance of Payment:* As the bank rate is raised, other interest rates in the money market go up. As a result, there will be movement of foreign capital into the country because of better returns and stoppage of capital going out of the country. Moreover, the demand for domestic currency will rise, raising its value and making the exchange rate more favourable.

Limitations of Bank Rate Policy

The effectiveness of the bank rate policy depends upon a number of assumptions which are not fully achieved in reality. Thus, the bank rate policy suffers from some limitations:

1. *Ineffective in Controlling Deflation:* When bank rate is lowered during a period of deflation, the resulting lower rates may not be able to induce the entrepreneurs to borrow and invest more because of falling prices and falling profits.

2. *Conflicting Effects:* The internal and external effects of the bank rate policy may be conflicting. If, the bank rate is raised to control domestic deflation, the resulting rise in the other rates may lead to an increase in the short term foreign funds into the country. This may lead to a decrease in the anti-inflationary effects of the bank rate.

3. *Ineffective in Controlling the Balance of Payments Disequilibrium:* The success of the bank rate to control the disequilibrium of the balance of payments depends upon the removal of any and all restrictions on the international capital inflow. This assumption however is not fulfilled.

4. *In Discriminatory:* The bank rate is in discriminatory in nature. In other words, it makes no distinction between the productive and unproductive activities in the country. For example, if the bank rate is raised to control speculative activities, it will adversely affect the productive activities of the country.

5. *Non-Dependence of Commercial Banks:* Now-a-days, the commercial banks have acquired enough liquid resources of their own, as a result of which they do not feel any need to approach the central bank for financial assistance.

Effectiveness of Bank Rate Policy in Underdeveloped Countries

In underdeveloped countries the bank rate has raised some serious doubts about its effectiveness due to the following reasons:

- In underdeveloped countries the money market comprises of two major entities: the modern banking sector and the indigenous bankers. Although the bank rate has some effect on the modern banking sector, the indigenous bankers remain unaffected by the changes in the bank rate as they do not approach the central bank for financial assistance.
- Many commercial banks have started keeping their cash reserves over and above the minimum level.
- In the underdeveloped sector, there is non-availability of eligible securities in large quantities to be rediscounted by the central bank.
- The presence of the barter system has also left the bank rate devoid of any meaning.
- The underdeveloped economies are far from elastic, i.e., the costs, prices, wages, etc. do not readily respond to any changes in the volume of credit.

Decline of Bank Rate Policy

After the Great Depression of 1929–1933, the bank rate has lost importance as a suitable method of credit control. Some of these factors are as follows:

1. *Decline in Bills of Exchange:* The bank rate operates through the rediscounting of bills of exchange. However, today bills of exchange is not being recognised as an instrument of financing trade mainly due to the contraction of international trade and the increasing use of treasury bills or short-term government securities.

2. *Economic Rigidities:* The growing tendency of all the countries towards economic rigidities, such as stabilisation of prices, wages, interests, etc., has reduced the importance of bank rate.

3. *Importance of Fiscal Policy:* The fiscal policy proved to be effective in offsetting the effects of depression during the period of economic recession of 1929–1933. Thus, henceforth, the fiscal policy has gained more and more importance while the monetary policy has been overshadowed.

4. *Increased Deposits:* The deposits have increased with the commercial banks due to the inflationary situations. With a strong financial position, the banks no longer approach the central bank for financial assistance.

5. *Other Methods:* In recent years, other and more effective means of credit control have been developed, as a result of which the bank rate has become more and more unimportant.

6. *Changing Methods of Business Financing:* Businessmen now resort more to the use of profits and accumulated funds for financing their activities and thus are less reliable on the commercial banks for financial assistance.

5. *Change in Liquidity Ratio:* Under this method every bank is required to keep a given proportion of its deposits as cash with itself. It is called *liquidity ratio*. When central is to contract credit it raise the liquidity ratio and when central bank is to expand credit it decrease the liquidity ratio.

6. *Net Liquidity Ratio:* In order to check excessive borrowings from the reserve bank by the commercial banks, reserve bank introduced the system of net liquidity ratio in Sep 1964. According to this system, a commercial bank can borrow from the reserve bank at the bank rate only if it maintains a minimum net liquidity ratio to its total demand and time liabilities; it will have to pay a penal rate of interest to the reserve bank.

7. *Repurchasing Option (REPO) Rate:* This rate is that rate on which commercial banks borrow from RBI to fulfill their short-term liabilities. As on 31st Mach 2014 it was 8%. As on December 13, 2019, REPO rate was 5.15%. At present as on 31 July 2021 REPO rate is 4.00%. When RBI wants to restrict the credit then RBI increased it or vice versa.

8. *Reverse RAPO Rate:* This rate is that rate on which RBI borrow from commercial banks for short term to control the credit in the economy. As on 31st Mach 2014 it was 7%. As on December 13, 2019, CRR was 4.9%. At present as on 31 July 2021 reverse RAPO rate is 3.35%. When RBI wants to restrict the credit then RBI increased it or vice versa.

9. *Call Rate (Inter bank borrowing rate):* Interest Rate paid by the banks for lending and borrowing funds with maturity period ranging from one day to 14 days. Call money market deals with extremely short term lending between banks themselves. After Lehman Brothers went bankrupt Call Rate sky rocketed to such an insane level that banks stopped lending to other banks.

10. *MSF (Marginal Standing Facility):* It is a special window for banks to borrow from RBI against approved government securities in an emergency situation like an acute cash shortage. MSF rate is higher than Repo rate. Current MSF Rate: 5.4%

Qualitative Instruments of Monetary Policy

1. *Change in Margin Requirements of Loans:* Banks never provides 100% loan amount against the securities. Banks take some margin and provide the less amount of loan in comparison to assets value. For example, banks provide 80% amount of loan of the total value of assets. In this situation 20% difference in amount is called *credit margin* requirements of loan. In the boom situation RBI can increase from 20% to 25%. Now banks will provide less amount of loan. In case of recession RBI can decrease from 20% to 10% than banks will provide more loans. Under this method credit grant for certain purpose is controlled. When the central banks feels that the trader are

stock piling certain commodities as a result of which their prices are rising then the central bank of India control the credit sanctioned for these goods by changing marginal requirements. As per the current system, an initial margin on collateral stands at 4% in case of government securities and 6% for state development loans. This system fails to differentiate between market risks across securities. Now, initial margin requirement would be in the range of 0.5–4% for benchmark government securities depending on their residual maturity. For state development loans, this requirement would range from 2.5–6%. To incentivise credit rating of development loans by state governments, their initial margin requirements will be 1% lower than other state development loans of the same maturity. In other words, central banks increase the minimum credit margin requirement and vice versa.

2. *Rationing of Credit:* Central bank is the lender of the last resort in a country. Rationing of credit can be done in following ways:

(*a*) it can decline loan to any given bank.

(*b*) Central bank reduces the amount of loan given to all the banks.

(*c*) Central bank can fix the quota of the credit given to different banks.

(*d*) Central bank can determine the limit if the credit granted to industry and trade.

(*e*) Central bank can fix the quota of the credit given for different commodities.

(*f*) Central bank can fix the quota of the credit given for different sectors as industry, commerce, trade, agriculture, etc.

3. *Direct Action:* Sometimes, central bank is obliged to take direct action against other banks. Central bank does not give any financial accommodation to any bank that does not comply with its instructions. Central banks cancelled the banking license and stopped their business.

4. *Moral Suasion:* Moral Suasion is just as a request by the RBI to the commercial banks to take so and so action and measures in so and so trend of the economy. RBI may request commercial banks not to give loans for unproductive purpose which does not add to economic growth but increases inflation.

5. *Direct Credit Control:* The Central Bank can give direction to banks on the maximum percentage or amount of loans (credit ceilings) to different economic sectors or activities, interest rate caps, liquid asset ratio and issue credit guarantee to preferred loans, etc. In this way the available savings is allocated and investment directed in particular directions.

6.2.3 Success of Monetary Policy

- *Creation and Expansion of Financial Institution:* Success and failure of monetary policy depends on the financial institution as like banks and non-banking financial institution. After the nationalisation of banks huge number of financial institute were expanded in cities and rural areas. This will help the people to take loan from various institutions if they have wider choice around them. More banks and financial institute have set to proper implementation of monetary policy.

- *Effective Central Banking:* It helps to meet the developmental needs of central bank in an underdeveloped country and monetary policy it must function effectively to control and regulate the volume of credit through various monetary instruments like bank rate, open market operations, cash reserve ratio, etc.
- *Integration of Organised and Unorganised Money Market:* Due to integration of organised and unorganised money market monetary policy will be functioning effectively. This also helps central bank to control the unorganised market.
- *Development of Banking Habits:* Banking habits in rural areas cannot developed before the proper development of financial infrastructure and proper implementation of monetary policy that depends on the development of banking habits in these countries. Proper monetary policy also helps to rural people to adopt banking habits.
- *Debt Management:* Monetary policy helps to fulfill gap in debt management. Debt management includes:
- *Deciding proper timing and issuing of government bonds.*
- *Stabilising their prices*
- *Minimising the cost of servicing public debt*
- *Maintaining Equilibrium Between Balance of Payment:* Monetary policy helps the developing countries to solve the problem of adverse balance of payments. Monetary policy also adopts direct foreign exchange controls and other measures to correct the adverse balance of payments.
- *Controlling Inflationary Pressure:* Developing economics are highly sensitive to inflationary pressures. The monetary policy helps to control inflationary tendencies by increasing savings by the people, checking expansion of credit by the developing banking system and discouraging deficit financing by the government.

6.2.4 Limitations of Monetary Policy

- *Unorganised Money Market:* In underdeveloped countries like India money market is unorganised. It is divided into two parts. One part includes, indigenous bankers, Banias, Landlord, moneylenders, etc. that is called the unorganised sector and other part considered of commercial banks, non-banking finance institutions, special financial institutions etc. those comes directly under the control of RBI. So that it is called the *organised sector* while Indigenous bankers, etc. are out of jurisdiction of central bank.
- *Less Importance of Demand Deposit:* Large part of currency is held by the people in term of currency in underdeveloped countries. A little portion of it is

kept in the banks in the form of demand deposits. As such, methods of credit control are operative in very limited sector of economy.

- *Black Money:* In under developed countries large quantity of black money is accumulated on account of political and economic factor. Black money is the main reason behind the failure of monetary policy.
- *Rate of Interest:* In order to promote domestic investment, rate of interest is kept low. Government is also in favour of low rate of interest so as to keep its monetary burden of public debt to minimum. However, due to low interest rate foreign capital is not attracted towords the country.
- *Non-Banking Financial Institutions:* Non-banking institution like life Insurance Corporation, investment trust, etc. also limit the effect of monetary policy by their activities.
- *Imbalance in Credit Allocation:* The credit facilities increased by central bank through the monetary policy which will bring negative effect in credit allocation and demand for credits increased. Thus, more people dependent on credit, which gives bad affect to the economy.
- *Limited Role of Capital Market:* Capital market provides credit for long term periods. But after the commencement of monetary policy by central banks role of capital market has declined.
- *Deficit Financing:* Central bank power of lending will decline after the commencement of monetary policy. Central bank cannot provide large funds at credit. So the funds of central bank deficit will be deficit due to monetary policy. Due to this reason government compel to central make to issue new notes through deficit financing and monetary policy would be failed to control the supply of credit and money.
- *Excess Credit Expansion:* Credit expansion has increased after the commencement of monetary policy. The demand of credit increases in the market and this will cross the limit of credit facilities. This gives negative impact on the economy as a hike in prices of goods and services.
- *Increase in Liquidity:* Liquidity means converting the assets into cash easily. The monetary policy increases the liquidity which gives negative effect to the economy.
- *Ineffective Control over Inflation:* During inflation time the prices of everything being increased. Monetary policy fails to control inflation. This is the biggest failure of monetary policy.

6.3 POLICY FRAMEWORK OF RBI

Monetary policy refers to the policy of the central bank of a country to regulate and control the volume, cost and credit with the aim of achieving the objectives of optimum levels of output and employment, price stability, balance of payment equilibrium, or any other goal set by the government. In a developing country like India, appropriate monetary policy can play a positive role in creating conditions those are necessary for rapid economic growth. Moreover, since these economies are highly sensitive to inflationary pressures, the monetary policy should also serve to control inflationary tendencies by increasing savings by the people, checking credit expansion by the banking system and discouraging deficit financing by the government.

1. The framework of monetary policy has undergone far reaching changes all over the world in the 1990s, mainly in response to the challenges and opportunities of financial liberalisation. There is, first of all, a clear focus on price stability as principles, though not necessarily the sole objective of monetary policy. Besides, with the deregulation of financial markets and globalisation, the process of monetary policy formulation has acquired a much greater market orientation than ever before, inducing a shift from direct to indirect instruments of monetary control. This has been accompanied by several institutional changes in the monetary-fiscal interface to ensure that central banks possess the autonomy to anchor inflation expectations.

2. Volatility in capital flows and exchange rate impacts not only domestic demand and inflation, but also has implications for the maintenance of financial stability. Central bank is thus concerned not only about price stability, but also financial stability. With exogenous shocks hitting the economy at different points of time, the stabilisation of the real economy as well as financial markets requires a multi-pronged response from central bank. In a way, central bank has, therefore, emerged as the primary shock absorbers in the system.

3. The process of globalisation and liberalisation has thus necessitated a widening of the mandate of central banks. At the same time, for their policies to be effective, monetary authorities have been required to modify the way in which they conduct monetary policy.

4. The Reserve Bank adopted a three pronged strategy of financial liberalisation. Improvement in allocation and efficiency of the financial system entailed deregulation of financial prices, including the institution of a market determined exchange rate regime in March 1993. This was supported by the development of financial markets. In tune with the process of financial liberalisation, the Reserve Bank, like other central banks in most emerging market economies (EMEs), has shifted from direct to indirect instruments of monetary policy. The Reserve Bank has been able to develop an array of monetary levers that are designed to manage market liquidity in order to achieve the overall objectives of price stability and credit availability for growth and to ensure orderly conditions in the financial markets. As a result, monetary policy emerged as a key instrument of stabilisation in the economy.

5. The inflationary consequences of the fiscal dominance of monetary policy brought into sharp focus the need to reduce fiscal imbalances as well as monetary and fiscal co-ordination that naturally raises the issue of its nature. A key issue in this context

is whether this co-ordination should be rule-based or discretionary. Frameworks based on clear mandates and rules are usually considered preferable to ad-hoc discretionary coordination, which could be clouded by problems of implementation and incentive distortions caused by electoral cycles. The draft of resources by the fiscal deficit on the central bank.

The key development that has enabled a more independent monetary policy environment was the discontinuation of automatic monetisation of the Government's fiscal deficit through an agreement between the Government and the Reserve Bank in 1997. The enactment of the Fiscal Responsibility and Budget Management (FRBM) Act, 2003 has strengthened this further.

Revision of Open Market Operations: The Reserve Bank revised its open market operations policy in October 1956, according to which it started giving discriminatory support to the sale and purchase of government securities. From 1948–51 banks made large purchases of government securities. In the subsequent period, bank's sales of the government securities to the public exceeded its purchases. This excess sales method was discounted between 1964 and 1969 with a purpose of expanding currency and credit in the economy.

Liberalisation of the Bill Market Scheme: Through the bill market scheme, the commercial banks receive additional funds from the reserve bank to meet the increasing credit requirements of their borrowers. Since 1957, the reserve bank has extended the bill market scheme to include export bills in order to help the commercial banks to provide credit to exporters liberally.

Facilities to Priority Sectors: The reserve bank continues to provide credit facilities to priority sectors such as small scale industries and co-operatives, even though the general policy of the bank is to control credit expansion. For instance, in October 1962, the banks were allowed to borrow additional funds from the reserve bank in order to provide finance to small scale industries and co-operatives. The reserve bank has also been providing short-term finance to the rural co-operatives.

Re-finance and Re-discounting Facilities: At present, the banks are permitted to refinance equal to one per cent of the demand and time liabilities at the rate of 10 per cent per annum. They are also available for food procurement credit and export credit.

Credit Facilities through Financial Institutions: The reserve bank has also been instrumental in the establishment of various financial institutions such as IDBI, IFCI, IRCI, ARDC and NABARD. Though these institutions, the reserve bank provides medium-term and long-term credit facilities for development.

Deficit Financing: Continuous increase in money supply in the country has been caused by adopting the method of deficit financing to finance the budgetary deficit of the government. This has been made possible through changes in the reserve requirements of the reserve bank.

Advantages

The followings are the advantages of deficit financing:

- Evidence shows that, in normal conditions, interest rates have a direct and powerful effect on household spending, which suggests that consumers are highly interest rate elastic.
- The developed country's monetary policy is independent from government and can make decisions free from political interference.
- Interest rates can be adjusted on a monthly basis, which contrasts with discretionary fiscal policy which cannot be adjusted at such regular intervals.
- While the full effects of interest changes may not be experienced for up to a year, there is often an immediate effect on confidence. The time-lag on output is estimated to be around one year, and on the price level, around two years.

Disadvantages

The followings are the disadvantages of deficit financing:

- There are still time lags to see the full effects, and there are some negative effects.
- Raising interest rates can negatively effect on investment spending and the housing market, and the exchange rate and hence the balance of payments.
- There is also the problem of the dual economy that are high rates set for the booming service sector, or low rates for the depressed manufacturing and export sector.
- The money supply is difficult to control in practice, so controlling interest rates are preferable.
- Interest rates may fall to very low levels during a deep recession, and while the demand for credit may rise, the supply may become trapped in the system, known as the liquidity trap.

6.3.2 Development Framework

A well-developed corporate bond market is critical for Indian economy as it:

- Enables Efficient Allocation of Funds
- Facilitates Infrastructure Financing
- Improves the Health of the Corporate Balance Sheets
- Promotes Financial Inclusion for the Small and Medium Enterprises (SMES) and the Retail Investors
- Safeguards Financial Stability and
- Enables Development of the Municipal Bond Market.

6.3.3 Latest Monetary Policy (2019)

The monetary policy is a policy formulated by the central bank, i.e., RBI and relates to the monetary matters of the country. The policy involves measures taken to regulate the supply of money, availability and cost of credit in the economy. The policy also oversees distribution of credit among users as well as the borrowing and lending rates of interest. In a developing country like India, the monetary policy is significant in the promotion of economic growth. The various instruments of monetary policy include variations in bank rates, other interest rates, selective credit controls, supply of currency, variations in reserve requirements and open market operations.

Throughout the year 2013–14, the monetary authorities continue to indicate seriousness and concern over inflationary pressures. The RBI has taken several rounds of tightening monetary measures during the year. The following are the main features of the monetary policy 2018–19:

1. The Repo Rate was raised 8.00% on March 31, 2014 from 5.25% on April 20, 2012, and from to 6.25% to 6.50% on January 25, 2011. As on July 2021 Current Repo Rate is 4%.

2. The Reverse Repo Rate was raised 7% on March 31, 2014 from 3.75% on April 20, 2012, and from 5.25% to 5.50% on January 25, 2012. As on July 2021 Current Reverse Repo Rate is 3.35%.

3. The CRR which was declined 4% on March 31, 2014 from 6% on April 20, 2011, remained unchanged throughout the year. As on July, 2021 Current CRR is 4%.

4. The bank rate remained at 9% as on March 31, 2014. As on July, 2021 Current Bank Rate is 4.25%.

5. Inflation, which was earlier pegged at 9% fourth financial year 2013–14, was later expected to touch 7.00% in March 2012 and as on June, 2021 Current Inflation Rate is 6.26%.

6. The GDP was projected to grow at 5.50% for the year 2013–14. GDP is projected for 2021–22 is 9.5%.

7. The RBI, in its review of the Monetary Policy 2021 observed that (*a*) there are signs of food and fuel inflation spilling over into generalised inflation and (*b*) anti-inflationary measures are to be pursued so as not to affect the growth prospects of adversely.

REVIEW QUESTIONS

1. What is the organizational structure of the Reserve Bank of India (RBI)?
2. What are the key functions and responsibilities of RBI's various departments and divisions?
3. How does the RBI's governance and decision-making process work?
4. Explain the role of the Central Board of Directors, the Monetary Policy Committee (MPC), and the various committees and subcommittees within the RBI's organizational framework.
5. Discuss the instruments of credit control.

Clean Note Policy: RBI December 5, 2002

7

7.1 INTRODUCTION

Shri Vepa Kamesam, Deputy Governor, Reserve Bank of India exhorted the banks to implement the Reserve Bank's instructions issued from November 2001 to do away with stapling of note packets and to introduce banding the packets with paper/polythene bands so that the life of the currency notes is increased. The Deputy Governor took a meeting of Chief Executives of public sector banks and other banks having currency chests in Delhi today to discuss matters connected with implementing the Reserve Bank of India's Clean Note Policy. *The objective of the Reserve Bank's Clean Note Policy is to give the citizens good quality currency notes and coins while the soiled notes are withdrawn out of circulation.* The Reserve Bank has also instructed the banks to issue only good quality clean notes to the public and refrain from recycling the soiled notes received by them over their counters. The Reserve Bank has installed high speed Currency Verification and Processing Systems (CVPS) machines at all its offices which deal with currency. These machines are capable of processing 50,000–60,000 pieces per hour and soiled notes are shredded and briquetted on-line. Ever since 1999, when the Governor announced the Clean Note Policy, several steps were taken for augmenting the supply of currency notes and coins. The members of public were urged not to write on the currency notes and banks were instructed to provide unrestricted facility for exchange of soiled and mutilated notes. As per the Reserve Bank instructions, currency chest branches of the banks must offer, even to non-customers, good quality notes and coins in exchange for soiled and mutilated notes. Complaints, however, continue to be received in this regard from the public and trade bodies that these instructions have not been given full effect. Some complaints of restrictive practices were also being received according to which some currency chest branches in the rural and semi-urban areas do not accept lower denomination notes. To mitigate the position, the Reserve Bank has given specific monthly targets for distribution of coins to these currency chests. The Reserve Bank monitors these targets from the feedback reports. Further in an experimental basis, the Reserve Bank had requested banks between September and November this year to open one currency chest branch on one Sunday in a month at selected centres to exclusively provide currency exchange and distribution of small coins and suck out the bad notes. The reports received from the banks show that this experiment received tremendous response from the public. It has, therefore, been decided that banks should run this scheme on a permanent basis with wholehearted participation. The choice of the centre and the choice of the Sunday in the month should be left to the individual bank to decide. The Deputy Governor emphasised that high degree of co-ordination is necessary between chest branches and non-chest branches and it was time that the currency chest branches also mechanised their operations by installing smaller desk top versions in addition to banding machines so that members of public receive good staple-free notes and the Reserve Bank also receives staple-free soiled notes ready for processing and destruction. He also stated that the Regional Directors of the Reserve Bank could be contacted for proper co-ordination of remittances of notes and coins. He hoped that the banks will extend full co-operation to the Reserve Bank in delivery of its Clean Note Policy and it may not have to think of any Regulatory intervention for this purpose.

The Reserve Bank has been extending facilities to the public for exchanging cut and mutilated notes at all its Issue Offices and currency chest branches of commercial banks. In order to make the Note Refund Rules easy to understand and to apply, these have been comprehensively revised and simplified. It has also been decided that any officer of the designated branch can adjudicate mutilated notes presented thereat. It is hoped that simplification and liberalisation of the Rules would help both, the prescribed officers as well as the tenderers of mutilated notes to easily comprehend the revised Rules and enable the former to apply the Note Refund Rules without leaving any scope for subjectivity.

While the facility for exchange of soiled notes is to be provided by all banks at all of their branches, the facility of exchange of mutilated notes would be available at designated bank branches (including co-operative banks and regional rural banks) to all tenderers whether they are account holders or not. This is a duty that the banking system as a whole owes to the public. It needs no emphasis that the object of simplification of RBI Note Refund Rules and its extension is to help members of the public exchange the cut/mutilated notes in their possession without difficulty. The designated bank branches should play an active role and ensure that the facility is operated for the benefit of the members of public at large and is not pre-empted by a group of persons.

This booklet contains Rules and Procedures to be followed under the Scheme. The procedure required to be followed by the branches for acceptance, adjudication, and maintenance of records of mutilated notes is also laid down in this booklet. All further instructions to be issued on the subject will be with reference to this booklet and branches of the banks shall update the booklet by making necessary amendments to it. If any clarification is needed on the scheme, a reference should be made either to the Issue Department of the Reserve Bank of India at its offices or the Chief General Manager, Reserve Bank of India, Central Office, Department of Currency Management, Mumbai.

Reserve Bank of India has been continuously making efforts to make good quality banknotes available to the members of public. The Clean Note Policy contains initiatives and instructions to make currency notes clean. To help RBI and banking system, the members of public are requested to ensure the following:

1. Not to staple the banknotes.
2. Not to write, mark and put rubber stamp on the banknotes.
3. Store the banknotes safely to prevent any damage of notes.

Basically, there are two categories of notes which are exchanged between banks and the Reserve Bank, soiled notes and mutilated notes.

a. Soiled notes are notes which have become dirty and limp due to excessive use or two-piece note. While soiled notes can be tendered and exchanged at all bank branches.

b. Mutilated note means a note of which a portion is missing or which is composed of more than two pieces. While, mutilated notes are exchanged at designated bank branches and such notes can be exchanged for value through an adjudication process which is governed by Reserve Bank of India (Note Refund) Rules, 2009.

Under current provisions, either full or no value for notes of denomination up to ₹ 20 is paid, while notes of ₹ 50 and above would get full, half, or no value, that depending on the area of the single largest undivided portion of the note. Special adjudication procedures exist at the Reserve Bank Issue offices for notes which have turned extremely brittle or badly burnt, charred or inseparably stuck together and therefore cannot withstand normal handling.

Currency Chests: Currency chests are branches of selected banks authorised by the RBI to stock rupee notes and coins. The responsibility for managing the currency in circulation is vested in the RBI. The central bank advises the Centre on the number of notes to be printed, the currency denominations, security features and so on. The number of notes that need to be printed is determined using a statistical model that takes the pace of economic growth, rate of inflation and the replacement rate of soiled notes. The Government has, however, reserved the right to determine the amount of coins that have to be minted.

The RBI offices in various cities receive the notes from note presses and coins from the mints. These are sent to the currency chests and small coin depots from where they are distributed to bank branches. The RBI has set up over 4,075 currency chests all over the country. Besides these, there are around 3,746 bank branches that act as small coin depots to stock small coins.

Clean Notes Policy: RBI Directs Banks not to Turn Away Soiled Notes

Reserve Bank of India has issued a fresh circular under which it has directed all banks including private lenders to accept spoiled, scribbled or torn-out currency notes.

Central bank's latest diktat comes in the backdrop of reports that suggested a number of banks were not accepting soiled notes causing hardship to customers. RBI has instructed 'faulting' banks to treat the notes coming in at their counters as 'soiled notes'.

Banks cannot turn away/denied to customers who come with soiled notes to deposit at their branches under RBI's 'clean notes policy'. The bankers' bank has also instructed lenders to avoid recycling of scribbled notes they get deposited at their counters.

In its earlier circular, RBI had asked bank staff not scribble or write on bank notes so as not to spoil them. However, the directive was misconstrued by bank staff that might have been a cause of worry for banks. In its consequence, some banks stopped accepting identified notes.

Reserve Bank of India has made exchange of soiled notes much easier for a customer and a non-customer of a bank who can make an over-the-counter exchange of these notes. The report added that RBI has installed high-speed Currency Verification and Processing Systems machines at all its offices which can process 50,000–60,000 pieces per hour. "Soiled notes are shredded and briquetted on-line," it said.

7.2 MASTER CIRCULAR, FACILITY FOR EXCHANGE OF NOTES AND COINS DATED JULY 02, 2018

7.2.1 Facility for Exchange of Notes and Coins at Bank Branches

(*a*) All branches of banks in all parts of the country are mandated to provide the following customer services, more actively and vigorously to the members of public so that there is no need for them to approach the RBI Regional offices for this purpose:

(*i*) Issuing fresh/good quality notes and coins of all denominations on demand,

(*ii*) Exchanging soiled/mutilated/defective notes,*

(*iii*) Accepting coins and notes either for transactions or exchange.

It will be preferable to accept coins, particularly, in the denominations. However, accepting coins packed in polythene sachets of 100 each would perhaps be more convenient for the cashiers as well as the customers. Such polythene sachets may be kept at the counters and made available to the customers.

(*b*) All branches should provide the above facilities to members of public without any discrimination on all working days. The scheme of providing exchange facility by a few selected currency chest branches on one of the Sundays in a month will remain unchanged. The names and addresses of such bank branches should be available with the respective banks.

(*c*) The availability of the above-mentioned facilities at the bank branches should be given wide publicity for information of the public at large.

* Small Finance Banks and Payment Banks may exchange mutilated and defective notes at their option.

(*d*) None of the bank branches should refuse to accept small denomination notes and / or coins tendered at their counters.

7.2.2 Reserve Bank of India (Note Refund) Rules, 2009–Delegation of Powers

(*a*) In terms of Section 28 read with Section 58 (2) of Reserve Bank of India Act, 1934, no person is entitled as a right to recover from the Government of India or RBI the value of any lost, stolen, mutilated or imperfect currency note of the Govt. of India (GOI) or banknote. However, with a view to mitigating the hardship to the public in genuine cases, it has been provided that the RBI may, with the previous sanction of the Central Government, prescribe the circumstances. Conditions and limitations subject to which, the value of such currency notes or banknotes may be refunded as a matter of grace.

(*b*) With a view to extending the facility for the benefit and convenience of public, all branches of banks have been delegated powers under Rule 2(j) of Reserve Bank of India (Note Refund) Rules, 2009 for exchange of mutilated / defective notes free of cost.

7.2.3 Liberalised Definition of A Soiled Note

In order to facilitate quicker exchange facilities, the definition of soiled note has been expanded. A 'soiled note' means a note which has become dirty due to normal wear and tear and also includes a two-piece note pasted together wherein both the pieces presented belong to the same note and form the entire note with no essential feature missing. These notes should be accepted over bank counters in payment of Government dues and for credit to accounts of the public maintained with banks. However, in no case, these notes should be issued to the public as re-issuable notes and shall be deposited in currency chests for onward transmission to RBI offices as soiled note remittances for further processing.

7.2.4 Mutilated Notes Presentation and Passing

A mutilated note is a note of which a portion is missing or which is composed of more than two pieces. Mutilated notes may be presented at any of the bank branches. The notes so presented shall be accepted, exchanged and adjudicated in accordance with Reserve Bank of India (Note Refund) Rules, 2009.

7.2.5 Extremely Brittle, Burnt, Charred, Stuck Up Notes

Notes which have turned extremely brittle or are badly burnt, charred or inseparably stuck-up together and therefore cannot withstand normal handling, shall not be accepted by the bank branches for exchange. Instead the holders may be advised to tender these notes to the Issue office concerned where they will be adjudicated under a Special Procedure.

(*a*) *Procedure for Exchange of Soiled/ Mutilated/Imperfect Notes*

1. *Exchange of soiled notes:* If there is all features in any notes banks can exchange such notes free of charge.
2. *Notes presented in small number:* Where the number of notes presented by a person is up to 20 pieces with a maximum value of ₹ 5000 per day, banks should exchange them over the counter, free of charge.
3. *Notes presented in bulk:* Where the number of notes presented by a person exceeds 20 pieces or ₹ 5000 in value per day, banks may accept them, against receipt, for value to be credited later. Banks may levy service charges as permitted in Master Circular on Customer Service in Banks (DBR.No.Leg.BC.21/09.07.006/2015–16 dated July 1, 2015). In case tendered value is above 50000, banks are expected to take the usual precautions.

(*b*) *Exchange of Mutilated and Imperfect Notes*

1. While designated branches may continue to follow the procedure as laid down in Part III of Note Refund Rule (NRR), 2009 for exchanging mutilated and imperfect notes and issue receipt for the notes presented for adjudication, non-chest branches are required to follow the following procedure for notes presented in small numbers and in bulk.
2. *Notes presented in small number:* Where the number of notes presented by a person is up to 5 pieces, non-chest branches should normally adjudicate the notes as per the procedure laid down in Part III of NRR, 2009 and pay the exchange value over the counter. If the non-chest branches are not able to adjudicate the mutilated notes, the notes may be received against a receipt and sent to the linked currency chest branch for adjudication. The probable date of payment should be informed to the tenderers on the receipt itself and the same should not exceed 30 days. Bank account details should be obtained from the tenderers for crediting the exchange value by electronic means.
3. *Notes presented in bulk:* Where the number of notes presented by a person is more than 5 pieces not exceeding 5000 in value, the tenderer should be advised to send such notes to nearby currency chest branch by insured post giving his/her bank account details (a/c no, branch name, IFSC, etc.) or get them exchanged thereat in person. All other persons tendering mutilated notes whose value exceeds ₹5000 should be advised to approach nearby currency chest branch. Currency chest branches receiving mutilated notes through insured post should credit the exchange value to the account of sender by electronic means within 30 days of receipt of notes.

(c) ***Grievance to Banking Ombudsman:*** Tenderers aggrieved with the service provided by the banks in this regard may approach Banking Ombudsman concerned, following the procedure as laid under Banking Ombudsman Scheme, 2006 with the bank /postal receipts as proof for necessary action.

7.2.6 Notes Bearing 'PAY' / 'PAID' / 'REJECT' Stamps

(a) Every Officer-in-charge of the branch, i.e., the Branch Manager and every Officer-in-charge of the Accounts or Cash Wing of the Branch shall act as 'Prescribed Officer' in each branch to adjudicate the notes received at the branch for exchange in accordance with Reserve Bank of India (Note Refund) Rules, 2009. After adjudicating mutilated notes, the Prescribed Officer is required to record his order by subscribing his initials to the dated 'PAY'/'PAID'/'REJECT' stamp. The 'PAY'/'PAID' and 'REJECT' stamps should also carry the name of the bank and branch concerned and held under the custody of the 'Prescribed Officer' to avoid misuse.

(b) Mutilated/defective notes bearing 'PAY'/'PAID' (or 'REJECT') stamp of any RBI Issue office or any bank branch, if presented for payment again at any of the bank branches should be rejected under Rule 6(2) of Reserve Bank of India (Note Refund) Rules, 2009 and the tenderer should be advised that the value of such note/s cannot be paid since the same has already been paid as is evident from the PAY/PAID stamps affixed on it/them. All bank branches have instructions not to issue notes bearing PAY/PAID stamps to the public even through oversight. The branches should caution their customers not to accept such notes from any bank or anybody else.

7.2.8 Notes Bearing Slogans/Political Messages, etc.

Any note with slogans and message of a political nature written across it ceases to be a legal tender and the claim on such a note will be rejected under Rule 6(3) (iii) of Reserve Bank of India (Note Refund) Rules, 2009. Similarly, notes which are disfigured may also be rejected under Rule 6(3) (ii) of Reserve Bank of India (Note Refund) Rules, 2009.

7.2.9 Deliberately Cut Notes

The notes, which are found to be deliberately cut, torn, altered or tampered notes if presented for payment of exchange value should be rejected under Rule 6(3) (ii) of the Reserve Bank of India (Note Refund) Rules, 2009. Although it is not possible to precisely define deliberately cut notes, a close look at such notes will clearly reveal any deliberate fraudulent intention, as the manner in which such notes are mutilated will follow a broad uniformity in the shape/location of missing portions of the notes, especially when the notes are tendered in large numbers. The details of the case such as the name of the tenderer, the number of notes tendered and their denominations should be reported thereafter to the Deputy/General Manager of Issue Department, under whose jurisdiction the branch falls. The matter should also be reported to local police in case a large number of such notes are tendered.

7.2.10 Training

Our Issue offices conduct training programmes for 'Prescribed Officers' of bank branches on a priority basis. As the training programmes are intended to provide knowledge and install confidence in the Prescribed Officers in the process of adjudication of defective notes, it is imperative that the Prescribed Officers of the branches are deputed for such programmes.

7.2.11 Display of Notice Board

All bank branches are required to display at their branch premises, at a prominent place, on a board indicating the availability of note and coin exchange facility with the legend, "Soiled/Mutilated Notes and Coins are Accepted and Exchanged Here" for information of general public. Banks should ensure that all their branches provide facility for exchange of notes and coins not only to their customers but also others. However, they should ensure that the note exchange facility is not cornered by money changers/dealers in defective notes.

7.2.12 Disposal of Notes Adjudicated at Bank Branches

Regarding audit of the notes adjudicated by bank branches, the full value paid notes have to be remitted by all branches to the chest branches with which they have been linked and there from to the Issue Offices concerned together with the next soiled note remittance in the manner already laid down. The half value paid notes and rejected notes, which are held by the chest branches in their cash balance, may either be remitted separately packed together with the full value paid notes or sent by registered and insured post as and when required. The full value paid notes will be treated as chest remittance by the Issue Office while the half value paid notes and rejected notes will be treated as notes tendered for adjudication and processed accordingly. All chest branches are required to submit to our Issue Offices a monthly statement showing the number of notes adjudicated during the month.

7.2.13 Uncurrent Coins

The coins of 25 paisa and below, issued from time to time, ceased to be legal tender for payments as well as account with effect from June 30, 2011 in terms of Gazette Notification No. 2529 dated December 20, 2010 issued by the Government of India.

7.2.14 Monitoring and Control

(*a*) The Regional Managers/Zonal Managers of the banks may pay surprise visits to the branches and report the position of compliance in this regard to the Head Office which will review such reports and take prompt remedial action, wherever necessary.

(*b*) Any non-compliance in this regard shall be viewed as violation of instructions issued by the Reserve Bank of India.

Master Direction on Currency Distribution and Exchange Scheme (CDES) based on performance in rendering customer service to the members of public. In terms of the Preamble, under Section 45 of the RBI Act, 1934 and 35 A of the Banking Regulation Act 1949, the Bank issues guidelines/instructions for realising the objectives of our Clean Note Policy. With a view to sustaining these objectives, the Bank has formulated a scheme of incentives titled (CDES in order to ensure that all bank branches provide better customer services to members of public.

1. The Master Direction enclosed incorporates updated guidelines/circulars on the subject. The direction will be updated from time to time as and when fresh instructions are issued.

2. Circular on CDES for bank branches including currency chests based on performance in rendering customer service to members of public.

3. The Currency Distribution and Exchange Scheme, for bank branches including currency chests has been formulated in order to ensure that all bank branches provide better customer service to members of public with regard to exchange of notes and coins, in keeping with the objectives of Clean Note Policy.

4. *Incentives:* As per the scheme, banks are eligible for the following financial incentives for providing facilities for exchange of notes and coins:

S.No.	Nature of Service	Particulars of Incentives
(*i*)	Opening and maintaining currency chests at centres that having population of less than 1 lakh in under banked States	(*a*) **Capital Cost:** Reimbursement of 50% of capital expenditure subject to a ceiling of 50 lakh per currency chest. In the North-Eastern region up to 100% of capital expenditure is eligible for reimbursement subject to the ceiling of 50 lakh. (*b*) **Revenue cost:** Reimbursement of 50% of revenue expenditure for the first 3 years. In the North Eastern region 50% of revenue expenditure will be reimbursed for the first 5 years.
(*ii*)	Exchange of soiled notes/ adjudication of mutilated banknotes over the counter at bank branches	(*a*) Exchange of soiled notes is ₹2 per packet for exchange of soiled notes up to denomination ₹50. (*b*) Adjudication of mutilated notes is ₹2 per piece

(*iii*)	Distribution of coins over counter	(*a*) ₹ 25 per bag for distribution of coins over the counter. (*b*) The incentives would be paid on the basis of withdrawal from currency chest, without waiting for claims from banks. (*c*) Banks may put in place a system of checks and balances to ensure that coins are distributed to retail customers in small lots and not to bulk customers. (*d*) The distribution of coins shall be verified by RBI Regional Offices through inspection of currency chest / incognito visits to branches, etc.

7.2.15 Operational Guidelines to Avail Performance-based Incentives

(*i*) The incentives will be paid on the soiled notes that actually received in the Notes Issue Office of the RBI. Banks need not submit a separate claim in this regard. Currency chest branch will have to pass on the incentive to the linked branches for the soiled notes tendered by them on a pro-data basis.

(*ii*) Similarly, incentive will be paid in respect of the adjudicated notes received along with the soiled note remittances/sent separately by registered/insured post in a sealed cover to the RBI. No separate claim is required to be made.

7.3 RESERVE BANK OF INDIA (NOTE REFUND) RULES 2009

7.3.1 Provisions in the Reserve Bank of India Act, 1934

Section 28: Notwithstanding anything contained in any enactment or rule of law to the contrary, no person shall of right be entitled to recover from the Central Government or the Bank, the value of any lost, stolen, mutilated or imperfect currency note, provided that the Bank may, with the previous sanction of the Central Government, prescribe the circumstances in and the conditions and limitations subject to which the value of such currency notes or banknotes may be refunded as of grace and the rules made under this provision shall be laid on the table of Parliament.

Section 58 (1): The Central Board may, with the previous sanction of the Central Government, by notification in the Official Gazette, make regulations consistent with this Act to provide for all matters for which provision is necessary or convenient for the purpose of giving effect to the provisions of this Act.

Section 58 (2): In particular and without prejudice to the generality of the foregoing provisions, such regulations may provide for all or any of the following matters. The circumstances in which, and the conditions and limitations subject to which the value of any lost, stolen, mutilated or imperfect currency note of the Government of India or banknote may be refunded.

7.3.2 Note Refund Rules

In exercise of the powers conferred by the provision to Section 28, read with clause (q) of the sub-section (1) and (2) of Section 58, of the Reserve Bank of India Act, 1934 (2 of 1934) and in supersession of the Reserve Bank of India (Notes Refund) Rules, 1975, except as respect things done or omitted to be done before such supersession, the Central Board with the previous sanction of the Central Government, hereby makes the following rules for specifying the circumstances in, and the conditions and limitations subject to which, the value of lost, stolen, mutilated or imperfect note may be refunded as a matter of grace, namely:

1. Short Title, Application and Commencement

(1) These rules may be called the Reserve Bank of India (Note Refund) Rules, 2009 and further amended vide Reserve Bank of India (Note Refund) Amendment Rules, 2018.

(2) They shall apply to a note, which is a legal tender on the date of its presentation before the Bank.

(3) They shall come into force on the date of their publication in the Official Gazette.

2. Definitions

In these rules, unless the context otherwise requires:

(A) The security features of a note, for deciding the genuineness or otherwise, include,

(*i*) Paper Quality;

(*ii*) Size and Shape of Numbers;

(*iii*) Security Thread;

(*iv*) Intaglio Printing;

(*v*) Latent Image in Vertical Band;

(*vi*) Electrotype Watermark (in watermark window);

(*vii*) Micro Lettering;

(*viii*) Fluorescence (number panels and central band);

(*ix*) Optically Variable Ink (in rupee five hundred and rupee one thousand denominations);

(*x*) See-Through Register, and

(*xi*) Any other security feature that may be introduced by the Bank.

(B) The essential features of a note have been enumerated with a view to help the prescribed officer to establish the genuineness or otherwise of a mutilated note;

'Government Note'; means any note issued by the Central Government or supplied by the Central Government to the Bank and issued by the Reserve Bank, provided the liability for the payment of the value in respect of such note has devolved on and been taken over by the Bank;

'Imperfect Note'; means any note, which is wholly or partially, obliterated, shrunk, washed, altered or indecipherable but does not include a mutilated note;

'Mutilated Note'; means a note of which a portion is missing or which is composed of more than two pieces;

'Mismatched Note'; means a mutilated note which has been formed by joining a half note of anyone note to a half note of another note:

(*i*) 'Note'; means a Banknote or a Government note;

'Prescribed Officer': means any officer of the Issue Department of the Bank or any officer of an agent of the Bank/designated by the Bank by arrangement through agreement in this behalf as authorised to receive mutilated notes for adjudication under these rules;

'Soiled Note:'; means a note which, has become dirty due to usage and also includes a two-piece note pasted together wherein both the pieces presented belong to the same note, and form the entire note.

3. Decision on Adjudication of Mutilated Note

If any dispute arises in relation to adjudication of mutilated note the same shall be referred to the Bank for its decision and its decision shall be binding on the claimant, his nominees and legal heirs or representatives as the case may be.

4. Presentation and Disposal of Claim

A claim in respect of any note may be presented before the Prescribed Officer for adjudication and payment of value under these rules.

5. Right to Call for Information or to Hold Enquiries

The prescribed officer may, if it is considered necessary so to do, call for any information or hold any inquiry relating to any claim presented before him under these rules, and where the genuineness of the note is doubtful, he shall send such doubtful note for expert opinion to the General Manager, Currency Note Press, Nashik Road or to any other authority as designated under any law in force for this purpose.

6. General Provisions in Relation to all Claims

(*a*) No claim in respect of a note, which is alleged to have been stolen, lost or wholly destroyed, shall be entertained.

(*b*) If the Prescribed Officer is satisfied that a mutilated note presented before him is one which appears to have been cancelled at any office of the Bank or the claim is one which appears to have already been paid under these rules, he may, after making enquiries under rule 5 above reject the claim on such note.

(*c*) A claim in respect of a note, which,

(*i*) It cannot be identified with certainty as a genuine note for which the Bank is liable under the Act;

(*ii*) It has been made imperfect or mutilated, thereby causing the note to appear to be of a higher denomination, or has been deliberately cut, torn, defaced, altered or dealt with in any other manner, not necessarily by the claimants, enabling the use of the same for making of a false claim under these rules or otherwise to defraud the Bank or the public,

(*iii*) It carries any extrinsic words or visible representations intended to convey or capable of conveying any message of a political or religious character or furthering the interest of any person or entity;

(*iv*) It has been imported into India by the claimant from any place outside India in contravention of the provision of any law;

(*v*) Any information called for by the Prescribed Officer or the Bank, as the case may be, is not furnished by a claimant within a period of three months from the date of receipt of the notice or letter asking for the information, or

(*vi*) The opinion of the Prescribed Officer, a deliberate fraudulent intention appears in respect of such a claim shall be rejected and shall not be eligible for consideration under any other law for the time being in force.

7. Imperfect Note

The value of an imperfect note may be paid for full value/half value as specified in the tables given in rule 8, if,

(*a*) The matter, which is printed on the note has not become totally illegible, and

(*b*) The Prescribed Officer is satisfied, having regard to the printed matter which is legible on the note, that it is a genuine note.

8. Mutilated Notes

(*a*) The adjudication of claims in respect of notes of less than fifty rupees denomination shall be made in the following manner, namely,

(*i*) if the area of the single largest undivided piece of the note presented is more than 50% of the area of the respective denomination, rounded off to the next complete square centimetre, full value on mutilated notes of the above denominations shall be payable;

(*ii*) If the area of the largest undivided piece of the note presented is less than or equal to 50% of the area of the note, the claim shall be rejected.

Explanation: For the purposes of this sub-rule, it is hereby clarified that the value of a mutilated note of less than rupees fifty denomination may be refunded in full if the undivided area of the single largest piece of the note is as specified.

(*b*) The payment of claim in respect of note of rupees fifty and above denominations shall be made in the following manner, namely,

(*i*) Full value of the mutilated notes of the above denominations shall be payable if the area of the single largest undivided piece of the note presented is more than 80% of the area of the respective denomination rounded-off to the next complete square centimeter;

(*ii*) If the undivided area of the single largest undivided piece of the note presented is equal to or more than 40% and less than or equal to 80% of the area of the respective denomination rounded-off to the next complete square centimetre, half the value of the note is payable.

(*iii*) If the area of the single largest undivided piece of the note is less than 40%, no value shall be payable, and the claim shall be rejected.

(*iv*) If the claim of mutilated notes of rupees fifty and above denominations consist of a note composed of two pieces of the same note and the two pieces, individually have an area equal to or more than 40% of the total area of the note in that denomination, then the claim may be refunded for full value of the note.

Explanation: For the purposes of this sub-rule, it is hereby clarified that the value of a mutilated note of equal to or more than rupees fifty denomination may be refunded in full or half, as the case may be, if the minimum undivided area of the single largest piece of the note is as specified.

9. Payment of Claim in Respect of Mismatched Note

The payment of claim in respect of a mismatched note may be dealt with as follows, namely,

(*a*) In case of notes up to rupees twenty denomination notes, the area of the larger of the two pieces presented may be measured and adjudicated as per the proviso of sub-rule (1) of Rule 8, ignoring the smaller half.

(*b*) If none of the two pieces presented meets the minimum area stipulated as per the proviso of clause (i) of sub-rule 1 of rule 8 above, the claim shall be rejected.

(*c*) In case of rupees fifty and above denominations, the two pieces may be treated as two separate claims and dealt with accordingly.

10. Claimants to Be Bound by Rules

(*a*) Any payment which is provided under these rules shall be made only as matter of grace and the Bank may, as it deems fit, from time to time issue such supplementary or detailed instructions for carrying out the provisions of these rules, for the guidance of the Prescribed Officer.

(*b*) Any person who makes any claim on account of an imperfect note or mutilated note shall be deemed to have made the said claim under the proviso to Section 28 of the Act and subject to the provisions of these rules, which shall be deemed to be binding on all claimants and their heirs or assigns.

11. Retention and Destruction of Note

Notwithstanding the denomination of a note or the decision of the Prescribed Officer on the claim, a note presented before the Prescribed Officer for the purpose of making a claim shall be retained and destroyed or otherwise disposed of by the Bank in the following manner, namely,

(*a*) in the case of a note in respect of which full payment is made, at anytime after the payment; and

(*b*) in the case of a note in respect of which no payment is made, or on which half value payment has been made, on the expiry of a period of three months from the date of the decision rejecting the claim or to pay half-value, as the case may be, unless within this period, an order from a competent Court is submitted to any office of the Bank or branch of the designated bank restraining the Bank from destroying or otherwise disposing of the said note.

12. Payment to Legal Heirs or Nominees

(*a*) If a claimant, who has submitted a claim under these rules, is dead, his legal representatives shall be eligible to receive the payment due to the claimant subject to the determination of the claim by the Prescribed Officer.

(*b*) The legal representatives shall be entitled to receive the payment due to the claimant, if any, upon furnishing to the Prescribed Officer an indemnity bond executed by the legal representative in favour of the branch or office of the Bank or any other institution or entity as designated by the Bank for this purpose;

Provided payment up to an amount of rupees five hundred may be made to the legal heir of the claimant on a declaration for this purpose.

(*c*) In case of mutilated note presented at the Bank through Triple Lock Receptacle (TLR) cover, the tendered shall indicate his name and address along with other details, such as, bank account number, etc. as specified on the cover, and the individual renderers, may, at their option, in addition, also indicate on the cover, the name and address of the nominee who may receive the amount that is determined to be due on the claim without production of indemnity, subject to proper identification.

13. Printed Forms

Where any indemnity bond as referred to in rule 12 is to be executed in favour of the Bank a printed copy of the bond shall be supplied free of cost to the claimant or the person eligible to receive the payment under these rules.

14. Stamp Duty

The value of the stamp duty on the indemnity bond shall be paid by the person executing the bond.

15. Procedure when Payee is Untraced

(*a*) In case of the note having been adjudicated at the office of the Bank, the value or part of the value of a note is payable to the claimant and if such claimant, is not found or is dead, his legal representatives or the nominee specified by him cannot be found or fails within a period of three months from the date of communication to him the decision to take steps to receive payment, the amount payable shall be paid to the Banking Department of the Bank.

(*b*) In case of the mutilated note having been adjudicated at the branch of designated bank or other entities, such payment may be credited with the Issue Office of the Bank after a period of three months from the date of communication to the tenderer of the decision to take steps to receive the exchange value.

Memorandum of Procedure for receipt, adjudication, payment and disposal of / mutilated notes at designated bank branches.

1. **Branches where Facilities are Available:** For the benefit and convenience of the public, Reserve Bank of India has authorised the designated branches of the banks to accept exchange and pay the admissible exchange value of mutilated notes in accordance with the Reserve Bank of India (Note Refund) Rules, 2009 or reject such mutilated notes as are not payable under these Rules.

2. **Notes shall be Accepted:** The branches shall accept notes in the denomination of ₹ 1, 2, 5, 10, 20, 50, 100, 200, 500, 2000 (and such other denominations of notes that may be issued in future) for exchange under the Rules.

Further, such notes which have turned extremely brittle or are badly burnt, charred, inseparably stuck together and therefore cannot withstand further handling or which may lose their original identity with the passage of time shall not be accepted by the branches for exchange. The holder/s of such notes may be advised to tender them to the In-charge, Issue Department of the Reserve Bank of India under whose jurisdiction the currency chest falls where such notes will be examined under Special Procedure.

3. **From whom Notes Shall be Accepted:** The branches shall freely accept the notes from anyone who wishes to get his/her mutilated notes exchanged from the branch. For serving a larger section of the public the branch may, if necessary impose

a reasonable restriction on the number of the notes to be tendered at a time by an individual tenderer. Large quantity of notes may be accepted from the Government Departments and banks by mutual arrangements. The branches shall take steps to see that the exchange facilities are not cornered by private money changers or professional dealers of defective notes.

4. **How the Notes Should be Accepted:** The notes may be accepted over the counter. On receipt of the notes, a paper token in form DN-I in duplicate indicating the number of pieces of notes and their value in each denomination may be prepared. The receiving staff /official should also authenticate the total pieces and values on both copies of the token by subscribing his initials. The original should be handed over to the tenderer. The duplicate should be attached to the notes and the token together with the notes should be passed onto the prescribed officer for adjudication. The notes should be securely fastened to the relative tokens to avoid mix-up of tenders covered by different tokens. It should further be ensured that the notes do not get damaged during receipt and transmission to the prescribed officer. The paper tokens should be serially numbered. To avoid disputes that may be raised by the tenderers in respect of rejected notes, it is advisable to write the token number on all the notes tendered. The details of each tender should be recorded in the register inform DN-2.

5. **Prescribed Officer-Adjudication and Payment:** Prescribed officer is the officer who has been authorised to adjudicate the mutilated notes by the designated branch as defined in Section 2(j) of the RBI (Note Refund) Rules 2009 for the purpose of adjudication of the mutilated notes under the Rules. He shall examine each and every mutilated note on its merit and decide its payability strictly according to the Rules. He shall record his 'Pay' order by subscribing his initial to a pay stamp, to be affixed on the notes, which are found payable by him under the Rules. Similarly, he shall, by subscribing his initials to dated 'Reject' stamp affixed on the note, record his rejection order indicating rules 6(3), 8(1) (ii) 8(2) (iii) and Explanation (d) under which the claim is rejected. The pay or rejection order should be put on front side of the note and not on any paper used for pasting the notes, etc. or on the reverse side of the note. The prescribed officer shall also record his orders on the duplicate paper token attached, etc. the notes and get the rejection advice in form DN-3 prepared. The notes with the covering token should then be sent back to the counter for making payment to the tenderer.

The Prescribed Officer may if necessary, get the badly pasted notes, re-pasted before their adjudication. He shall act with due diligence while exercising the powers under these Rules in order to ensure that no notes payable under them are rejected and no notes not payable are paid. If any paid notes are later on found by Reserve Bank of India not to be payable under the above Rules, the Bank may recover the value of loss from such of the authorised bank. The authorised bank branch shall abide by the decisions of the Reserve Bank of India, in this regard, who in pursuance of the above Rules is the ultimate authority in whom the powers to make, issue, amend, interpret and enforce the Rules are vested.

6. **Payment:** After receipt of the notes with the covering paper token from the prescribed officer, the counter staff shall check that the PAY and REJECT orders have been properly recorded on all the notes and the paper token. He shall then pay to the tenderer the exchange value of the notes ordered to be paid and also issue him rejection advice in form DN-3 in respect of rejected notes, if any, on his surrendering the original token issued to him with his name and address duly written on the reverse of it. He shall then affix the dated 'PAID' stamp on the notes (on the obverse side) on which the exchange value is paid. In no case the rejected notes shall be given back to the tenderer. After completion of payment, the paid and the rejected notes should be segregated. The original token surrendered by the tenderer should be attached to the rejected notes. It should be carefully noted that notes on which half value has been paid should be kept with the rejected notes for easy retrieval, should the tenderer choose subsequently to question the payment of half value instead of full value. In the branches which do not have a currency chest of the Reserve Bank of India, the paid and rejected notes shall be held separately along with branch cash balance. The Branch Manager shall have, however, overall responsibility for the proper and safe custody of the notes. It must be clearly understood that both paid and rejected notes are to be retained by the bank on behalf of the Reserve Bank of India and their disposal in any manner will be subject to such directions that the Reserve Bank may give in this regard.

In the branches having currency chests, the 'paid' notes only shall be deposited in the currency chest in multiples of ₹ 500/- with a minimum of ₹ 1000/-. The half value paid notes and rejected notes shall, however, be held separately along with the cash balance of the branch.

7. **Accounting for Notes Adjudicated:** The full value paid notes may be treated on par with non-issuable notes and shall be kept as part of the currency chest balances following the procedure prescribed for depositing non-issuable notes. These notes should be shown in the currency chest slip as non-issuable notes. The paid notes shall be held distinct by segregating them from soiled notes to be sent to the Reserve Bank of India and storing them in separate receptacle. These notes may be packed separately and sent along with soiled notes at the time of remitting soiled notes to the Issue Department of Reserve Bank of India. The half value notes and the rejected notes shall be kept separately along with the cash balance of the branch and in no case they shall be kept deposited with the full value paid notes in the chest.

The non-chest branches shall send notes adjudicated by them for deposit to the linked currency chest that in turn will remit to the Reserve Bank of India along with soiled note remittance.

8. **Verification and Transfer of Adjudicated Notes:** Notes adjudicated for full value may be sent along with the soiled note remittance separately. A qualitative and quantitative verification of such notes would be undertaken in Reserve Bank of India. Such notes would be treated as a chest remittance and accounted for accordingly.

Half value paid notes and Rejected notes may be sent separately to Claim Section, Issue Department of RBI. The prescribed officer should ensure that the preservation period of three months as laid down in para 11(b) of the Rules note is over, before sending them to RBI. However, the detail of the tenderer in DN-2 has to be preserved for payment to him. These notes would be accounted as a receipt from that currency chest-holding branch. These notes would be subject to audit at the Reserve Bank of India to ensure that none of the rejected notes are payable for any value and none of the half value paid notes payable for full value. As the half value paid and rejected notes would have already completed the required period of preservation, they would be destroyed by the Issue Department of Reserve Bank of India as deemed appropriate.

9. **Forged Notes:** If during the course of adjudication of mutilated notes, any note is suspected to be forged or is found to be forged, it should be impounded by the Prescribed Officer by affixing 'COUNTERFEIT NOTE IMPOUNDED' stamps with his initial therein. The procedure laid down in regard to handling of forged notes may be followed.

10. **Miscellaneous:**

(*i*) Only those notes which are mutilated should be examined and adjudicated by the Prescribed Officer. Soiled notes (which include two-piece notes having middle or near middle cut either horizontally or vertically) should be freely accepted and exchanged at all branches including currency chest branch.

(*ii*) Every effort should be made to pay the exchange value in minimum possible time, but in any case it should be on the same day. To facilitate banking habits, exchange value should be credited to the account through Electric clearance service (ECS) or paid by way of Banker Cheque or Demand Drafts.

(*iii*) The Prescribed Officer should examine the tendered notes with due care. Notes appear to be doubtful or built-up should be examined against a table-lamp to establish the size of the largest undivided piece of the note which is the basic criteria of exchange of notes.

(*iv*) The Prescribed Officer should record his pay order in red ink and arrange to have the 'PAY' stamp affixed on it immediately. The 'PAY stamp should be held in his custody to avoid misuse.

(*v*) Requests for expression of opinion on defective notes regarding their payability or otherwise should not be entertained.

(*vi*) No requests for inspection of or return of the notes tendered for exchange or for any information relating to them should be entertained.

11. **Accessories for Prescribed Officers:** The Prescribed Officers should be equipped with the following accessories to enable them to exercise better judgement while handling defective notes:

(*i*) Table lamp of medium intensity.

(*ii*) Magnifying glass.

(*iii*) Measuring centimetre plate (in plastic)

(*iv*) A set of genuine notes in all denominations of different patterns (for the purpose of comparison in case of doubt).

12. **Display over Notice Board:** The Branch Manager shall arrange to display outside the branch premises the following board for information of the public in Hindi, English and local language; Mutilated notes are accepted and exchanged here;

Inside the banking hall and above the counter where mutilated notes will be accepted, the following board will be displayed:

(*i*) Mutilated notes are accepted here for exchange under Reserve Bank of India (Note Refund) Rules.

(*ii*) Exchange value, if any, must be collected on the same day.

(*iii*) Notes on which exchange value is not payable will be retained by us.

(*iv*) In case of difficulty, please see Branch Manager.

7.3.3 Security Features of Indian Banknotes

Watermark

The Mahatma Gandhi Series of banknotes contain the Mahatma Gandhi watermark with a light and shade effect and multi-directional lines in the watermark window.

Security Thread

₹1000 notes introduced in October 2000 contain a readable, windowed security thread alternately visible on the obverse with the inscriptions 'Bharat' (in Hindi), '1000' and 'RBI', but totally embedded on the reverse. The ₹500 and ₹100 notes have a security thread with similar visible features and inscription 'Bharat' (in Hindi), and 'RBI'. When held against the light, the security thread on ₹1000, ₹500 and ₹100 can be seen as one continuous line. The ₹5, ₹10, ₹20 and ₹50 notes contain a readable, fully embedded windowed security thread with the inscription 'Bharat' (in Hindi), and 'RBI'. The security thread appears to the left of the Mahatma's portrait. Notes issued prior to the introduction of the Mahatma Gandhi Series have a plain, non-readable fully embedded security thread.

Latent Image

On the obverse side of ₹1000, ₹500, ₹100, ₹50 and ₹20 notes, a vertical band on the right side of the Mahatma Gandhi's portrait contains a latent image showing the respective denominational value in numeral. The latent image is visible only when the note is held horizontally at eye level.

Micro Lettering

This feature appears between the vertical band and Mahatma Gandhi portrait. It contains the word 'RBI' in ₹5 and ₹10. The notes of ₹20 and above also contain the denominational value of the notes in micro letters. This feature can be seen better under a magnifying glass.

Intaglio Printing

The portrait of Mahatma Gandhi, the Reserve Bank seal, guarantee and promise clause, Ashoka Pillar Emblem on the left, RBI Governor's signature are printed in intaglio, i.e., in raised prints, which can be felt by touch, in ₹20, ₹50, ₹100, ₹500 and ₹1000 notes.

Identification Mark

A special feature in intaglio has been introduced on the left of the watermark window on all notes except ₹10/- note. This feature is in different shapes for various denominations (₹20-Vertical Rectangle, ₹50-Square, ₹100-Triangle, ₹500-Circle, ₹1000-Diamond) and helps the visually impaired to identify the denomination.

Fluorescence

Number panels of the notes are printed in fluorescent ink. The notes also have optical fibres. Both can be seen when the notes are exposed to ultraviolet lamp.

Optically Variable Ink:

This is a new security feature incorporated in the ₹ 1000 and ₹ 500 notes with revised colour scheme introduced in November 2000. The numeral 1000 and 500 on the obverse of ₹ 1000 and ₹ 500 notes respectively is printed in optically variable ink viz., a colour-shifting ink. The colour of the numeral 1000/500 appears green when the note is held flat but would change to blue when the note is held at an angle.

See through Register

The small floral design printed both on the front (hollow) and back (filled up) of the note in the middle of the vertical band next to the Watermark has an accurate back to back registration. The design will appear as one floral design when seen against the light.

7.4 DETECTION AND IMPOUNDING OF COUNTERFEIT NOTES

7.4.1 Introduction

Everyone has once in his lifetime received a counterfeit note. In day-to-day life, people don't take the pain to report one or two fake notes received, to the police and tend to pass them off to others. However, doing such a thing is a crime punishable with imprisonment. The Reserve Bank of India from time to time comes out with various notifications regarding detection and impounding of counterfeit currency. The latest notification was issued by the RBI on July 20, 2017. In the Master Circular for Detection and Impounding of Counterfeit notes, RBI issues guidelines on impounding such currencies.

Counterfeit Notes: Counterfeit money, goods, or documents are not genuine, but have been made to look exactly like genuine ones in order to deceive people. He admitted possessing and delivering counterfeit currency.

7.4.2 Meaning of Impounding

Impounding means to take into 'lawful custody'. In India, RBI has designated various authorities to impound counterfeit currency. Authority to impound counterfeit notes:

- All Banks.
- All treasuries and sub-treasuries.
- Note Issuing office of the RBI.

Steps to be followed while impounding counterfeit currency:

Step 1: Detection of Counterfeit Currency

- All banknotes which are presented by customers at the bank counters or received directly in currency chest should be examined through machines.
- According to the guideline issued by the RBI on May 11, 2010, on Installation of Note Sorting Machines–Note Authentication and Fitness Sorting Parameter all bank branches, as well as bank offices, should be equipped with ultraviolet lamp detection machine. The guidelines also provide other requirements to be fulfilled. At all currency chest branches of banks, there should be verification, processing, and sorting machines. Such machines help in detecting the counterfeit currency.
- The customer's account should not be credited with the amount of fake currency.
- The fake currency should not be returned to the tenderer or customer and should not be destroyed by the branch.
- If the banks do not follow these guidelines, it will be considered that the bank is wilfully involved in circulating the counterfeit currency.

Step 2: Impounding of Counterfeit Notes

All counterfeit notes received at the bank branches cannot be destroyed by the bank. Counterfeit notes should be stamped as "COUNTERFEIT NOTE." The size of the Stamp Should be 5 cm × 5 cm, and the following should be inscribed:

- Counterfeit Banknote Impounded.
- Bank/Treasury/Sub-Treasury.
- Branch/Currency Chest.
- Signature
- Date

Step 3: Issue of Receipt to Tenderer

- If any counterfeit currency is detected, an acknowledgment slip is to be given by the bank to the customer, mentioning the serial number of notes and signed by the cashier and counter-signed by the customer.
- The receipt is to be issued even when the customer is unwilling to sign it.

Step 4: Reporting to the Police

- In case where, in a single transaction four pieces of counterfeit currency are detected, a report is sent by the Nodal Bank Officer to the Nodal Police Station along with the counterfeit notes, at the end of every month. Every bank should appoint a Nodal Officer at the district level, and the same should be notified to the regional office of the RBI.
- In a case where, in a single transaction five or more pieces of counterfeit notes are detected, the notes are sent to the police station by the Nodal Bank Officer. The police after that register an First Information Report (FIR) and start investigation.
- A copy of all FIRs registered in a month is sent by the police to the Forged Note Vigilance Cell. A Forged Note Vigilance Cell is established by all banks at its Head Office. The Forged Note Vigilance Cell submits a quarterly report on counterfeit notes to the Chief General Manager, Department of Currency Management, RBI.
- In order to identify persons circulating counterfeit currencies and to help police in investigation banks should have Close Circuit Television (CCTV) cameras at cash counters.
- The data on counterfeit notes is to be forwarded by the banks to the Issue Office of the RBI every month.

Step 5: Preservation and Disposal of Counterfeit Notes

- All forged notes received back from the police by the bank should be kept in a safe custody and record of such notes needs to be maintained.
- They should be preserved for a period of three years from the date of receipt from the police.
- After three years these notes are sent to the Issue Office of the RBI with full details.
- In cases where the counterfeit note is a subject matter of litigation in the court, it should be preserved till the time court gives it decision.

Para 1: Authority to Impound Counterfeit Notes:

The Counterfeit Notes can be impounded by:

(*i*) All branches of Public Sector Banks.

(*ii*) All branches of Private Sector Banks and Foreign Banks.

(*iii*) All branches of Co-operative Banks and Regional Rural Banks.

(*iv*) All Treasuries and Sub-Treasuries.

(*v*) Issue Offices of Reserve Bank of India.

Para 2: Detection of Counterfeit Notes

Banknotes tendered over the counter/received directly at the back office/currency chest through bulk tenders should be examined for authenticity through machines. No credit to customer's account is to be given for counterfeit notes, if any, detected in the tender received over the counter or at the back-office/currency chest.

If there is no case, the counterfeit notes should be returned to the tenderer or destroyed by the bank branches/treasuries. Failure of the banks to impound counterfeit notes detected at their end will be construed as willful involvement of the bank concerned, in circulating counterfeit notes and penalty will be imposed for violation of Directive No. 3158/09.39.00 (Policy)/2009–10 dated November 19, 2009 issued by the Reserve Bank.

Para 3: Impounding of Counterfeit Notes

Notes determined as counterfeit shall be stamped as "COUNTERFEIT NOTE" and impounded in the prescribed format. Each such impounded note shall be recorded under authentication, in a separate register.

Para 4: Issue of Receipt to Tenderer

When a banknote tendered at the counter of a bank branch/back office and currency chest or treasury is found to be counterfeit, an acknowledgement receipt in the prescribed format must be issued to the tenderer, after stamping the note as in Paragraph 2. The receipt, in running serial numbers, should be authenticated by the cashier and tenderer. Notice to this effect should be displayed prominently at the offices/branches for information of the public. The receipt is to be issued even in cases where the tenderer is unwilling to countersign it.

Para 5: Detection of Counterfeit Notes

(*a*) **Reporting to Police and Other Bodies:** The following procedure should be followed while reporting incidence of detection of counterfeit note to the Police:

For cases of detection of counterfeit notes up to 4 pieces, in a single transaction, a consolidated report in the prescribed format should be sent by the Nodal Bank Officer to the police authorities or the Nodal Police Station, along with the suspect counterfeit notes, at the end of the month.

For cases of detection of counterfeit notes of 5 or more pieces, in a single transaction, the counterfeit notes should be forwarded by the Nodal Bank Officer to the local police authorities or the Nodal Police Station for investigation by filing FIR in the prescribed format.

A copy of the monthly consolidated report/FIR shall be sent to the Forged Note Vigilance Cell constituted at the Head Office of the bank (only in the case of banks), and in the case of the treasury, it should be sent to the Issue Office of the Reserve Bank concerned.

Acknowledgement of the police authorities concerned has to be obtained for note/s forwarded to them both as consolidated monthly statement and FIR. If the counterfeit notes are sent to the police by insured post, acknowledgement of receipt thereof by the police should be invariably obtained and kept on record. A proper follow-up of receipt of acknowledgement from the police authorities is necessary. In case, any difficulty is faced by the Offices/Branches due to reluctance of the police to receive monthly consolidate statement/file FIRs, the matter may be sorted out in consultation with the Nodal Officer of the police authority designated to co-ordinate matters relating to investigation of counterfeit banknotes cases. The list of Nodal Police Station may be obtained from the respective Regional Office of Reserve Bank.

Banks should also monitor the patterns/trends of such detection and suspicious trends/patterns should be brought to the notice of RBI /Police authorities immediately.

The progress made by banks in detection and reporting of counterfeit notes to Police, RBI, etc. and problems thereof, should be discussed regularly in the meetings of various State Level Committees, viz. State Level Bankers' Committee (SLBC), Standing Committee on Currency Management (SCCM), State Level Security Committee (SLSC), etc.

The data on detection of counterfeit Indian notes at bank branches and treasuries should be included in the monthly Returns forwarded to the Reserve Bank Issue Offices as indicated in para 10 below.

The definition of 'counterfeiting' in the Indian Penal Code (IPC) covers currency notes issued by a foreign government authority as well. In case of suspected foreign currency note received for opinion from the police and government agencies, etc., they should be advised to forward the case to the Interpol Wing of the CBI, New Delhi after prior consultation with them.

Para 6: Examinations of the Banknotes before Issuing over Counters, Feeding ATMs and Remitting to Issue Offices of the Reserve Bank

The banks should re-align their cash management in such a manner so as to ensure that cash receipts in the denominations of ₹ 100 and above are not put into re-circulation without the notes being machine processed for authenticity. The said instructions shall be applicable to all bank branches, irrespective of the volume of daily cash receipt. Any non-compliance will be construed as violation of the Directive No. 3158/09.39.00 (Policy)/2009–10 dated November 19, 2009 issued by the Reserve Bank.

In order to obviate complaints regarding receipt of counterfeit notes through ATMs, and to curb circulation of counterfeits, it is imperative to put in place adequate safeguards/checks before loading ATMs with notes. Dispensation of counterfeit notes through the ATMs would be construed as an attempt to circulate the counterfeit notes by the bank concerned.

Detection of counterfeits in chest remittances is also liable to be construed as willful involvement of the chest branches concerned in circulating Counterfeit Notes and may attract special investigation by police authorities, and other action like suspending the operation of the chest concerned.

Penalty at 100% of the notional value of counterfeit notes, in addition to the recovery of loss to the extent of the notional value of such notes, will be imposed under the following circumstances:

(*a*) When counterfeit notes are detected in the soiled note remittance of the bank.

(*b*) If counterfeit notes are detected in the currency chest balance of a bank during Inspection/Audit by RBI.

Para 7: Designating Nodal Bank Officer

Each bank should designate Nodal Bank Officer, district-wise and notify the same to the concerned Regional Office of RBI and Police Authorities. All cases of reporting of counterfeit note detection as indicated in Para 5 should be through the Nodal Bank Officer. The Nodal Bank Officer will also serve as the contact point for all counterfeit note detection related activities.

Para 8: Establishment of Forged Notes Vigilance Cell at Head Office of Bank

Each bank shall establish at its Head Office, a Forged Note Vigilance Cell (FNVC) to undertake the following functions:

(*i*) Dissemination of instructions issued by the Reserve Bank on counterfeit notes to bank's branches. Monitoring the implementation of these instructions. Compilation of data on detection of counterfeit notes, and its submission to Reserve Bank and Financial Intelligence Unit-India (FIU-IND) as per extant instructions. Follow-up of cases of counterfeit notes, with police authorities/ designated Nodal Officer.

(*ii*) Sharing of the information thus compiled with bank's (CVO) and report to him/her all cases of acceptance/issue of counterfeit notes over the counters.

(*iii*) Conducting periodic surprise checks at currency chests where shortages/ defective/counterfeit notes, etc. are detected.

(*iv*) Ensuring operation of Note Sorting Machines (NSM) of appropriate capacity at all the currency chests/back offices and closely monitoring the detection of Counterfeit Notes and maintaining the record of the same. Ensuring that only properly sorted and machine examined bank notes are fed into the ATMs/ issued over the counters and to put in place adequate safeguards, including surprise checks, both during the processing and in transit of notes.

Para 9: Provision of Ultraviolet Lamp and Other Infrastructure

With a view to facilitating the detection of counterfeit notes, all bank branches/ identified back offices should be equipped with ultraviolet lamps/ other appropriate banknote sorting/detection machines. In addition, all currency chest branches should be equipped with verification, processing and sorting machines and should be used to their optimum capacity. Such machines should conform to the guidelines on 'Note Authentication and Fitness Sorting Parameters' prescribed by the Reserve Bank in May 2010.

The banks shall maintain a daily record of the notes processed through the Note Sorting machines, including the number of counterfeits detected.

The banks should also consider providing at least one counting machine (with dual display facility) for public use at the counter.

Para 10: Reporting of Data to RBI

I. **By Bank Branch:** Data on counterfeit notes detected by all the branches of the bank shall be reported in the prescribed format, on a monthly basis. A statement showing the details of counterfeit notes detected in the bank branches during the month shall be compiled and forwarded to the Issue Office of Reserve Bank concerned so as to reach them by 7th of the next month.

   A "nil" report may be sent in case no counterfeit has been detected during the month.

II. **By Co-operative Banks and Regional Rural Banks:** Data on Counterfeit Notes detected by branches of Co-operative Banks and Regional Rural Banks should be furnished on monthly basis to the respective Issue Office of Reserve Bank in prescribed format.

Para 11: Preservation of Counterfeit Notes Received from Police Authorities

All Counterfeit Notes received back from the police authorities/courts may be carefully preserved in the safe custody of the bank and a record thereof be maintained by the branch concerned. Forged Note Vigilance Cell of the bank shall also maintain a branchwise consolidated record of such Counterfeit Notes.

These Counterfeit Notes at branches should be subject to verification on a half-yearly basis (on 31st March and 30th September) by the Officer-in- Charge of the bank office concerned. They should be preserved for a period of three years from the date of receipt from the police authorities.

They may there-after be sent to the concerned Issue Office of Reserve Bank of India with full details.

Counterfeit notes, which are the subject matter of litigation in the court of law, should be preserved with the branch concerned for three years after conclusion of the court case.

Para 12: Detection of Counterfeit Notes—Training of Staff

It is necessary to ensure that the cash handling staff in banks and treasuries/sub-treasuries is fully conversant with the security features of a banknote. With a view to educating the branch staff on detection of counterfeit notes, the design and security features of all the banknotes shown in Annex VII have been supplied to all the banks/treasuries with instructions to display them prominently at the branches for information of the public. Posters of the 2005–06 series of banknotes have also been supplied to bank branches for display at the branches. The Controlling Offices/Training Centres should also organise / conduct training programmes on the security features of banknotes for members of staff to enable detection of counterfeit notes at the point of receipt itself. The banks should ensure that all bank personnel handling cash are trained on features of genuine Indian bank notes. The Reserve Bank will also provide faculty support and training materials.

7.5 ATMS DISPENSING COUNTERFEIT NOTES REPORT

- For currencies of denomination more than Indian Rupee (INR) 100, all notes are to be examined by machines before putting it into the ATMs. This instruction is applicable to all banks. Non-compliance with this instruction will be taken as a violation of the Directive No.3158/09.39.00 (Policy)/2009–10 dated November 19, 2009, issued by the Reserve Bank.
- If ATM of any bank dispenses forged currencies, it will be considered as an attempt by the banks to circulate counterfeit note.

7.5.1 Complaint if ATM is Dispensing Forged Currency

ATM machines dispensing forged currency have become common these days. It becomes difficult for customers to prove their case and they lose their money. To protect consumers, RBI has issued guidelines to be followed by banks before filling cash in the ATMs (rules to be followed by banks have been discussed above). If someone gets a fake currency from an ATM here is what he should do:

- Identify fake notes.
- Write down the serial number of the notes.
- Present the transactional slip and the passbook to the police.
- The police will register an FIR, followed by an investigation.
- If the bank is found guilty RBI will penalise the bank and refund your money.
- ATM security guard cannot be an evidence for supporting your claim while filing an FIR. Thus, it is advisable that if you spot a fake currency, show it in the CCTV of the ATM.

7.5.2 Security Features of the New 2000 and 500 Rupee Note

- Numeral 2000 can be seen when the note is held against the light.
- A latent image of 2000 when the note is tilted.
- Micro letters 'RBI' and '2000'.
- Colour shift security thread.
- Numeral panel growing big from left to right.
- Seven angular lines in raised print for ₹ 2000 notes and five angular lines in raised print for ₹ 500 notes.

Under Section 489A to 498E of the Indian Penal Code (IPC), possessing or circulating counterfeit currency has been made an offence.

Section 498A: This section states that any person who tries to counterfeit any bank note or performs any part related to counterfeiting shall be punished with imprisonment for life and shall also be liable to pay fine.

Section 489B: The section states that any person who buys anything from another person using a forged currency, knowing such currency to be forged or having reason to believe the same to be forged shall be imprisoned for life and shall also be liable to pay a fine.

Section 498C: The section states that any person possessing forged currency having reason to believe it to be forged shall be liable for imprisonment for life along with fine.

Section 498D: The section states that any person having any material which can be used for forged currency like paper, machine, inks, etc. or in anyway he is related to the process of counterfeiting can be imprisoned for life.

If you receive a forged note from someone, and instead of filing a complaint you are thinking to pass it off, then you can be in serious trouble if you are caught.

To avoid this, you need to go to your nearest police station and report the matter to the police who will register an FIR against the accused for violation of Section 489 of the IPC. Then the police will carryout further investigation, and the court will prosecute him.

7.5.3 Problem of Cross-Border Trafficking of Fake Currency Notes

To deal with the problem of cross-border trafficking of fake currency, India has signed the International Convention for the Suppression of Counterfeiting Currency in 1929. Under this convention, the parties to the convention criminalise the creation, use, and exportation or importation of counterfeit currency. Under the agreement, no distinction is to be made as to what currency is the subject of the crime. Under the treaty, currency counterfeiting is an extraditable offence. States also agree to establish a central office that will forward to all other state parties cancelled specimens of their state's currency and notify the other states when changes to their currency are implemented. The Financial Action Task Force (FATF) is the statutory body which frames policies to prevent illegal trafficking.

7.6 CURRENCY MANAGEMENT IN INDIAN BANKS:

"Currency management essentially relates to planning, designing, issue and withdrawal of currency, ensuring its integrity, availability and the maintenance of quality". The paper currency in India was first issued by the private banks like Bank of Hindustan and the Presidency Banks in the era of East India Company in late 18th century during the British rule. The Paper Currency Act of 1861 brought the monopolistic right to the British Government of India in the field of currency management which ended the power of private banks and presidency banks to issue notes. After introducing the Paper Currency Act 1861, the British Govenment of India authorised the Presidency Banks as agents to circulate and distribute the paper notes throughout the whole British India. Soon circulation and redemption of currency faced a lot of problems due to the vastness of the undivided British India; as a result the British Govenment of India terminated the agreements with the Presidency Banks in 1867 for rearranging the whole currency issuing system for smooth circulation and redemption of currency notes throughout the nation. The Controller of Currency were engaged as the promoting agency and made responsible for the circulation and redemption of the currency. With the assistance of officials and agencies like Mint Masters, Accountant General and the Controller of Currency, the British Government of India arranged the management of the issuance of paper currency. Thus, the British Government of India controlled the whole currency management system throughout the span between 1861–1935.

The Reserve Bank was initially established in Calcutta on the 1st April 1935 under the provisions of the Reserve Bank of India Act, 1934, enacted by the Parliament of India. It started its operations in full swing and it took over the charges from the Office of the Controller of Currency, Govenment of India and began the functions of issuing currency notes.

7.6.1 Functions of RBI Under the Provision of the RBI Act

As per the Section 22 of The RBI Act, 1934 and according to the preamble of the RBI Act, the Reserve Bank is the solitary authorised institution of India for issuance of currency notes in the country and thus it holds a monopolistic status as RBI has the sole right to issue the banknotes of all denominations. As of now, valid paper currency in India is existing in the denomination of 5, 10, 20, 50, 100, 200, 500 and 2,000. Recently the paper currency notes of denomination of ₹1000 have been withdrawn and the denomination of ₹2000 is introduced. Printing of paper currency of denomination of ₹1 and ₹2 have been stopped, though those currency notes are still in circulation and are treated as valid currencies by RBI. As per RBI act 1934, Reserve Bank of India can issue any denomination of currency paper note provided, it should not exceed ₹10,000.

The currency note of certain denomination is notified by Government and RBI issues and circulates accordingly. According to RBI Act, circulation and redemption of currency notes are major functions and responsibility of RBI. Coins of all denominations are also distributed and circulated by the Reserve Bank of India though they are issued by the Government of India. Coins up to 50 paisa are called "small coins" and coins of Rupee one and above are called "Rupee coins". The RBI Act 1934 assigns the Reserve Bank of India, the role to act as a responsible authority of designing, producing, distributing and overall managing the currency of the country.

The Reserve Bank of India, according to the RBI Act, is responsible not only for providing sufficient quantity of bank currency, but also maintaining the quality and genuinity of currency in circulation throughout the country. The Reserve Bank of India regularly looks into the security related issues and gives attentions to reduce the chances of counterfeiting or forgery of currency. The Reserve Bank of India, from time to time, increases security features of banknotes by enhancing the technology, design and materials of banknotes, in consultation with the Government of India. For example, Reserve Bank of India introduces Machine-readable security features in currency notes in the year 2005. RBI routinely examines incremental needs, replacement needs and reserve needs of the currency, and takes actions to deal with these issues in accordance with the Government of India. RBI also mechanises the currency processing in the year 2000 in accordance of the demand of new modern technology.

7.6.2 Right to Issue Bank Notes Under Section 22 of the RBI Act, 1934

"The Bank shall have the sole right to issue banknotes in India and may, for a period which shall be fixed by the Central Government on the recommendation of the Central Board, issue currency notes of the Government of India supplied to it by the Central Government, and the provisions of this Act applicable to banknotes shall, unless a contrary intention appears, apply to all currency notes of the Government of India issued either by the Central Government or by the Bank in like manner as if such currency notes were banknotes, and references in this Act to banknotes shall be construed accordingly".

7.6.3 Infrastructure for Currency Management

According to section 23 of the RBI Act, the issuance of currency and the general business affairs of the Reserve Bank of India are carried on through two different specialised departments; Issue Department and Banking Department.

Issue Department

This department is responsible for the total value of the currency notes in circulation and to safely keep the total assets of desired value. This department is liable in issuance of banknotes in exchange of other denominations and against assets and instrumental in the process of getting currency notes or coins from printing presses or mints and distributing currency among public across the country. It is also responsible for withdrawing unfit and improper currency from the circulation.

But the mechanism of doing the above-mentioned activities, i.e., placing the required currency into circulation and the withdrawal of currency from circulation are done effectively through the Banking Department of the RBI.

7.6.4 The Objectives of Currency Management Areas

- To assure the smooth cash flow by making available sufficient quantity and desirable quality of currency to meet country's demand.
- To print notes and mint coins from Govenment owned and self-run Note Printing Presses and Mints.
- To distribute and circulate sufficient notes and coins throughout the country by arranging the proper and secured infrastructure.
- To maintain desired quality of notes fit and appropriate for circulation.
- To withdraw unfit and inappropriate notes from circulation and to destroy them and replace them with new currencies without hampering the demand and supply balance of desired quantity of currency.
- To maintain secured and effective processes for accounting.
- To manage foreign exchange efficiently.

7.6.5 The Functions of Department of Currency Management

The Reserve Bank of India fulfills the above-mentioned objectives and duties through its well-organised and efficient department called *Department of Currency Management* (DCM). The Department of Currency Management is headed by a Chief General Manager (CGM). The Department has planning division, resource management and remittance of treasure division, note processing and data analysis division, inspection follow-up division, currency chest division, note exchange division, forged note vigilance cell, security cell, co-ordination and development division, and administration division. The Department of Currency Management of the Reserve Bank of India makes monetary policies and addresses operational issues and takes actions in managing the planning, process of issuance and distribution of currency within the country:

1. **To design Currency notes.** It recommends designs of banknotes to the Central Government and prints them in accordance.
2. To forecast the demand for Currency notes and coins of the country.
3. To circulate and distribute currency smoothly throughout the nation.
4. To withdraw the dirty, unfit and improper paper notes and incorrect coins from circulated currency.
5. To ensure the integrity of banknotes.
6. To administer the provisions of RBI ('Notes Refund') Rules 2009, that deals with the payment of value of the soiled or mutilated notes.
7. To rationalise the work procedures of the issue offices on regular basis.

8. To Identify, evaluate and manage the security risks of the issuance, circulation and distribution of currency.
9. To co-ordinate and ensure the protection and safety of the currency management system and assets as a whole.
10. To spread information on matters which are related to currency to the general public as—'The guiding principle for a Central Bank, whatever function or group of functions it performs at any particular moment, is that it should act only in public interest and without regard to profit as a primary consideration'.

7.6.6 The Process of Movement of Currency

Reserve Bank of India gets new currency notes from four currency note printing presses and gets coins from mints. Among the four currency note printing presses, two currency printing presses are owned by the Security Printing and Minting Corporation of India Limited (SPMCIL) which is wholly owned by the Indian Government which are situated at Nasik, Maharashtra and Dewas, Madhya Pradesh and the other two are run by the Reserve Bank of India and owned by its subsidiary named the Bharatiya Reserve Bank Note Mudran Ltd. (BRBNML) which are situated at Mysore in Karnataka and Salboni in West Bengal. There are four mints in India where coins are minted. All mints are owned by the Government of India and they are situated at Mumbai, Hyderabad, Kolkata and Noida. Currency notes move from printing presses to currency chests or from chests to bank branches or vice versa, in specially-built secured trucks accompanied by RBI officials and security. Banks officials are responsible for the movement of the currency from currency chests to bank branches. Currency chest distributes currencies to a particular bank branch to fulfill a specific demand based on the certain business volume created by that particular bank branch in its local business area of operation. Currency flow looks like this:

Printing Presses → RBI Offices → Currency Chests → Bank Branches → Public.

7.6.7 The Currency Chest Mechanism

The Reserve Bank performs the systematic operations, formulates the policies and functions as the authority of currency management of the country through its specific and specialised department called *Department of currency management* (DCM) which is situated at its Central Office in Mumbai where the Governor sits and 19 Issue Offices situated at all over the country and a sub-office located at Kochi. RBI distributes notes and coins through its authorised selected bank branches. Those bank branches act as chests and called *Currency Chests* which facilitate the distribution of currency throughout the country. The Currency Chests are actually the extensions of the Issue Department of RBI which provide the availability of the services of Issue Bank at different places to counter the needs of public. Currency chests are storehouses of currency where currency notes and rupee coins are stored by Reserve Bank. Currency

Chests required refilling which are drawn from them to maintain the cash balance. Unfit and non-issuable or surplus to the circulation banknotes and rupee coins are deposited into the currency chests. If such types of currency are accumulated sufficiently to the chests, they are transferred to the Issue Department. Banknotes and rupee coins are deposited as well as withdrawn simultaneously in the currency chests on everyday basis to meet the requirement of the bank branch and these types of transactions are called *currency transfer transactions*. Each deposit of currency to the chest reduces the liability and increases the assets of the Issue Department; on the contrary, each withdrawal increases the liability and decreases the assets of the Issue Department.

Same currency chests are authorised for small coin depots also which is established by a few selected bank branches to stock small coins. Those small coin depots act as the storehouses to reserve the small coins and distribute them to other bank branches throughout the country. Small coins are minted in Government owned mints and issued by Govenment of India and distributed by Reserve Bank of India as an authorised agency of the Central Government.

7.6.8 Infrastructure for Distribution and Circulation of Currency

The RBI established Integrated Computerised Currency Operations and Management System (ICCOMS) in Central Office, regional Issue Departments and Currency Chest which consists of three components: Currency Chest Reporting System (CCRS), ICCOMS-Issue Department (ICCOMS-ID) and Currency Management Information System (CMIS). The objectives of this systems are:

- Improve operational efficiency;
- Faster and accurate accounting;
- Improve Management Information System (MIS) and planning;
- Better monitoring and control;
- Better customer service.

This system provides computerisation and network connection of the Currency Chests with the Issue Offices which alleviate prompt and accurate reporting's, immediate action and creates a seamless smooth flow of information's between all the offices. It helps to detect problems immediately and accurately and take action accordingly. The scopes of this very modern and integrated system are:

1. Planning for Currency Issue,
2. Allocation and Distribution of Currency,
3. Better Monitoring overall processes from currency stock to distribution to accumulation of currency, etc.
4. Infrastructure Planning,
5. Dissemination of live data on currency in circulation.

Reserve Bank of India has established a huge network and at presents it consisting of 4281 Currency Chests (CCs), 488 repositories and 4044 small coin depots (SCDs) with other banks. Currency chests and coin depots are managed by commercial, co-operative and regional rural banks. State Bank of India manages the highest number of currency chests–2192. The currency chests and small coin depots are established with Treasuries (11 chests) State Bank of India (2192 chests and 2118 small coin depots), six associate banks (778 chests and 775 small coin depots), nationalised banks (1124 chests and 1009 small coin depots), private sector banks (107 chests and 107 small coin depots), foreign bank (5 chests and 5 small coin depots), a state co-operative bank (1 chest and 1 small coin depot), and regional rural bank (3 chests and 3 small coin depots).

More than 64,000 bank branches and more than 43,000 ATMs are engaged in distributing currency to be circulated across the country. Coin Vending Machines (CVMs) are used in banks for distributing coins. For smooth processing of currency 54 high capacity currency verification and processing system (CVPS), 28 currency disintegration and briquetting system (CDBS), 40 desktop note sorting machines are installed and activated across its offices.

The currency chests and high business branches are upgraded with the installation of improved machines like note sorting machines (NSM), desktop note sorters, and notes counting machines, ATMs, cash recyclers and note detectors which increased the quality of circulation of currency and made it more punctual.

7.6.9 Proportional Reserve System vs Minimum Reserve System

As per the RBI Act, the Issue Department should never keep assets less than the liability of it which is the banknotes in circulation. As per the Section 33 of Reserve Bank of India Act, 1934 the circulation of currency is endorsed with assets like gold (in form of coin and bullion), foreign securities, rupee coin and securities. At first, the assets of the Issue department of Reserve Bank of India must had to consist Gold or securities which might not be less than two-fifths of the total assets, provided a valuation of total Gold would be at least ₹40 Crore in any given point of time. Remaining three-fifths of the assets of Issue department of RBI might be rupee coins. This system was known as "Proportional Reserve System". In 1956, this system has been changed. At present, RBI is required to consist of Gold and Foreign Exchange Reserves of ₹200 Crore of which the total valuation of gold reserve should be at least ₹115 crores of rupees at any given point of time and ₹85 crore rupees foreign assets. This system is known as *Minimum Reserve System*. This system is followed by RBI till date. As per RBI Act, followings are regarded as eligible assets for the Issue Department:

1. Gold coins and bullions,
2. Foreign securities,
3. Rupee coins,
4. Government securities,
5. Internal bills of exchange and other commercial paper.

Deposits of the currency from circulation or from the printing presses or mints into the currency chests increase the reserves and are admitted in the Cash Reserve Ratio of the Reserve Bank of India. Similarly, withdrawal of currency from the currency chests decreases the reserves and increases the currency in the circulation and increases the liability of the issue department of the Reserve Bank of India. Thus equilibrium of liability and asset get imbalanced due to the currency transfer transactions. When liability of Issue Department pushes up, it is compensated by the Banking Department through the transfer of required amount of currency to the Issue Department to make-up the deficit. On the other hand, when the liability of Issue Department decreases, it is counter balanced by the transfer of bank notes from Issue Department to Banking Department.

7.6.10 Current Scenario

Inspite of increased use of non-cash modes of transactions due to improvement of technology, the demand of the country for currency in circulation for smooth running has increased continuously and proportionately to the constant growth of the Indian economy. To provide good quality and proper banknotes in the circulation, the Reserve Bank of India undertook various effective steps, such as continuous supply of fresh banknotes in sufficient amount, quicker disposal of unfit currency and built up vast mechanised cash processing system. RBI has undertaken different actions according to its 'Clean Note Policy' and to counter the threat of fake notes like: (*a*) Creating Awareness, (*b*) Raising the Security Features, and (*c*) Introducing Improved Modern Technology to Detect Counterfeit Notes.

7.6.11 Currency in Circulation in the Country

Currency notes in circulation stood at ₹21.71 lakh crore as of May end 2019, showing an increase of more than 22% over the pre-demonetisation level. The notes in circulation as on November 4, 2016 were ₹17,74,187 crore, which have now increased to ₹21,71,385 crore as on May 31, 2019. The government had announced demonetisation of ₹500 and ₹1,000 notes on November 8, 2016. The total value of currency in circulation was ₹10,663 billion in the year 2012. The total volume of currency was 56,549 billion pieces in the year 2010; 64,577 billion pieces in 2011 and 69,382 billion pieces in the year 2012. Coins in circulation were 105,306 billion pieces in 2010; 112,184 billion pieces in 2011 and 78,029 billion pieces in the year of 2012.

The demonetisation was done with a view to eliminate black money, curb fake currency and thereby to create deterrence to funding of terror and left-wing extremism, facilitate transition of India's non-formal economy into a formal economy and to give boost to digitalisation, among other objectives. As reported by the Reserve Bank of India, 762,072 pieces of counterfeit bank notes were detected in the banking system during 2016–17; 522,783 pieces in 2017–18; and 317,389 pieces in 2018–19. Hence, demonetisation resulted in curbing of the counterfeit currency. There is a significant growth has been observed in digital transactions in the country post-demonetisation. Growth of digital transactions in terms of value has increased to ₹188.07 lakh crores in September 2018 from ₹112.27 lakh crores in November 2016.

7.6.12 Note Refund Rule

As per Section 28, RBI Act, "Notwithstanding anything contained in any enactment or rule of law to the contrary, no person shall of right be entitled to recover from the Central Government or the Bank, the value of any lost, stolen, mutilated or imperfect currency note, provided that the Bank may, with the previous sanction of the Central Government, prescribe the circumstances in and the conditions and limitations subject to which the value of such currency notes or bank notes may be refunded as of grace and the rules made under this proviso shall be laid on the table of Parliament".

7.6.13 Mutilated notes

The payment of claim against mutilated notes shall be made if the area of single largest undivided piece of the note presented is more than 50% of the area of the respective denomination in case of one rupee, two rupees, five rupees and ten rupees note. Full value of the mutilated notes of the denomination of fifty and above shall be payable if the area of the single largest undivided piece of the note presented is more than 65% of the area of the respective denomination rounded-off to the next complete square centimetre.

7.6.14 Counterfeit or Fake Banknotes

Counterfeit or fake banknotes created a huge problem and had a great impact to the Indian economy. In the year of 2008–2009, increased numbers of counterfeit notes were detected. Out of the total number of detected fake notes, more than 401,000 pieces, which is as much as 86.9% of the total ceased notes, were found at bank branches. The Reserve Bank of India has been working on for long-time to check the menace of counterfeit notes. The Bank took some steps to achieve the goal like:

1. Creating awareness through publicity campaigns,
2. Enhancing the security features, and
3. Introducing improved modern technology to detect counterfeit notes.

Recently made Demonetisation by Government of India in accordance with RBI, is a big step to counter the menace of counterfeit notes.

7.7. DEMONETISATION IN INDIA (2016)

On 8 November 2016, the Government of India announced the demonetisation of all ₹500 and ₹1,000 banknotes of the Mahatma Gandhi Series. It also announced the issuance of new ₹500 and ₹2,000 banknotes in exchange for the demonetised banknotes. The Prime minister of India Narendra Modi claimed that the action would curtail the shadow economy and reduce the use of illicit and counterfeit cash to fund illegal activity and terrorism.

The announcement of demonetisation was followed by prolonged cash shortages in the weeks that followed, which created significant disruption throughout the economy. People seeking to exchange their banknotes had to stand in lengthy queues and several deaths were linked to the rush to exchange cash.

According to a 2018 report from the Reserve Bank of India, approximately 99.3% of the demonetised banknotes, or ₹15.30 lakh crore (15.3 trillion) of the ₹15.41 lakh crore that had been demonetised, were deposited with the banking system. The banknotes that were not deposited were only worth ₹10,720 crore (107.2 billion), leading analysts to state that the effort had failed to remove black money from the economy. The BSE SENSEX and NIFTY 50 stock indices fell over 6% on the day after the announcement. The move reduced the country's industrial production and its GDP growth rate.

Initially, the move received support from several bankers as well as from some international commentators. The move was also criticised as poorly planned and unfair and was met with protests, litigation and strikes against the government in several places across India. Debates also took place concerning the move in both houses of the parliament.

The Indian government had demonetised banknotes on two prior occasions; once in 1946 and once in 1978 and in both cases, the goal was to combat tax evasion via 'black money' held outside the formal economic system. In 1978, the Janata Party coalition government demonetised banknotes of ₹1,000, ₹5,000 and ₹10,000, again in the hopes of curbing counterfeit money and black money.

In 2012, the Central Board of Direct Taxes recommended against demonetisation, saying in a report that "demonetisation may not be a solution for tackling black money or shadow economy, which is largely held in the form of benami properties, bullion and jewellery." According to data from income tax probes, black money holders kept only 6% or less of their wealth as cash, suggesting that targeting this cash would not be a successful strategy.

7.7.1 Preparation and Announcement

The plan to demonetise the ₹500 and ₹1,000 banknotes was initiated between six and ten months before it was a report by the State Bank of India analysed possible strategies and effects of demonetisation. In May 2016, the Reserve Bank of India had started preparing for new banknotes and confirmed the design of ₹2,000 banknotes in August 2016. The printing of new banknotes started in October when the news stories of forthcoming new banknotes appeared in the media. On 27 October, 2016, the Hindi daily Dainik Jagran published a report quoting RBI sources speaking of the forthcoming of ₹2,000 banknotes alongside withdrawal of ₹500 and ₹1,000 banknotes. On 21 October 2016, *The Hindu* Business Line had also published a report on forthcoming ₹2,000 banknote.

The Union cabinet was informed about the plan on 8 November 2016 in a meeting in the evening called by the Indian Prime Minister Narendra Modi. Soonafter the meeting, Modi announced the demonetisation in an unscheduled live national televised address at 20:15 Indian Slandered Time (IST). He declared circulation of all ₹500 and ₹1,000 banknotes of the Mahatma Gandhi Series as invalid effective from the midnight of the same day and announced the issuance of new ₹500 and ₹2,000 banknotes of the Mahatma Gandhi New Series in exchange for the demonetised banknotes.

7.7.2 Information Leaks

Prominent businessmen stated after the announcement of demonetisation that they had received prior warning of the move, allowing them to convert their money into smaller denominations. A BJP MLA from Rajasthan, Bhawani Singh Rajawat, claimed in a video that wealthy businessmen were informed about the demonetisation before it occurred. He later denied making the comments.

7.7.3 Cash Exchange and Withdrawal

The Reserve Bank of India stipulated that the demonetised banknotes could be deposited with banks over a period of fifty days until 30 December 2016. The banknotes could also be exchanged for legal tender over the counter at all banks. The limit for such exchange was ₹4,000 per person from 8 to 13 November, was increased to ₹4,500 from 14 to 17 November and reduced to ₹2,000 from 18 to 25 November. The exchange of banknotes was stopped completely on 25 November, although the government had previously stated that the volume of exchange would be increased after that date. International airports also facilitated an exchange of banknotes for foreign tourists and out-bound travellers, amounting to a total value of ₹5,000 per person. Fuel pumps, government hospitals, railway and airline booking counters, state-government recognised dairies and ration stores, and crematoriums were allowed to accept the demonetised banknotes until 2 December 2016.

Cash withdrawals from bank accounts were restricted to ₹10,000 per day and ₹20,000 per week per account from 10 to 13 November. This limit was increased to ₹24,000 per week from 14 November 2016. Limits on cash withdrawals from Current accounts/ Cash credit accounts/ Overdraft accounts were withdrawn later. RBI increased the withdrawal limit from Savings Bank account to ₹50,000 from the earlier ₹24,000 on 20 February 2017 and then on 13 March 2017, it removed all withdrawal limits from savings bank accounts.

A daily limit on withdrawals from ATMs was also imposed varying from ₹2,000 per day until 14 November and ₹2,500 per day until 31 December. This limit was increased to ₹4,500 per day from 1 January and again to ₹10,000 from 16 January 2017. From 17 November, families were allowed to withdraw ₹250,000 for wedding expenses. Farmers were permitted to withdraw ₹25,000 per week against crop loans.

7.7.4 Ordinance and Act

The Specified Bank Notes (Cessation of Liabilities) Ordinance, 2016 was issued on 28 December 2016, ending the liability of the government for the demonetised banknotes.

The ordinance also imposed fines on people found carrying out transactions with them after 8 November 2016, or holding more than ten of them after 30 December 2016. It provided for the exchange of the banknotes after 30 December for people who had been outside India between 9 November and 30 December. The Specified Bank Notes (Cessation of Liabilities) Act, 2017 was notified on 1 March 2017, replacing the ordinance.

7.7.5 Objectives and Outcomes of Demonitisation

The government said that the main objective of the exercise was curbing black money which included income which had not been reported and thus was untaxed; money gained through corruption, illegal goods sales and illegal activities such as human trafficking; and counterfeit currency. Other stated objectives included expanding the tax base and increasing the number of taxpayers; reducing the number of transactions carried out by cash; reducing the finances available to terrorists and radical groups such as Maoists and Naxalites; and integrating the formal and informal economies.

7.7.6 Black Money

The government estimated that ₹3 lakh crore, or approximately 20%, of the demonetised banknotes would be permanently removed from circulation. However, according to a 2018 report from the RBI, approximately 99.3% of the demonetised banknotes, or ₹15.30 lakh crores of the ₹15.41 lakh crores that had been demonetised, were deposited with the banking system. The banknotes that were not deposited were only worth ₹10,720 crores. Commentators concluded that the government failed in its aim of purging black money from the economy.

7.7.7 Evasion

A jewellery store in a shopping mall with a notice "We accept ₹500 and ₹1,000 notes", even after they were no longer valid banknotes.

There have been reports of people circumventing the restrictions imposed on exchange transactions by conducting multiple transactions at different bank branches and also sending hired people, employees and followers in groups to exchange large amounts of demonetised banknotes at banks. In Gujarat, Delhi and many other major cities; sales of gold increased post-demonetisation, with an increased 20 to 30% premium surging the price as much as ₹45,000 (US$ 650) from the ruling price of ₹31,900 (US$ 460) per 10 grams (0.35 oz). The Enforcement Directorate raided several forex establishments making backdated entries. Money laundering using backdated accounting was carried out by co-operative banks, jewellers, sellers of mobile phones, and several other businesses.

The cash deposited into hundis, or cash collection boxes in temples and gurudwaras are exempted from inquiry by the tax department which is sometimes misused to launder money. After the demonetisation, there was a spike in donations in the form of the demonetised banknotes in temples. People had booked large number of railway tickets to dispose of unaccounted cash. It came to notice of the Indian Railways authorities which imposed restrictions to check evasion.

7.7.8 Counterfeit Banknotes

After demonetisation, there was an increase in the number of counterfeit ₹100 and ₹50 banknotes. The number of counterfeit ₹500 and ₹1,000 (demonetised version) banknotes saw an increase in 2016–17 and subsequently a decline in 2017–18. But in 2017–18, there was an increase in counterfeit ₹500 and ₹2,000 (new version) banknotes than the previous year. There has been no significant change in the number of counterfeit banknotes detected. In 2017–18, the number of detected counterfeit banknotes was close to the number before demonetisation. Additionally, after demonetisation, only 0.0035% of the ₹1,000 banknotes were found to be counterfeit.

7.7.9 Tax Collection

The number of income tax returns filing increased from ₹43.3 million to ₹52.9 million between financial year 2016 and 2017 which was not a significant increase compared to increase between 2015 and 2016. The tax compliance had increased with number of income tax returns filing increased but majority of them were from salaried and non-business class. The income tax collections increased in financial year 2017 due to Income Disclosure Scheme 2016. If adjusted for it, the increase in tax collection was modest. The tax-to-GDP ratio has increased due to expanding tax base. An analysis of the economic data shows that there has been no substantial increase in the number of new tax payers or direct tax collection due to demonetisation.

The use of demonetised banknotes was allowed for the payment of municipal and local civic body taxes, leading to a jump in their revenue collections. For example, the Greater Hyderabad Municipal Corporation reported collecting about ₹ 160 crore (US$ 23 million) in cash payments of outstanding and advance taxes, within first four days of demonetisation.

7.7.10 Digital Payments

The push for the digital payments was one of the stated intentions of the demonetisation. There was immediate and sharp jump in the digital payments in November–December 2016 owing to shortage of cash. The debit card point of sale transactions was twice the size of value suggested by trend before the demonetisation. The value of credit card increased but no sharp growth was seen. The mobile wallet transactions picked up immediately after the demonetisation followed by dip in mid-2017 due to easing cash shortage. There was again sharp rise thereafter. By April 2018, the volume of the digital payments had doubled. After return of the cash, the growth in digital payment had been modest.

The currency-to-GDP ratio was 12.1% in 2015–16. It declined to 8.8% in 2016–17 due to demonetisation but increased again to 10.9% in 2017–18. The currency-to-GDP ratio was only marginally lower compared to level before demonetisation.

7.7.11 Banknotes in Circulation

On 28 October, 2016 the total banknotes in circulation in India were valued at ₹17.77 lakh crore (US$ 260 billion); what proportion of this derived from ₹500 and ₹1,000 banknotes was unknown. In its annual report of March 2016, the Reserve Bank of India (RBI) stated that total banknotes in circulation valued ₹16.42 lakh crore (US$ 240 billion) of which nearly 86% (around ₹14.18 lakh crore (US$ 210 billion)) derived from ₹500 and ₹1,000 banknotes. In terms of volume, the report stated that 24% (around 22.03 billion) of the total ₹9026.6 crore (90.26 billion) banknotes in circulation were ₹500 and ₹1,000 banknotes.

Before demonetisation (November 2016), there were banknotes worth ₹17.97 lakh crore (US$ 260 billion) in the market. The demonetised banknotes constituted 86.4% of it. The banknotes in circulation had reached to the level before demonetisation in March 2018. By March 2018, there were banknotes worth ₹18.03 lakh crore (US$ 260 billion) in the market; increase of 9.9%. New banknotes of ₹2,000 and ₹500 constitute 80.6% of it. So, there was only 5.8% increase in small domination banknotes. Due to demonetisation volume of banknotes in the market has increased by 2.1%. The banknotes in circulation had further increased to ₹ 19.5 lakh crore (US$ 280 billion) in September 2018 and ₹21.41 lakh crore (US$ 310 billion) in March 2019, 19.14% higher than the level before demonetisation.

7.7.12 Terrorism and Internal Security

Initially there was a decrease in the activities and attacks by Maoist and Naxalite radical groups which was attributed to lack of finance following demonetisation. The surrender rate had reached its highest. The activities returned within few months. There was a decrease in the terror activities in Jammu and Kashmir.

7.7.13 Other Effects

Cash Shortage: The scarcity of cash due to demonetisation led to chaos and people faced difficulties in depositing or exchanging the demonetised banknotes due to long queues outside banks and ATMs across India. The ATMs were short of cash for months after demonetisation.

During the demonetisation, the unaccounted money worth ₹610 crore were seized by the police and tax officials across India which included ₹110 crore in new banknotes. Reports in the media noted that although the general public faced a severe cash shortage, some individuals were able to amass crores in new banknotes; they thus described the demonetisation exercise as being futile.

Transportation: The All India Motor Transport Congress claimed that about 800,000 truck drivers and conductors were affected due to shortage of cash, with around 400,000 trucks stranded at major highways across India. While major highway toll junctions on the Gujarat and Delhi-Mumbai highways also saw long queues as toll plaza operators refused the demonetised banknotes. The Ministry of Road Transport and Highways subsequently announced a suspension of toll collections on all national highways across the country until 2 December as well as acceptance of demonetised ₹500 banknote as a toll from 2 to 15 December.

Stock Market: As a combined effect of demonetisation and US presidential election, the stock market indices dropped to an around six-month low in the week following the announcement. The day after the demonetisation announcement, BSE SENSEX crashed nearly 1,689 points and NIFTY 50 plunged by over 541 points. By the end of the intraday trading section on 15 November 2016, the BSE SENSEX index was lower by 565 points and the NIFTY 50 index was below 8100 intraday. There was a marginal effects on stock market during November–December 2016. A data study (July 2016–February 2017) of 54 companies across 13 sectors listed with the NSE showed that companies in cement, cotton and rubber sectors showed an increase in total trades while companies in automotive, clothing, foods, paper, real estate, retail, steel, sugar, tea and textiles sectors showed a decrease in total trades after demonetisation. Demonetisation had a negative impact on stock market returns evidenced from NIFTY 50 and other NIFTY sectoral indices.

Industrial Output: There was a reduction in industrial output as industries were hit by the cash shortage. The Purchasing Managers' Index (PMI) fell to 46.7 in November 2016 from 54.5 in October 2016, recording its sharpest reduction in three years. A reading above 50 indicates growth and a reading below shows contraction. This indicates a slowdown in both, manufacturing and services industries. The PMI report also showed that the reduction in inflation in November 2016 was due to shortage in money supply.

The growth in eight core sectors such as cement, steel and refinery products, which constitute 38% of the Index of industrial production (IIP), was only to 4.9% in November 2016 as compared with 6.6% a month ago.

Agriculture: Transactions in the agriculture sector are heavily dependent on cash and were adversely affected by the demonetisation. Due to scarcity of the new banknotes, many farmers have insufficient cash to purchase seeds, fertilisers and pesticides needed for the plantation of Rabi crops usually sown around mid-November. Farmers and their unions conducted protest rallies in Gujarat, Amritsar and Muzaffarnagar against the demonetisation as well as against restrictions imposed by the Reserve Bank of India on district co-operative central banks which were ordered not to accept or exchange the demonetised banknotes.

The shortage of cash led to plunge in demand which in turn led to a crash in the prices of crops. Farmers were unable to recover even the costs of transportation from their fields to the market from the low prices offered. Some farmers dumped their produce in protest against the government. Demonetisation resulted in the relative erosion of agricultural wages and weak bargaining power of farmers for their produce.

Real Gross Domestic Product (GDP) Growth Rate: Global analysts cut their forecasts of India's real GDP growth rate for the financial year 2016–17 by 0.5 to 3% due to demonetisation. India's GDP in 2016 is estimated to be US$ 2.25 trillion, hence, each 1 per cent reduction in growth rate represents a shortfall of US$ 22.5 billion (₹1.54 lakh crore) for the Indian economy. According to Society General, quarterly GDP growth rates would drop below 7% for an entire year at a stretch for the first time since June 2011. The Q4'16–17 growth rate was 6.1% as against a forecast of 7.1% by economists. The rate for the financial year 2016–17 was 7.1%, a reduction from the 8% in 2015–16. This drop was attributed to demonetisation by economists.

The GDP growth rate for Q1'17–18 dropped to 5.7%, compared to 7.9% a year ago, the lowest since March 2014. This drop was attributed to demonetisation as well as inventory drawdown by companies due to the forthcoming implementation of the Goods and Service Tax (GST). The GDP started to recover from Q2'17–18 and clocked 8.2% in Q2'18–19.

Employment: There was a huge loss of jobs and decline in wages due to demonetisation, particularly in the unorganised and informal sector and in small enterprises. Migrant workers were adversely affected by demonetisation.

According to the report prepared by Centre for Monitoring Indian Economy (CMIE), the number of employed people was 401 million in January–April 2016, 403 million during May–August 2016, ₹ 406.5 million in September–December 2016. After demonetisation in November 2016, the number fell to 405 million in January–April 2017. So, there was fall of 1.5 million in number of people employed. CMIE also reported that the number of persons employed was 406.7 million in 2016–17 which fell by 0.1% to 406.2 million in 2017–18. So, the employment had stagnated which resulted in employment rate decline. The employment rate fell from 42.59% in 2016–17 to 41.45% in 2016–17. The unemployment rate also declined from 7.51% in 2016–17 to 4.66% in 2017–18 because of the shrinking employed force. The number of employed force fell from 439.7 million in 2016–17 to 426.1 million in 2017–18. CMIE attributed the impact to demonetisation as well as implementation of GST in July 2017.

Cost to Banks: Before demonetisation, the RBI had spent ₹ 3,421 crore to print banknotes in 2015–2016 (July to June). The cost of printing new banknotes escalated to ₹7,965 crore in 2016–17 and ₹4,912 crore in 2017–18. This resulted in a decline in the dividend paid to the government from ₹ 65,876 crore in 2015–16 to ₹ 30,659 crore in 2016–17 and ₹ 50,000 crore in 2017–18. It was estimated that this decrease in income for the government could cause the fiscal deficit for the financial year 2016–17 to increase from the targeted 3.2% to 3.4%. The Indian Air Force was paid ₹ 29.41 crore to move banknotes after demonetisation. The banks incurred the cost in collection, storage and movement of banknotes across the country as well as in re-calibrating the ATMs.

Welfare Schemes: Demonetisation negatively impacted the Mid-day Meal Scheme due to shortage of funds.

Deaths: Several people were reported to have died from standing in queues for hours to exchange their demonetised banknotes. Deaths were also attributed to lack of medical help due to refusal of demonetised banknotes by hospitals. By the end of December 2016, political opposition leaders claimed that over 100 people had died due to demonetisation. In March 2017, the government stated that they received no official report on deaths connected to demonetisation. Later in December 2018, the Finance Minister Arun Jaitley reported in parliament that four people, three bank personnel and one customer of the State Bank of India, died during the demonetisation.

Legal Issues: A public interest litigation (PIL) was filed in Madras High Court by M. Seeni Ahamed, General Secretary of the Indian National League, to scrap the decision of demonetisation. The High Court dismissed the PIL stating that it could not interfere in monetary policies of the government. Similar PILs were also filed in the Supreme Court of India. In November 2017, the Supreme Court of India referred all cases related to demonetisation to constitutional bench to review the legality of the demonetisation, implementation irregularities and violation of people's rights by limits on cash withdrawals.

The government had initially announced that any person who is unable to deposit the demonetised banknotes by 31 December 2016 would be given an opportunity to do so until a later date. However, the government allowed only Non-Resident Indians (NRIs) to deposit demonetised banknotes after 31 December 2016. As a result, many people were left stranded with demonetised banknotes. People petitioned the courts to allow deposit of the demonetised banknotes. In November 2017 the Supreme Court dismissed 14 petitions related to demonetisation, and asked petitioners to file pleas with a constitutional bench which would deal with cases related to demonetisation.

7.7.14 Reactions

Reactions of Economists: Most economists across the ideological spectrum, except some prominent ones, were broadly critical of the demonetisation as an economic policy.

Indian-American economist Jagdish Bhagwati praised the demonetisation. Nobel laureate Amartya Sen, severely criticised the demonetisation move calling it a "despotic action" among other things. Former Senior Vice-President and Chief Economist of the World Bank, Kaushik Basu, called it a 'major mistake' and said that the 'damage' is likely to be much greater than any possible benefits.

Reactions of Industrialists: The decision met with mixed initial reactions. Several bankers appreciated the move in the sense that it would help curb black money. Businessmen also supported the move adding that it would also accelerate e-commerce.

Political Reactions: Opposition parties criticised and led major protests against the decision in their states and in parliament. Initially, the move to demonetise and try to hinder black money was appreciated, but the manner in which it was carried out by causing hardships to common people was criticised.

A Parliamentary panel report in April 2017 stated that rural households and honest taxpayers were the worst hit by demonetisation. It said that it was not just the poor that suffered, but the manufacturing sector was impacted too. According to the panel, demonetisation created significant disruption throughout economy, because it was carried out without prior study or research. A Indian National Congress led opposition which includes 13 political parties, opposed the government on the issue of demonetisation in the Winter Session of the Indian Parliament.

International Reactions: By and large, initial international response was positive which saw the move as a bold crackdown on corruption. The International Monetary Fund's spokesperson Gerry Rice told that it supported the efforts to fight corruption and illegal finances but cautioned about the disruptions.

Political Impact: Akshay Mangala, an Assistant Professor at Harvard Business School, called the move "the politics of visible disruption". He noted that the people might attribute the implementation shortcomings to institutional weakness while the government could take credit for its attempt to curb the black money. He also noted that it may result in the public opinion in favour of the government which is led by the BJP if the opposition parties, led by INC, fail to form the countervailing narrative. MIT associated academics Abhijit Banerjee and Namrata Kala also opined the same.

REVIEW QUESTIONS

1. Give a gist of -- the objective of the Reserve Bank's Clean Note Policy for giving the citizens good quality currency notes and coins while the soiled notes are withdrawn out of circulation.
2. Discuss about -- the Master Circular, Facility For Exchange of Notes and Coins Dated July 02, 2018.
3. Give a short explanation about -- Notes Bearing 'PAY' / 'PAID' / 'REJECT' Stamps.
4. What do you mean by – a soiled note?
5. What are the Reserve Bank of India's (Note Refund) Rules, 2009?

Commercial Banks in India

8

8.1 CONCEPT OF COMMERCIAL BANK

Banking is a business of accepting deposits and lending money. It is carried out by financial intermediaries, which performs the functions of safeguarding deposits and providing loans to the public. In other words, Banking means accepting the deposits for the purpose of lending or investment for profit motives and gives the facility to customers to withdrawn money by cheque, draft order and so on.

The main objective of a commercial bank is to generate profitability for its ownership by providing quality based products and services to the residents of the communities and regions that they represent. Aside from offering traditional banking products, commercial banks must be highly competitive and provide specialized products.

Banking Regulation Act of India, 1949 defines Banking as "accepting, for the purpose of lending or investment of deposits of money from the public, repayable on demand or otherwise and withdrawable by cheques, draft, and pay order or otherwise."

Finance is the basic necessity of commerce and industry. All companies need funding for various reasons. Some need long term funding for purchasing fixed assets like land, building, machinery etc. while some need short term funding for their day to day operations (working capital requirements). Banks provide these finances to companies and in their absence, it is almost impossible to make commercial progress. They lend funds and provide opportunities of investment and safe custody of deposits. They promote habit of savings amongst the public. It promotes growth and development of economy by mobilizing savings and channeling them for more productive purposes. They facilitate wealth creation by providing funds to companies who need them for productive uses. Thus, banking and finance form an indispensable component of an economy.

Commercial Bank: Commercial banking activities are different than those of investment banking, which include underwriting, acting as an intermediary between an issuer of securities and the investing public, facilitating mergers and other corporate reorganizations, and also acting as a broker for institutional clients. Some commercial banks, such as Citibank and JPMorgan Chase, also have investment banking divisions, while others, such as Ally, operate strictly on the commercial side of the business.

Banking is a business of accepting deposits and lending money. It is carried out by financial intermediaries, which performs the functions of safeguarding deposits and providing loans to the public. In other words, Banking means accepting the deposits for the purpose of lending or investment for profit motives and gives the facility to customers to withdrawn money by cheque, draft order and so on.

Banking Company: Any company, which transacts the business of banking, is called a bank. Banking System is a PRINCIPLES mechanism through which the money supply of the country is created and controlled. The banking system enables us to understand Commercial Banks, Secondary Banks, Central Banks, Merchant Bank or Accepting Houses and Discount Houses but to exclude the Saving Banks and Investment and other intermediaries.

Objectives of a Commercial Bank: The main objective of a commercial bank is to generate profitability for its ownership by providing quality based products and services to the residents of the communities and regions that they represent. Aside from offering traditional banking products, commercial banks must be highly competitive and provide specialized products.

8.2 FEATURE OF THE BANKING SYSTEM

Banks are the backbone of any economy.

- **Base for capital formation:** They provide huge capital for capital formation like road project, metro project.
- **Economic Stability:** Economic stability depends on financial infrastructure.
- Helpful to develop the money and capital market.
- **Helpful in Innovation:** They provide finance to research & development work.
- **Quality Services:** They provide quality services like payment of bill, discounting of bill etc.
- Adaptation of new techniques like ATMs, E-banking.
- Helpful to remove the business cycle or trade cycle.
- Helps in stabilization of price.
- Development of banking infrastructure.

8.3 CHARACTERISTICS OF A BANK

Bank has the following features:

1. **Deals in Money:** Banks deal with depositors' in money.

2. **Stores Money:** One of basic function is to provide a safe and valuables place to investors. Banks are fireproof and nearly impenetrable. Moreover banks have insurance against losses as a result of theft.

3. **Saving Money/Accept Deposits:** They offer various means of saving of money (current account, saving account etc.). They pay interest in a percentage of money in these accounts.

4. **Lend Money/Offer Loans:** Like they receive deposits, they lend money to those who need as well and charge interest and fees. They can however issue only certain amount of loan due to Fractional Reserve System, which states banks should keep certain % of value of loans in form of deposits.

5. **Establishes a Connecting Link:** It acts as a link between those who need money and those who have surplus funds.

6. **Profit/Service Oriented:** Just like any other business, banks are also profit oriented. They earn profit by charging interest on loans and fees on various banking services which they provide.

7. **Business:** The business of banking cannot function as a subsidiary to any business.

8. **Name:** In order to enable people to understand that xyz is a bank and transacts in money, it must add "bank" to its name.

8.4 IMPORTANCE OF COMMERCIAL BANK

Commercial Banks are considered as important due to following reasons:

Accepting Deposits: Commercial banks have evolved from a long tradition, dating back at least to Italian money lenders and merchants in the 12th century, of accepting deposits and writing checks. Checks allow cheaper transaction costs, by reducing costs associated with transporting money for long-distance commerce, and by reducing risks of money from theft. By accepting deposits, offering interest on savings accounts, and offering inexpensive checking, banks lure customers to supply funds to drive their revenue-creating activities. Bank customers also receive an economic bonus.

Financial Hubs that Lower Cost: Banks reduce transaction costs in the economy by aggregating settlement of payments among multiple parties, as those parties (bank customers, other banks and third parties) engage in financial transactions. Interbank systems help banks to collect payments from multiple sources. Banks not only acquire business due to their convenience, but they also serve to reduce the average cost of settlement between various parties. The globalization and integration of the economy make this effect more pronounced.

Lending and Credit: When banks accept personal deposits and aggregate them, they typically only keep a low percentage of deposits one-hand and lend out as much as possible. Loans earn the bank money in interest payments, but they also help the economic system to function by increasing the availability of capital and allowing business to use debt to expand. Banks are important sources of typically high-quality credit, especially when we compared it with other agents in the economy. Even though some percentage of issued debt will go bad, the bank can (generally) still meet all of its obligations to depositors by using the revenues from diversified earnings.

Banking and Credit Creation: Banks are highly important for the economy because by engaging in their activities, they actually create credit. The fractional-reserve system, universal in modern banking, means that banks only hold a certain percentage of deposits on-site. The fractional amount held is large enough to cover day-to-day withdrawals from accounts, but not enough to cover all claims by depositors. For example, if the reserve requirement is 10 percent and the bank receives a deposit of ₹ 100 crore, it could loan out ₹ 90 crore, than total money supply will equal ₹ 190 crore in the economy. If the loaned amount ₹ 90 crore is deposited again in the banks, again banks will provide loan amount ₹ 81 crore, and banks will be capable to generate ₹ 1000 crore from the amount ₹ 100 crore. This process is called the credit creation and under this process banks could be create ₹ 900 crore additional credits in the economy without printing new money.

Modern Banking: Besides the esoteric arguments about the money supply, commercial banks are also important because they reduce transaction costs using modern technology. For example, electronic money transfer, on-line banking, internet banking, telephone banking etc reduces the costs for sending money in many cases, both in shipping and security costs as well as risks of theft. ATMs allow their citizens to access accounts every day, and the rise of drive-through banking has made using bank services even faster. As banks increasingly reach out to the Internet to connect with customers, this factor of convenience (which saves time and money).

Significance

Commercial banks are different from other types of banks due to their close knit community relationship and the specialized local products that they offer to their customer base. They are not able to effectively compete with large money Centre banks or multinational banks that engage in money dealing activities such as buying and selling overnight federal funds, hedging of foreign exchange contracts or trading in securities.

8.5 TYPES OF LOANS GRANTED BY COMMERCIAL BANKS

Secured loan

A secured loan is a loan in which the borrower pledges some asset (e.g. a car or property) as collateral for the loan, which then becomes a secured debt owed to the creditor who gives the loan. The debt is thus secured against the collateral in the event that the borrower defaults, the creditor takes possession of the asset used as collateral and may sell it to regain some or the entire amount originally lent to the borrower, for example, foreclosure of a home. From the creditor's perspective this is a category of debt in which a lender has been granted a portion of the bundle of rights to specified property. If the sale of the collateral does not raise enough money to pay off the debt, the creditor can often obtain a deficiency judgment against the borrower for the remaining amount. The opposite of secured debt/loan is unsecured debt, which is not connected to any specific piece of property and instead the creditor may only satisfy the debt against the borrower rather than the borrower's collateral and the borrower.

Unsecured loan

Unsecured loans are monetary loans that are not secured against the borrower's assets (i.e., no collateral is involved). There are small business have unsecured loans such as credit cards and credit lines to large corporate credit lines. These may be available from financial institutions under many different guises or marketing packages.

Bank overdrafts

An overdraft occurs when money is withdrawn from a bank account and the available balance goes below zero. In this situation the account is said to be "overdrawn". If there is a prior agreement with the account provider for an overdraft, and the amount overdrawn is within the authorized overdraft limit, then interest is normally charged at the agreed rate. If the positive balance exceeds the agreed terms, then additional fees may be charged and higher interest rates may apply.

8.6. FUNCTIONS OF COMMERCIAL BANKS

Commercial bank being the financial institution performs diverse types of functions. It satisfies the financial needs of the sectors such as agriculture, industry, trade, communication, etc. That means they play a very significant role in a process of economic social needs. The functions performed by banks are changing according to change in time and recently they are becoming customer centric and widening their functions. Generally the functions of commercial banks are divided into two categories viz. primary functions and the secondary functions. The following chart simplifies the functions of banks.

8.6.1 Commercial Banks Engage in the Following Activities

Traditionally, large commercial banks also underwrite bonds, and make markets in currency, interest rates, and credit-related securities, but today large commercial banks usually have an investment bank arm that is involved in the mentioned activities:

1. Processing of payments by way of telegraphic transfer, EFTPOS, internet banking, or other means
2. Issuing bank drafts and bank cheques
3. Accepting money on term deposit
4. Lending money by overdraft, instalment loan, or other means
5. Providing documentary and standby letter of credit, guarantees, performance bonds, securities underwriting commitments and other forms of off balance sheet exposures

6. Safekeeping of documents & other items in safe deposit boxes
7. Sales, distribution or brokerage, with or without advice, of: insurance, unit trusts and similar financial products as a "financial supermarket"
8. Cash management and treasury
9. Merchant banking and private equity financing

8.6.2 Functions of a Bank

The functions of bank can be divided into two categories: primary functions and secondary functions.

1. Primary Functions of Banks:

(*a*) **Accepting Deposits:** The most significant function of a bank is to mobilize deposits from the public. The persons having surplus funds and savings find it handy to deposit the amounts with banks. On the basis of the nature of deposits, funds that have been deposited with bank also earn interest. Thus, deposits with the bank grow along with the interest earned. If the rate of interest is higher, people are encouraged to deposit even more money with the bank. Banks also ensure safety of funds deposited with the bank. Following are the types of account bank use to open:

(*i*) **Savings account:** Meant for those people who wish to save money for future. Generally, here there are no restrictions on the amount that can be withdrawn at any point of time and also how often can it be withdrawn (frequency of withdrawals). Savings account holder receives a pass book which includes rules with respect to its operations. Minimum amount for account opening in a nationalized bank: ₹ 500. If you want cheque book facility as well, then it may cost ₹ 1000. The interest rates range from 4-6%. In private banks, minimum balance required is generally higher and can be as high as ₹ 5000/ 10, 000. One can have single or joint accounts.

(*ii*) **Fixed Deposits/Time Deposits/Long Term Deposits:** As the name suggests, they have been made for a specific time period and one cannot withdraw funds before maturity of that period for which they have been deposited in the bank. One earns higher rate of interest depending on the period of deposit. For this account, one does not get a pass book or cheque book, instead he will receive a Fixed deposit Receipt that will be duly signed by manager of the bank and will contain details like name/address of depositor, amount deposited, rate of interest, maturity date, etc. On maturity, the holder can claim his funds by producing this receipt.

(*iii*) **Current Deposits/Demand Deposits:** Businessmen generally open these accounts. Here, one can withdraw funds anytime by means of cheques. Here, deposits can be made to any extent and bank does not pay interest on current deposits. In fact, it charges a small amount as fees from operators of this account on the basis of transactions they carry out. They also enjoy overdraft facilities. They are provided with cheque book, pass book and a pay-in slip book. Cheque book contains blank printed cheques with counterfoils which are used to withdraw money from banks. Pass book is copy of customer's accounts in bank's ledger. It shows entries of all deposits and withdrawal of money and balance outstanding on any particular day. It is written by the bank from its own record and is meant for use of customer. Pay in slip book contains printed forms with perforated counterfoils which are meant to deposit cash or cheque into the bank. The pay in slip contains details of deposit and also serves as a receipt for the deposit made. Opening of this account not only requires an introduction from old customer of the bank, but also maintenance of minimum balance in this account at all times.

(*iv*) **Recurring Deposits:** Normally salaried employees and small traders open this account. Periodically, they deposit a certain amount of money in the bank. On the expiry of certain time period, withdrawals are allowed. This account earns a higher rate of interest.

(*b*) **Grant of loans and advances:** Loans and advances are given to people and to companies at a higher rate of interest than what banks give on various deposit accounts. The rate of interest charged on loans and advances shall vary on the purpose, period and the mode of repayment. The difference between the rate of interest allowed on deposits and the rate charged on the Loans is the main source of a bank's income.

(*i*) **Loans:** A loan is given for a certain time period. Normally, banks give short-term loans. Though term loans, meaning, loans for more than one year, shall also be given. The borrower/debtor can pull out the total amount in lump sum or in instalments. Nonetheless, interest will be charged on the entire loan amount. Loans are normally given against the security of certain assets i.e. collateral. A loan can be repaid either in lump sum or in instalments.

(*ii*) **Advances:** An advance is a credit facility provided by the bank to its customers. It differs from loan in the sense that loans may be granted for longer period, but advances are normally granted for a short period of time. Further the purpose of granting advances is to meet the day to day requirements of business. The rate of interest charged on advances varies from bank to bank. Interest is charged only on the amount withdrawn and not on the sanctioned amount. Following are the advance facilities provided by banks:

- **Cash Credit:** It is a financial arrangement through which banks allow borrower to borrow money upto a certain limit. Cash Credit arrangement is ordinarily made against the security of commodities hypothecated or pledged with the banker. The borrower has to pay interest on the total amount of advance.
- **Bank Overdraft:** Overdrafts are advanced to holders of current accounts. If borrower requires temporary finance, banker may allow him to overdraw on

his account with or without security. As compared to Cash Credit, overdraft is advantageous to borrower as he has to pay interest only on the actual amount withdrawn by him and not total amount.

- **Letter of Credit:** A letter of credit is an assurance from a bank that a particular debt will be honoured by the bank if the borrower defaults/fails to pay. Letters of credit are beneficial when dealing with new, unfamiliar vendors who might not be sure of a company's credit worthiness.

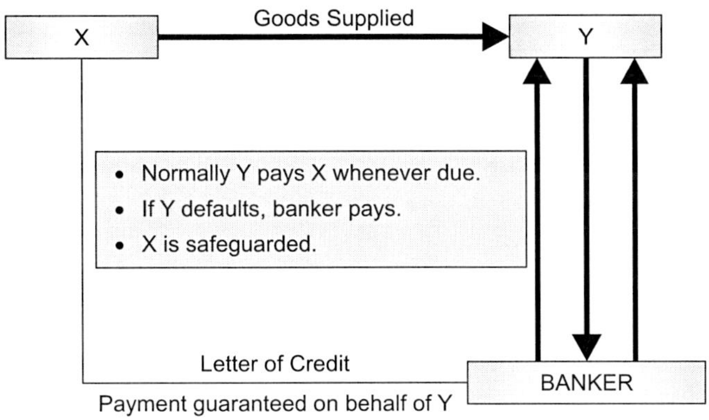

Fig. 8.1 Letter of Credit

If company X were supplying goods to company Y, company Y would wish to get credit from company X. Company X does not have regular supply to Y and hence does not have enough comfort to extend credit to Y. In such case, banker of Y may come forward to guarantee payments to X on behalf of Y. Since the payments are now guaranteed by a bank, X would not hesitate to extend credit to Y. It is evident that bank does not supply any funds in this facility. It is only the contingent risk that is assumed by the bank. So, risk of bank is lower as compared to cash credit facility where bank's funds are also involved in addition to the risk assumed. Hence, it is an indirect way of financing working capital.

- **Discounting of Bills:** In a particular transaction, company A supplies goods to company B. Company B accepts the goods , also accepts the bill of company A and agrees to pay after a specified credit period. However, A requires money immediately. He approaches a banker who pays him up front against the accepted bill. Banker does not pay him full amount but adjusts its interest payment for the value and period and pays A. This is called as banker discounts the bill. This is a fund based facility as banker actually pays upfront. Suppliers' working capital is thus not stuck up for that credit period. Supplier has to get prior limit set for such bill discounting facility. Discounting may be done either by supplier's banker or purchaser's banker. It is diagrammatically represented as follows:

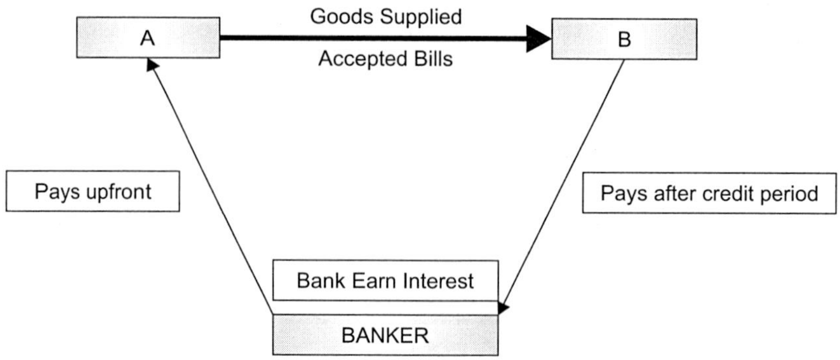

Fig. 8.2 Discounting of Bills

Bankers sanction the above mentioned facilities based on their assessment of the business entity. The creditworthiness of the business, profitability, sales projections, and promoter's track record are some of the considerations for sanctioning any of these facilities. Usually the inventory is either hypothecated or pledged to the lender/banker to avail of such facility. Thus banker's funds are provided against adequate security cover.

2. Secondary Functions of Banks:

The bank performs a number of secondary functions, also called as non-banking functions. These important secondary functions of banks are explained below.

(*a*) **Agency Functions:** The bank acts as an agent of its customers. The bank performs a number of agency functions which includes:-

- **Transfer of Funds:** The bank transfer funds from one branch to another or from one place to another.
- **Collection of Cheques:** The bank collects the money of the cheques through clearing section of its customers. The bank also collects money of the bills of exchange.
- **Periodic Payments:** On standing instructions of the client, the bank makes periodic payments in respect of electricity bills, rent, etc.
- **Portfolio Management:** The banks also undertake to purchase and sell the shares and debentures on behalf of the clients and accordingly debits or credits the account. This facility is called portfolio management.
- **Periodic Collections:** The bank collects salary, pension, dividend and such other periodic collections on behalf of the client.
- **Other Agency Functions:** They act as trustees, executors, advisers and administrators on behalf of its clients. They act as representatives of clients to deal with other banks and institutions.

(*b*) **General Utility Functions:** The bank also performs general utility functions, such as:

- **Issue of Drafts and Letter of Credits:** Banks issue drafts for transferring money from one place to another. It also issues letter of credit, especially in case of, import trade. It also issues travelers' cheques.
- **Locker Facility:** The bank provides a locker facility for the safe custody of valuable documents, gold ornaments and other valuables.
- **Underwriting of Shares:** The bank underwrites shares and debentures through its merchant banking division.
- **Dealing in Foreign Exchange:** The commercial banks are allowed by RBI to deal in foreign exchange.
- **Project Reports:** The bank may also undertake to prepare project reports on behalf of its clients.
- **Social Welfare Programmes:** It undertakes social welfare programmes, such as adult literacy programmes, public welfare campaigns, etc.
- **Other Utility Functions:** It acts as a referee to financial standing of customers. It collects creditworthiness information about clients of its customers. It provides market information to its customers, etc. It provides travelers' cheque facility.

Modern Functions (Recent Trends) In Banking

1. **Electronic Payment Services – E-Cheques:** Now-a-days we are hearing about e-governance, e-mail, e-commerce, e-tail etc. In the same manner, a new technology is being developed in US for introduction of e-cheque, which will eventually replace the conventional paper cheque. India, as harbinger to the introduction of e-cheque, the Negotiable Instruments Act has already been amended to include; Truncated cheque, E-Rupe and E-cheque instruments.

2. **Real-time Gross Settlement (RTGS):** Real-time Gross Settlement system, introduced in India since March 2004, is a system through which electronics instructions can be given by banks to transfer funds from their account to the account of another bank. The RTGS system is maintained and operated by the RBI and provides a means of efficient and faster funds transfer among banks facilitating their financial operations. As the name suggests, funds transfer between banks takes place on a 'Real-time' basis. Therefore, money can reach the beneficiary instantaneously and the beneficiary's bank has the responsibility to credit the beneficiary's account within two hours.

3. **Electronic Funds Transfer (EFT):** Electronic Funds Transfer (EFT) is a system whereby anyone who wants to make payment to another person/company etc. can approach his bank and make cash payment or give instructions/authorization to transfer funds directly from his own account to the bank account of the receiver/beneficiary. Complete details such as the receiver's name, bank account number,

account type (savings or current account), bank name, city, branch name etc. should be furnished to the bank at the time of requesting for such transfers so that the amount reaches the beneficiaries' account correctly and faster. RBI is the service provider of EFT.

4. **Electronic Clearing Service (ECS):** Electronic Clearing Service is a retail payment system that can be used to make bulk payments/receipts of a similar nature especially where each individual payment is of a repetitive nature and of relatively smaller amount. This facility is meant for companies and government departments to make/receive large volumes of payments rather than for funds transfers by individuals.

5. **Automatic Teller Machine (ATM):** Automatic Teller Machine is the most popular devise in India, which enables the customers to withdraw their money 24 hours a day 7 days a week. It is a devise that allows customer who has an ATM card to perform routine banking transactions without interacting with a human teller. In addition to cash withdrawal, ATMs can be used for payment of utility bills, funds transfer between accounts, deposit of cheques and cash into accounts, balance enquiry etc.

6. **Point of Sale Terminal:** Point of Sale Terminal is a computer terminal that is linked online to the computerized customer information files in a bank and magnetically encoded plastic transaction card that identifies the customer to the computer. During a transaction, the customer's account is debited and the retailer's account is credited by the computer for the amount of purchase.

7. **Tele Banking:** Tele Banking facilitates the customer to do entire non-cash related banking on telephone. Under this devise Automatic Voice Recorder is used for simpler queries and transactions. For complicated queries and transactions, manned phone terminals are used.

8. **Electronic Data Interchange (EDI):** Electronic Data Interchange is the electronic exchange of business documents like purchase order, invoices, shipping notices, receiving advices etc. in a standard, computer processed, universally accepted format between trading partners. EDI can also be used to transmit financial information and payments in electronic form.

8.6.2 E-RUPI

RBI starts a e-rupi voucher on dated 02/08/2021. In this digital transaction there is no need of card or net banking to redeem this voucher. Prime Minister Narendra Modi on Monday launched e-RUPI, an electronic voucher promoting digital payment solution, via video conferencing. The platform, developed by the National Payments Corporation of India in collaboration with the Department of Financial Services, Ministry of Health and Family Welfare and National Health Authority, claims to be a person and purpose-specific digital payment solution. e-RUPI voucher will play a role in boosting digital transactions and Direct Benefit Transfer (DBT) in the country. This will help everyone in targeted, transparent and leakage-free delivery, PM Modi said at the launch event.

"e-RUPI is an example of how India is moving forward an connecting people in the 21st century with the help of advanced technology. I'm glad that it has started in the year when India is celebrating its 75th year of Independence," the prime minister added. He also said that not only govt. but if a non-govt organisation wants to support anyone in their education or medical treatment, then they can use e-RUPI instead of giving cash. "This will assure that the amount donated is being used only for the said work." More than 300 cr transactions happened through UPI in July with over 6 lakh crore being transacted, said PM Modi, adding that government is using direct-benefit transfer to provide benefits of 300 schemes ranging from LPG to ration to pension directly to beneficiaries. "The new digital payment mode –e-RUPI– is basically a prepaid voucher that can be issued directly to citizens after verifying mobile number and identity. e-RUPI voucher will be delivered in the form of a QR code or SMS string-based e-voucher to the beneficiary's mobile number," said Bharat Panchal, CRO - APAC, Middle-east and Africa, FIS.

The beneficiary can redeem the voucher without a card, digital payments app or internet banking access, at the service provider. "This would be very useful instrument for those who are not privy to use the digital platform yet the government can extend monetary support in digital form directly to citizens in a "leak-proof manner" in the form of prepaid e-voucher powered by UPI," added Panchal. e-RUPI is a cashless and contactless instrument for digital payment.

It is a QR code or SMS string-based e-voucher, which is delivered to the mobile of the beneficiaries, a statement said earlier. The users of this seamless one-time payment mechanism will be able to redeem the voucher without a card, digital payments app or internet banking access, at the service provider, it said. e-RUPI connects the sponsors of the services with the beneficiaries and service providers in a digital manner without any physical interface. It also ensures that the payment to the service provider is made only after the transaction is completed.

Being pre-paid in nature, it assures timely payment to the service provider without involvement of any intermediary, the statement said. The PMO said it is expected to be a revolutionary initiative in the direction of ensuring a leak-proof delivery of welfare services. It can also be used for delivering services under schemes meant for providing drugs and nutritional support under Mother and Child welfare schemes, TB eradication programmes, drugs and diagnostics under schemes like Ayushman Bharat Pradhan Mantri Jan Arogya Yojana, fertiliser subsidies etc. Even the private sector can leverage these digital vouchers as part of their employee welfare and corporate social responsibility programmes, the statement said.

8.6.3 Objectives Behind Nationalisation of Banks in India

The nationalisation of commercial banks took place with an aim to achieve following major objectives.

Social Welfare: It was the need of the hour to direct the funds for the needy and required sectors of the Indian economy. Sector such as agriculture, small and village industries were in need of funds for their expansion and further economic development.

Controlling Private Monopolies: Prior to nationalisation many banks were controlled by private business houses and corporate families. It was necessary to check these monopolies in order to ensure a smooth supply of credit to socially desirable sections.

Expansion of Banking: In a large country like India the numbers of banks existing those days were certainly inadequate. It was necessary to spread banking across the country. It could be done through expanding banking network (by opening new bank branches) in the un-banked areas.

Reducing Regional Imbalance: In a country like India where we have an urban-rural divide; it is necessary for banks to go in the rural areas where the banking facilities are not available. In order to reduce this regional imbalance nationalisation is justified.

Priority Sector Lending: In India, the agriculture sector and its allied activities are the largest contributor to the national income. Thus these are labelled as the priority sectors. But unfortunately they are deprived of their due share in the credit. Nationalisation is urgently needed for catering funds to them.

Developing Banking Habits: In India more than 70% population used to stay in rural areas. It is necessary to develop the banking habit among such a large population.

8.6.4 Demerits, Limitations – Bank Nationalisation in India

Though the nationalisation of commercial banks was undertaken with tall objectives, in many senses it failed in attaining them. In fact it converted many of the banking institutions in the loss making entities. The reasons were obvious lethargic working, lack of accountability, lack of profit motive, political interference, etc. Under this backdrop it is necessary to have a critical look to the whole process of nationalisation in the period after bank nationalisation.

8.7 ADVANTAGES OF COMMERCIAL BANKS

Commercial Banks offer following advantages to the customers:

Investment: For any new business to get off the ground and begin operations there must be capital available that can be used to purchase necessary equipment and property. Commercial banks make this capital available to new entrepreneurs through the great number of loans that they provide. If it isn't for the role that commercial banks play, capital for starting a business would only be available to the very rich.

Mortgages: The flat price of a home is beyond the purchasing power of most people. Only through the creation of mortgages by commercial banks is the ability to purchase a house that given to the average person. A mortgage of assets involves a fixed series of annual payments to a bank over a long period of time in exchange for the bank paying the full price of the purchase in the short.

Savings: Rather than merely keeping your money in a safe place, by placing your money in a bank account you add to your wealth as the bank pays interest on the amount. This has a further advantage for society at large. As money saved in the bank isn't merely dead capital but money that the bank is actively investing in other enterprises, it helps to grow the wealth of society overall.

Payment: Commercial banks have devised a number of ways to aid clients in the payment of their debts. The first paper currency was created by commercial banks as issued credits on physical wealth, such as gold kept in bank vaults. Commercial bank customers can use checks as well as debit cards and online bill-paying services to make payments in a quick, easy way.

8.8 DISADVANTAGES OF COMMERCIAL BANKS

Delay in Loan Approvals: One disadvantage of using a large, commercial bank can easily be seen if you're trying to get a loan. Unlike a local bank, or a relatively small bank, a larger, commercial bank will have to put a loan through several different departments. Beyond that, you may have to have dozens of people sign off on a single loan. This can lead to many more people getting involved in saying yes or no to your loan, and it may lead to a lot more negotiation than you are hoping to conduct. This is especially true for a simple, relatively straightforward home or business loan.

Rigid Standards: Another downside of using commercial banks is that they have very rigid standards more often than not. All banks have to follow the financial laws put forth by the U.S. government, but commercial banks may treat their own, additional rules as if they're set in stone. Again, this is most often seen in the loan process. Commercial banks, due to their size and the sheer volume of the market that they command, are often less likely to make concessions to customers. This can lead to a very "my way or the highway" attitude from a commercial bank.

Security: One of the biggest concerns that a person has with their bank is whether or not their money is insured. If you put ₹ 10,0000 in a savings account, you want to be sure that money will be available, regardless of what expenses your bank has to deal with. Your deposits are secured by RBI. Many commercial banks, because of how they choose to run their business, forgo this government insurance and instead offer private insurance. This private insurance isn't as reliable as the government's insurance, and it makes many depositors nervous to be out from under the government's protection.

Inadequate Banking Facilities: Even though banks have spread across the country; still many parts of the country are unbanked. Especially in the backward states as like Uttar Pradesh, Madhya Pradesh, Chhattisgarh and north-eastern states of India.

Limited Resources Mobilized and Allocated: The resources mobilized after the nationalisation is not sufficient if we consider the needs of the Indian economy. Sometimes the deposits mobilized are enough but the resource allocation is not as per the expansions.

Lowered Efficiency and Profits: After nationalisation banks went in the government sector. Many times political forces pressurized them. Banking is not done on professional and ethical grounds. It resulted into lower efficiency and poor profitability of banks.

Increased Expenditure: Due to huge expansion in a branch network, large staff administrative expenditure, trade union struggle, etc. banks expenditure increased to dangerous levels.

Political and Administrative Interference: Many public sector banks badly suffered due to the political interference. It was seen in arranging loan meals. It ultimately resulted in huge non-performing assets (NPA) of these banks and inefficiency.

These are several limitations faced by the banks nationalisation in India. Apart from this there are certain other limitations as well, such as weak infrastructure, poor competitiveness, etc.

But after Economic Reform of 1991, the Indian banking industry has entered into the new horizons of competitiveness, efficiency and productivity. It has made Indian banks more vibrant and professional organizations, removing the bad days of bank nationalisation.

8.9 DEMERITS OF INDIAN BANKING SYSTEM

- Poor Efficiency: Financial institutions takes more time in clearing of Cheques or pass book entry.
- Unable to fulfill the credit requirement.
- They charge High rate of interest.
- Financial institutions or banks have less efficient staff.
- Poor banking infrastructure.
- Lack of control on unauthorized sector by the RBI.
- High non-performing assets (NPA): According to national standards NPA should not increase upto 15% but NPA is very high particularly in case of vehicle loan.
- Banks have failed to maintain rural development.
- Lack of innovation or new technique: A Public sector banks does not adopt new techniques.
- Banking Frauds

- Corruption
- Financial institutions charge high rate of interest.
- Political interference & red-tapism.
- Financial institution or banks are unable to fulfill the credit requirements.

8.10 CHALLENGES FACED BY INDIAN BANKING INDUSTRY

India's banking sector has made rapid strides in reforming and aligning itself to the new competitive business environment. The major challenges faced by banks today are as to how to cope with competitive forces and strengthen their balance sheet. Today, banks are groaning with burden of NPA's. It is rightly felt that these contaminated debts, if not recovered, will eat into the very vitals of the banks.

1. **High transaction costs:** A major concern before the banking industry is the high transaction cost of carrying non- performing assets in their books. The growth led to strains in the operational efficiency of banks and the accumulation of non-performing assets (NPA's) in their loan portfolios.

2. **IT revolution:** The Indian banks are subject to tremendous pressures to perform as otherwise their very survival would be at stake. The application of IT and e-banking is becoming the order of the day with the banking system heading towards virtual banking.

3. **Timely technological up gradation:** Already electronic transfers, clearings, settlements have reduced translation times. To face competition it is necessary for banks to absorb the technology and upgrade their services.

4. **Intense Competition:** The RBI and Government of India kept banking industry open for the participants of private sector banks and foreign banks. The foreign banks were also permitted to set up shop on India either as branches or as subsidiaries. Due to this lowered entry barriers many new players have entered the market such as private banks, foreign banks, non-banking finance companies, etc. The foreign banks and new private sector banks have spearhead the hi-tech revolution. For survival and growth in highly competitive environment banks have to follow the prompt and efficient customer service, which calls for appropriate customer centric policies and customer friendly procedures.

5. **Privacy and Safety:** Among the most important aspects of savings, i.e., safety, liquidity and profitability, safety is at the top most priority. The areas which might endanger security in e-banking can be:

- Credit risk
- Liquidity, interest rate risk, market risks
- Legal risk

6. **Global banking:** The impact of globalization becomes challenges for the domestic enterprises as they are bound to compete with global players. If we look at the Indian Banking Industry, then we find that there are 36 foreign banks operating in India, which becomes a major challenge for Nationalized and private sector banks.

7. **Financial inclusion:** Financial inclusion has become a necessity in today's business environment. Whatever is produced by business houses, that has to be under the check from various perspectives like environmental concerns, corporate governance, social and ethical issues. In India, RBI has initiated several measures to achieve greater financial inclusion, such as facilitating no-frills accounts and GCCs for small deposits and credit.

REVIEW QUESTIONS

1. What is the concept of a commercial bank? What are the objectives of a commercial bank?
2. What are the features of a banking system?
3. What are the characteristics of a commercial bank?
4. What is the importance of a commercial bank?
5. What are the types of loans granted by commercial banks?

Social Responsibilities of Commercial Banks in India

9

The financial system is the lifeline of any economy. The changes in the economy can show performance of the financial system, more or less through the banking industry. Banks over the years have become a significant aspect of an economy. The banking sector forms a portion of the financial sector, primarily works as a financial intermediary to generate the money supply. From the different macroeconomic models, banks have been found to be a part of the supply side of money in the economy. However, over time banks have transformed from merely money generating organisations to a multi-tasking entity.

Financial Sector Reforms set in motion in 1991 have greatly changed the face of Indian banking system. The banking industry has moved gradually from a regulated environment to a deregulated market in the economy. The market developments by liberalisation and globalisation have resulted in changes in the intermediation role of banks. The pace of transformation has been more significant in recent times, with technology acting as a catalyst.

9.1 SOCIAL RESPONSIBILITY OF BANKS

Commercial banks fulfil their social responsibility through following means:

1. **Rural Branch Expansion:** This variable is used to measure the extent up to which the banks are following the financial inclusion policy formulated by the Reserve Bank of India to promote balanced growth of the economy.

2. **Priority Sector Lending:** As described by the Reserve Bank of India, Priority Sector lending means lending to the agriculture, small scale and ancillary industries, new and renewable sources of energy, cottage industries, artisans, food and agro-based processing, education, housing and the weaker sections. While for domestic banks, both the public and private sectors are required to lend 40 per cent of their net bank credit (NBC) to the priority sector, foreign banks are required to lend 32 per cent of their NBC to the priority sector. It has been observed that while banks often tend to meet the overall priority sector targets, they sometimes tend to miss the sub-targets. This is particularly true in case of domestic banks failing to meet their sub-targets for agricultural advances. One of the reasons banks often site for not lending to this sector is that recovery is often difficult.

3. **Environment Protection:** This variable includes all the activities carried out by the banks for the purpose of environment protection or to reduce the environmental harm by adopting different initiatives, replacing traditional activities by eco-friendly processes or activities in day to day business. The major activities performed by banks in this field are as follows:

- No credit to businesses involved in Ozone depletion, human rights violation, controversial weapons, gambling or pornography activities.
- Awareness programs about 'avoiding the usage of plastic bags' and 'reduced use of paper in offices'.
- Promoting and financing energy saving and solar energy projects.
- Encouraging, financing and setting up of non-conventional energy generation units,
- Assistance for rain water harvesting tanks
- Wild animal protection projects
- Tree plantation drives
- Projects related to reduction of carbon emissions

4. **Education:** This variable is used to measure the contribution of banks in the field of education. In India, Rao (1964) and the Education Commission (1966) emphasised the links between education and development. Fields (1980) and Tilak (1978) explained that education and poverty are inversely related: the higher the level of education of the population, the lower would be the proportion of poor people in the total population, as education imparts knowledge and skills that are associated with higher wages. The major activities carried out by the banks in the field of education are as follows:

- Support to low income family students with financial assistance, free uniform and books
- Motivational camps for rural students to attend schools.
- Concession in interest on education loans for backward class students
- Creating library-cum-reading rooms in rural areas and providing fans, water coolers, etc., to schools.
- Promotion and financial support for special children's education.
- Collaborations with educational institutes to provide educational loans and interest.
- School adoption initiatives.
- Special educational sponsorships for the girl child
- Donations for educational assistance.
- Establishments of pre-schools and assistance in mid-day meal programmes for the under priviledged.

5. **Community Welfare:** This variable is used to measure the activities performed by the banks for the welfare of the community. As per the data, highest number of banks have contributed in this CSR activity. Some of the common activities in this field are:

- Donations to orphanages
- Free food distribution to the poor patients of government health care centers
- Health awareness programmes
- Free health checkups
- Campaigns against usage of drugs, alcohol and smoking
- Construction of toilets, community halls and dispensaries
- Providing free medical facilities to the poor people
- Community welfare through helping NGOs
- Blood donation camps
- Donations for disaster relief and accident victims

6. **Financial Literacy:** As per the Reserve Bank of India, Financial literacy is providing familiarity with and understanding of financial market products, especially rewards and risks, in order to make informed choices. It is the ability to know, monitor, and effectively use financial resources to enhance the well-being and economic security of oneself, one's family and one's business. Financial literacy has assumed greater importance in the recent years, as financial markets have become increasingly complex and as there is information asymmetry between markets and the common man, leading to the latter finding it increasingly difficult to make informed choices. In India, the need for financial literacy is even greater considering the low levels of literacy and the large section of the population, which still remains out of the formal financial set-up.

Credit Counselling can be defined as counselling that explores the possibility of repaying debts outside bankruptcy and educates the debtor about credit, budgeting, and financial management. In view of the above two points, the RBI has initiated a scheme for setting up of Financial Literacy and Credit Counselling (FLCC) Centres by the banks. Certain banks have not just opened the FLCC centres but have also taken other measures to promote finance education among people.

New Initiatives related to CSR: This variable is used to measure the new CSR initiatives taken by the banks in the respective year for which CSR has been measured. Some of the major initiatives taken by the banks are listed below:

- Programs for promotion of women entrepreneurs
- Village adoption schemes
- Green initiatives like electricity audit of bank office
- Establishment of Butterfly park which houses medicinal plants
- Tree plantation drives
- Spreading awareness on Climate Change and Global Warming, joining hands with 'World Wide Fund of Nature' (WWF) and 'The Indus Entrepreneurs' (TIE)

7. **Women Welfare:** This variable indicates the activities done in the direction of welfare of women and girl child. Some of the activities which banks are performing in the field of the women welfare are as follows:

- Free or concessional education for poor girls, scholarships to girl students
- Concessions on the interest rate for girl student
- Project for Women Weavers in Varanasi
- Insurance policies specially for rural and urban poor women
- Special credit cards issued for women
- Women empowerment through donation of sewing machines for self-employment
- Maternal Nutrition Project
- Support to Indian School of Microfinance for Women (ISMW)

8. **Farmer's Welfare:** Indian economy has always been an agriculture based economy. Although, the contribution of agriculture to the GDP of the country has decreased in past years, a large portion of population still depends upon agriculture for its survival. However, the agriculture sector is still in a meagre state. Due to the poor economic health of agriculture sector, India observes a large number of cases of suicide among the farmers. It has been felt that there is an urgent requirement to promote investments in this sector and welfare of the farmers. Some of the major activities done by the banks under the farmer's welfare are as follows:

- Agriculture Debt Waiver & Debt Relief Scheme
- Loan for Solar Water Heating Systems at concessional rate
- Rural Extension Education Programmes enabling farmers and entrepreneurs to improve their productivity/production
- Establishment of Farmers clubs
- Farmers' Training Centres (FTCs)
- Special credit cards for farmers
- Agriculture knowledge sharing Programs
- National insurance programs for agriculture
- Financing rural godowns and cold storages/warehouses
- Debt Swap Schemes
- Setting up agriculture clusters for better farming
- Commodity finance against pledge of warehouse receipts of agro commodities

9.2 SOME OTHER SOCIAL RESPONSIBILITY FOLLOWED BY BANKS

1. **Responsibility towards Public**

- **Customers:** Business relationships with customers are founded on mutual respect and confidence and are in a proper manner strengthened by informal, social relations. As professional advisers, the bank helps their customers to acquire additional skills, facilitate contacts, find new opportunities for their business and encourage them in different ways to exercise social responsibility.
- **Investors:** The Bank's reporting is transparent, up-to-date and non-discriminatory and complies with the highest communication standards.
- **Media:** The Banks proactively communicates with journalists and responds quickly to their requests.
- **Suppliers:** The Banks endeavors to establish long-term cooperation and partner relations with suppliers. The Bank aims as far as possible to develop collaboration between employees and suppliers and to establish mutual responsibility for timely accomplishment of agreed services. Good partner relationships, involving mutual respect and trust, provide a good basis for better productivity and faster accomplishment of agreed-upon tasks.

2. **Responsibility towards Environment:** We are aware that providing for sustainable development represents a valuable contribution that is being created by our proper attitude towards natural environment. When purchasing new fixed assets, the Bank follows its policy that investments in equipment, premises, computer infrastructure, heating and air-conditioning equipment should be made by placing the minimum possible burden on the environment.

The Bank encourages employees, customers and business partners to use electronic banking channels and e-mail for all types of communication, which reduces the consumption of paper.

In collecting and carting off waste material the Bank fully complies with applicable legislation and regulations and delivers all ecologically harmful waste for disposal or recycling to organisations legally engaged in this activity.

There are many individuals among Bank employees that participate as volunteers in various organisations and activities the mission of which is to preserve natural resources as well as healthy and clean natural environment.

3. **Responsibility towards Social and Economic Environment:** The Bank actively recognises the opportunities where it can contribute with its know-how, financial resources and other assets to the development of social and economic environment, which surpasses its involvement based merely on sponsorships and grants.

4. **Responsibility towards Employees:** Banks offers each employee opportunities for professional and personal growth. The conduct of management serves as a model of good internal relations. It fully observe provisions of the Code of Conduct and take care

of well-regulated internal communication, thus, contributing to more effective working processes, better motivation, commitment and satisfaction of our employees.

In addition to their regular work, the Bank employees often meet at sports, social and cultural events. This helps us preserve our mutual interaction and pursuit of a sound mind in a sound body. Active in the Bank are a sports club, a choir and a trade union, while our ex-employees meet at pensioners' clubs on different occasions.

Banks also take care of safe and healthy working environment and promote awareness regarding the prevention of illness and injuries at work. By paying supplementary voluntary pension insurance, the Bank wants to assure its employees greater financial security in their old age.

9.3 SOCIAL CONTROL OF BANKS

Prior to nationalisation of 14 major banks in 1969, the government experimented briefly (for 19 months from Dec 1967 onwards) with the social control of banks. The basic objective of such control was to ensure, in the immediate future, equitable and purposeful distribution, within the resources, keeping in view the relative priorities of development needs.

The main features of social control are as follows:

1. Under social control, the Board of Directors were to be reconstituted and the majority of the directors of banks had to be persons having special knowledge or practical experience in agriculture, small scale industries, corporation and economics.
2. New loans were prohibited to directors and the concerns in which they might be interested.
3. The outstanding loans to such director must be paid back within 3 years.
4. National credit council composed of representatives from various sectors was set up in 1967 to determine priorities of bank loans and advances. Three priorities were recognised: agriculture, small scale industries and export.
5. The government could acquire control over any commercial bank, if it fails to abide by the social control policies and directions given by RBI.

9.4 SOCIAL BANKING

After nationalisation, the commercial banks in India have adopted a new policy orientation to meet the socio-economic obligations of the country.

The important aspects of this social orientation are given below:

1. Alignment of credit policy with the overall objective of the government.
2. Allocation of credit in accordance with the requirements of the planned economic development of the country.

3. Reduction of regional disparities in the spread of banking to achieve the balanced development of the country.
4. A lead role in the development of credit at the district level.
5. Greater financial assistance to the priority sectors of the economy and weaker sections of the society on easy and convenient terms.

In order to achieve the new social reorientation of banking, the banking system was developed and its functioning changed in the following directions:

1. Expansion of bank offices in the rural and hitherto unbanked areas.
2. Gradual decline in the security and guaranty-oriented approach and laying more emphasis on the purpose, viability and creditworthiness of the project for which the loan is required.
3. Decline in the share of bank credit to large and medium industry and rise in that to the small scale industries.
4. Greater provision of bank credit has been made to the priority sectors like agriculture, small and cottage industry, small road transport, export, etc.
5. Differential interest rate scheme was introduced in 1972 to provide financial assistance to the economically weaker sections of the society, the physically handicapped persons and the orphanages and women's houses at a nominal interest rate of 4% p.a.
6. Lead Bank scheme was introduced in December 1969 to evolve a consortium approach on the part of the commercial banks to develop on the basis of area approach the lead banks are expected to formulate district-wise plans for branch expansion, deposit mobilisation and credit allocation, after conducting economic service in the district.

REVIEW QUESTIONS

1. What are the social responsibilities of commercial banks?
2. Give a gist about the social control of banks?
3. What is social banking?
4. What is a bank's responsibility towards – customers, investors, media and suppliers.
5. Give a gist of -- the nationalization of 14 major banks in 1969.

Role of Banks in Economic Development

10

10.1 INTRODUCTION

Commercial banks play an important and active role in the economic development of a country. If the banking system in a country is effective, efficient and disciplined, it brings a rapid growth in the various sectors of the economy. The economic significance of commercial banks is given in brief.

Commercial banks are considered not merely as dealers in money but also the leaders in economic development. They are not only the storehouses of the country's wealth but also the reservoirs of resources that are necessary for economic development. A well-developed banking system is essential for the economic development of a country. The 'Industrial Revolution' in Europe in the 19th century would not have been possible without a sound system of commercial banking. In case of developing countries like India, the commercial banks are considered to be the backbone of the economy. Commercial banks can contribute to a country's economic development in the following ways:

Capital Formation: Banks collect ideal saving of the people and invest the same in productive activities thus they help in accelerating the rate of capital formation enhancing the economic development. The commercial banks play an important role in raising the financial resources. They encourage savings by giving various types of incentives to the savers. They expand branches of the banks in rural and urban areas and mobilise savings, even at far of places. These savings are then made available to the business which use of them for productive purposes in the country. The banks provide stream of resources that are necessary for economic development.

Provision of Finance and Credit: Commercial banks are a very important source of finance and credit for big industry, trade, service, small scale industry, village industry, cottage industry and agriculture and allied activities. Credit is a pillar of development. Credit lubricates all commerce and trade. Banks become the nerve centre for all credit facilitation. Banks are instruments for developing internal as well as external trade.

Monetisation of Economy: An underdeveloped economy is characterised by the existence of a large non-monetised sector. The existence of this non-monetised sector is a hindrance in the economic development of the country. The banks, by opening branches in rural and backward areas can promote the process of monetisation (conversion of debt into money) in the economy.

Inducement to Innovation: Innovations are an essential prerequisite for the economic development. By providing credit to entrepreneurs banks encourage innovation. These innovations are mostly financed by bank credit in the developed countries. But in underdeveloped countries, entrepreneurs hesitate to invest in new ventures and undertake innovations largely due to lack of funds. Facilities of bank loans enable the entrepreneurs to step up their investment in innovation activities, adopt new methods of production and increase productive capacity of the economy.

As a result, production of new goods is increased. It has a favourable effect on the economic development the country. Innovations are an essential prerequisite for the economic progress. These innovations are mostly financed by bank credit in the developed countries. But the entrepreneur in the underdeveloped countries cannot bring about these innovations for lack of bank credit in an adequate measure. The banks should, therefore, pay special attention to the financing of business innovations by providing adequate and cheap credit to entrepreneurs.

Implementation of Monetary Policy: An organised banking system is a precondition for the effective implementation of the monetary policy of the government and central bank of an underdeveloped country to achieve the objectives of the monetary policy of the country. Economic development needs an appropriate monetary policy. But a well-developed banking is a necessary pre-condition for the effective implementation of the monetary policy. Control and regulation of credit by the monetary authority is not possible without the active co-operation of the banking system in the country. Cooperation of the commercial banks has a great significant.

Encouragement of Right Type of Industries: Banks generally provide financial resources to the right type of industries to secure the necessary material, machines and other inputs. In this way they influence the nature and volume of industrial production.

Development of Agriculture: Underdeveloped economies are primarily agricultural economies. Majority of the population in these economies live in rural areas. Therefore, the economic development in these economies require the development of agriculture and small scale industries in rural areas. So far banks in underdeveloped countries have been paying more attention to trade and commerce and have almost neglected agriculture and industry. Banks must provide loans to agriculture for development and modernisation of agriculture. In recent years, the State Bank of India and other commercial banks are granting short term, medium-term and long-term loans to agriculture and small-scale industries.

Regional Development: Banks can also play an important role in achieving balanced development in different regions of the country. They transfer surplus capital from the developed regions to the less developed regions, where it is scarce and most needed. This reallocation of funds between regions will promote the economic development in underdeveloped areas of the country.

Promote Industrial Development: Industrial development needs finance. In some countries, commercial banks encouraged industrial development by granting long-term loans also. Loan or credit is a pillar for development. In underdeveloped countries like India, commercial banks are granting short-term and medium-term loans to industries. They are also underwriting the issue of shares and debentures by industrial concerns. This helps industrial concerns to secure adequate capital for their establishment, expansion and modernisation. Commercial banks are also helping manufacturers to secure machinery and equipment from foreign countries under instalment system by guaranteeing deferred payments. Thus, banks promote or encourage industrial development.

Promote Commercial Virtues: The businessmen are more afraid of a banker than a purchaser. The businessmen should have certain business qualities like industry, forethought, honesty and punctuality. These qualities are called 'commercial virtues' which are essential for rapid economic progress. The banker is in a better position to promote commercial virtues. Banks are called 'public conservators of commercial virtues'.

Full-fillment of Socio-economic Objectives: In recent years, commercial banks, particularly in developing countries, have been called upon to help achieve certain socio-economic objectives laid down by the state. For example, nationalised bank in India have framed special innovative schemes of credit to help small agriculturists, self-employed persons and retailers through loans and advances at concessional rates of interest. Banking is thus used to achieve the national policy objectives of reducing inequalities of income and wealth, removal of poverty and elimination of unemployment in the country.

Thus, banks in a developing country have to play a dynamic role. Economic development places heavy demand on the resources and ingenuity of the banking system. It has to respond to the multifarious economic needs of a developing country. Traditional views and methods may have to be discarded. "An Institution, such as the banking system, which touches and should touch the lives of millions, has necessarily to be inspired by a larger social purpose and has to sub serve national priorities and objectives." A well-developed banking system provides a firm and durable foundation for the economic development of the country.

Finance for Priority Sectors: The commercial banks in underdeveloped countries generally hesitate in extending financial accommodation to sectors such as agriculture and small scale industries, on account of the risks involved. They mostly extend credit to trade and commerce where the risk involved is far less. But for the development of these countries it is essential that the banks take risk in extending credit facilities to the priority sectors, such as agriculture and small scale industries.

Investment in New Enterprises: Businessmen normally hesitate to invest their money in risky enterprises. The commercial banks generally provide short and medium term loans to entrepreneurs to invest in new enterprises and adopt new methods of production. The provision of timely credit increases the productive capacity of the economy.

Provision for Medium and Long term Finance: The commercial banks in underdeveloped countries invariably give loans and advances for a short period of time. They generally hesitate to extend medium and long term loans to businessmen. It is well known, the new business need medium and long term loans for their proper establishment. The commercial banks should, therefore, change their policies in favor of granting medium and long term accommodation to business and industry.

Impact on the Rate of Interest: Banks determine the rate of interest as to encourage Entrepreneurs and traders to make new investments. There is development of industry and trade. It also has a favourable impact on the economic development.

Role in the Development of Rural Sector: Banks play a significant role in the development of rural areas. They provide loans to the farmers at low rate of interest for the purchase of agricultural product and tools.

Helpful in Pushing up the Demand: People have low income and low standard of living in under develop countries and their demand for consumer goods is very low. Banks provide loans to their customers and make able them to buy consumer durables.

Promotion of Trade and Industry: With the growth of commercial banking in the 19th and 20th centuries, there is vast expansion in trade and industry. The use of bank draft, cheque, bill of exchange credit cards etc. has revolutionized both national and international trade.

Development of Agriculture: The commercial banks, particularly in developing countries, are now providing credit for the development of agriculture and small scale industries in rural areas. The provision of credit to agriculture sector has greatly helped in raising agricultural productivity and income of the farmers. This has led to increased demand for industrial goods and expansion of industry

Balanced Development of Different Regions: The commercial banks play an important role in achieving balanced in different regions of the country. They help in transferring surplus capital from developed regions to the less developing regions. The traders, industrialists etc of less developed regions are able to get adequate capital for meeting their business needs. Thus, in turn, increases investment, trade and production in the economy.

Influencing Economy Activity: The banks can also influence the economic activity of the country through its influence on (*a*) availability of credit and (*b*) the rate of interest. If the commercial banks are able to increase the amount of money in circulation through credit creation or by lowering the rate of interest, it directly affects economic development. A low rate of interest can encourage investment. The credit creation activity can raise aggregate demand which leads to more production in the economy.

Employment Generation: Commercial banks help to increase the opportunities of employment directly as well indirectly. By obtaining loans at reasonable rate of interest, unemployed youth can arrange for their self-employment.

Implementation of Monetary Policy: The central bank of the country controls and regulates volume of credit through the active cooperation of the banking system in the country. If helps in bringing price stability and promotes economic growth within shortest possible period / time.

Monetisation of the Economy: The commercial banks by opening branches in the rural and backward areas are reducing the exchange of goods through barter. The use of money has now greatly increased the volume of production of goods. The non-monetized sector (barter economy) is now being converted into monetized sector with the help of commercial banks.

Export Promotion Cells: In order to increase the exports of the country, the commercial banks have established export promotion cells. They provide information about general trade and economic conditions both inside and outside the country to its customers. The banks are, therefore, making positive contribution in the process of economic development.

Cheap Money Policy: The commercial banks in an underdeveloped economy should follow cheap money policy to stimulate economic activity or to meet the threat of business recession. In fact, cheap money policy is the only policy which can help to promote the economic growth of an underdeveloped country.

Role of Banks in the 21st Century: Commercial banks are now not confined to local banking. They are fast changing into global banking, i.e., understanding the global customer, using latest information technology, competing in the open market with high technology system, changing from domestic banking to investment banking etc. The commercial banks are now considered the nerve centre of all economic development in the country. The use of online banking is now increasing day by day. It has brought revolution in banking industry.

10.2 SOURCES OF CAPITAL

Commercial bank gets their capital from various sources. Based on their capital they advance loan to earn interest income.

- **Share Capital:** Organisation of commercial bank is largely like joint stock companies these shares may be off rupees 10, 50 or 100. Authorised capital of the bank is the maximum permissible capital that it can collect by selling shares. Shares of authorised capital which are offered for sale to the general public is called issued capital. This issued capital the value of shares actually purchased by the people is called subscribed capital.

- **Reserve Fund:** The banks also maintain their cash reserve. The bank does not distribute all their profits among the share holders. Part of the profit are retain in the form of reserve fund to meet accidental situation.
- **Deposits:** Deposits are accepted from the people in various form or accounts. These may be current account, time account or saving account. Deposits obtained from the people in the form of cash.
- **Loans:** In abnormal condition commercial banks raised loan for their working capital. This loan can be obtained from central government, RBI and other financial institutes. Commercial bank generally seek loan from the RBI.
- **Credit Creation:** Credit creation is yet another important source of working capital for the commercial bank. Whenever a commercial bank advances loan it is not paid in cash. Two accounts are opened by the bank. One the loan account and the other the personal account of the browser. Through this method banks creates credit.
- **Fee-Based Services:** In the present era banks earn a huge amount from the services which are provided by banks to their customers' as like ATM charges, DD charges, fund transfer charges, charges from various bills and charges from discount of bills etc.

10.3 CREDIT CREATION BY COMMERCIAL BANKS

Central bank is the first source of money supply in the form of currency in circulation. The Reserve Bank of India is the note issuing authority of the country. The RBI ensures availability of currency to meet the transaction needs of the economy. The Total Volume of money in the economy should be adequate to facilitate the various types of economic activities such as production, distribution and consumption. The commercial banks are the second most important sources of money supply. The money that commercial banks supply is called credit money. The process of 'Credit Creation' begins with banks lending money out of primary deposits. Primary deposits are those deposits which are deposited in banks. In fact banks cannot lend the entire primary deposits as they are required to maintain a certain proportion of primary deposits in the form of reserves with the RBI under RBI and Banking Regulation Act. After maintaining the required reserves, the bank can lend the remaining portion of primary deposits. Here bank's lend the money and the process of credit creation starts. Suppose there are a number of Commercial Banks in the Banking System – Bank 1, Bank 2, Bank 3, and so on. To begin with let us suppose that an individual "A" makes a deposit of ₹ 100 in bank 1. Bank "1" is required to maintain a Cash Reserve Requirement of 5% (Prevailing Rate) which is decided by the RBI's Monetary Policy from the deposits made by 'A'. Bank "1" is required to maintain a cash reserve of ₹ 5 (5% of 100). The bank has now lendable funds of ₹ 95 (100 – 5). Let the Bank '1' lend ₹ 95 to a borrower; say B. the method of lending is the same that is bank 1 opens an account in the name of the borrower cheque for the loan amount. At the end of the process of deposits and lending, the balance sheet of bank reads as given below:

It can be seen from the combined balance sheet that a primary deposits of ₹ 100 in a bank 1 leads to the creation of the total deposit of ₹ 2,000. The combined balance sheet also shows that the banks have created a total credit of ₹ 2,000. And maintained a total cash reserve of ₹ 100. Which equals the primary deposits. The total deposit created by the commercial banks constitutes the money supply by the banks.

These two sources of credit are now discussed in below.

10.3.1 Non-Institutional Sources of Credit

The major non-institutional sources of farm credit are money-lenders, friends, relatives, landlords, shopkeepers and commission agents. Before 1947, the money lenders mostly non-Muslims were the main suppliers of loans to the farmers. After Partition however their importance has decreased to a great extent and the short term credit needs of the farmers are met from commission agents, friends and relatives which supply roughly more than 50% of total rural borrowings.

The traders and commission agents advance loans to the farmers for short period. These loans are provided mostly for productive purposes before the maturity of crops. The commission agents force the farmers to sell the product to them which generally is purchased at low rates.

The lenders of the informal sources (friends, relatives etc.) have certain advantages over the formal credit sources. The informal lenders usually know the borrowers personally. They require little security for advancing loans. The loans are given for consumption as well as production purposes. The lenders are approachable at all times. They are also lenient in rescheduling loans. However, the informal lenders are also accused of charging higher rates of interest. They extract monopoly profits from the borrowers. As such a need was felt to organize and develop the institutional sources of credit.

10.3.2 Institutional Sources of Credit

Commercial Banks: The interest of commercial banks in rural finance first started when the State Bank of India was established in 1955 to provide, among others, credit facilities for co-operative processing and marketing societies. After nationalization, a rapid expansion in branch banking in rural and semi-urban areas was started. Now there are 16 million agricultural borrowing accounts with total outstanding advances to agriculture by public sector commercial banks accounting to ₹ 53690 corers as compared to a mere 0.2 million accounts with total outstanding advances to the extent of ₹ 162 corers in June 1969. A large number of village co-operatives societies are among the borrowers.

There are two ways to provide finance for the rural area:

1. Direct Financing by Commercial Banks
2. Indirect Financing by Commercial Banks

1. Direct Financing by Commercial Banks: It was conceded that the commercial banks did not have the necessary experience or the personnel to deal with the farmers directly while the co-operatives had been specializing in rural credit since the beginning of the century. Even then the commercial banks were expected to go vigorously in support of the farmers in general and small cultivators in particular. In the initial stages, for various reasons the nationalized banks concentrated their attention on cultivators and other special category farmers such as those engaged in raising high-yielding varieties of food grains. At present short-term crop loans account for nearly 45 to 47 percent of the total loans given and discoursed by the commercial banks. Term loans for varying periods are given for purchasing pump-sets, tractors and other agricultural machinery, for construction of wells and tube wells, for development of fruit and garden crops, for leveling and development of land, for the purchase of ploughs, animals, etc. Finally, commercial banks extend loans for allied activities, for dairying, poultry, piggery, bee keeping, fisheries and others.

2. Indirect Financing by Commercial Banks: Even though the scope for direct financing by commercial banks would be limited for some years to come, there is considerable scope for indirect financing by them:

- Commercial banks finance to co-operative societies to enable them to extern their production, credit to the farmers. Especially, they finance to those co-operatives societies which engaged in marketing and processing of agricultural product or activities such as dairy poultry, etc.
- Commercial banks are undertaking indirect provision of production in credit through agencies which managed in the supply of inputs for marketing or processing of agricultural product.
- They finance to the operations of the food corporation of India, the state governments and others in the procurement, storage and distribution of food grains.
- Commercial banks are increasing subscribing to debentures of the central land development banks and also extend advances to the latter.

This enables land development banks to expand their medium and long-term advances to farmers for the purpose of land improvement and land development.

10.3.3 Problems of Commercial Banks in Rural Credit

The annual credit needs of the agricultural sector in the next few years are estimated to rise to ₹ 90,000 to ₹ 100,000 crore. To meet these needs is an enormous task and the responsibility must rest mainly with the co-operatives and commercial banks. As resources available to commercial banks in the agricultural sector will naturally be limited, it is important that every commercial bank attempts to make optimum use of its limited recourses in this sector.

In field of financing of agriculture, the problem is not merely quantitative but also of coverage viz-a-viz the organization and the personnel available to the commercial banks. The majority of population consists of small farmers, further, there are 5,50,000 villages spread throughout the country to reach all of them with only 33,000 rural bank offices is, no doubt, a stupendous task. Even with the completion of the ruler branch expansion programs of the commercial banks now in hand or those which may be undertaken during the next 5 to 10 years, banks may not in be a position to cover most of the villages in the country.

Moreover, in recent years, the rural branches of commercial banks in general and branches of regions rural banks in particular, have been under severe financial strain on account of:

- Higher transaction costs involved in handling of large number of a small sized loan accounts.
- Lower income as result of concessional rates of interest on small fixed loans. The lower proportion of current deposits in total deposits of rural branches has also placed them at a disadvantage in regard to best of resources,

Finally, the presence of overdue particularly after implementation of agricultural and rural credit debt relief scheme, 1990 has further adversely affected the viability of rural branches. Under these conditions, small and marginal farmers have been forced to rely increasingly on money lenders.

10.4 RECOMMENDATIONS OF THE NARASIMHAM COMMITTEE

The banking system is expected to reorient its approach to rural lending. "Going as Rural" could be the new market mantra. Rural market comprises 74% of the population, 41% of Middle class and 58% of disposable income. Consumer growth is taking place at a fast pace in 17,113 villages with a population of more than 5000. Of these, 9,989 villages are in Seven States, namely Andhra Pradesh, Bihar, Kerala, Maharhtra, Tamilnadu, Uttar Pradesh and West Bengal. Banks' approach to the rural lending will be guided mainly by commercial considerations in future.

Commercial Banks, Co-operatives and Regional Rural Banks are the three major Segments of rural financial sector in India. Rural financial system, in future has a challenging task of facing the drastic changes taking place in the banking sector, especially in the wake of economic liberalisation. There is an urgent need for rural financial system to enlarge their role functions and range of services offered so as to emerge as one stop destination for all types of credit requirements of people in rural/ semi-urban centers.

Barring commercial banks, the other rural financial institutions have a weak structural base and the issue of their strengthening requires to be taken up on priority. Co-operatives will have to be made viable by infusion of capital. Bringing all cooperative institutions under the regulatory control of RBI would help in better control and supervision over the functioning of these institutions. Similarly Regional Rural banks (RRBs) as a group needs to be made structurally stronger. It would be desirable if NABARD takes the initiative to consolidate all the RRBs into a strong rural development entity.

1Small Scale Industries have, over the last five decades, emerged as a major contributor to the economy, both in terms of employment generation and share in manufactured output and exports. SSIs account for 95% of the industrial units and contribute about 40% of the value addition in the manufacturing sector. There are more than 32 lac units spread all over the country producing over 7500 items and providing employment to more than 178 lac persons. The employment generation potential and favorable capital-output ratio would make small scale sector remain important for policy planners.

Removal of quantitative restrictions on a large number of items under the WTO and opening up of Indian market to greater international competition have thrown both challenges and opportunities for the SSI sector. Low capital base and weak management structure make these units vulnerable to external shocks, more easily. However the units which can adopt to the changing environment and show imagination in their business strategy will thrive in the new environment. Instead of following the narrow definition of SSI, based on the investment in fixed assets, there is a move to look at Small and Medium Enterprises (SME) as a group for policy thrust and encouragement. For SMEs, banks should explore the option of e-banking channels to develop web-based relationship banking models, which are customer-driven and more cost-effective. Government is already considering legislation for the development of SME sector to facilitate its orderly growth.

In the next ten years, SME sector will emerge more competitive and efficient and knowledge-based industries are likely to acquire greater prominence. SMEs will be dominating in industry segments such as Pharmaceuticals, Information Technology and Biotechnology. With SME sector emerging as a vibrant sector of the Indian economy, flow of credit to this sector would go up significantly. Banks will have to sharpen their skills for meeting the financial needs of this segment. Some of the Banks may emerge as niche players in handling SME finance. Flow of credit to this Sector will be guided purely by commercial considerations as Banks will find SMEs as an attractive business proposition.

The Annual Policy Statement of the Reserve Bank for 2005-06 had stated that:

- RBI would implement policies to encourage banks, which provide extensive services while dis-incentivising those, which are not responsive to the banking needs of the community, including the underprivileged.

- The nature, scope and cost of services would be monitored to assess whether there was any denial, implicit or explicit, of basic banking services to the common person.

In keeping with these objectives, the Reserve Bank's approach to Financial Inclusion is:

- Aim at 'connecting' people with the banking system and not just credit dispensation
- Aim at giving people access to the payments system
- Use multiple channels such as civil service organizations, NGOs, post offices, farmers' clubs, panchayats, MFIs, etc. to expand the outreach of banks
- Adopt a decentralized approach, which is state and region specific and has close involvement and cooperation between the respective State Governments and banks
- Make use of ICT using biometric smart cards and mobile hand held electronic devices for receipts and disbursement of cash by agents of banks, such as business facilitators/correspondents
- Astray Financial Inclusion as a viable business model and opportunity
- Aim at continuous evaluation, sharing of experiences, feedback and improvement

REVIEW QUESTIONS

1. What is the important role that the Commercial banks play in the economic development of a country?
2. How is a monetary policy implemented?
3. What are the sources of capital for commercial banks?
4. What do you mean by credit creation by commercial banks?
5. What are the non-institutional sources of credit?

Credit Creation 11

11.1 CONCEPT OF CREDIT CREATION

Credit creation refers to the unique power of the banks to expand secondary deposits as a multiple of their cash reserve either by giving loans and advances or by investing in securities. Central bank is the first source of money supply in the form of currency in circulation. The Reserve Bank of India is the note issuing authority of the country. The RBI ensures availability of currency to meet the transaction needs of the economy. The total volume of money in the economy should be adequate to facilitate the various types of economic activities such as production, distribution and consumption. The commercial banks are the second most important sources of money supply. The money that commercial banks supply is called credit money. The process of 'Credit Creation' begins with banks lending money out of primary deposits. Primary deposits are those deposits which are deposited in banks. In fact banks cannot lend the entire primary deposits as they are required to maintain a certain proportion of primary deposits in the form of reserves with the RBI under RBI and Banking Regulation Act. After maintaining the required reserves, the bank can lend the remaining portion of primary deposits. Here bank's lend the money and the process of credit creation starts. Suppose there are a number of Commercial Banks in the Banking System – Bank 1, Bank 2, Bank 3, and so on. To begin with let us suppose that an individual 'A' makes a deposit of ₹ 100 in bank 1. Bank '1' is required to maintain a Cash Reserve Requirement of 5% (Prevailing Rate) which is decided by the RBI's Monetary Policy from the deposits made by 'A'. Bank '1' is required to maintain a cash reserve of ₹ 5 (5% of 100). The bank has now lendable funds of ₹ 95 (100 – 5). Let the Bank '1' lend ₹ 95 to a borrower; say B. the method of lending is the same that is bank 1 opens an account in the name of the borrower cheque for the loan amount. At the end of the process of deposits and lending, the balance sheet of bank reads as given below:

It can be seen from the combined balance sheet that a primary deposits of ₹ 100 in a bank 1 leads to the creation of the total deposit of ₹ 2,000. The combined balance sheet also shows that the banks have created a total credit of ₹ 2,000 and maintained a total cash reserve of ₹ 100 which equals the primary deposits. The total deposit created by the commercial banks constitutes the money supply by the banks.

Basic Concepts of credit creation:

1. **Bank as a business institution:** Bank is financial institution which aims at maximizing profits through loans and advances.

2. **Bank deposits:** These are the basis of credit creation. They are of two types:-

(*a*) **Primary deposits:** When a bank accepts cash from the customers and opens a deposit account in his name is called primary or passive account.

(*b*) **Secondary or derivative deposits:** When a bank grants loans and advances, it instead of giving cash to borrower, opens a deposit account in his name. This is secondary deposit. It is also called derivative deposit since it has been derived from loan transaction of bank.

3. **Cash Reserve Ratio (CRR):** Banks keep a fraction of the total deposit for meeting the depositor's requirement for cash, which is called Cash Reserve Ratio. If there is high CRR there will be low credit creation and vice-versa.

4. **Excess Reserves:** These are the reserves that a bank holds above the required cash reserves. These are the reserves which are used to lend money or create credit. In other words those amount hold by banks to central bank is called excess reserve.

5. **Credit Multiplier:** It is the reciprocal of the Cash Reserve Ratio. It gives us the number of times a given amount of deposit can be multiplied by banks by the process of credit creation. If there is high multiplier there will be high credit creation and vice-versa.

Credit creation can be analysed in two ways:

(A) **Credit creation by a single bank:** In the single bank system only one bank operates cheques and cash deposits are to be made with this bank only. This can be explained with a hypothetical example. Suppose the CRR maintained by the banks is 20%. Now if a person (P) deposits ₹ 1000 in a bank, the bank doesn't keep entire amount as reserve for meeting the day to day expenses. Thus, after keeping ₹ 200 as reserve, the bank lends ₹ 800 to Q by opening a credit account in his name. Again keeping 20% of 800 (i.e. ₹ 160) the bank advances the remaining ₹ 640 to a person R. This process will continue till the time the primary deposits become 5 times the initial primary deposit (since credit multiplier is 5). This can also be explained with the help of a table.

Table 11.1 Credit Creation with the Help of a Single Bank

Rounds	Primary Deposits	Cash Reserve (CRR 20%)	Credit Creation
1. Person (P)	₹ 1000 (Initial Deposits)	₹ 200	₹ 800
2. Person (Q)	₹ 800	₹ 160	₹ 640
3. Person (R) ...	₹ 640 ...	₹ 128 ...	₹ 512 (Deposits Same Process Continues on Till Primary Total ₹ 5000) ...
Total	₹ 5000	₹ 1000	₹ 4000

$$m = 1/(0.2) = 5$$

Credit Multiplier:

The most common method used to measure the amount of credit creation or the increase in money supply is money multiplier. It helps us determine the maximum amount of money that a particular amount of deposit will yield. The money multiplier (m) is the inverse of the cash reserve ratio (r), PD is primary deposit.

$$m = 1/r *PD$$

Assumptions of credit multiplier are:

- Cash reserve ratio remains constant through all the stages of credit creation.
- There exists normal business condition in the country.
- The central bank doesn't adopt any credit control policy,

(B) **Credit Creation by Multiple Banking System:** In real world there are many banks in existence comprising multiple banking systems. A single bank cannot lend as much money that a multiple banking system can. The process of credit creation in multiple banking systems can be explained with the help of an example. Suppose the initial deposit is ₹ 1000 and the CRR is 20%. Bank A generates credit of ₹ 800 (200 kept as reserve), the bank creates derivative deposits of this amount. The borrowers make payments by cheque to people who are customers of bank B. Now the CRR being 20%, bank B has excess reserve of ₹ 640 (i.e. 800–160). Bank B creates credit to the extent of ₹ 640 and again the borrower makes payment to people of bank C by cheque. This will continue till the primary deposit of ₹ 1000 with bank a lead to creation of total deposit of ₹ 5000.

Table 11.2 Credit Creation with the help of Multiple Banks

Banks	Primary Deposits	Cash Reserves	Credit Creation (CRR = 20%)
A	₹ 1000	₹ 200	₹ 800
B	₹ 800	₹ 160	₹ 640
C	₹ 640	₹ 128	₹ 512
N	...	...	...
Total	₹ 5000	₹ 1000	₹ 4000

Destruction of Credit

Banks create credit by granting loans to public or creating derivative deposits. Similarly, the banks can destroy credit by reducing loans. The extent of destruction of credit depends upon the cash reserve ratio (CRR). Higher the cash reserve ratio higher will be the credit destruction and vice versa. This is so as if the CRR is high, more amounts of the deposits needed to be kept as reserve and hence the banks will have less amount of money to lend.

11.2 FACTORS INFLUENCING CREDIT CREATION

1. **Amount of Deposit:** The most important factor which decides credit creation is the amount of deposits made by the depositor. There is a direct relation between the two. Higher the amount of deposits higher will be the credit creation and vice versa.

2. **Cash Reserve Ratio (CRR):** There exists an indirect relationship between credit creation and CRR. Higher the CRR more will be the reserves to be maintained and less amount of credit will be created and vice versa.

3. **Banking Habits:** If people have well developed banking habits then most of the transactions of people will be through banks and thus deposits with bank will increase. This will lead to an increase in credit creation and vice versa.

4. **Willingness of People to Borrow:** Commercial banks may be having enough funds but if consumers are not willing to borrow no credit creation will take place. Thus if less number of people are willing to borrow money from banks then credit creation will be low and vice versa.

5. **Monetary Policy of Central Bank:** While credit is created by commercial banks, it is controlled by the Central Bank. Credit control is one important function of the central bank. Central Bank uses various methods of Credit Control from time to time and thus influences the banks to expand or contract credit.

6. **Availability of Securities:** Bank loans are granted against securities. Banks converts other forms of wealth into money. Thus the power of banks to turn other assets into money is restricted by the availability of securities.

7. **Credit Policy of other Banks:** All banks may not adopt same credit policy. If some banks decide not to utilise their full capacity for credit creation and keep large reserves, the credit creation in the country will be limited.

8. **Business Conditions:** Credit creation is further limited by business condition. During depression, when due to low profit expectation businessmen do not come forward to borrow from banks; credit creation will be small and vice versa. Hence, credit creation will be smaller during depression and higher during business prosperity.

11.3 BALANCE SHEET OF BANK

In financial accounting, a balance sheet or statement of financial position is a summary of the financial balances of a sole proprietorship, a business partnership, a corporation or other business organisation at the end of the year.

Banks take deposits from savers, paying interest on some of these accounts. They pass these funds on to borrowers, receiving interest on the loans. Their profits are derived from the spread between the rate they pay for funds and the rate they receive from borrowers. This ability to pool deposits from many sources that can be lent to many different borrowers creates the flow of funds inherent in the banking system.

By managing this flow of funds, banks generate profits, acting as the intermediary of interest paid and interest received and taking on the risks of offering credit.

A total overview of a bank's balance sheet: The table below ties together the bank's balance sheet with the income statement and displays the yield generated from earning assets and interest bearing deposits. Most banks provide this type of table in their annual reports. The following table represents the balance sheet of bank:

Table11.3 Balance Sheet of a Bank

Liabilities	Assets
Share Capital	Cash: (*a*) Cash in Hand (*b*) Cash with Central Bank (*c*) Cash with other Bank
Reserve Fund	Money at Call and short notice
Deposits: (*a*) Demand Deposit (*b*) Time Deposit (*c*) Saving Deposit	Bills Purchased or Discounted
Borrowing from other Banks	Investments
Acceptance and Endorsements	Loans and Advances
Other Liabilities	Acceptance and Endorsements
	Building and other fixed Assets
Total	Total

An asset is anything that can be sold for value. A liability is an obligation that must eventually be paid, and, hence, it is a claim on assets. The owner's equity in a bank is often referred to as bank capital, which is what is left when all assets have been sold and all liabilities have been paid. The relationship of the assets, liabilities, and owner's equity of a bank is shown by the following equation:

Bank Assets = Bank Liabilities + Bank Capital. A bank uses liabilities to buy assets, which earns its income. By using liabilities, such as deposits or borrowings to finance assets such as loans to individuals or businesses, or to buy interest earning securities, the owners of the bank can leverage their bank capital to earn much more than would otherwise be possible using only the bank's capital.

Assets: Uses of Funds

Assets earn revenue for the bank and include cash, securities, loans, and property and equipment that allow it to operate.

1. **Cash:** Cash is the most liquid but non-earning asset and is considered as the first line of defence. Every bank keeps certain amount of cash to meet the cash

requirement of their customers. In cash bank includes three items: (a) Cash (currency and coins) in hand; (b) Cash kept with central bank; and (c) Cash kept with other banks. One of the major services of a bank is to supply cash on demand, whether it is a depositor withdrawing money or writing a check, or a bank customer drawing on a credit line. A bank also needs funds to pay bills, but while bills are predictable in both amount and timing, cash withdrawals by customers are not.

2. **Money at Call and Short Notice:** These loans are for a period of one day to 15 days. Such loans are earning as well as highly liquid assets which can be converted into cash quickly and without loss. These assets are of two types: (*a*) Call and short notice loans to the brokers in the stock market (*b*) Short-term treasury bills i.e. borrowing of the government for very short period. Bills purchased or discounted: The bank utilises its funds in trade bills and treasury bills which it discounts. The amount of bills is collected by the bank on maturity. The commercial bank generally prefers these bills because of the following reasons: (*a*) they are highly negotiable and can be easily bought and sold. (*b*) They are eligible for rediscounting with the central bank in case the bank needs cash before the maturity of the bills. (*c*) They bring to the banks good earning in the form of interest. Thus the bills are considered the ideal bank assets because they satisfy both the objectives of liquidity and profitability.

3. **Investments:** Some funds are invested in profit-yielding assets, mainly the government securities. Government securities are relatively safe because there is certainty of repayment after maturity. Moreover, the banks can borrow from the central bank against these securities. The banks also invest in fixed interest yielding debentures or bonds of well-established industrial concerns. Such investments are highly shift able and yield good income. But they also involve risk.

4. **Loans and Advances:** Loans and advances are the most profitable and the least liquid assets of the banks. Banks provide loan and advances to the businessmen either through overdraft or by discounting of bills of exchange. The difference between loans and advances is that the advances are for the short period and loans are for relatively longer period. Loans and advances earn high rate of interest, carry greater risk and are generally non-shiftable. Thus, while loans and advances are mostly preferred by the banks because of their high yields, they are not popular from the consideration of liquidity and safety of the bank.

5. **Acceptance and Endorsements:** When a bank accepts or endorses exchange bills for its customers the amount of the bill becomes customer's liability and the bank's asset.

6. **Building and other fixed Assets:** Bank's assets also include the value of the moveable and immoveable properties of the bank, such as office buildings, furniture etc. These assets do not contribute to the income of the bank and constitute very small properties of the assets of the bank.

Liabilities: Sources of Funds

Liabilities are either the deposits of customers or money that banks borrow from other sources to use to fund assets that earn revenue. Deposits are like debt in that it is money that the banks owe to the customer but they differ from debt in that the addition or withdrawal of money is at the discretion of the depositor rather than dictated by contract.

1. **Share Capital:** A joint stock bank initially raises its funds by issuing share capital. In other words, share capital is contributions made by the shareholders. Share capital is in the form of

(*a*) Authorised Capital i.e. the maximum amount of capital that bank is authorised to raise in the form of share; (*b*) Issued Capital, i.e., the part of authorised capital that issued in the form of share for public subscription; (*c*) Subscribed Capital i.e. the part of issued capital that actually subscribed by the public and; (*d*) Paid-up Capital i.e. the part of subscribed capital that actually paid by the subscribers. It is actually paid-up share capital which constitutes the liability of the bank.

2. **Reserve Fund:** Reserve fund is the amount accumulated over the years out of undistributed profits. Normally all the profit of bank are not distributed to the shareholders, this undistributed profit is called reserve fund.

3. **Deposits:** Deposits from the public organisation constitute the major portion of the banks working capital. Various type of deposits accepted by the banks are (*a*) Demand deposits which can be withdrawn at any time and on which no interest is paid by banks (*b*) Time deposits which can be withdrawn after a fixed time and on which banks paid high rate of interest and (*c*) Saving deposits which can be withdrawn to the limited amount in a given period and on which some interest is paid. All deposits are the liabilities of the banks towards the depositors. But they are also assets of the banks because after keeping a fixed amount (CRR) the bank invests the balance amount in securities or advancing loans and earns income.

4. **Borrowing from Banks:** Sometimes banks borrow some amount from other banks to meet the high demand of money. Central bank is the lender of the last resort and provides the loan facilities to the all commercial banks in special circumstances. All these borrowings are the liability of the borrower banks.

5. **Acceptance and Endorsements:** The bank also creates liabilities by accepting or endorsing the bills of exchange on behalf of its customers. Through this facility the bank assumes the liability to pay the amount of the bill of maturity.

6. **Other Liabilities:** Some other miscellaneous liabilities are incurred by the banks. For example, acting as an agent the bank makes collections on behalf of its customers and thus creates liabilities.

11.3.1 Importance of Balance Sheet of the Banks

Balance sheet play very important role in Banks due to following reasons:

1. It represents the complete functioning of bank. It tells how the bank raises money and how it invests it.
2. It through light on the financial position (liquidity and solvency) of bank because it contains all information about the liabilities and assets of the bank.
3. The progress of the bank over time can be determined by comparing the balance sheet of different periods.
4. A comparison of balance sheet of different banks gives comparative picture of financial position of a bank.
5. It brings out an important fact that banks buy assets primarily by creating liabilities in the form of deposits. These deposits are simply debt claims against the assets of the banks.
6. It gives an estimate of the confidence of the public in the bank. Increasing saving or time deposits of the bank represent that the confidence of the people in the bank is also increasing.
7. It shows the loans and investment policy of the bank.
8. It provides information about the interest of various persons, such as shareholders, debtors, creditors etc.

REVIEW QUESTIONS

1. Discuss the basic concepts of credit creation.
2. What are the factors influencing credit creation?
3. Discuss about the Balance sheet of a bank.
4. What is the importance of the Balance sheet of banks?
5. What do you mean by destruction of credit?

Banker-Customer Relationship

12

12.1 INTRODUCTION

Customer relationship management (CRM) is a technology for managing all your company's relationships and interactions with customers and potential customers. The goal is simple: Improve business relationships. A CRM system helps companies stay connected to customers, streamline processes, and improve profitability. When people talk about CRM, they are usually referring to a CRM system, a tool that helps with contact management, sales management, productivity and more. A CRM solution helps you focus on your organisation's relationships with individual people including customers, service users, colleagues, or suppliers- throughout your lifecycle with them, including finding new customers, winning their business, and providing support and additional services throughout the relationship.

12.1.1 Methods Used by Banks to Increase Customer Retention (CRM)

Today, anyone with a Smart phone or computer can compare rates, read reviews and open accounts in a matter of minutes. To remain competitive, banks need to develop a customer-centric retention approach that incorporates data insights, personnel training and added product value. In banking, a well-designed CRM can serve as the foundation for this transformation. With these some tips, banks can gain valuable insight into the benefits of CRM in banking and improve customer service and retention. According to Dave Horstein there are 10 methods to increase CRM in banks. These methods are like as:

1. **Gain a 360 Degree View:** Banking CRMs provide a 360-degree view of customer data, including accounts, service inquiries and marketing segmentation. A well-designed system will provide an instantaneous, at-a-glance view of a customer, allowing employees to:

- Provide faster service to customers
- Make informed decisions
- Understand how a customer prefers to communicate
- View recent interactions the customer has had with the bank

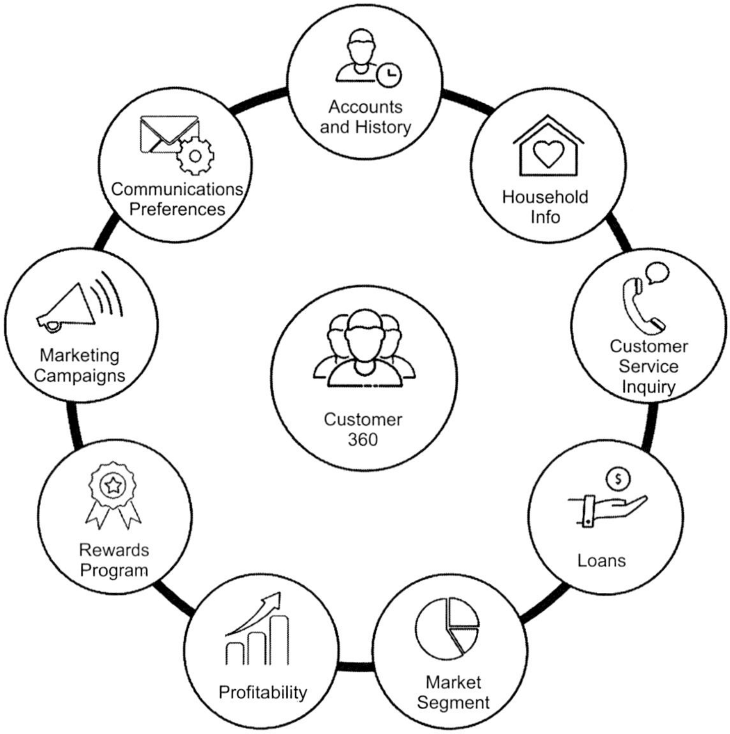

Fig. 12.1

Essentially, a CRM in banking provides a 360 degree view of the customer relationship to front-line employees, improving your services and thus improving customer retention.

2. **Provide Top-Notch Service:** There are multiple communication channels available to customers. Each point of contact provides an opportunity to address questions, complaints, or compliments. Ensuring all customer-facing personnel have access to the banking CRM allows them to quickly capture their customer interactions, record follow-ups and provide fast resolution.

Since customers have embraced social media as a platform to leave reviews or vent frustrations, marketing departments have been looking for ways to identify and respond to customer sentiments. Utilizing CRM as a tool to quickly identify and respond to customer posts will make a tangible impact on retention.

3. **Offer Self-Service Options:** Innovative banks are giving their customers more opportunities to access knowledge-based articles, submit questions/issues online or interact with a customer service representative or catboats. Through the use of a self-service portal, customers are able to access self-help resources; view data stored in CRM (their service inquiries, contact information and account summaries) and communicate with their bank. As an added benefit, portals reduce the amount of time

personnel need to spend supporting customers, since many simple banking activities can be performed on them.

4. **Promote Rewards:** Customer-facing banking for CRM users should have visibility into customer rewards balances, whether it be available cash back, travel miles or statement credits. Consider adding a validation and reminder of rewards balances into customer interaction scripts and coaching. Customers that leverage rewards programs gain additional value in their relationship with their bank and are less likely to leave for a competitor.

5. **Identify the Next Best Product:** Leveraging the power of a CRM database, banks can make highly-educated product recommendations to customers. For example, Hitachi Solutions for Banking includes powerful tools to help bankers to understand the most relevant product, to offer a customer based on their demographics, current product mix and life circumstances. Every bank should establish a formula for identifying the next best products for their customers. Storing the next best product for each customer in your CRM for banking will give employees a great source of referrals. Additionally, providing this tailored experience will result in a deeper relationship between a bank and its customers.

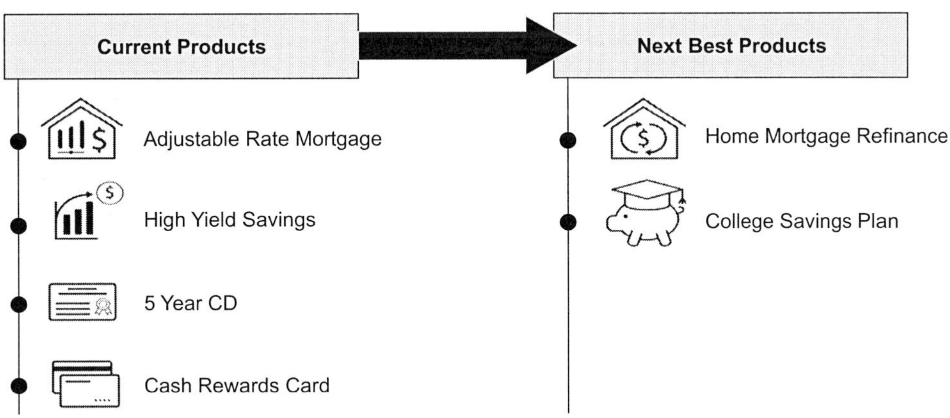

Fig. 12.2

A comprehensive banking solution CRM will include logic that recommends the next best product, given a customer's current product mix.

6. **Cross-Sell/Up-sell:** Whereas the next best product concept uses an algorithm to determine a customer's most relevant next product need, a well-designed bank CRM system will offer recommendations of complimentary products to customers, based on product relationships configured by a CRM administrator. This provides personnel with additional opportunities to interact with customers and grow their product mix.

7. **Execute Tailored Marketing Campaigns:** Through integration with an automated platform, such as Click Dimensions, marketing departments can create highly customized e-mail campaigns to increase customer awareness, reinforce brand

integrity and inform customers of products and promotions straight from your CRM for banking. With the ability to segment, score and analyze customer data, you can offer targeted communications regarding:

- Rate changes
- New products
- Products targeted towards specific life events
- Rewards redemptions

Communicating targeted information, based on a customer's life situation and current financial needs, increases the likelihood of engagement.

8. **Take Action through Predictive Analytics:** Over the past few years banks have been busy building rich CRM databases that enable them to better understand their customers. The next evolution of business intelligence involves deep analysis of existing data to identify trends, predict customer behavior and proactively take action.

9. **Collaborate with Colleagues:** Whether by phone or personally, customers will often need to interact with multiple employees regarding a product or issue. Modern bank CRM systems include powerful collaboration functionality that empowers banking teams to seamlessly collaborate on customer issues, sales opportunities and referrals, improving overall customer service. For example of providing a smooth transition for customers include:

- A customer service representative takes a call regarding an incorrect balance shown on the customer's most recent statement. The representative, unable to make the necessary changes due to security, captures the statements made by the customer in CRM, attaches the latest bank statement to the customer's case and assigns it to her supervisor. Upon receiving the transferred call, the supervisor is immediately able to see all comments made by the customer to the customer service representative and is able to quickly resolve the issue.

10. **Understand the Voice of the Customer:** When it comes to retention, listening to and acting on customer feedback goes a long way. CRM for banking systems can include survey functionality, offering institutions a way to design surveys, distribute them to a targeted audience and track responses directly within the application, all tied back to the customer record. Surveys should be conducted regularly to maintain an understanding of the customer-base.

12.2 BANKER-CUSTOMER RELATIONSHIP

Today, many businesses such as banks, insurance companies and other service providers realize the importance of Customer Relationship Management (CRM) and its potential to help them acquire new customers retain existing ones and maximize.

Debtor and Creditor: The true relationship between a banker and the customer is primarily of a debtor and creditor. When customer deposits money with a bank, the bank then is the debtor and the customer is the creditor. The customer expects from the bank that:

- His money will be kept safe by the bank.
- It will be returned on demand in business hours.
- The money would earn some form of return such as interest.

The position is reversed if the customer is advanced loan then the banker becomes creditor and the customer is the debtor.

Principal and Agent: The special relationship between the banker and the customer is that of **principal** and **agent**. The customer deposits cheques, drafts, dividends for collection with the bank. He also gives instructions to the bank to purchase securities, pay insurance premium, installments of loans etc. on his behalf. When the bank performs such services, he becomes an agent of his customer.

Bailer and Bailment: The relationship between banker and customer can be that of Bailor and Bailee. Bailment is a contract for delivering goods by one party to another to be held in trust for a specific period and returned when the purpose is ended. A bailment is delivery of goods on trust. During certain circumstances banker becomes bailee. When he receives gold ornaments and important documents for safe custody he takes charge of it as bailee and not trustee or agent. He cannot make use of them as he is bound to return the identical articles on demand. So, when a customer gives a sealed box to the bank for safe keeping, the customer became the bailor and the bank became the bailee. Bailor (customer) is the party that delivers property to another. Bailee (bank) is the party to whom the property is delivered. The bank charges a very nominal amount for the safe custody of the valuables from his customer.

Relationship of Pledger and Pledgee: The relationship between customer and banker can be that of Pledger and Pledgee. This happens when customer pledges (promises) certain assets or security with the bank in order to get a loan. In this case, the customer becomes the Pledger and the bank becomes the Pledgee. Under this agreement, the assets or security will remain with the bank until a customer repays the loan. The pledged goods are to be returned intact to the pledge/ pawner after the debt is repaid by him.

Mortgage and Mortgagor: The relation between a banker as mortgagee and his customer as mortgagor arises when the latter executes a mortgage deed in respect of his immovable property in favour of the bank or deposits the title deeds of his property with the bank to create an equitable mortgage as security for an advance.

Lessee and Lessor: When a customer hires a locker in the bank's safe deposit vault, the bank undertakes to take necessary precaution for the safety of the articles in the locker. The relation between the parties is that of a lessor and lessee.

Guarantor and Guarantee: a bank as guarantor gives guarantee to its customer by issuing a 'letter of credit'. It is a kind of credit facility to its customer to facilitate international trade. A bank guarantee contains an undertaking to pay the amount without any demur on mere demand of the PRINCIPLES amount on the ground for non-performance or breach of contract.

Bank as a Trustee: The bank acts as a trustee for his customer in those cases where he accepts securities and other valuables for safe custody. In such cases, the customer continues to be the owner of the valuables deposited with the bank.

Obligation to Honour Cheques: Bank accepts the deposits from the customer with an obligation to repay it to him on demand or otherwise. The drawee of a cheque having sufficient funds of the drawer in his hands properly applicable to the payment of such cheque must pay the cheque when duly required so to do and in default of such payment, must compensate the drawer for any loss or damage caused by such default.

Obligation to Maintain Secrecy and Disclosure of Information Required by Law: The banker is under an obligation to take utmost care in keeping secrecy about the accounts of the customers since it may affect his reputation, credit-worthiness and business. It was firmly laid down and in India it was made compulsory after 1970. The duty to maintain secrecy will be continuing even after the account is closed or the death of the customer.

Obligation to Keep a Proper Record of Transactions: The banker must keep a proper record of transactions of the customer. If he wrongly credits the account of the customer and intimates him with the same and the customer acts upon the intimation bonafide and withdraws cash the banker cannot contend that the entries were wrongly made. He shall not succeed in recovery of money from the customer.

Obligation to abide by the Instructions of the Customer: The banker must abide by any express instructions of the customer provided; it is within the scope of their banker-customer relationship. In the absence of any express instructions, the banker must according to prevailing usages at the place where the banker conducts his business.

Relationship of Licensor and Licensee: The relationship between banker and customer can be that of a Licensor and Licensee. This happens when the banker gives a (sale) deposit locker to the customer. So, the banker will become the Licensor and the customer will become the Licensee.

Relationship of Hypothecator and Hypothecatee: The relationship between customer and banker can be that of Hypothecator and Hypotheatee. This happens when the customer hypothecates (pledges) certain movable or non-movable property or assets with the banker in order to get a loan. In this case, the customer became the Hypothecator and the Banker became the Hypothecatee.

Relationship of Trustee and Beneficiary: A trustee holds property for the beneficiary and the profit earned from this property belongs to the beneficiary. If the customer deposits securities or valuables with the banker for safe custody, banker becomes a trustee of his customer. The customer is the beneficiary so the ownership remains with the customer.

Relationship of Agent and Principal: The banker acts as an agent of the customer (principal) by providing the following agency services:

1. Buying and selling securities on his behalf,
2. Collection of cheques, dividends, bills or promissory notes on his behalf.
3. Acting as a trustee, attorney, executor, correspondent or representative of a customer.
4. Banker as an agent performs many other functions such as payment of insurance premium, electricity and gas bills, handling tax problems, etc.

Relationship of Advisor and Client: When a customer invests in securities, banker acts as an advisor. The advice can be given officially or unofficially. While giving advice the banker has to take maximum care and caution. Here, the banker is an advisor and the customer is a client.

Other Relationships: Other miscellaneous banker-customer relationships are as follows:

Obligation to honour cheques: As long as there is sufficient balance in the account of the customer, the banker must honour all his cheques. The cheques must be complete and in proper order. They must be presented within six months from the date of issue. However, the banker can refuse to honour the cheques only in certain cases.

Secrecy of Customer's Account: When a customer opens an account in a bank, the banker must not give information about the customer's account to others.

Banker's Right to Claim Incidental Charges: A banker has a right to charge a commission, interest or other charges for the various services given by him to the customer, e.g., an overdraft facility.

Law of Limitation on Bank Deposits: Under the law of limitation, generally, a customer gives up the right to recover the amount due at a banker if he has not operated his account since last 10 years.

12.3 CUSTOMER RELATIONSHIP MANAGEMENT (CRM)

Today, many businesses such as banks, insurance companies and other service providers realise the importance of Customer Relationship Management (CRM) and its potential to help them acquire new customers retain existing ones and maximise their lifetime values. Customer relationship management (CRM) is a model for managing a company's interactions with their current and future customers. It involves using technology to organise, automate and synchronise sales, marketing, customer service and technical support. It enables Business firms to:

- Understand the customer.
- Retain customers through better customer experience.
- Attract new customer.

- Win new clients and contracts.
- Increase profitably.
- Decrease customer management costs.

In banking, CRM is a sound business strategy to identify the bank's most profitable customer's prospects and devote time and attention to expand account relationships with those customers through individualised marketing, re-pricing, discretionary decision making and customized service-all delivered through the various sales channels that the bank uses. The idea of CRM is that it helps businesses to use technology and human resources gain insight into the behaviour of customers and the value of those customers. Competition and globalisation of banking services are forcing banks to be productive and profitable. To retain High Net Worth, individual's banks should focus strongly on relationship management with customers. Innovative Customer Relationship Management (CRM) strategies and cutting edge software can help, to a great extent, in achieving the desired results.

Steps Involved in CRM: For great and effective CRM an organisation should follow some steps. Some steps are as like:

First, bank decides what kind of customer information he is looking and what importance for bank is. Second, bank must look into all of the different ways of information about customers that comes into a business. Third, where and how this data is stored and how it is currently used information. Fourth, collected data flows between operational systems and analytical systems that can help sort through these records for patterns. Fifth, data analysts should go through the data, to obtain an emphasised view of each customer and pinpoint areas where better services are they needed.

12.4 UTILITY OF CRM IN BANKS

Campaign Management: Banks need to identify customers, tailor products and services to meet their needs and sell these products to customers. CRM achieves this through Campaign Management by analysing data from banks internal applications or by importing data from external applications to evaluate customer profitability and designing comprehensive customer profiles. Based on these profiles, banks can identify the most profitable/gainful customers, customer segments and execute targeted, personalised multi-channel marketing campaigns to reach these customers and maximize the lifetime value of those relationships.

360 Degree View of the Company: This means that whoever the bank speaks to, the bank is aware of the interaction. Removal of inconsistencies of data makes the client interaction processes smooth and efficient, thus leading to enhanced customer satisfaction.

Enhanced Productivity: CRM can help in enhanced productivity of customers, partners and employees.

Centralized Sales Home Page: CRM can provide a single view where Sales Mangers and agents can get all the most up-to-date information in one place, including opportunity, account, news and expense report information. This would make sales decision fast and consistent.

Activity Management: It helps managers to assign and track the activities of various members. Thus improved transparency leads to improved efficiency.

Operational Efficiency Removal: CRM can help in Strategy Formulation to eliminate current operational inefficiencies. An effective CRM solution supports all channels of customer interaction. It also links these customer touch points to an operations center and connects the operations center with the relevant internal and external business partners.

12.5 BENEFITS OF CRM FOR BANKING BUSINESS

One of the unique challenges of business banking in a digital world is to meeting customer expectations. With all that's expected of banks, a Customer Relationship Management (CRM) solution is no longer optional. It's critical to your success. A great CRM can help any bank/company market to capture new customers, close the deal and provide excellent customer service, but the benefits of a CRM in banking business are especially lucrative. Here are some of those benefits and how you can become the bank that customers love with the right banking CRM solution.

Benefits of CRM in Banking: There are various benefits of CRM. Some are as like:

Boosted Sales: On an average, business of banks loan outstanding money increased more than 15 times in comparisons to consumer lend money. The stakes are high if you want to earn those big business accounts and you need a great CRM to launch that you ahead of the competition in present era. Identification, nurture and convert leads into deals ahead than the others even they know what will hit them.

Increased Lead Conversion: Good CRM is helpful to increase land conversion. Implementing CRM in banking enables deeper and more customised customer interactions. CRM in banking with new technology, each department of bank can access the same information across to all customer profiles, while setting up individual triggers for offering additional services. Employees can look up rich customer profiles compiled from marketing, sales and service data to identify new opportunities to convert leads. They won't have to start from scratch every time an interdepartmental lead that comes through the funnel, so they'll create a seamless and personalised experience for the customer and a streamlined conversion process for you.

Personalised Customer Journeys: Customer retention play a critical role in bank business growing. A CRM for financial services can help your bank with a steady stream of new and ready leads. A great banking CRM allows you to create reports and graphic representations of key data points and trends, which makes it easy to share with your team, drive your marketing strategy and keep your customers happy all the while.

A bank's CRM solution can help keep track of customer behaviors, predict needs and automatically send out suggestions for how the bank can fulfill those needs with a tailored product offering.

Increased Productivity and Efficiency: In the present era CRM help to cut costs by minimizing repetitive administrative tasks, streamlining proposals and keeping your sales team in the loop with just a few clicks. With the right technology, bankers are capable of handling more accounts in less time.

More Efficient Communication: A CRM can help you monitor the web for conversations about your brands and products. It can also make it easier for you to respond quickly in a way that puts out the fire instead of stoking the flames.

Inter-Department Data Tracking: In the present era marketing is a data-driven field. The right CRM can track data from several departments, so a call to customer service or a lost account becomes an opportunity to prepare potential customers to love banking with you before they ever speak to a banker.

Better Service: With the right and latest banking technology, you may be able to offer quality and advanced services such as mobile check deposits, fraud alerts, paperless statements, customer service chat and more. You may already offer many of these digital services. Imagine what you could do if you paired them with a great CRM that could keep track of all of your customer interactions.

Improved Customer Experience: Even if your bank has only a few dozen distinct products, than your customer service depends on answering questions and solving problems quickly, without handing the customer off to department after department. With a good banking CRM, you can easily keep all departments on the same page and quickly provide each customer with solutions.

Increased Customer Loyalty: Your customers helps to run businesses, so asking them to repeat their issue or customer history every time, they speak to a new representative stretches their patience and wasting your and theirs time. Through CRM you can instantly pull up every service ticket, purchase and data point at the precise moment customers need help so you can swoop in to save the day. When you use a CRM solution to stay on top of customer service tickets and personalize your response, you can turn issues into opportunities for increasing loyalty and satisfaction.

12.6 DISADVANTAGES OF CRM

There are some disadvantages of CRM are like as:

Record Loss: There is a fear of the loss of data due to customers. They can transfer the data to their rival's and they can misuse these data against them.

Training: Banks have to give training to their employees for these purposes and for this they have to spend a lot of money for this purpose.

Require Additional Data: They required additional data base for this and they have also required additional workforce and resources.

Require Continuous Maintenance: They required continuous maintenance or updating the CRM data and required time to time some additional information from the customers and they have to update data according to customers test and preferences.

Costly Maintenance and Up-Gradation: It is very costly to maintain and updating of data in the origination.

Difficult to Integrate: Deferent department of origination have different type of data. To integrate these different types of data with all department is very difficult.

REVIEW QUESTIONS

1. What is Customer Relationship Management?
2. What are the methods used by banks to increase customer retension?
3. "Banking CRMs provide a 360-degree view of customer data, including accounts, service inquiries and marketing segmentation." Explain this statement.
4. What is Top-Notch Service?
5. Explain the banker-customer relationship as a -- debtor-creditor relationship

Know Your Customer

13

13.1 INTRODUCTION

KYC means "Know Your Customer". It is a process by which banks obtain information about the identity and address of the customers. This process helps to ensure that banks' services are not misused. The KYC procedure is to be completed by the banks while opening accounts and also periodically updating the same. Know Your Customer, alternatively known as know your client or simply KYC, is the process of a business verifying the identity of its clients and assessing their suitability, along with the potential risks of illegal intentions towards the business relationship. The term is also used to refer to the bank regulations and anti-money laundering regulations which govern these activities. Know your customer processes — are also employed by companies of all sizes for the purpose of ensuring their proposed customers, agents, consultants, or distributors are anti-bribery compliant. Banks, insurers, export creditors and other financial institutions are increasingly demanding that customers provide detailes which are due diligence information.

To open a bank account, one needs to submit an Aadhaar/enrolment number and PAN as 'proof of identity' and 'proof of address' together with a recent photograph.

If you do not provide the required documents for KYC, the bank may not be able to open your account.

If you have opened an account with a bank, which is KYC compliant, then for opening another account with the same bank, furnishing of documents is not necessary.

Full KYC exercise is necessary for Credit/Debit/Smart/for purchaser of Gift Cards and also in respect of add-on/supplementary cards.

KYC exercise needs to be done for all those who want to make domestic remittances of ₹ 50,000 and above and all foreign remittances.

Demand Draft/Payment Order/Travellers Cheques for ₹ 50,000 and above can be issued only by way of debiting the customer's account or against cheques.

All customers who do not have accounts with the banks (known as walk-in customers) have to produce proof of identity and address while purchasing third party products from banks if the transaction is for ₹ 50,000 and above. KYC exercise may not be necessary for bank's own customers for purchasing third party products. However, instructions to make payment by debit to customers' accounts or against cheques for remittance of funds/issue of travellers' cheques, sale of gold/silver/platinum and the requirement of quoting PAN number for transactions of ₹ 50,000 and above would be applicable to purchase of third party products from banks by bank's customers as also to walk-in customers.

Banks are required to periodically update KYC records. This is a part of their ongoing due diligence on bank accounts. The periodicity of such updation would vary from account to account or categories of accounts depending on the bank's perception of risk. Periodical updation of records also helps prevent frauds in customer accounts.

Banks are required to classify the customers into 'low', 'medium' and 'high' categories depending on their AML risk assessment.

Different periodicities have been prescribed for updation of KYC records depending on the risk perception of the bank. KYC is required to be done once in every two years for high risk customers, once in every eight years for medium risk customers and once in every ten years for low risk customers. This exercise would involve all formalities normally taken at the time of opening the account.

During the process, the following are carried out.

- PAN verification from the verification facility available with the issuing authority
- Authentication, of Aadhaar Number already available with the RE with the explicit consent of the customer in applicable cases.
- In case identification information available with Aadhaar does not contain current address an Officially Valid Documents (OVDs) containing current address may be obtained.
- Certified copy of OVD containing identity and address shall be obtained at the time of periodic updation from individuals not eligible to obtain Aadhaar, except from individuals who are categorised as 'low risk'. In case of low risk customers when there is no change in status with respect to their identities and addresses, a self-certification to that effect shall be obtained.
- Customers who are minors have to submit fresh photograph on becoming major.
- REs may not insist on the physical presence of the customer for the purpose of furnishing OVD or furnishing consent for Aadhaar authentication/Offline Verification unless there are sufficient reasons that physical presence of the account holder/holders is required to establish their bona-fides. Normally, OVD/Consent forwarded by the customer through mail/post, etc., shall be acceptable.

Proof of Identity and Proof of Address

- For an individual who is eligible for enrolment of Aadhaar, the Aadhaar number; the Permanent Account Number (PAN) or Form No. 60 as defined in Income-tax Rules, 1962, as amended from time to time is required.
- Where an Aadhaar number has not been assigned to an individual, proof of application of enrolment for Aadhaar shall be obtained wherein the enrolment is not older than 6 months and in case PAN is not submitted, certified copy of an Officially Valid Document (OVD) containing details of identity and address and one recent photograph shall be obtained.
- For residents of the State of Jammu and Kashmir or Assam or Meghalaya, and who do not submit Aadhaar or proof of application of enrolment for Aadhaar, the following shall be obtained:

  (*i*) Certified copy of an OVD containing details of identity and address

  (*ii*) One recent photograph

  The Government of India has notified following documents as 'Officially Valid Documents (OVDs)'.

  - Passport,
  - Driving Licence,
  - Voters' Identity Card
  - PAN Card
  - Aadhaar Card issued by UIDAI and
  - Job card issued by NREGA duly signed by an officer of the State Government
  - Letter issued by the National Population Register containing details of name and address

In case the identity information relating to the Aadhaar number or Permanent Account Number submitted by the customer does not have current address, any of the following documents is to be submitted.

(*i*) Utility bill which is not more than two months old of any service provider (electricity, telephone, post-paid mobile phone, piped gas, water bill)

(*ii*) Property or Municipal tax receipt

(*iii*) Pension or family pension payment orders (PPOs) issued to retired employees by Government Departments or Public Sector Undertakings, if they contain the address

(*iv*) Letter of allotment of accommodation from employer issued by State Government or Central Government Departments, statutory or regulatory bodies, public sector undertakings, scheduled commercial banks, financial institutions and listed companies and leave and licence agreements with such employers allotting official accommodation

Provided further that the customer shall submit Aadhaar or OVD updated with current address within a period of three months of submitting the above documents.

You can still open a bank account known as 'Small Account' by submitting your recent photograph and putting your signature or thumb impression in the presence of the bank official if you have no documents. The Small Account entails the following limitations:

- the aggregate of all credits in a financial year does not exceed rupees one lakh;
- the aggregate of all withdrawals and transfers in a month does not exceed rupees ten thousand; and
- the balance at any point of time does not exceed rupees fifty thousand.

The account shall remain operational initially for a period of twelve months which can be extended for a further period of twelve months, provided the account holder applies and furnishes evidence of having applied for any of the OVDs during the first twelve months of the opening of the said account.

You can open a bank account in Chennai even if your permanent address is in New Delhi and you do not have a proof of address for your Chennai address. In that case, you can submit an officially valid document (proof of address document) of your New Delhi address together with a declaration about your Chennai address, for communication purposes. However, you need to submit Aadhaar or OVD updated with current address within a period of three months of submitting the above documents.

It is possible to transfer an account from one branch to another branch of the same bank. There is no need for KYC exercise again to transfer a bank account from one branch to another branch of the same bank. However, if there is a change of address, then you would have to submit a declaration about the current address. If the address in the 'officially valid documents'/ 'proof of address' is neither permanent nor current address, a new proof of address would be required within three months.

In case of opening an account in another bank, however, you would have to undergo KYC exercise afresh.

The 'Small Accounts' have certain limitations such as:

- Balance in such accounts at any point of time should not exceed ₹ 50,000
- Total credits in one year should not exceed ₹ 1,00,000
- Total withdrawal and transfers should not exceed ₹ 10,000 in a month.
- Foreign remittance shall not be allowed to be credited into the account

Such accounts remain operational initially for a period of twelve months and thereafter, for a further period of twelve months, if the holder of such an account provides evidence to the bank of having applied for any of the officially valid documents within twelve months of the opening of such account. The bank will review such account after twenty four months to see if it requires such relaxation and introduction is not required.

PAN number needs to be quoted for transactions, such as, account opening, transactions above ₹ 50,000 (whether in cash or non-cash), etc. A full list of transaction where PAN number needs to be quoted can be accessed from website of Income Tax Department.

Payment of cheques/drafts/pay orders/banker's cheques, if they are presented beyond the period of three months from the date of such instruments, shall not be made.

13.2 KYC PROCESS IN BANKS

Banks have to perform thorough investigation and identity verification before client on boarding in order to mitigate risk associated with money laundering. They do it with different levels of customer due diligence process depending on the risk profile of a potential client.

Customer due diligence: Customer due diligence is the procedure to establishing trust in a client and assessing associated risk. Customer Due Diligence can help banking and financial organizations mitigate risk presented by money laundering attempts from Politically Exposed Persons (PEPs), terrorist organizations or criminals.

Customer due diligence can be performed at three levels:

Simplified due diligence: when risk of money laundering is low and a full due diligence is not required.

Basic due diligence: basic information obtained for all customers for identity verification and assessment of the risk associated.

Enhanced due diligence: high risk customers are processed with enhanced due diligence, in which additional information is collected to provide a deeper understanding of customer activity to mitigate associated risks.

KYC Norms in Banking: Due to their importance in economic stability, banking and financial services firms are one of the highly important and regulated institutions. These institutions are not only the potential targets of fraud and scams, but also the potential channels for getting illegal or tax-unpaid money laundered. No wonder government regulators lay strict guidelines for them to operate.

Usually a superior body likes a central bank, Federal Reserve, etc. sets forth the KYC norms in banking, which may differ from one country to another. In many countries, KYC can be a part of more comprehensive regulations. For example, in the United States Customer Identification Program (CIP) is a requirement and provision of the USA Patriot Act, in which financial institutions need to verify the identity of individuals wishing to conduct financial transactions with them.

KYC norms in banking may differ from country to country, however they typically involves the following formalities:

KYC Process in Banks: Banks have to process KYC formalities as defined by the regulatory requirements. There may be variations how banks in a particular jurisdiction process the KYC formalities, it typically involves the following:

- Collection of documents and proof of identity, address (normally done with the photocopies of the government issued IDs)
- Establishment and verification of customer identity
- Screening the identity information against watchlists, political exposure, etc.
- Understanding the customer profile and nature of his/her activities to ensure that source of customer's money is not illegal.
- Assessment of the risks and creation of the customer profile on the basis of risks assessed.
- Monitoring of the transactions performed by the customer in accordance with the risk profile and expected behaviour.

13.3 IMPORTANCE OF KYC IN BANKING SECTOR

Following are the reasons why KYC is extremely important in banking sector:

- Some people may not want to show how much money they are earning, even if they are doing it legally, especially, when their income attracts high taxes imposed by the government. They can perform high value transactions in cash, which stays undetected from government's tax collection agencies. These individuals can use bank or financial institutions to clean their money with money laundering tactics. This activity results in loss of revenue and eventually hindered growth of the country.
- If source of the funds is illegal, people may use money laundering tactics to make this illegally obtained money legal.

Undetected money earned out of criminal activities can make way to terror funding and/or similar activities after laundering. It compromises the national security.

Performing KYC ensures compliance to regulatory requirements and facilitates a standard and easy on-boarding process for new clients.

KYC-done customers results in higher level of trust, efficient monitoring of customer behaviour as per their risk profile and standardisation of customer identification /authentication.

e-KYC and Working of e-KYC: e-KYC refers to electronic KYC. e-KYC is possible only for those who have Aadhaar numbers. While using e-KYC service, you have to authorise the Unique Identification Authority of India (UIDAI), by explicit consent, to release your identity/address through biometric authentication to the bank branches/ business correspondent (BC). The UIDAI then transfers your data comprising name, age, gender and photograph of the individual, electronically to the bank/BC. Information thus provided through e-KYC process is permitted to be treated as an 'Officially Valid

Document' under PML Rules and is a valid process for KYC verification. Accounts opened using OTP based e-KYC, in non-face-to-face mode are subject to the following conditions:

Nowadays, e-KYC or electronic KYC is taking over manual KYC methods, in which verification and screening of a customer used to be performed with manual methods. In the last couple of decades, biometrics has emerged as a potential solution of the problems associated with traditional identification, authentication and verification methods. Banks have to spend a lot of time and resource to verify the documents and IDs provided by a client. In some cases, accessing database of issuing authority (which is often a government agency), may not be easy, especially when you have to make manual requests.

Biometrics can help overcome problems associated with manual KYC procedures.

1. Mitigate the problem of forged or manipulated IDs
2. Biometrics require a real person to present for a biometric scan
3. Since it is done electronically, it is quick and efficient
4. There are virtually no chances of human errors
5. There must be a specific consent from the customer for authentication through OTP.
6. The aggregate balance of all the deposit accounts of the customer shall not exceed rupees one lakh. In case, the balance exceeds the threshold, the account shall cease to be operational, till CDD as mentioned at (v) below is complete.
7. The aggregate of all credits in a financial year, in all the deposit accounts taken together, shall not exceed rupees two lakh.
8. As regards borrower accounts, only term loans shall be sanctioned. The aggregate amount of term loans sanctioned shall not exceed rupees sixty thousand in a year.
9. Accounts, both deposit and borrower, opened using OTP based e-KYC shall not be allowed for more than one year within which identification as per Section 16 is to be carried out.
10. If the CDD procedure as mentioned above is not completed within a year, in respect of deposit accounts, the same shall be closed immediately. In respect of borrower accounts no further debits shall be allowed.
11. A declaration shall be obtained from the customer to the effect that no other account has been opened nor will be opened using OTP based KYC in non-face-to-face mode with any other RE. Further, while uploading KYC information to CKYCR, REs shall clearly indicate that such accounts are opened using OTP based e-KYC and other REs shall not open accounts based on the KYC information of accounts opened with OTP based e-KYC procedure in non-face-to-face mode.

12. REs shall have strict monitoring procedures including systems to generate alerts in case of any non-compliance/violation, to ensure compliance with the above mentioned conditions.

Biometrics has already been deployed in many identification and authentication applications. Biometrics not only makes a perfect use case in banking KYC requirement, it also enhances overall security and efficiency in banking operations. In fact biometrics for banks and financial institutions has already been deployed by many leading banks around the globe.

Following are the some of the methods used for biometric KYC in banks:

KYC biometric machine: KYC can be performed on a biometric recognition setup configured to scan modalities like face, iris or fingerprint recognition. KYC biometric machine allow bank employees to take the new applicants to quickly take through the otherwise lengthy and bothersome KYC process. Existing customers, who were processed with manual KYC mechanism, can also be revivified with KYC biometric machine.

KYC biometric machine includes a biometric scanner, e.g. fingerprint scanner, camera, etc. a computer system that connects to the scanner and connection to a database of established identities (e.g. civil biometric database, watch-list, etc.).

KYC biometric machine connects to a biometric database of already established identities with the help of the software running on the connected computer system. Biometric KYC fetches the identity details like name, date of birth, address, etc. out of the database, and verifies against what the customer claims.

Many banks and financial services companies have already started performing KYC with KYC biometric machines or similar setup, in which customers can just have their biometric scanned to perform KYC instantly.

KYC Kit: In many scenarios, banks and financial may have to perform on-site or remote KYC. A financial firm can also do it for the sake of customer convenience. In such scenarios, a KYC kit can be useful. KYC kit (also known as e-KYC kit or biometric KYC kit) is a set of equipment to enable remote KYC.

A biometric KYC kit can consist of the following:

- A biometric scanner (e.g. fingerprint scanner, iris scanner, camera, etc.)
- A portable computer or Smartphone with internet connectivity
- Biometric KYC app or e-KYC app

In remote KYC process, biometric identifiers of a customer is scanned and verified against a pre-existing database of biometric identities. If the fetch identity data post biometric scan matches with the customer's claim of the identity, KYC is deemed done. Customer due diligence can be performed once KYC is done.

Biometric KYC app: Inception of biometrically enabled mobile devices is arguably one the major milestones in the field biometric technology. Before landing on the mobile phones, biometrics had already been deployed in a wide array of identification and authentication applications. It is already on its way replacing PINs and passwords on devices like smart phones, tablets and mobile computers.

Present day mobile devices natively support biometric authentication using multiple modalities like face, voice, iris and fingerprint recognition. Many software solution providers and app development firms have started offering biometric KYC apps, which can be used for performing KYC on the mobile device.

Ability to store and process biometric data has turned mobile devices into on-the-go biometric scanner and you do not need expensive setup to perfume KYC. Biometric KYC app on a connected mobile device and a fingerprint scanner is all you need to turn your phone into an e-KYC kit. Even low-end mobile devices feature a camera, which can be used to perform biometric face scan. Most smart phones now launch with a fingerprint sensors to perform fingerprint authentication, however sensors used on these devices are small and only capture partial fingerprints. So you may still need an external fingerprint reader compatible with the biometric KYC app that scan and process full fingerprints.

Jumio is one of such Biometric KYC app that enables online mobile payments and identity verification by performing KYC right on your phone. Jumio biometric KYC app also provides card and ID scanning and validation products for mobile and web transactions. These ID verification apps use mobile technology prowess to store identity information of physical IDs on mobile phones.

The objective of KYC: The objective of KYC guidelines is to prevent banks from being used, intentionally or unintentionally, by criminal elements for money laundering activities. Related procedures also enable banks to better understand their customers and their financial dealings. This helps them manage their risks in a well-judged manner. Today not only the banks but also different online businesses can implement KYC. They usually frame their KYC policies incorporating the following four key elements:

- Customer Acceptance Policy;
- Customer Identification Procedures;
- Monitoring of Transactions; and
- Risk management.

Requirement of KYC: The stringent regulatory environment establishes KYC as a mandatory and crucial procedure for financial institutions. As it minimizes the risk of fraud, by identifying suspicious elements earlier on in the client-business relationship lifecycle. For the purposes of a KYC policy, a customer/user may be defined as:

- a person or entity that maintains an account and/or has a business relationship with the bank;
- one on whose behalf the account is maintained (i.e. the beneficial owner);
- beneficiaries of transactions conducted by professional intermediaries such as stockbrokers, Chartered Accountants or solicitors, as permitted under the law; or

- any person or entity connected with a financial transaction which can pose significant reputational or other risks to the bank, for example, a wire transfer or issue of a high-value demand draft as a single transaction

Typical Controls: KYC controls typically include the following:

- Collection and analysis of basic personally identifiable information (PII).
- (Referred to in US regulations and practice as a "Customer Identification Program" or CIP).

Screening of identity particulars (PII) against global watch-lists to determine the status of public exposure (politically exposed person or PEP) and adverse media.

Determination of the customer's risk in terms of the tendency to commit money laundering, terrorist finance or identity theft.

Creation and assessment of a 'Customer Profile' on the basis of a customer's transactional behaviour.

Monitoring of a customer's transactions against expected behaviour and recorded profile as well as that of the customer's peers.

Laws by Country:

Australia: The Anti-Money Laundering and Counter-Terrorism Financing Act 2006 (AML/CTF Act) gives effect to KYC laws. The Anti-Money Laundering and Counter-Terrorism Financing Rules Instrument 2007 provides guidance for applying the powers and requirements of the Act. Compliance is governed by the Australian Government agency, Australian Transaction Reports and Analysis Centre, established in 1989, known as AUSTRAC.

Canada: The Financial Transactions and Reports Analysis Centre of Canada, also known as FINTRAC, was created in 2000 as Canada's financial intelligence unit. FINTRAC updated its regulations in June 2016 regarding acceptable methods to determine the identity of individual clients to ensure compliance with AML and KYC regulations. A pending lawsuit is active in Canada challenging the legality of the new legislation.

India: The Reserve Bank of India introduced KYC guidelines for all banks in 2002. In 2004, RBI directed all banks to ensure that they are fully compliant with the KYC provisions before December 31, 2005.

Italy: The country's Central Bank (Banca d'Italia), which also exercises regulation power for the financial industry, has enacted in 2007 the KYC requirements and rules that financial institutions have to comply with on the Italian territory.[6]

South Korea: Act on Reporting and Use of Certain Financial Transaction Information regulates due diligence in the country.

Namibia: Financial Intelligence Act, 2012 (Act No. 13 of 2012) published as Government Notice 299 in Gazette 5096 of 14 December 2012.

New Zealand: Updated KYC laws were enacted in late 2009 and entered into force in 2010. KYC is mandatory for all registered banks and financial institutions (the latter has an extremely wide meaning).

South Africa: The Financial Intelligence Centre Act 38 of 2001 (FICA).

United Kingdom: The Money Laundering Regulations 2017 are the underlying rules that govern KYC in the UK. Many UK businesses use the guidance provided by the European Joint Money Laundering Steering Group along with the Financial Conduct Authority's 'Financial Crime: A guide for firms' as an aid to compliance.

United States of America: Pursuant to the USA Patriot Act of 2001, the Secretary of the Treasury was required to finalize regulations before October 26, 2002 making KYC mandatory for all US banks. The related processes are required to conform to a customer identification program (CIP)

Luxembourg: KYC is governed in the Anti-Money Laundering (AML) laws and regulations, which became effective in 1993 and were amended for the last time in 2015.

Singapore: Various industries in Singapore are subject to AML/CFT requirements, including requirements promulgated by the Monetary Authority of Singapore applicable to financial institutions.

Japan: Act on identification of customers by financial institutions 2003.

Enhanced due diligence: Enhanced due diligence (EDD) is a more comprehensive set of procedures for customers with a higher risk profile, either through sources of origin or transactions that exhibit irregular behaviour. The USA PATRIOT Act dictates that institutions "shall establish appropriate, specific and where necessary, enhanced, due diligence policies, procedures and controls that are reasonably designed to detect and report instances of money laundering through those accounts." US regulations require that Enhanced due diligence (EDD) measures are applied to account types such as private banking, correspondent account and offshore banking institutions. Because regulatory definitions are neither globally consistent nor prescriptive, financial institutions are at risk of being held to differing standards dependent upon their jurisdiction and regulatory environment. An article published by Peter Warrack in the July 2006 edition of ACAMS Today (Association of Certified Anti-Money Laundering Specialists) suggests the following:

A rigorous and robust process of investigation over and above (KYC) procedures, that seeks with reasonable assurance to verify and validate the customer's identity; understand and test the customer's profile, business and account activity; identify relevant adverse information and risk; assess the potential for money laundering and/ or terrorist financing to support actionable decisions to mitigate against financial, regulatory and reputational risk and ensure regulatory compliance.

Use-Cases of KYC

- Client on-boarding.
- User Registration.

- Processing of high-profile transactions.
- Re-verification of existing users.
- Ensure regulatory compliance.
- Replacement of outdated authentication mechanisms.

Characteristics

Rigorous and Robust: Generally this means consistent, thorough and accurate. The process must be documented and available for inspection by regulators. The process must be SMART (Specific, Measurable, Achievable, Relevant and Time-bound, scalable and proportionate to the risk and resources.

Over and above KYC Procedures: Enhanced due diligence (EDD) files rely upon initial client screening. EDD processes should use a tiered approach dependent upon the risk. Crucial to the integrity of any EDD process is the reliability of information and information sources, the type and quality of information sources used, properly trained analysts who know where to look for information, how to look and how to corroborate, interpret and decide the results. Commercial intelligence companies aggregate this information and compile it daily into a comprehensive database. Many of these commercial intelligence companies are serviced by in-country providers with researchers on the ground who can obtain information that is not otherwise easily accessible.

Reasonable Assurance: Reasonable depends upon factors including jurisdiction, risk, resources and state of the art technology. For sanction matches it depends upon information provided by regulators. In all cases the suggested standard is to the civil standard of proof i.e. on the balance of probability.

Relevant Adverse Information: Information obtained from any source, including the Internet, free and subscription databases and the media, which is directly or indirectly indicative of involvement in money laundering, terrorist financing or predicate offences. Examples include fraud and other dishonesty, drug trafficking, smuggling or other proscribed offences, references to money laundering or conducting business, residing in or frequenting countries deemed by the Financial Action Task Force and/or (institution) as being countries under sanction or countries with which (institution) does not do business; to official sanctions or watch lists; and to investigations, convictions or disciplinary findings by authorized regulatory bodies.

KYCC: KYCC or Know Your Customer's Customer is a process that identifies a customer's customer activities and nature. This includes the identification of those people, assessing their associated risk levels and associated activities the customer's customer (business) is involved in. KYCC is a derivative of the standard KYC process, that was necessitated from the growing risk of fraud originating from fraudulent individual or companies that might otherwise be hiding in second-tier business relationships. i.e. a customer.

KYC requirements in banks for individual customers

- Obtaining identity documents, address proof and photograph
- Verification of the identity and the documents provided by the customer.
- Details of social / financial status, origin of income to be transacted, expected value and volume of transactions, etc.

KYC requirements in bank for business customers

- Collecting documents like business registration certificates, financial statements (e.g. P/L accounts and/or Balance Sheet).
- Identity of individuals operating the business
- Understanding the nature of business activity, sources of wealth or income, information about the clients' business and their location, the purpose of opening the account, social/financial status, the expected origin of the funds to be used within the relationship and details of occupation/employment, expected monthly withdrawals, expected monthly remittance, etc.

Advantages of KYC

- Helps establish trust in customer profile
- Helps understand nature of client activities
- Provides protection from fraud and losses
- Helps mitigate risk associated with money laundering
- Standardizes on boarding process
- Makes it easy to monitor the customer behaviour depending on the risk profile

Controversies: Controversies over this legislation/regulation/policy include:

- Know your customer places an incredible costly burden on businesses operating in the financial industry, especially smaller financial companies where compliance costs are disproportionately heavy.
- Customers may feel the information requested to be extremely intrusive and burdensome.

Innocent, law abiding individuals such as digital nomads are very likely disproportionately disadvantaged as living a nomadic life makes it increasingly difficult or even impossible to hold any formal banking relationship anyplace in the world due to lack of proof of address, bills, and/or debt documentation required by KYC.

Retired people who travel within their own country without having a permanent fixed address may also be disproportionately disadvantaged for the same reason.

Jurisdictions across the Americas, EMEA and Asia Pacific indicated that all of these jurisdictions permit a form of reliance on customer information provided by third parties. In many instances this data is incorrect, potential bank customers may be unaware of the error and there is no grievance procedure to correct or sanction the bad data provider.

Some citizens in other countries (Canada) are fighting back against USA over-reach into their sovereign banking system and have challenged new USA law in their courts.

The intelligence division at the Treasury Department has repeatedly and systematically violated domestic surveillance laws by snooping on the private financial records of US citizens and companies, according to government sources.

You remember the collapse of Lehman Brothers in 2008. Failure of the investment bank started a chain reaction that caused global financial crisis and eventually the government had to step-in to assist the troubled financial services firm. This single event told us that how important banks and financial services institutions have become in today's extremely complex yet delicate economic structure.

Banks are one of the highly regulated institutions and they have to comply with the set of rules and guidelines prescribed by a governing regulatory, which is often a government agency. These regulations come in the form in strict requirement to adhere to and procedures to follow.

KYC (Know Your Customer) is one of such requirements, in which banks and other financial institutions have to adhere to certain guidelines for the verification, identification and authentication of their clients. KYC and inclusion of biometrics to improve the KYC process in banks will be our points of discussion in the subsequent sections.

REVIEW QUESTIONS

1. What is KYC procedure?
2. What is Pan Card? Explain in brief.
3. What are the necessary requirements for an individual who is eligible for enrolment of Aadhaar?
4. What is OVD? Explain.
5. List out the notified government OVDs.

Principles of Lending

14

14.1 INTRODUCTION

Bank follows certain basic **principles of lending** while doing carrying out their lending and credit operations. Banks deals with public money accepting deposit and lend to their borrowers to earn profit. Banks follow some fundamental principles of lending in order to ensure safety, security and profitability on money it lend. Lending is one of the most important functions performed by the commercial banks and is major source of income of bank. Borrower may differ in terms of their purpose of advance, activities, financial health, repayment capacity, risk so some important principles/ considerations are followed by bank before taking lending decision.

Types of Consumer Credit and Loans

Loan contracts come in all kinds of forms and with varied terms, ranging from simple promissory notes between friends and family members to more complex loans like mortgage, auto, payday and student loans.

Banks, credit unions and other people lend money for significant but necessary items like a car, student loan or home. Other loans, like small business loans and those from the Department of Veterans Affairs, are only available to select groups of people.

Regardless of type, every loan and its conditions for repayment is governed by state and federal guidelines to protect consumers from unsavory practices like excessive interest rates. In addition, loan length and default terms should be clearly detailed to avoid confusion or potential legal action.

In case of default, terms of collection of the outstanding debt should clearly specify the costs involved in collecting upon the debt. This also applies to parties of promissory notes as well.

If you need of money for an essential item or to help make your life more manageable, it's a good thing to familiarize yourself with the kinds of credit and loans that might be available to you and the sorts of terms you can expect.

Types of Credit

The two basic categories of consumer credit are open-end and closed-end credit.

Open-end Credit: open-end credit known as revolving credit, can be used repeatedly for purchases that will be paid back in monthly installment, though paying the full amount due every month is not required. The most common form of revolving credit are credit cards, but home equity loans and home equity lines of credit (HELOC) also comes in this category.

Credit cards are used for daily expenses, such as food, clothing, transportation and small home repairs. Interest charges are applied when the monthly balance is not paid in fully once. The interest rates on credit cards charges on an average 15 percent, but it can be as low as zero percent (temporary, introductory offers) and it may be high as 30 percent or more, depending on the consumer's payment history and credit score. Loans for bad credit may be hard to find, but lower interest rates are available within nonprofit debt management programs, even for credit scores below 500.

Closed-End Credit: Closed-end credit is used to finance a specific purpose for a specific period of time. They also are called installment loans because consumers are required to follow a regular payment schedule (usually monthly) that includes interest charges, until the principles is paid off.

The interest rate for installment loans varies by lender and is tied closely to the consumer's credit score. The lending institution can seize the consumer's property as compensation if the consumer defaults on the loan.

Examples of closed-end credit include:

- Mortgages
- Car loans
- Appliance loans
- Payday loans

Types of Loans

There are various types of loans because each loan has a specific intended use. They can vary by length of time, by low interest rates are calculated, by when payments are due and by a number of other variables.

Debt Consolidation Loans: A consolidation loan is meant to simplify your finances. Simply put, a consolidation loan pays off all or several of your outstanding debts, particularly credit card debt. It means fewer monthly payments and lower interest rates. Consolidation loans are typically in the form of second mortgages or personal loans.

Learn More About Debt Consolidation Loans

Student Loans/ Education Loan: Student loans are offered to college students and their families to help cover the cost of higher education for professional's courses. There are two main types: federal student loans and private student loans. Federally funded loans are better, as they typically come with lower interest rates and more borrower-friendly repayment terms.

Mortgages: Mortgages loans distributed by banks to allow consumers to buy homes they can't pay for upfront. A mortgage is tied to your home, meaning you risk foreclosure if you fall behind on payments. Mortgages have among the lowest interest rates of all loans.

Auto Loans: Auto loans are tied to your property. They can help you afford a vehicle, but you risk losing the car if you miss payments. This type of loan may be distributed by a bank or by the car dealership directly but you should understand that while loans from the dealership may be more convenient, they often carry higher interest rates and ultimately cost more overall.

Personal Loans: Personal loans can be used for any personal expenses and don't have a designated purpose. This makes them an attractive option for people with outstanding debts, such as credit card debt, who want to reduce their interest rates by transferring balances. Like other loans, personal loan terms also depend on your credit history.

Loans for Veterans: The Department of Veterans Affairs (VA) has lending programs available to veterans and their families. With a VA-backed home loan, money does not come directly from the administration. Instead, the VA acts as a co-signer and effectively vouches for you, helping you earn higher loan amounts with lower interest rates.

Small Business Loans: Small business loans are granted to entrepreneurs and aspiring entrepreneurs to help them start or expand a business. The best source of small business loans is the Small Business Administration (SBA), which offers a variety of options depending on each business's needs.

Payday Loans: Payday loans are short-term, high-interest loans designed to bridge the gap from one paycheck to the next, used predominantly by repeat borrowers living paycheck to paycheck. The government strongly discourages consumers from taking out payday loans because of their high costs and interest rates.

Borrowing from Retirement and Life Insurance: Those have retirement funds or life insurance plans may be eligible to borrow from their accounts. This option has the benefit that you are borrowing from yourself, making repayment much easier and less stressful. However, in some cases, failing to repay such a loan can result in severe tax consequences.

Borrowing from Friends and Family: Borrowing money from friends and relatives is an informal type of loan. This isn't always a good option, as it may strain a relationship. To protect both parties, it's a good idea to sign a basic promissory note.

Cash Advances: A cash advance is a short-term loan against your credit card. Instead of using the credit card to make a purchase or pay for a service, you bring it to a bank or ATM and receive cash to be used for whatever purpose you need. Cash advances also are available by writing a check to payday lenders.

Home Equity Loans: If you have equity in your home and the house is worth more than you owe on it. You can use that equity to help pay for big projects. Home equity loans are good for renovating the house, consolidating credit card debt, paying off student loans and many other worthwhile projects.

Home equity loans and home equity lines of credit (HELOCs) use the borrower's home as a source of collateral so interest rates are considerably lower than credit cards. The major difference between the two is that a home equity loan has a fixed interest rate and regular monthly payments are expected, while a HELOC has variable rates and offers a flexible payment schedule. Home equity loans and HELOCs are used for things like home renovations, credit card debt consolidation, major medical bills, education expenses and retirement income supplements. They must be repaid in full if the home is sold.

Whenever you decide to borrow money whether it is to pay the bills or buy a luxury item. Make sure you understand the agreement fully. Know what type of loan you're receiving and whether it is tied to any of your belongings.

Also, familiarize yourself with your repayment terms: what your monthly obligation will be how long you have to repay the loan and the consequences of missing a payment. If any part of the agreement is unclear to you, don't hesitate to ask for clarifications or adjustments.

14.2 FACTORS AFFECTING BANK LENDING POLICY

1. **The Importance of Character:** Foremost on the list is character. If bank doesn't trust you or think you're not an honest person, they will not approve your loan request. It doesn't matter how much collateral you have, it will not be enough to offset a lack of trust. The lender needs the confidence that the borrower has the experience, education and industry knowledge to successfully manage the business. The borrower's reputation plays a significant part in getting a bank loan. Your credit history will show your track record for repaying debts.

2. **The Need for Collateral:** When a bank makes a loan, it determines a plan of how the borrower will repay the loan. If the borrower defaults on the loan, then the bank falls back on the collateral. A lender never wants to use the collateral to repay a loan, because the sale of the collateral may not be enough to pay off the loan. Banks like to take property and assets as collateral as a way to recover their loan in the event the borrower fails to pay as planned.

3. **Capacity to Repay the Loan:** The borrower must show that he can repay the loan out of the company's cash flow. The bank will analyze a company's debt-to-income ratio and the amount of its free cash flow. Lenders like these ratios to provide a cushion in case the business takes a downturn.

4. **The Need for Capital:** Banks feel more comfortable when the owner has his own money invested in the business. Lenders like to know the owner will lose something if the business fails. Banks like lending to companies with a lot of capital because it

means the owners have some "skin in the game." When owners have more personal capital in the business, they will fight harder and sacrifice more to save a business and repay their debts.

5. **Overall Economic Conditions:** Besides analyzing the borrower, bankers will look at the overall economy, industry trends and even the direction of politics. They are thinking about factors beyond the control of the business owner that will affect the performance of the company. It is almost impossible to start a new business and finance its growth solely with internally generated funds and owners' capital. At some point, small business owners will have to approach their banks for loans. Understand the process that bankers go through to evaluate their risks before you apply for a loan. Unless these deposits are prudently utilized banks are destined to incur losses. Banks cannot effort to either keep the deposits idle in the vaults or lend the deposits and not recollect. Hence, it is essential that a proper lending policy is in place. Commercial Bank will carefully analyze and consider factors before sanctioning loans to its customers.

14.3 IMPORTANT PRINCIPLES OF LENDING IN BANKING PRINCIPLES OF CREDIT

A banker follows certain basic **principles of lending** while doing carrying out their lending and credit operations. Banks deals with public money accepting deposit and lend to their borrowers to earn profit. Banks follow some fundamental principles of lending in order to ensure safety, security and profitability on money it lend. Lending is one of the most important functions performed by the commercial banks and is major source of income of bank.

Borrower may differ in terms of their purpose of advance, activities, financial health, repayment capacity, risk so some important principles / considerations are followed by bank before taking lending decision.

1. Liquidity.
2. Profitability
3. Safety and Security.
4. Purpose.
5. Sources of Repayment.
6. Diversification of Risk.
7. Social Responsibility.
8. Security
9. Stability

1. **Liquidity:** Liquidity is an important principle of bank lending. Bank lend for short period only because they lend public money which can be withdrawn at any time by depositors. They therefore advances loans on security of such assets which are easily marketable and convertible into the cash at short notice. A bank chooses such securities in its investment portfolio which possess sufficient liquidity. It is essential because if the bank needs cash to meet the urgent requirement of its customers, it should be in position to sell some of the securities at a very short notice without disturbing their market prices much. There are certain securities such as central, states and local govt. bonds which are easily saleable without affecting the price of market.

2. Profitability: This is the cardinal principle for making investment by a bank. Its must earn sufficient profits. It should therefore invest in such securities which was sure a fair and stable return on the funds invested. The earning capacity of securities and share depends upon the interest rate and the dividend rate and the tax benefits they carry. It is largely the govt. securities of the centre, state and local bodies that largely carry the exemptions of their interest from taxes. The bank should invest more in such securities rather than in the shares of new companies which also carry tax exemption. This is because shares of new companies are not the safe investment.

3. Safety: Safety is the most important fundamental principle of lending. Banks deal with public money so safety of money from public is first priority of bank. Safety means that the borrower should be able to repay the loan and interest in time at regular intervals without default. The repayment of the loan depends upon the nature of the security, character of the borrower, his capacity to repay and his financial standing. Like other investment bank investments involves risk but the degree of risk varies with the type of the securities of the central govt. are safer than those of the state govt. and local bodies. When a banker lends, he must be sure about that the money is in safe hand and will definitely come back at regular interval as per repayment schedule without any default. The banker should ensure that the borrower has the ability and the willingness to repay the advances as par agreement. If it is an unsecured advance, its repayment depends on the creditworthiness of the borrower and that of the guarantor.

4. Purpose: The banker has to carefully examine the purpose for which the advance has been applied for. The underlying purpose for which an applicant is seeking a loan should be productive. The purpose of loan helps in determining level of risk and also impact interest rate on loan. Purpose of loan should be productive in order to ensure safety of funds while it should be extended for short term to ensure liquidity.

5. Sources of Repayment: Before giving financial accommodation, a banker should consider the source from which repayment is promised. In some instances, debentures which are to be redeemed in a few months' time or a life insurance policy which is to mature in near future may be offered as security. Advances against such security give no trouble.

Sometimes customers may apply for loans for additional working capital for their business and undertake to repay out of the profits over a period. In such cases, the rate at which the customer can reasonably hope to repay should be ascertained.

6. Diversification of Risk: Do not put all eggs in one basket – In choosing its investment portfolio a commercial bank should follow the principle of diversity. It should not invest its surplus funds in a particular type of securities. Its aim is to minimizing risk of the investment portfolio of a bank. It also applies to the advancing of loans to varied types of firms, industry, business and trades. "Do not keep all eggs in one basket".

A banker must follow principle of diversity also while choosing its investment portfolio. He must invest the funds over different share and debentures of different industries rather than investing in particular type of security.

7. Social Responsibility: While admitting that banks are essentially commercial ventures, a bank should not forget the fact that it is not enough that only people of means are given bank finance. Through productive effort, bank finance should make people creditworthy and turn them into people of means. Technical competence of the borrower, operational flexibility and economic viability of the project, rather than the security which the borrower can offer, should be considered in evaluating a loan proposal. The identification of priority sectors for the purpose of extending bank credit should be considered as a positive development in the banking system, aimed at effectively discharging its responsibility towards society.

8. Security: A banker avoids lending to a borrower without any security. Securities act as insurance to lender bank in case of default by the borrower. The banker carefully scrutinizes all the different aspects of an advance before granting it. At the same time, he provides for an unexpected change in circumstances which may affect the safety and liquidity of the advances. It is only to provide against such contingencies that he takes security, so that he may realize it and reimburse himself if the well-calculated and almost certain source of repayment unexpectedly fails.

9. Stability: Another important principle of a bank's investment policy should be to invest in those stocks and securities which possess a high degree of stability in their prices. The bank cannot afford any loss on the value of its securities. It should, therefore, invest it funds in the shares of reputed companies where the possibility of decline in their prices is remote. Government bonds and debentures of companies carry fixed rates of interest. Their value changes with changes in the market rate of interest. But the bank is forced to liquidate a portion of them to meet its requirements of cash in cash of financial crisis. Otherwise, they run to their full term of 10 years or more and changes in the market rate of interest do not affect them. Thus bank investments in debentures and bonds are more stable than in the shares of companies.

Some other Principle of lending:

Principles of Solvency: Commercial banks must be financially sound. Further, they need to maintain a certain required capital for running the business.

Principles of Safety: A commercial bank accepts deposits from its customers and then invests it. However, since it is investing the investor's money it keeps the safety of the money first.

Principles of Collection of Savings: This is one of the most important principles in the current banking scenario. Commercial banks seek huge amounts of idle money from their clients. In fact, bank employees are given targets to collect more savings from people.

Principles of Loans and Investment Policy: A commercial bank primarily earns money through its lending and investing activities. It also ensures that the investor's money is invested in viable projects. Therefore, banks need strong loans and investment policies to earn a good profit.

Principles of Economy: Commercial banks always try to avoid any unnecessary expenditure. Therefore, they try to manage their functions within a set budget and increase their profits.

Principles of Providing Services: Commercial banks are usually service-focused banks. After all, good service ensures a better reputation and therefore, profits.

Principles of Secrecy: Commercial banks ensure that they keep the accounts of their clients secret. Also, access to the accounts is given only to legitimized persons.

Principles of Modernization: We live in an era of technology as well as modernization. Therefore, to cope with the advancements in the world, commercial banks adopt modern technical services like online banking, mobile banking, etc.

Principles of Specialization: Apart from modernization, we also live in the age of specialization as well as super-specialization. Therefore, commercial banks segment their entire functions into smaller units and place their employees according to their efficiencies.

Principles of Location: Usually, commercial banks choose a location where they think they can find many customers.

Principles of Relation: All commercial banks try to maintain good relations with their existing clients as well as potential customers.

Principles of Publicity: Any successful business needs good publicity. Therefore, most successful businesses advertise to get the attention of more customers. Hence, commercial banks follow the principles of publicity.

14.4 CONTRIBUTION OF SERVICES IN BANK'S INCOME

Increasingly banks are witnessing a growth in their non-interest or fee-based incomes. With interest spreads decreasing, banks have little option but to ramp up their revenues from fee-based income.

Fee-based income constitutes a major portion of a bank's other income. The ratio of other income to total income is an indicator of the size of fee-based income. Treasury incomes of public sector banks are no longer the major revenue driver and have been coming down as a result of rising interest rates. Volatility of interest rates is compelling banks to increase their fee based income.

Services Offered by Bank

Banks offer the following services to account holders at their specified branches, multicity / Payable at Par (PAP) cheque facility, anywhere banking facility, trade services, phone banking facility, internet banking facility, credit card, debit/ATM card, mobile banking and Real-time Gross Settlement (RTGS).

Credit Cards: A credit card is a payment card issued to users as a system of payment. It allows the cardholder to pay for goods and services based on the holder's promise to pay for them. The issuer of the card creates a revolving account and grants a line of credit to the consumer (or the user) from which the user can borrow money for payment to a merchant or as a cash advance to the user.

Debit Card: A debit card (also known as a bank card or check card) is a plastic card that provides the cardholder electronic access to his or her bank account at a financial institution. Some cards have a stored value with which a payment is made, while most relay a message to the cardholder's bank to withdraw funds from a payee's designated bank account. The card, where accepted, can be used instead of cash when making purchases. In some cases, the primary account number is assigned exclusively for use on the Internet and there is no physical card.

ATM Card: An ATM card (also known as a bank card, client card, key card, or cash card) is a card issued by a financial institution, such as a bank, credit union, or building society, that can be used in an automated teller machine (ATM) for transactions such as: deposits, withdrawals, obtaining account information, and other types of transactions, often through interbank networks. Banks charge some amount annually and some amount against damage of cards. Banks also charge some money from those customers who used the ATM of another banks more than five times in a month.

Online Banking: Online banking (or Internet banking or E-banking) allows customers by a financial institution to conduct financial transactions on a secure website operated by the institution, which can be a retail or virtual bank, credit union or building society. Sometime some banks charge some nominal amount against these services.

To access a financial institution's online banking facility, a customer having personal Internet access must register with the institution for the service, and set up some password (under various names) for customer verification. The password for online banking is normally not the same as for telephone banking. Financial institutions now routinely allocate customer numbers (also under various names), whether or not customers intend to access their online banking facility. Customer numbers are normally not the same as account numbers, because a number of accounts can be linked to the one customer number. The customer will link to the customer number any of those accounts which the customer controls, which may be cheque, savings, loan, credit card and other accounts. Customer numbers will also not be the same as any debit or credit card issued by the financial institution to the customer.

To access online banking, the customer would go to the financial institution's website, and enter the online banking facility using the customer number and password. Some financial institutions have set up additional security steps for access, but there is no consistency to the approach adopted.

Real-time Gross Settlement: Real-time gross settlement systems (RTGS) are funds transfer systems where transfer of money or securities takes place from one bank to another on a "real-time" and on "gross" basis. Sometime some banks charge some nominal amount against these services. Settlement in "real-time" means payment transaction is not subjected to any waiting period. The transactions are settled as soon as they are processed. "Gross settlement" means the transaction is settled on one to one basis without bunching or netting with any other transaction. Once processed, payments are final and irrevocable.

Multicity: This facility has helped many of our corporate/commercial clients in their business. Multi-city cheques are often known as 'at par' cheques payable at all branches of the bank, within the framework of the clearing norms. Banks charge some money against the clearance the multicity cheque.

Safe Custody of Valuables: Banks are well equipped with safes and strong rooms and can accept the valuables of their customers for safe custody and charge some amount against these services. Lockers are installed at extension counters. Adequate publicity should be given about the availability of Safe Custody and Lockers.

Merchant Banking: Banks charge some amount against these services. It is a tremendous scope of increasing income and it includes the following:

- Project counseling.
- Preparation of feasibility report.
- Arranging term finance and underwriting business.
- Obtaining requisite permission from various statutory bodies for starting industrial ventures.

Letters of Credit (LC) and Letters of Guarantee (LG): Opening of letters of credit and issue of guarantee is an important service provided by bank to facilitate trade and commerce. Banks lend their creditworthiness to the beneficiaries by issuing LCs and LGs and collect commission from the customers.

Phone Banking Facility: Banks charge some nominal amount against such type of services. Telephone banking is a service provided by a financial institution that enables customers of the financial institution to perform financial transactions over the telephone, without the need to visit a bank branch or automated teller machine. Telephone banking times can be longer than branch opening times, and some financial institutions offer the service on a 24 hour basis. From the bank's point of view, telephone banking reduces the cost of handling transactions by reducing the need for customers to visit a bank branch for non-cash withdrawal and deposit transactions. The types of financial transactions which a customer may transact through telephone banking include obtaining account balances and list of latest transactions, electronic bill payments, and funds transfers between a customer's or another's accounts. Cash withdrawals and deposits require the customer to visit an automated teller machine or bank branch.

Trade Services: A customer may not be able to use telephone banking on particular bank accounts with a financial institution, such as loan accounts, but bank rules vary in this respect. Trade in Services refers to the sale and delivery of an intangible product, called a service, between a producer and consumer. Trade in services takes place between a producer and consumer that are, in legal terms, based in different countries, or economies, this is called International Trade in Services.

Monthly Account Charges: Banks may charge their customers a fixed monthly charge for the provision of the account. In the UK, this was not common practice until the 1990s when banks began to introduce this type of bank charges as a means of product differentiation – often offering additional services bundled with the bank account itself (e.g. travel insurance, mobile phone insurance, preferential rates on other products).

Charges for Specific Transactions: Until the 1980s, most banks charged for all transactions. A number of newer entrants to the personal current account market took a "no fees whilst in credit" approach, leading very rapidly to a situation where no bank could compete with others without offering the same deal.

Whilst the loss of income incurred was, to some extent, covered by the interest earned on carrying balances in current accounts, the banks' profitability on personal current accounts was severely impacted by this change in the charging structure. In turn this led to the banks' increased use of charges for exceeding overdraft limits as a means of generating their required level of profitability.

Bill Business: Collection of outstation and inward cheques/bills is an important source of revenue for the bank. Bills are also purchased by the bank by charging hundi which add to the non-interest income of the branch.

Forex Business: Remuneration from exchange transaction is a major source of revenue to the bank. The quantum of export turnover and import turnover and the exchange rates of the currencies determine the export profits. It plays an important role in increasing the exchange profit.

Government Business: Handing of government business not only earns commission but is also a source of deposit for the bank. Commission is claimed from RBI on quarterly basis on turnover of government business.

Depository: It is a recently introduced concept which facilitates scrip less trading of shares. A depository is an organization where the securities of the shareholders are held in electronic form at the request of the shareholders through the medium of depository participants. It offers substantial income by way of levying charges for opening of accounts of shareholders and also on every share transaction in the account.

Interest in Respect of Overdrafts: Most banks charge interest to their customers in respect of overdrafts. It is common to charge differentially for authorized and unauthorized overdrafts, with unauthorized overdrafts often bearing an interest rate two or three times higher than authorized ones.

In order to gain customers from competitors, banks will sometimes offer introductory 0% or low interest rates on authorized overdrafts, together with generous initial overdraft limits. As part of the development of the personal current account market, certain banks have altered their overdraft charging structure to a fixed daily charge, irrespective of the size of the overdrawn balance.

Charges for Exceeding Authorized Overdraft Limits: As banks' income from transaction charges declined, due to the "free banking" that had become the de-facto standard in the personal current account market and the banks' income from carrying balances fell due to declining interest rates, banks sought to increase the profitability of their businesses by significantly increasing the charges levied for exceeding authorised overdraft limits, or when customers make payments (or attempt to make payments), including direct debits, cheque payments or standing orders, where no authorised overdraft limit exists.

These charges are commonly referred to as penalty charges, although penalty charges are explicitly forbidden under the law. Many individuals were able to retrieve money paid in such fees through the courts on these grounds.

Transfer Redirection Charges: A Redirection of Transfer charge is included in bank charges and are only required on specific transfer occasions only. A redirection fee is a bank charge that is only paid to a bank when a mistake is made by another bank and a sum of amount is transferred into a wrong bank account in another bank. This may occur between continents, countries or states. A redirection fee is often expensive when required as the bank requiring this may not have legal rights to freeze the account the funds are mistakenly transferred into. It may also require urgent attention depending on the banking rules of the country and it takes a period of 30–45 minutes for a redirected transfer to be completed. This is normally caused in a Bank Wire Transfer, Telegraphic Transfer also known as Telex Transfer (T/T) and most times, local bank to bank transfer. Most banks calculate this type of bank charge according to the amount in question.

Services Charges on Local Clearing: At present, banks are collecting the local cheques free of cost to the customers. As profitability has become an important criteria banks cannot afford to give service free of cost. All the banks should consider levying of a nominal fee for collection of local cheques to at least cover the cost incurred for clearing business.

Smart Cards: A smart card, typically a type of chip card, is a plastic card that contains an embedded computer chip–either a memory or microprocessor type – that stores and transacts data. This data is usually associated with either value, information, or both and is stored and processed within the cards chip. The card data is transacted via a reader that is part of a computing system. System that are enhanced with smart cards are in use today throughout several key applications, including healthcare, banking, entertainment, and transportation.

Safe lockers: Strong storage container maintained in the vault area of a bank and rented to bank customers for safekeeping of valuables documents and goods. These boxes are said to be impervious to fire, flood, theft, and their contents are covered by the banks insurer. Access to individual boxes is secured through two different keys: one kept by the customer, the other by the bank. Banks charge rental fee for providing lockers to customers.

Issuing Cheque Book: Banks charges money against the issuing of a cheque book more than 10 cheque yearly. As on 30th June 2021 SBI charges for more than 10 leaf cheque book ₹ 40 plus GST and bank charges ₹ 75 plus GST for the leaf of 25 cheque book.

Demand Draft: A method used by individuals to make transfer payments from one bank account to another. Demand drafts are marketed as a relatively secure method to cash checks. Banks charged fee for making demand draft.

Foreign Exchange Services: Banks earn commission in exchanging currency for customers and earn income.

Agency Services: Agency services make payments on behalf of customers like electricity bill, telephone bill and charge fees for the same.

SMS Alert: Banks charge some money from the customers against the services of SMS alert. It very from bank to bank. SBI charges ₹ 17 per Quarter.

Letter of Credit: Banks offer importer as well as domestic Letter of Credit facility to our clients for procurement of goods on DA/DP basis as per their needs at very competitive rates. Considering our international network of branches/offices coupled with worldwide correspondent relationship arrangements, our clients enjoy market acceptability and comfort in business deals.

Bank Guarantee: Banks offer Guarantee facility to their clients guaranteeing their performance /financial obligations in the domestic as well as international market.

LC Advising/Confirming Services: In case of Letters of Credit received by clients, banks offer LC advising as well as LC confirmation services under our correspondent relationships with domestic as well as international banks.

Co-acceptance Facilities: Sometimes in business deals on credit basis, buyers are required to offer adequate comforts to the sellers such as bank guarantee or co-acceptance of bills by the bankers. Bank of Baroda offers co-acceptance of bills facility to the top rated clients.

Bancassurance: A lot of banks have tie-up with various Insurance Companies, under which we arrange for issuance of general insurance policies to our clients thereby taking away their worries of timely and adequate insurance cover of the assets.

Solvency Certificate: Banks are charging some money against providing Solvency Certificate to their clients in case it is required for providing to Government authorities, other corporate in business deals/bids etc.

Credit Reports: Banks charges some money as a fee to provide Credit Reports of their clients to other banks/FIs and banks also obtain Credit information that required to our clients on their counter parties, through their correspondent relationship.

Miscellaneous Income

The share of non-interest income can also be improved by collecting the following service charges also:

- Collection of handling charges for return of bills.
- Collection of charges for issue of MICR cheque leaves.
- Collection of ledger folio charges from Current a/c and Cash credit a/c holders.

Banks Make Investments

Bank financing and fees comprise most of a bank's profits, but there is one more strategy they employ. As many businesses do, banks attempt to maximize profits by making their own investments that will hopefully earn good returns. However, they cannot simply make any purchase as they wish. Banks must keep a certain amount of deposits liquid at all times, which is defined by the FDIC, and then must primarily invest in loans. Anything other venture must be very low-risk.

If you are concerned that banks are gambling your money on investments you never authorized, rest assured that they are limited in what they can do. Banks do not invest depositors' money in anything but loans. They use "extra" money for doing so. Banks are investing their funds in various fee based activities. Those areas like as:

Equipment Leasing: A lease is an agreement under which a company or a firm acquires a right to make use of a capital assets like machinery, on payment of a prescribed fee called 'rental charges'.

Hire Purchase: Hire purchase is a mode of financing the price of the goods to be sold on a future date. In a hire purchase transaction, the goods are let on hire, the purchase price is to be paid in installments and hirer is allowed an option to purchase the goods by paying all the installments.

Bill Discounting: Bill discounting is a short tenure financing instrument for companies willing to discount their purchase/sale bills to get funds for the short run.

Account Receivable Financing/Factoring: A type of asset-financing arrangement in which a company uses its receivables-which is money owed by customers-as collateral in a financial agreement. The company receives an amount that is equal to a reduced value of the receivable pledged.

Factoring is similar to the above, the only difference is that the factoring firms purchase the receivables and takes the ownership of the receivables. The entire responsibility of collecting the book debts passes on to the factor.

Venture Capital: Venture capital is a financial capital provided to early stage, high-potential, high risk, growth start-up companies. The venture capital fund makes money by owning equity in the companies it invests in, which usually have a novel technology.

Housing Finance: Housing finance refers to providing finance to an individual or a group of individuals for purchase, construction or related activities of house etc.

Mutual Funds: A mutual fund refers to a fund raised by a financial service company by pooling the savings of the public. It is invested in a diversified portfolio with a view to spreading and minimizing the risk.

Issuance of Stock-Invest: Stock-invest are a non-negotiable instrument used for subscribing to capital issues in the primary capital market. The investor send the application money through a stock-invest instead of cheque or draft. The benefit to the investor is that he continues to earn interest in his deposit account till it is en-cashed.

14.5 METHODS OF BANK CHARGES

Typically, the bank fee is an ongoing or single use fee. Many banks assess a monthly fee to customers. These fees are frequently associated with having a checking account, and not all banks charge them. Sometimes banks waive fees if people use direct deposit, or alternatively, they charge them for specific types of services, like using online bill pay or Internet checking. Other common fees are assessed on a per use basis, and customers might be charged for ATM use, if they wish to get a money order or cashier's cheque, and sometimes if they call or visit their bank and want to talk to a teller.

A bank charge is for services that a customer ordinarily wouldn't expect a bank to offer. For example, if a customer writes a cheque that can't be covered by funds in an account, the bank can assess an overdraft charge. Some people pay a monthly fee to purchase overdraft protection, which means the bank won't return the cheque but will advance money to pay it. A bank charge typically also applies if a person deposits a cheque that bounces. Banks may construct this charge by percentage of the cheque deposited or they can assess it as a flat fee. This is why merchants are entitled to payment above a bounced cheque from customers. They've lost money from their bank because a cheque was returned for insufficient funds.

It's very important for customers to understand the bank charge and fee structure of their bank. Some banks have a reputation for minimal fees, but over the top charges that can swamp customers if they're not extremely careful in their banking habits. It's advised people inquire about any unusual charges or fees, such as those that might be assessed for early withdrawal of funds or account cancellation.

Various Indian banks have announced various changes in the service charges which will effective from October 1, 2019. These service charges include number of free transactions per month via ATM, including both financial and non-financial transactions, issue of multi-city cheque books for savings bank account, stopping a payment instruction, revision of charges per month for non-maintenance of Average Monthly Balance (AMB) and so on.

Number of ATM Withdrawals: You cannot make unlimited cash transactions from your ATM. There is a limit to it. According to RBI rules from your own ATM you can make at least first five transactions in a month free. From other ATMs you can make three free transactions per month in six metro cities and five in other cities.

For accounts having AMB up to ₹ 25,000, the bank will be offering up to 8 ATM transactions including financial and non-financial ones. Similarly for account holders having AMB between ₹ 25,000 and ₹ 50,000 can avail unlimited ATM transaction at the SBI's own ATMs.

However, for the financial transactions conducted at other bank's ATMs beyond the set limit, you will be charged ₹ 20 plus GST. For non-financial transactions, you will be charged ₹ 9.55 plus GST.

For financial transactions at SBI's own ATMs, financial transactions will be charged at ₹ 17 plus GST and non-financial transactions will be charged at ₹ 6 plus GST. If the transaction is declined due to insufficient balance irrespective of whether card was wiped at SBI ATM or other bank, then you will be charged ₹ 20 plus GST.

Issue of Multi-City Cheque Book

SBI will issue only 10 cheque leaves free in a financial year for savings bank account holders. Thereafter, additional 10 leaf cheque books will be issued at ₹ 40 plus GST. For 25 leaf cheque books, the bank will charge you ₹ 75 plus GST. For senior citizens, no such charges have been imposed. Similarly, for salaried accounts, no restrictions have been imposed on number of cheque leaves except for bulk requirement.

Stopping Payment Instructions: If you wish to stop a payment from your savings bank account, then you will be charged ₹ 100 plus GST per instrument, maximum ₹ 500 plus GST per instance.

Non-maintenance Charges: Non-maintenance charges have always been a point of dispute between a customer and a bank. It is always advisable to ask your banker at the time of opening an account about the minimum balance required. If your bank branch is in Metro and Urban Centre, then you are required to maintain Average Minimum Balance (AMB) of ₹ 3,000. For semi-urban centre, savings account holders are required to maintain AMB of ₹ 2,000. In rural centre branches, the AMB requirement is ₹ 1,000.

For example, HDFC Bank charges ₹ 600 if the minimum balance (₹ 10,000) falls below ₹ 2,500. If the balance is between ₹ 7,500 and ₹ 10,000, the penalty is ₹ 150.

In metropolitan areas, there will be a charge of ₹ 100 plus service tax if the balance falls below 75 per cent of the minimum available balance of ₹ 5,000. If the shortfall is 50 per cent or less, the bank will charge ₹ 50 plus service tax. SBI used to have such charges in 2021.

Banks calculate the MAB by adding daily closing account balance and dividing by the number of days in the period. Considering the method involved you might meet the minimum balance limit just by keeping your salary for a few days in your bank account.

Account Closure Charges: Closing your bank account after 14 days of opening and before one year of completion will cost you ₹ 500 plus GST. However, there will be no charges if account is closed after one year of account opening.

Internet Banking Transactions: NEFT transaction up to ₹ 2 lakh done via net banking or mobile banking will be free of cost. Similarly, RTGS transactions up to ₹ 5 lakh done via net banking or mobile banking will be free of cost. However, this will apply only for transactions originated and payable in India. For NEFT and RTGS transactions, done at bank branch, the charges will be as follows

Cash Deposit Transactions: SBI is offering three transactions free every month for deposit of cash. If the cash deposit transaction exceeds three, then ₹ 50 plus GST will be charged per transaction.

Cash withdrawal at Home and Non-Home Branch: Though the banking industry has adopted core banking, several banks still distinguish between home and non-home-branch transactions. Large transactions are generally not encouraged at non-home branches and therefore charges are levied on them. The number of free cash withdrawals at a branch will be dependent on the AMB of your account. If the transaction exceeds beyond the specified limit, then you will be charged ₹ 50 plus GST per transaction. As a savings bank account holder, you can withdraw up to ₹ 50,000 at non-home branch. For instance, HDFC Bank has capped the amount that can be transacted in the home branch at ₹ 2 lakh. Above ₹ 2 lakh, it charges ₹ 5 per ₹ 1,000. At non-home branches, there is a cap of ₹ 25,000; above this, customers are charged ₹ 5 per ₹ 1,000, subject to a minimum charge of ₹ 150.

It is always good to shift your bank account to the place you reside so that there is less cost to the transaction.

Overdraft Fees: Banks levy this fee when consumers withdraw more from an account than is available. For example, an ₹ 1500 transaction on an account that holds just ₹ 1000 may trigger an overdraft charge.

Transfer Redirection Charges: A Redirection of Transfer charge is included in bank charges and are only required on specific transfer occasions only. A redirection fee is a bank charge that is only paid to a bank when a mistake is made by another bank and a sum of amount is transferred into a wrong bank account in another bank. A Redirection of Transfer charge is very important subject for the all banks. This is play vital role during the Transfer. These charges are applied by the all types of Banks. There is also including Nationalized Bank.

Banks charge from their clients for services to recover their costs. It is not a recent phenomenon. There are charges for PIN generation, demand draft, duplicate bank statement, and even account balance updates that you get via SMS on your phone.

Here are some common bank charges that we all should know about.

Cash Transactions: You cannot do unlimited cash transactions from your bank account. There is a cost to it and banks charge from you for that. SBI Bank allows just three free cash transactions per month for saving account holders and thereafter charges ₹ 50 plus service tax for every transaction. The charges were introduced last year by the bank.

Similarly, India's biggest private sector bank, ICICI Bank, reintroduced cash transaction charges post demonetization at branches from January 1, 2017.There are no charges for first four transactions in a month at branches in the same city. Thereafter, ₹ 5 per ₹ 1,000 is charged.

International Transactions: If you make payments abroad through debit or credit card, a charge of 3-4 per cent is added to the exchange rate. So, before swiping the cost abroad, add 3-4 per cent extra cost on the transaction amount. Next time when you do any banking transactions do keep the above-mentioned charges in mind. As like: Overdraft fees, Monthly maintenance fees, Paper statement fees, Account closure fees, Inactivity or escheatment fees, Card replacement fees and Returned item fees.

Card Replacement Fees: Your bank may charge you if you ask to replace a debit card before it's expired. **Debit card re-issuance/replacement fee charged by** SBI, ICICI, HDFC, PNB and Axis bank charges a fee of ₹ 200 for replacement of a lost card. Yes bank charges a fee of ₹ 149 while Bank of India charges a fee of ₹ 120.

Annual Maintenance Charges: The annual maintenance charges vary with the cards issued. For the classic cards, most banks like SBI, HDFC, PNB, Axis bank charges between ₹ 100-150, while bank of India charges ₹ 60 for semi urban and rural area and ₹ 120 for metro and urban area. ICICI Bank charges no fee towards annual maintenance charge for its debit cards. For the Coral debit card, the bank charges a joining fee of ₹ 499 and an annual fee of the same amount, according to its website. For its Platinum debit card, HDFC Bank charges a fee of ₹ 750 as an annual renewal fee. The annual card fee of Yes Bank's First World debit card is ₹ 2499. However, it is waived off for some customers. An annual fee for the Platinum card in Yes bank is ₹ 599.

Regeneration of Debit Card PIN: Most banks like SBI, HDFC, PNB, yes bank and Axis bank charges a fee of ₹ 50 for its debit card. However, there are no charges applicable to customers generating an instant PIN, wherein the customer sets up the PIN using net banking or mobile banking, according to the bank's website. ICICI Bank has stipulated a fee of ₹ 25 as debit card PIN regeneration charges. These charges are "not applicable if request through Instating at Branch/Customer Care.

SMS Charges: SBI will charge ₹ 15 for SMS alerts per quarter from debit card holders who maintain average quarterly balance of up to ₹ 25,000 during the three months. There will be no charge for UPI/USSD transactions of up to ₹ 1,000.

Other Charges: Getting your signature verified will cost ₹ 150 plus GST in per instance. If your ATM Card or ATM kit returned by courier due to wrong address, then you will be charged ₹ 100 plus GST.

14.6 PROMOTING FEE-BASED SERVICE

The top five user groups which respond most successfully to advertising and promotion materials are law firms; business firms; local residents; alumni; and science, medicine, and technology firms. In their marketing efforts, fee-based services highlight strong and unique collections; fast turnaround times; knowledge, skills, and expertise of their staff; and the accuracy and quality of services.

Services Charged by Banks

(*i*) **Overdraft Facility:** An overdraft facility is a formal arrangement with a bank that allows an account holder to draw on funds in excess of the amount on deposit. This type of financing is most commonly used by businesses as a way of making their working capital more flexible, although it can also be available to individuals.

Normal Charges: The interest rate differs from bank to bank and the interest is charged on the excess amount withdrawn.

(*ii*) **Failure to Maintain an Accurate Account Register:** The account holder doesn't accurately account for activity on their account and overspends through negligence. This results in additional charges for overdrawing money.

(*iii*) **ATM Overdraft:** Banks or ATMs may allow cash withdrawals despite insufficient availability of funds. The account holder may or may not be aware of this fact at the time of the withdrawal. If the ATM is unable to communicate with the cardholder's bank, it may automatically authorize a withdrawal based on limits.

(*iv*) **Unexpected Electronic Withdrawals:** Some time account holder may have authorized electronic withdrawals by a business. This could occur in good faith of both parties if the electronic withdrawal in question is made legally possible by terms of the contract, such as the initiation of a recurring service following a free trial period. The debit could also have been made as a result of a wage garnishment, an offset claim for a taxing agency or a credit account or overdraft with another account with the same bank, or a direct-deposit chargeback in order to recover an overpayment.

(*v*) **Merchant Error:** A merchant may improperly debit a customer's account due to human error. For example, a customer may authorize an ₹ 500 purchase which may post to the account for ₹ 5000. The customer has the option to recover these funds through chargeback to the merchant.

(*vi*) **Bank Fees:** The bank charges fees from the customer's account for not leaving sufficient amount for the necessary debits to take place. For example ₹ 1000 is the minimum balance amount in the bank account and sometimes account holder has less than above said amount. In that case bank charge some amount.

(*vii*) **Playing the Float:** The account holder makes a debit while insufficient funds are present in the account believing they will be able to deposit sufficient funds before the debit clears. While many cases of playing the float are done with honest intentions, the time involved in cheque clearing and the difference in the processing of debits and credits are exploited by those committing cheque kiting.

(*viii*) **Returned Check Deposit:** The account holder deposits a cheque or money order and the deposited item is returned due to non-sufficient funds, a closed account, or being discovered to be counterfeit, stolen, altered, or forged. As a result of the cheque chargeback and associated fees, an overdraft results or a subsequent debit which was reliant on such funds causes one. This could be due to a deposited item that is known to be bad, or the customer could be a victim of a bad cheque or a counterfeit cheque scam. If the resulting overdraft is too large or cannot be covered in a short period of time, the bank could sure or even press criminal charges.

(*ix*) **Intentional Fraud:** An ATM deposit with misrepresented funds is made or a cheque or money order known to be bad is deposited by the account holder, and enough money is debited before the fraud is discovered to result in an overdraft once the chargeback is made. The fraud could be perpetrated against one's own account, another person's account, or an account set up in another person's name by an identity thief.

(*x*) **Bank Error:** A cheque debit may post for an improper amount due to human or computer error, so an amount much larger than the maker intended may be removed from the account or less or more amount of money received from ATM etc. Some bank errors can work to the account holder's detriment, but others could work to their benefit.

(*xi*) **Credit Card Charges: Joining and Annual Fees:** In order to entice customers into buying a credit card, many credit card companies offer credit cards free of cost, i.e. no joining fees and perhaps exemption from annual fees for a particular period, say, 1 year after which they will start charging an annual fees. The joining and annual fees could range from ₹ 1,000 to ₹ 3,000 depending on the type of card.

Duplicate Statement Fees: While monthly statements are delivered free of cost to the address of the card holder, request for a duplicate statement in the physical form attracts charges which is typically a fixed sum. Some credit card issuers also charge for a duplicate e-statement. e.g. ₹ 100 for a bill over 3 months.

Interest: It is primarily the interest rate levied by the credit card company on the outstanding amount if it is not repaid before the expiry of the due date. This charge can range anywhere between 4 per cent to 5 per cent per month which in annualized percentage rate (APR) turns out to be as high as 30–48 per cent.

(*xii*) **Traveller Cheque:** A traveller's cheque is a preprinted, fixed-amount cheque designed to allow the person signing it to make an unconditional payment to someone else as a result of having paid the issuer for that privilege.

(*xiii*) **Exchanging Foreign Currency and Foreign Transactions:** Bank charge commission on the exchange of foreign currency.

(*xiv*) **Online Banking, Money Transfer:** Bank charge some money on the online transaction and money transfer through online and internet banking.

(*xv*) **International Shopping, Money Orders and Bank Draft:** Bank also charges some money on the international shopping, issuing international money order and bank draft.

REVIEW QUESTIONS

1. What is open-end credit? What is HELOC?
2. What is closed end credit?
3. What is a debit card? What is a credit card?

Universal Banking

15

15.1 CONCEPT OF UNIVERSAL BANKING

Universal banking is a combination of Commercial banking, Investment banking, Development banking, Insurance and many other financial activities. It is a place where all financial products are available under one roof. So, a universal bank is a bank which offers commercial bank functions plus other functions such as Merchant Banking, Mutual Funds, Factoring, Credit cards, Housing Finance, Auto loans, Retail loans, Insurance, etc.

Universal banking is done by very large banks. These banks provide a lot of finance to many companies. So, they take part in the Corporate Governance (management) of these companies. These banks have a large network of branches all over the country and all over the world. They provide many different financial services to their clients.

In 1998 two reports Narasimham Committee Report and the S.H. Khan Committee Report mentioned the concept of universal banking. Both these reports advised to consolidate (bring together) the banking industry through mergers and integration of financial activities. That is, they advised a combination of all banking and financial activities. That is, they suggested a Universal banking. In 2000, ICICI asked permission from RBI to become a universal bank. RBI wants some big domestic financial institutions to become universal banks.

15.2 ADVANTAGES OF UNIVERSAL BANKING

The **benefits** or advantages of universal banking are:

Investors' Trust: Universal banks hold stakes (equity shares) of many companies. These companies can easily get other investors to invest in their business. This is because other investors have full confidence and faith in the Universal banks. They know that the Universal banks will closely watch all the activities of the companies in which they hold a stake.

Economies of Scale: Universal banking results in economic efficiency. That is, it results in lower costs, higher output and better products and services. In India, RBI is in favour of universal banking because it results in economies of scale.

Resource Utilization: Universal banks use their client's resources as per the client's ability to take a risk. If the client has a high risk taking capacity then the universal bank will advise him to make risky investments and not safe investments. Similarly, clients with a low risk taking capacity are advised to make safe investments. Today, universal banks invest their client's money in different types of Mutual funds and also directly into the share market. They also do equity research. So, they can also manage their client's portfolios (different investments) profitably.

Profitable Diversification: Universal banks diversify their activities. So, they can use the same financial experts to provide different financial services. This saves cost for the universal bank. Even the day-to-day expenses will be saved because all financial services are provided under one roof, i.e. in the same office.

Easy Marketing: The universal banks can easily market (sell) all their financial products and services through their many branches. They can ask their existing clients to buy their other products and services. This requires less marketing efforts because of their well-established brand name. For e.g. ICICI may ask their existing bank account holders in all their branches, to take house loans, insurance, to buy their Mutual funds, etc. This is done very easily because they use one brand name (ICICI) for all their financial products and services.

One-stop Shopping: Universal banking offers all financial products and services under one roof. One-stop shopping saves a lot of time and transaction costs. It also increases the speed or flow of work. So, one-stop shopping gives benefits to both banks and their clients.

15.3 DISADVANTAGES OF UNIVERSAL BANKING

The **limitations** or disadvantages of universal banking are:

Different Rules and Regulations: Universal banking offers all financial products and services under one roof. However, all these products and services have to follow different rules and regulations. This creates many problems. For e.g. Mutual Funds, Insurance, Home Loans, etc. have to follow different sets of rules and regulations, but they are provided by the same bank.

Effect of failure on Banking System: Universal banking is done by very large banks. If these huge banks fail, then it will have a very big and bad effect on the banking system and the confidence of the public. For e.g. Recently, Lehman Brothers a very large universal bank that was failed. It had very bad effects in the USA, Europe and even in India.

Monopoly: Universal banks are very large. So, they can easily get monopoly power in the market. This will have many harmful effects on the other banks and the public. This is also harmful to economic development of the country.

Conflict of Interest: Combining commercial and investment banking can result in conflict of interest. That is, Commercial banking versus Investment banking. Some banks may give more importance to one type of banking and give less importance to the other type of banking. However, this does not make commercial sense.

15.4 OTHER BANKING SYSTEM USED IN INDIA

Following are the other banking system available in India:

1. **Retail Banking:** Retail banking is when a bank executes transactions directly with consumers, rather than corporations or other banks. Services offered include savings and transactional accounts, mortgages, personal loans, debit cards, and credit cards. The term is generally used to distinguish these banking services from investment banking, commercial banking or wholesale banking. It may also be used to refer to a division of a bank dealing with retail customers and can also be termed as Personal Banking services. In the US the term Commercial bank is used for a normal bank to distinguish it from an investment bank. After the great depression, through the Glass-steagall Act, the US Congress required that banks only engage in banking activities, whereas investment banks were limited to capital markets activities. This separation was repealed in the 1990s. Commercial bank can also refer to a bank or a division of a bank that mostly deals with deposits and loans from corporations or large businesses, as opposed to individual members of the public (retail banking).

2. **Wholesale Banking:** Wholesale banking is the provision of services by banks to organizations such as Mortgage Brokers, large corporate clients, mid-sized companies, real estate developers and investors, international trade finance businesses, institutional customers (such as pension funds and government entities/agencies), and services offered to other banks or other financial institutions. (Wholesale finance means financial services, which are conducted between financial services companies and institutions such as banks, insurers, fund managers, and stockbrokers.) Modern wholesale banks are engaged in: finance wholesaling, underwriting, market making, consultancy, mergers and acquisitions, fund management.

Wholesale banking will include the task of providing a broad suite of services to large corporations, mid-sized companies, and small businesses. Often, a financial institution will provide these services as discounted rates, based on the number of services included in the package. This approach makes it more attractive for a company to place all financial matters with the single institution, rather than using different banks and agencies for each banking service that the business needs in order to function.

Wholesale banking is also an option that is open for real estate developers, market investors, and others that operate in the buying and selling of properties and other forms of investment. The advantage of wholesale banking in this application is the easy access to the total financial portfolio, which makes transfers between accounts much simpler. Wholesale banking also includes features that allow for efficient transfers of stock ownership, funds, and other financial instruments between financial institutions.

REVIEW QUESTIONS

1. Explain the concept of Universal banking.
2. What is investor's trust?
3. What are the advantages of universal banking?

Venture Capital

16

16.1 CONCEPT OF VENTURE CAPITAL

Venture capital (VC) is financial capital provided to early-stage, high-potential, growth and start-up companies. The venture capital fund earns money by owning equity in the companies it invests in, which usually have a novel technology or business model in high technology industries, such as biotechnology, IT and software. The typical venture capital investment occurs after the seed funding round as the first round of institutional capital to fund growth (also referred to as Series A round) in the interest of generating a return through an eventual realization event, such as an IPO or trade sale of the company. Venture capital is also type of private equity.

Venture capital is attractive for new companies with limited operating history that are too small to raise capital in the public markets and have not reached the point where they are able to secure a bank loan or complete a debt offering. In exchange for the high risk that venture capitalists assume by investing in smaller and less mature companies, venture capitalists usually get significant control over company decisions, in addition to a significant portion of the company's ownership (and consequently value).

16.2 FEATURES OF VENTURE CAPITAL

Under venture capital finance the lender provides financial support to a company which is in early stage of development, though it involves risk but at the same time is has the potential for generating abnormal returns for venture capitalist. Given below are some of the features of venture capital.

1. Venture capital involves not only investing money but also active participation in the management of the company by the person who has made investments in the company.
2. Venture capitalist divests his or her holding once the investments has generated returns in accordance with the venture capitalist desired return.
3. Venture Capital Financing is in the form of equity participation rather than giving it as loan or debt.

4. Venture Capital Financing is usually done for companies which are small level or medium level and also relatively newly formed companies are the preferred choice of venture capitalist.
5. Venture capitalist does Venture Capital Financing in order to make a capital gain on equity investment at the time of exit.

16.3 STAGES OF VENTURE CAPITAL FINANCING

Following are the steps involved in venture capital funding:

1. **Business Plan Submission:** The first step in approaching a VC is to submit a business plan. At minimum, plan should include:
   - a description of the opportunity and market size;
   - resumes of your management team;
   - a review of the competitive landscape and solutions;
   - detailed financial projections and
   - a capitalization table.

   Once the venture capitalist has received the plan, it will discuss opportunity internally and decide whether or not to proceed. This part of the process can take up to three weeks, depending on the number of business plans under review at any given time.
2. **Introductory Conversation/Meeting:** If firm has the potential to fit with the VC's investment preferences, he will be contacted in order to discuss his business in more depth. If, after this phone conversation, a mutual fit is still seen, he might be asked to visit with the venture capitalist for a one-to-two hour meeting to discuss the opportunity in more detail. After this meeting, the venture capitalist will determine whether or not to move forward to the due diligence stage of the process.
3. **Due Diligence:** The due diligence phase will vary depending upon the nature of your business proposal. The process may last from three weeks to three months, and borrower should expect multiple phone calls, emails, management interviews, customer references, product and business strategy evaluations and other such exchanges of information during this time period.
4. **Term Sheets and Funding:** If the due diligence phase is satisfactory, the venture capitalist will offer borrower a term sheet. This is a non-binding document that spells out the basic terms and conditions of the investment agreement. The term sheet is generally negotiable and must be agreed upon by all parties, after which you should expect a wait of roughly three to four weeks for completion of legal documents and legal due deligence before funds are made available.

16.4 ADVANTAGES OF VENTURE CAPITAL FINANCING

Venture capital funding offers following advantages:

1. Since VC funding is not a loan scheme, there is no repay schedule; which means you don't have to repay debt as a cost of doing business.
2. Many VCs have consultants and professionals on their staff that has deep knowledge of specific markets. These experts can help your business avoid many of the pitfalls that are usually associated with start-ups.
3. Being an entrepreneur does not automatically make you a good business manager. However, since VCs will hold a percentage of equity in your business, they will most likely have a say in how it is managed. So if you are really not a good manager, this can be a significant benefit.
4. Because they are obligated to make profit from their investment in your business, VCs often provide HR consultants (who are specialists in hiring talents) to hire the best staff for your business. This can help you avoid hiring the wrong people.
5. Because VC firms are under strict supervision by regulatory bodies, there are very few or no unscrupulous VCs.
6. VC firms are very easy to locate because they are documented in business directories.

16.5 LIMITATIONS OF VENTURE CAPITAL FINANCING

Venture capital financing suffers from following limitations:

1. Some VC firms require much more ROI than expected. In many cases, it can be as much 60 percent of the equity in your company. This, in effect, means the VC firm is controlling your business; not you, the owner.
2. Usually, VC firms will want to add a member of their team to your company's management team. While this is generally to ensure the success of your business, it can create internal problems.
3. Another big problem you will most likely face when you opt for VC funding is that you will give up many key decisions on how your company will operate. This is because the VC firm will require to be informed of any major decision you make, and they usually have the power to override such decisions.
4. Though they generally treat information confidentially, VC firms usually refuse to sign a non-disclosure agreement due to the legal ramifications of doing so. This can put your ideas at risk, especially when it's new.
5. Because they are keen on making profit, and they invest huge funds (which means they take large risks), venture capitalists take too long to decide whether to invest in your business or not.

6. Most VC firms do not release all the needed funds up front. Rather, they usually release funds in stages with an eye on the expansion of your business. Because this approach may not be suitable for your funding plans, it may ruin your business.
7. Usually, VC firms want to close the deal and get their investment back within three to five years. If your business plan contemplates a longer timetable before providing liquidity, VC funding may not be suitable for you.

REVIEW QUESTIONS

1. Explain the concept of Venture capital.
2. What are the various stages of venture capital financing?
3. List the advantages of Venture capital financing.
4. What are the Limitations of venture capital financing?
5. Explain –" VC firms require much more ROI than expected."

17 Project Financing

17.1 CONCEPT OF PROJECT FINANCING

Project financing is the long term financing of infrastructure and industrial projects based upon the projected cash flows of the project rather than the balance sheets of the project sponsors. Usually, a project financing structure involves a number of equity investors, known as sponsors, as well as a syndicate of banks or other lending institutions that provide loans to the operation. The loans are most commonly non-recourse of banks, which are secured by the project assets and paid entirely from project cash flow, rather than from the general assets or creditworthiness of the project sponsors, a decision in part supported by financial modeling. The financing is typically secured by all of the project assets, including the revenue-producing contracts. Project lenders are given a lien on all of these assets, and are able to assume control of a project if the project company has difficulties complying with the loan terms.

Generally, a special purpose entity is created for each project, thereby shielding other assets owned by a project sponsor from the detrimental effects of a project failure. As a special purpose entity, the project company has no assets other than the project. Capital contribution commitments by the owners of the project company are sometimes necessary to ensure that the project is financially sound, or to assure the lenders of the sponsors' commitment. Project finance is often more complicated than alternative financing methods. Traditionally, project financing has been most commonly used in the extractive (mining), transportation, telecommunications and energy industries. More recently, particularly in Europe, project financing principles have been applied to other types of public infrastructure under public–private partnerships (PPP) or, in the UK, Private Finance Initiative (PFI) transactions (e.g., school facilities) as well as sports and entertainment venues.

Project financing in the developing world peaked around the time of the Asian financial crisis, but the subsequent downturn in industrializing countries were offset by growth in the OECD countries, causing worldwide project financing to peak around 2000. The need for project financing remains high throughout the world as more countries require increasing supplies of public utilities and infrastructure. In recent years, project finance schemes have become increasingly common in the Middle East, some incorporating Islamic finance.

The new project finance structures emerged primarily in response to the opportunity presented by long term power purchase contracts available from utilities and government entities. These long term revenue streams were required by rules implementing PURPA, the Public Utilities Regulatory Policies Act of 1978. Originally envisioned as an energy initiative designed to encourage domestic renewable resources and conservation, the Act and the industry it created lead to further deregulation of electric generation and, significantly, international privatization following amendments to the Public Utilities Holding Company Act in 1994. The structure has evolved and forms the basis for energy and other projects throughout the world.

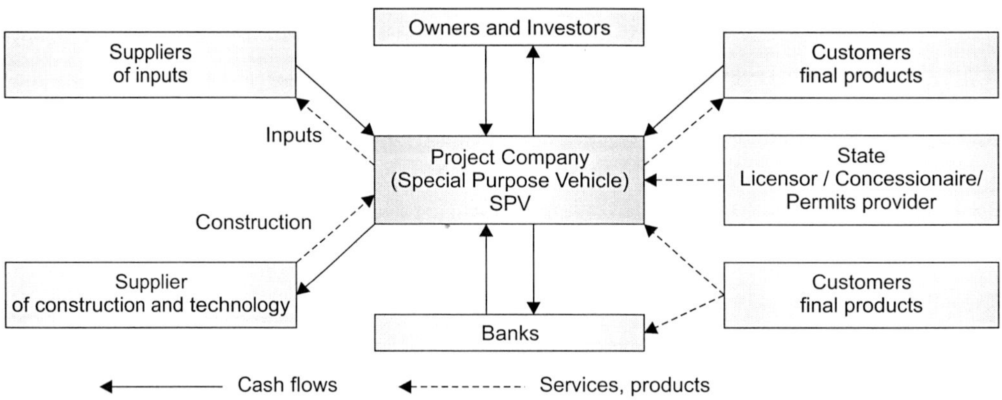

Notes: Sponsors may be beside an investor also in a role of a supplier, a customer or the state – accordingly how much the subject is interested on a particular project and what risks it bears. Some roles may overlap (e.g. investor and customer).

Fig. 17.1 Concept of Project Financing

17.2 CHARACTERISTICS OF PROJECT FINANCING

Following are the some common characteristics of Project financing:

1. **Capital-intensive:** Project financings tend to be large-scale projects that require a great deal of debt and equity capital, from hundreds of millions to billions of dollars. Infrastructure projects tend to fill this category. A World Bank study in late 1993 found that the average size of project financed infrastructure projects in developing countries was $440 million. However, projects that were in the planning stages at that time had an average size $710 million.

2. **Highly leveraged:** These transactions tend to be highly leveraged with debt accounting for usually 65% to 80% of capital in relatively normal cases.

3. **Long term:** The tenure for project financings can easily reach 15 to 20 years.

4. **Independent entity with a finite life:** Similar to the ancient voyage-to-voyage financings, contemporary project financings frequently rely on a newly established legal

entity, known as the project company, which has the sole purpose of executing the project and which has a finite life "so it cannot outlive its original purpose." In many cases the clearly defined conclusion of the project is the transfer of the project assets. For example, in a build-operate-transfer (BOT) project, the project company ceases to exist after the project assets are transferred to the local company.

5. **Non-recourse or limited recourse financing:** The project company is the borrower. Since these newly formed entities do not have their own credit or operating histories, it is necessary for lenders to focus on the specific project's cash flows. That is, "the financing is not primarily dependent on the credit support of the sponsors or the value of the physical assets involved." Thus, it takes an entirely different credit evaluation or investment decision process to determine the potential risks and rewards of a project financing as opposed to a corporate financing. In the former, lenders "place a substantial degree of reliance on the performance of the project itself. As a result, they will concern themselves closely with the feasibility of the project and its sensitivity to the impact of potentially adverse factors." Lenders must work with engineers to determine the technical and economic feasibility of the project. From the project sponsor's perspective, the advantage of project finance is that it represents a source of off-balance sheet financing.

6. **Controlled dividend policy:** To support a borrower without a credit history in a highly-leveraged project with significant debt service obligations, lenders demand receiving cash flows from the project as they are generated. This aspect of project finance recalls the Devon silver mine example, where the merchant bank had complete access to the mine's output for one year. In more modern major corporate finance parlance, the project has a strictly controlled dividend policy, though there are exceptions because the dividends are subordinated to the loan payments. The project's income goes to servicing the debt, covering operating expenses and generating a return on the investors' equity. This arrangement is usually contractually binding. Thus, the reinvestment decision is removed from management's hands.

7. **Many participants:** These transactions frequently demand the participation of numerous international participants. It is not rare to find over ten parties playing major roles in implementing the project.

8. **Costly:** Raising capital through project finance is generally more costly than through typical corporate finance avenues. The greater need for information, monitoring and contractual agreements increases the transaction costs. Furthermore, the highly-specific nature of the financial structures also entails higher costs and can reduce the liquidity of the project's debt. Margins for project financings also often include premiums for country and political risks since so many of the projects are in relatively high risk countries. Or the cost of political risk insurance is factored into overall costs.

17.3 PARTIES TO PROJECT FINANCING

There are several parties in a project financing depending on the type and the scale of a project. The most usual parties to a project financing are:

1. **Project Company:** The Company that needs to be financed and which is in need of funds for further course of action in its agenda.

2. **Sponsor:** It is the person, institute or an enterprise which finances or provides funds to the project company.

3. **Borrower:** It is basically the capital investor or the owner of the project company.

4. **Financial Adviser:** A person who guides both the parties in dealing with monetary terms and making them aware of further legal consequences and also the profit, loss and partnerships.

5. **Equity Investors:** These are the person who is involved in money and funds investment in various market shares.

6. **Regulatory Agencies:** These are the institutes or agencies that set rules and guidelines for proper and lawful functioning of this financing and borrowing process and also to resolve disputes related to this matter.

17.4 PROCEDURE OF PROJECT FINANCING

The project financing involves following steps:

1. Client will send Project Summary to finance advisor with ROI statement to review.
2. After reviewing the Summary and ROI statement, if finance advisor have any question arises; the same will be sent to client for getting the answers to questions along with fee and Agreement to sign.
3. On getting reply and signed Agreement from the client, project will be submitted to lender.
4. On satisfaction of lender, conference call will be arranged among lender, client and finance advisor for introduction and during that both parties can ask question to each other.
5. On request of lender, client will submit the Detailed Project Report (DPR).
6. On getting DPR, lender will conduct the Due Diligence, which is consist of various aspects like Reviewing DPR with underwriters, Discussions, Inspection, submission of documents asked, Appraisal, Title work etc.
7. On satisfaction, lender will give the term sheet, mentioning the terms and conditions of financing.
8. On getting the reply with signed term sheet from client, lender will prepare all the documents for closing.

9. Lender will inform the date of closing.
10. On inform date, closing will be arranged by lender/lender's lawyer and funds will be released according to agreed terms.

17.5 ADVANTAGES OF PROJECT FINANCING

Following are the benefits offered by project financing:

1. Eliminate or reduce the lender's recourse to the sponsors.
2. Permit an off -balance sheet treatments of the debt financing.
3. Maximize the leverage of the project.
4. Avoid any negative impact of a project on the credit standing of the sponsors.
5. Avoid any restrictions or covenants binding the sponsors under their respective financial obligations.
6. Obtain better financial conditions when the credit risk of the project is better than the credit standing of sponsors.
7. Allow the lenders to appraise the project on a segregated and standalone basis.
8. Obtain a better tax treatment for the benefits of the project, the sponsors or both.

17.6 DISADVANTAGES OF PROJECT FINANCING

Project financing suffers from following limitations:

1. Often take longer to structure than equivalent size corporate finance, since it involves monetary transactions and legal issues, paper work make the whole procedure more time taking and lengthy.
2. Higher transaction cost due to creation of an independent entity, since the regulatory agency is also involved in this process, so it becomes more costly. Also because of longer time, execution time expands and hence, cost, budgeting also gets disturbed.
3. Project debt is substantially more due to its non-recourse nature.
4. Extensive contracting restricts managerial decision making, since the authority at top level increases and delegation and distribution of authority contracts.
5. It requires greater disclosure of proprietary information and strategic deals because the regulatory agency is involved in this whole process that follows and allows the parties to work according to the law and its practices.

REVIEW QUESTIONS

1. Discuss the concept of Project Financing.
2. What are the characteristics of Project Financing?
3. Who are the parties to project financing?
4. What is the procedure of Project Financing?
5. What are the advantages and disadvantages of Project financing?

Merchant Banking

18

18.1 INTRODUCTION

Merchant banking as a term originated from the London (UK) which initiated financing foreign trade by accepting bills and soon the service was spread out to help under developed countries government to raise long term funds. This service later got know by its name "Merchant Banking and Securities House Association" as an association. Merchant banking can be defined as a financial institution which includes a vast array of activities such as shares underwriting, managing portfolio, project counselling, insurance etc. and all of these services are complimentary i.e. free.

A merchant bank is a financial institution which provides capital to companies in the form of share ownership instead of loans. A merchant bank also provides advisory on corporate matters to the firms they lend to. In the United Kingdom, the term "merchant bank" refers to an investment bank. Today, according to the U.S. federal deposit insurance corporation (FDIC), "the term merchant banking is generally understood to mean negotiated private equity investment by financial institutions in the unregistered securities of either privately or publicly held companies." Both commercial banks and investment bank may engage in merchant banking activities. Historically, merchant banks' original purpose was to facilitate and/or finance production and trade of commodities, hence the name "merchant". Few banks today restrict their activities to such a narrow scope. In banking, a merchant bank is a bank primarily engaged in offering financial services and advices as to advice its wealthy customers and corporations as to how to utilize their resources properly and efficiently. According to cox. D. Merchant banks are those banks which provide special advice regarding to corporate finance, bills of exchange, portfolio management etc.

Merchant Banking Services in India:

There are several different banks in India both domestic and foreign which provide services of Merchant Banking to client in India:-

- Commercial banks such as Canara Bank
- Development banks such as ICICI, IDBI, and IFCI.
- Foreign banks such as Citibank, HSBC bank, and National Grindlays Bank.

- Private companies such as JM Financial and Investment service, Create Financial Services, Kotak Mahindra.

18.2 FUNCTIONS OF MERCHANT BANKS

Functions of merchant banking are as follows:

1. **Raising Finance for Clients:** Merchant banking helps its clients in raising finance through issue of shares, bonds, debentures etc. It also help its clients to raise loans from national as well as international market. This finance is basically used for commencement or expansion of business.

2. **Brokers in Stock Exchange:** Merchant bankers act as a broker in the stock exchange. They buy and sell their shares on behalf of their clients. They conduct research on equity shares. They give advices to their clients as to how much shares to buy and sell. Large brokers, mutual companies, venture capital, and investment banks offer merchant banking services.

3. **Project Management:** Merchant bankers help their clients in many ways such as, advising about project locations, project preparations, feasibility studies, advising about concessions etc.

4. **Advising about Modernization and Expansions:** Merchant bankers give advice about expansions and modernization of the business of their clients. They also give advices on mergers and acquisitions, amalgamation and expansions, diversifications of the business, foreign collaborations, and joint ventures etc.

5. **Managing Public Issue of Companies:** Merchant banks also help in management of public issue of companies. They also provide the following services:

- Advice on timing of public issue.
- Advice on the size of the public issue.
- Acting as manager to the issue.
- Help in appointing underwriters and brokers etc.

6. **Special Assistance to Small and Medium Companies:** Merchant bankers help small businessmen to know about business opportunities, govt. policies, various incentives etc. It also help them to take advantage of such opportunities.

7. **Services to Public Sector Units:** Merchant banks offer many servicers to public sectors and public utilities. They help in long-term loans, marketing of securities, foreign collaborations from the market.

8. **Revival of Sick Industrial Units:** Merchant banks help in recovery of sick industrial units. It also plans and executes full revival package.

9. **Portfolio Investments:** Merchant banks make portfolio investments of the investors through safety, profitability, and liquidity. It offers expert decisions regarding safety of investments by the investors.

10. **Money Market Operations:** Money market operations deal with short term operations such as:

- Govt. Bonds.
- Certificate of deposits issued by commercial banks.
- Commercial papers issued by large cooperate firms.
- Treasury bills issued by the central bank.

11. **Leasing Services:** Merchant bankers also help in leasing services. Lease is a contract between the lesser and the lessee, whereby the lesser allows the lessee to use the particular asset for a certain period of time. The lesser charges in lieu of this service as fees or rent.

18.3 IMPORTANCE OF MERCHANT BANKING

With the increase of funds for the smooth functioning of the commercial banks, there was a pressure in the capital market that embossed the commercial banks, capital market, and financial broker and consultancy firms to enter in the field of merchant banking. As a result many nationalized banks of India have opened their merchant bank operations and are competing in this field. There has been a mushroom growth in the financial consultancy firms and other broker firms which doing functions in syndication with other merchant banks. Merchant banking became very important nowadays due to following reasons:

1. Merchant banks play a significant role by mobilizing funds of investors into investible channels assuring promising return on investment. Thus merchant banks can help in meeting the widening demand for investible funds for economic activity.
2. With the growth of the profession of merchant banking, both public and private sector would be able to raise the amount of funds from capital market to meet the growing requirements of funds for commencement/expansion/diversification of business. This emphasizes vigorously the role of commercial banks.
3. Merchant banks have been procuring impressive support from capital market for the corporate sectors financing their projects. As a result there has been an increase in the fund of the capital market year by year.
4. Merchant bankers, with their knowledge, skills and updated information, provide the services of skilled agency and knowledge to the corporate units and gives advise them as such requirements to be compiled with for raising of funds from the capital market under different enhancement viz. companies act, securities regulation act.

18.4 SERVICES PROVIDED BY MERCHANT BANKING

Merchant bankers differ from normal banks when we take in consideration the services that they render. Let's understand these services offered more in details:

1. **Corporate Counseling:** A merchant banker provides a whole range of financial services to corporate to give a jump to its performance and to maintain a steady growth for the company to attract investors. Usually a merchant banker will figure out the problems of an enterprise, including its organizational goals, size of the organisation/ operation, choice of product, pricing etc and also will provide suggestions to deal with these issues.

2. **Project Counseling:** It basically includes project report preparation, financing pattern decision making, appraising the project relating to its technical, commercial and financial viability and also for obtaining funds from financial institutions, it helps with filling up of application forms.

3. **Credit Syndication:** Under credit syndication, a merchant banker helps to locate the various sources of funds and looks after the formalities required for the procurement of the funds for the undertaken project. These funds are for both the project cost and the working capital that's required.

4. **Underwriting:** A merchant banker works as an underwriter so it helps with the procedure of IPO (initial public offering) by buying the stocks of the client company and then reselling it to the general public. It falls under his shoulders to do proper valuing of the company's stocks and also to insure that all the legal requirements are met timely.

5. **Portfolio Management:** Portfolio management deals with efficient management of the investments in securities (shares/debentures) of a client by a merchant banker. The merchant banker undertakes the management of the portfolio of securities (shares/ debentures) and provides unique services keeping in mind that its aimed at maximizing returns on such investment with minimal risk of loss for the client.

6. **Advice related to Business Takeovers and Merging Business:** A merchant banker helps a firm to think through the procedure of taking over or merging with other businesses though looking at the company's objective is from this action. He helps to negotiate the dealing with the different parties and decides over the mode of payment and the consideration that is to be paid. It also to be noted that all the legal requirements for the same are fulfilled by him only.

7. **NRI Investment:** Merchant bankers provide services of giving advice related to investment to the NRIs. The services include providing understanding of investment opportunities, grabbing the best opportunity, portfolio management etc.

8. **Off-Shore Finance:** Merchant banker's advice/help to its clients with foreign currency finance in terms of:

- Joint ventures situated in foreign countries.
- Long duration loans in foreign currencies.
- Finance for imports and exports.
- Helping to mergers and takeovers with foreign firm.

18.5 GUIDING PRINCIPLES FOR MERCHANT BANKS IN INDIA

There are certain guidelines drafted by SEBI following of which is a must to fit in the criteria of a Merchant Banker. These guidelines include:

1. Professional qualification in finance/law/business management (BBA, BBS).
2. Adequate capital.
3. Good past track record/experience.
4. Office infrastructure/equipments/manpower.
5. Should maintain proper Income Statement and Balance sheet
6. Unaudited half yearly outcomes must be submitted to SEBI
7. Not allowed to buy/sell stocks of client on the basis of unpublished pricing information.
8. SEBI may collect an initial authorization charge or an annual fee.

REVIEW QUESTIONS

1. Explain the concept of Merchant banking.
2. What are the functions of Merchant banks?
3. What is the importance of Merchant banking?
4. What are the services provided by Merchant banks?

Anti Money Laundering (AML) 19

19.1 INTRODUCTION

Money Laundering

Anti-money Laundering (AML) refers to a set of laws, regulations and procedures intended to prevent criminals from disguising illegally obtained funds as legitimate income. Though AML laws cover a relatively limited range of transactions and criminal behaviours, their implications are far-reaching. For example, AML regulations require that banks and other financial institutions that issue credit or allow customers to open deposit accounts follow rules to ensure they are not aiding in money-laundering.

"Any act or attempted act to conceal or disguise the identity of illegally obtained proceeds so that they appear to have originated from legitimate sources". In other words, it is the process used by criminals through which they make 'dirty' money appear clean.

Money Laundering

- It is a process of making dirty money clean.
- Money is moved around the financial system again and again in such a manner that its origin gets hidden.
- Money generated from illegitimate source is converted into that derived from legitimate source.

Sec. 3 of PML Act, 2002 defines 'money laundering' as:

"Whosoever directly or indirectly attempts to indulge or knowingly assists or knowingly is a party or is actually involved in any process or activity connected with the proceeds of crime and projecting it as untainted property shall be guilty of the offence of money laundering.

Definition of Money Laundering

Money launderers are big time criminals who operate through international networks without disclosing their identity. The money laundered every year could be in the range of $600 billion to $2 trillion. This gives money launderers enormous financial power to engage or coerce or bribe people to work for them. Generally, money launderers use professionals to create legal structure/entities which act as 'front' and use them for laundering of funds.

Money laundering is the process by which the proceeds of the crime and the true ownership of those proceeds are concealed or made opaque so that the proceeds appear to come from a legitimate source. Generally, money laundering is the process through which one conceals the existence, illegal source or illegal application of income to make it appear legitimate. In other words, it is the process used by criminals through which they make 'black' money appear 'white' or the profits of criminal activities are made to appear legitimate.

Money Laundering Process:

- **Placement:** entry of funds in banking system
- **Layering:** distancing of funds from point of entry
- **Integration:** usage of funds
- Some ways of ML Number of cash deposits in same a/c/numerous accounts
- Increase in turnover in dormant a/c
- Receipts and payments of cash from/to unrelated to business/relationship
- Reluctance in providing fictitious/minimal/normal information
- Deposits of third party cheques
- Sudden increase in cash deposit in a/c from abroad

Money Laundering consists of three stages:

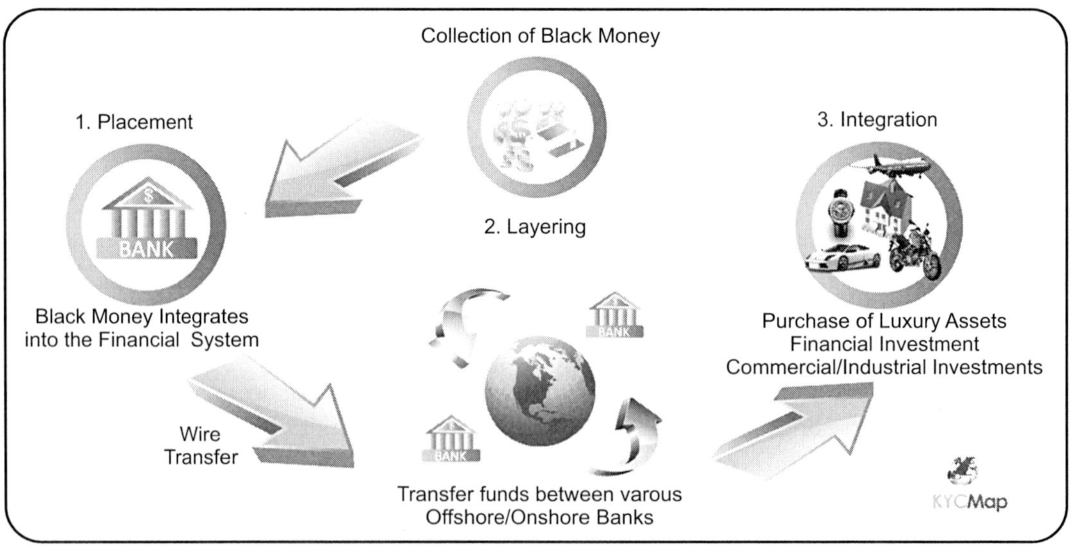

Fig. 19.1 A Typical Money Laundering Scheme

Placement: It is the first stage in money laundering where the cash proceeds of criminal activity enters into the financial system. This is most critical stage for any money launderer as the criminal that can effectively mask his 'black' funds by his 'clean' funds and creating an aura of legitimacy.

Examples of Placement include:

- Exchanging small notes/bills for large notes/bills.
- Foreign bank accounts physically taking small amounts of cash from abroad, below the customs declaration threshold, then lodging in foreign bank accounts and sending back to country of origin.
- Aborted transactions funds are lodged with a lawyer or accountant to hold in their client account to settle a proposed transaction. After a short time, transaction is aborted. Funds are repaid to the client from an unimpeachable source.
- False invoicing putting through dummy invoices to match cash lodged, making it look like payment in settlement of the false invoice.
- Smurfing lodging small amounts of money below the Anti Money Laundering (AML) reporting threshold to bank accounts or credit cards, then using these to pay expenses etc.
- Trusts and offshore companies useful for hiding the identity of the real beneficial owners.
- Blending funds – Using a legitimate cash focused business to co-mingle dirty funds with the day's legitimate of sales receipts.
- Loan repayment – Repayment of loans or credit cards with illegal proceeds.
- Gambling – Purchase of gambling chips or placing bets on sporting events.

Smurfs: A popular method used to launder cash in the placement stage. This technique involves the use of many individuals (the "smurfs") who exchange illicit funds (in smaller, less conspicuous amounts) for highly liquid items such as traveller cheques, bank drafts or deposited directly into savings accounts. These instruments are then given to the launderer who then begins the layering stage.

Layering: It is the second stage in money laundering where attempts are made to distance the money from its illegal source through layers of financial transactions.

Examples of Layering include:

- Sending funds to different onshore and offshore bank accounts
- Creating complex financial transactions
- Loans and borrowing against financial and non-financial assets
- Letters of credit, Bank Guarantees, Financial instruments, etc.
- Investments and investment schemes
- Insurance products

Integration: It is the third stage of money laundering. This stage involves the re-introduction of the illegal proceeds into legitimate commerce by providing a legitimate-appearing explanation for the funds.

Examples of Integration include:

- Buying businesses
- Investing in luxury goods
- Buying commercial property
- Buying residential property
- Fake employees – a way of getting the money back out.
- Usually paid in cash and collected Loans - to directors or shareholders, which will never be repaid.
- Dividends – paid to shareholders of companies controlled by criminals.

The first stage is called Placement: Immersion or Soaking. The physical disposal of bulk cash proceeds derived from illegal activity, the movement of proceeds, frequently currency, from the scene of the crime to a place or into a form, less suspicious and more convenient for the criminal.

The second stage is called Layering: "Soaping/Scrubbing", It involves the separation of proceeds from illegal source through the use of complex transactions designed to obscure the audit trail and hide the proceeds. The criminals frequently use shell corporations, offshore banks or countries with loose regulation and secrecy laws for this purpose.

The third stage is called Integration: Repatriation/Spin Dry, It represents the conversion of illegal proceeds into apparently legitimate business earnings through normal financial or commercial operations. Integration creates the illusion of a legitimate source for criminally derived funds and involves techniques as numerous and creative as those used by legitimate businesses. For e.g false invoices for goods exported, domestic loan against a foreign deposit, purchasing of property and co-mingling of money in bank accounts.

Reinjecting laundered proceeds into economy so that they re-enter in financial system as normal business funds provides an apparently legitimate explanation to criminally derived wealth:

Typologies/Techniques employed deposit structuring or surfing:

1. Connected accounts
2. Payable through accounts
3. Loan back arrangements
4. Forex money changers
5. Credit/ Debit cards
6. Investment banking and the securities sector
7. Insurance and personal investment products
8. Companies trading and business activity

9. Correspondent banking
10. Lawyers, accountants & other intermediaries
11. Misuse of non-profit organisations

Financing of terrorism: Money to fund terrorist activities moves through the global financial system via wire transfers in out of personal and business accounts. It can sit in the accounts of illegitimate charities and be laundered through buying and selling securities and other commodities or purchasing and cashing out insurance policies.

Although terrorist financing is a form of money laundering, it doesn't work the way conventional money laundering works. The money frequently starts out clean i.e. as a 'charitable donation' before moving to terrorist accounts. It is highly time sensitive requiring quick response.

Working of Anti Money Laundering (AML)

Anti-money-laundering laws and regulations target criminal activities including market manipulation, trade in illegal goods, corruption of public funds and tax evasion, as well as the methods that are used to conceal these crimes and the money derived from them.

Area of Money Laundering

Money laundering generally refers to 'washing' of the proceeds or profits generated from:

(*i*) Drug trafficking
(*ii*) Arms, antique, gold smuggling
(*iii*) Prostitution rings
(*iv*) Financial frauds
(*v*) Corruption
(*vi*) Human trafficking
(*vii*) Illegal sale of wild life products and other specified predicate offences

Key Take Away

- Criminals use money laundering to conceal their crimes and the money derived from them.
- Anti Money Laundering seeks to deter criminals by making it harder for them to hide the loot.
- Financial institutions are required to monitor customers' transactions and report on anything suspicious.

Criminals often try to "launder" the money they obtain illegally through acts such as drug trafficking so that it can't easily be traced back to them. One of the most common techniques is to run the money through a legitimate cash-based business owned by the criminal organization or its confederates. The supposedly legitimate business can deposit the money, which the criminals can then withdraw.

Financial Institution used as conduit by

- By offshore shell corporations
- By trusts located at multiple jurisdiction with "banking secrecy" and "corporate secrecy" clauses
- By Directors, shareholders, authorized signatories

  Banking secrecy – delay in investigation, no direct information

  Corporate secrecy – ownership information is not easily revealed-

  - AML & CFT practices policies
  - Procedures
  - Controls
  - Compliances
  - Training
  - Internal audit
  - Risk based processes use of AML Software

Identification of high risk areas such as:

- cash intensive businesses
- import export businesses
- Politically exposed persons (PEPs)
- correspondent banking
- non face to face businesses
- charitable institutions

Aim: identification of beneficial ownership of various accounts

- Monitoring of accounts linking of multiple accounts in multiple jurisdictions with number of people.
- Comparing account activity against transaction history and comparison with peer accounts. AML transaction trend monitoring software, Link Analysis software, good data base & name recognition software.

  1. AML skills development customer information- building up to date KYC design
  2. Training & awareness
  3. Flagging high risk accounts
  4. Transaction monitoring

  Ways available for exchange of information access of information from countries where mutual legal assistance treaty is signed

  1. Financial Intelligence Unit (FIU) MOU
  2. Supervisory gateway

19.2 CRITICAL VIEW OF AML PROGRAMME

- Compliance overhead
- No value addition
- Delivers little
- Contributes little to bottom line
- Increased compliance cost
- Excessive regulation
- Competitive disadvantage
- Case of misplaced energies

Bank officers – do's and don'ts

- Exercise constant vigilance right from opening of new accounts.
- Know your customer and know your colleagues
- Separate legitimate business and illegitimate/irregular/ suspicious business
- Always think of bank's reputation/clean image.
- Develop risk aware culture – a good customer today may not be good tomorrow
- Do not exercise willful blindness.

19.3 SOURCES/ COMBATING FINANCING OF TERRORISM

(*i*) State sponsored

(*ii*) Other activities-legal or non-legal

A. Legal Sources of terrorist financing

- Collection of membership dues
- Sale of publications
- Cultural of social events
- Door to door solicitation within community
- Appeal to wealthy members of the community
- Donation of a portion of personal savings

B. Illegal Sources

- Kidnap and extortion
- Smuggling
- Fraud including credit card fraud
- Misuse of non-profit organisations and charities fraud
- Thefts and robbery and
- Drug trafficking
- Human trafficking

Macroeconomic impact: Money laundering can have a range of severe macroeconomic consequences on countries.

1. IMF has cited unpredictable changes in money demand, prudential risks to the soundness of banking systems, contamination of legal financial transactions and increased volatility of international capital flows and exchange rates due to unanticipated cross-border asset transfers.

2. The economic and political influence of criminal organizations can weaken the social fabric; collective ethical standards and ultimately the democratic institutions of the society. Organized crime can infiltrate financial institutions; acquire control of large sectors of the economy through investment or other bribes to public officials and indeed governments.

3. Money Laundering can also have a dampening effect on FDI if a country's financial sectors are perceived to be under control and influence of organized crime.

Money Laundering Risks to Banks

(*i*) Reputational risk

(*ii*) Legal risk

(*iii*) Operational risk (failed internal processes, people and systems and technology)

(*iv*) Concentration risk (either side of balance sheet)

All risks are inter-related and together have the potential of causing serious threat to the survival of the bank.

Reputational Risk: The potential that adverse publicity regarding a bank's business practices, whether accurate or not, will cause a loss of confidence in the integrity of the institution. It is a major threat to banks as confidence of depositors, creditors and general market place to be maintained. Banks vulnerable to reputational risk as they can easily become a vehicle for or a victim of customers' illegal activities.

Operational Risk: The risk is a direct or indirect loss resulting from inadequate or failed internal processes, people and systems or from external events. It weaknesses in implementation of banks' programmes, ineffective control procedures and failure to practise due diligence.

Legal Risk: The possibility that lawsuits, adverse judgments or contracts that turn out to be unenforceable can disrupt or adversely affect the operations or condition of a bank. Banks may become subject to lawsuits resulting from the failure to observe mandatory KYC standards or from the failure to practice due diligence. Banks can suffer fines, criminal liabilities and special penalties imposed by supervisors.

Concentration Risk: Mostly applies on the assets side of the balance sheet: Information systems to identify credit concentrations; setting prudential limits to restrict banks' exposures to single borrowers or groups of related borrowers.

On Liabilities Side: Risk of early and sudden withdrawal of funds by large depositors- damages to liquidity.

Penalties imposed on banks

- Jan. 2006 ABM AMRO US$ 80 million
- Aug. 2005 Arab Bank US$ 24 million
- Feb. 2005 City National Bank US$ 750,000
- Jan. 2005 Riggs Bank US$ 41 million
- Oct. 2004 AmSouth Bank US$ 50 million
- Sep. 2004 City Bank Japan Licence cancelled
- May. 2004 Riggs Bank US$ 25 million

Suspicious Transaction

(*a*) Suspicious transaction means a transaction whether or not made in cash which, to a person acting in good faith:

1. It gives rise to a reasonable ground of suspicion that it may involve the proceeds of crime; or
2. It appears to be made in circumstances of unusual or unjustified complexity; or
3. It appears to have no economic rationale or bonafide purpose.

(*b*) Providing misleading information/information not easily verifiable while opening an Account.

(*c*) Large cash withdrawals from: a dormant or inactive account or account with unexpected large credit from abroad.

(*d*) Sudden increase in cash deposits of an individual with no justification.

(*e*) Employees leading lavish lifestyles that do not match their known income sources.

(*f*) Large cash deposits into same account.

(*g*) Substantial increase in turnover in a dormant account.

(*h*) Receipt or payment of large cash sums with no obvious purpose or relationship to Account holder/his business.

(*i*) Reluctance to provide normal information when opening an account or providing minimal or fictitious information.

Role of cash in money laundering:

- disguise the audit trail
- provide anonymity
- concealing true ownership and origin of money
- control over money
- changing the form of money

Cash Transaction Report:

Maintenance of records of transactions:

- valued below rupees ten lakh or its equivalent in foreign currency where such
- series of transactions have taken place within a month and
- the aggregate value of such transactions exceeds rupees ten lakh
- Furnishing of CTR
- individual transactions below rupees fifty thousand may not be included

Due Dates:

- cash transaction report
- by 15th of the succeeding month.
- suspicious transaction report
- Within 7 days of arriving at a conclusion that any transaction is of suspicious nature.

19.4 GUIDELINES FOR PREVENTING ANTI MONEY LAUNDERING

Know Your Customer guidelines and advise banks to follow certain customer identification procedures for opening of accounts and monitoring transactions of a suspicious nature for the purpose of reporting it to the appropriate authority. These guidelines have been framed in the context of the recommendations made by the Financial Action Task Force (FATF) on Anti Money Laundering (AML) standards and on combating financing of terrorism.

The objective of the KYC guidelines is to prevent banks from being used, intentionally or unintentionally, by criminals for money laundering activities. These guidelines also enable banks to know/understand their customers and their financial dealings better, which in turn help them to manage their risk. Compliance with these guidelines both by banks/FIs and the country has become necessary for international financial relationships.

The guidelines on prevention of AML lay down the bank's obligations to appoint a PRINCIPLES Officer and put in place a system of internal reporting of suspicious transactions and cash transactions of ₹ 10 lakh and above to the fraud intelligence unit. The banks are also expected to maintain all records of the customer including the record pertaining to identification for at least ten years from the date of cessation of transactions between the bank and the customer.

19.5 PREVENTION OF MONEY LAUNDERING ACT, 2002

It was brought into force with effect from 1st July 2005. As per the provision of the Prevention of Money Laundering Act (PMLA), every banking company, financial institution (which includes chit fund company, a cooperative bank, a housing finance institution and non banking financial) and intermediary (which includes a stock-broker, sub-broker, merchant banker etc.) shall have to maintain a record of all the transactions, the nature and value of which has been prescribed in the rules notified under the PMLA. Such transactions include:

- All cash transactions of the value of more than ₹ 10 lakhs or its equivalent in foreign currency.
- All series of cash transactions integrally connected to each other which have been valued below ₹ 10 lakhs or its equivalent in foreign currency where such series of transactions take place within one calendar month.
- All suspicious transactions whether or not made in cash. Each registered intermediary should adopt written procedures to implement the anti-money laundering provisions. Such provisions should include the following three specific parameters which are related to the overall 'client due diligence process'.
- Policy for acceptance of clients
- Procedure for identifying the clients
- Transaction monitoring and reporting especially suspicious transactions reporting.

REVIEW QUESTIONS

1. Explain the concept of Money Laundering.
2. What are the three stages of Money laundering?
3. What are the legal and illegal forces combating Finance terrorism?
4. What are the Money laundering risks to banks?
5. Discuss the -- Prevention of Money Laundering Act, 2002.

Electronic Fund Transfer System

20

20.1 INTRODUCTION

Electronic Funds Transfer (EFT) is a system of transferring money from one bank account to another bank account directly without any paper money changing hands to hands. It does not involve any physical exchange of money, but it's all done electronically from one account to another using the internet. Internet banking is just like normal banking with one big exception. You don't have to go to the bank for transactions. Instead, you can access your account anytime anywhere in any part of the world. For busy executives, students, and homemakers, e-banking is virtual blessing. No more talking precious time off from work to get a demand draft made or a cheque book issued.

One of the most widely-used EFT programs is direct deposit, through which payroll is deposited straight into an employee's bank account. However, EFT refers to any transfer of funds initiated through an electronic terminal, including credit card, ATM, Fed-wire, and Point-Of-Sale (POS) transactions. It is used for both credit transfers, such as payroll payments and for debit transfers, such as mortgage payments.

Working of Electronic Funds Transfer (EFT)

Electronic Funds Transfer (EFT) Transactions are processed by the bank through the Automated Clearing House (ACH) network, the secure transfer system that connects all banking sector/ financial institutions in the country. For payments, funds are transferred electronically from one bank account to the billing company's bank account, usually less than a day after the scheduled payment date.

The Automated Clearing House (ACH) Network operates as a batch processing system. Financial institutions accumulate Automated Clearing House (ACH) transactions throughout the day, which are handled via batch processing later on. The ACH network is one of the largest and most reliable payment systems in the world. To complete an EFT, the receiving party must provide the following information:

- Name of customer
- The name of the funds receiving bank
- The type of account (e.g. current or savings)
- The bank's IFC code

- The recipient's account number
- Phone number optionally

The growing popularity of Electronic Funds Transfer (EFT) for online bill payment is paving the way for paperless transactions where checks, stamps, envelopes, and paper bills are obsolete. The benefits of EFT include reduced administrative costs, high efficiency, less time, simplified bookkeeping, and high security. However, the number of companies that send and receive bills through the Internet is still relatively small.

20.2 ADVANTAGES AND LIMITATIONS OF ELECTRONIC FUNDS TRANSFER (EFT)

20.2.1 Advantages of Electronic Funds Transfer (EFT)

The main advantage of an electronic funds transfer is time saving. Since all the transaction is done automatically and electronically, the bank doesn't need to pay a person to do it, a person to drive the loans to the other bank, the cost of the transport, the cost of the maintenance of the transport, insurance and the gas of the transport. EFT's have revolutionized modern banking.

Another benefit is the immediate payment, which brings an up to date cash flow. You won't hear either about lost cheques causes by the inefficiency of normal mail (nowadays known as snail mail for its velocity compared to emails) and up to date bookkeeping.

Advantages of Electronic Funds Transfer (EFT) can be seen from both customers' and bank's point of view.

Benefits to Customers:

1. Consumers can use their computers and telephone modem to dial in from home or any sit where they have access to computer.
2. The services are available 24 × 7 day.
3. Transactions are executed and confirmed quickly, although not instantaneously.
4. In general, the customer will find lower fees and higher interest rates on deposits due to the reduced cost of operating online and not needing numerous physical bank branches.
5. The range of transactions available is fairly broad. Customers can do everything from simply checking on an account balance to applying from a mortgage.
6. The interface is very user-friendly and often intuitive.

Benefits to the Bank:

1. **Ability to Increase Revenue:** Financially, the bank can benefit a great deal from providing their customers with an online banking service. The bank has the ability to increase revenue by generating user and transaction fees for the use of a bill payment product and has the option of charging an account access fee for the use of the online system. Online banking provides an excellent promotional opportunity to generate revenue by helping the bank to cross-sell products such as credit cards, loans, certificate of deposits, and other financial services.
2. **Save Money:** In addition to making money, the bank can save money with an Electronic Funds Transfer (EFT). Online banking can actually decrease operating costs by reducing the daily reproduction and distribution of paper-drawn transaction and delivering and processing statements for accounts, credit cards and bills. Performing transactions via Internet also provides saving of costs, as indicated by a study done by Booz, Allen and Hamilton that shows a transaction over the phone cost $ 54, at an ATM it cost $ 27 and via the Internet the cost is $ 0.1 using the Internet to perform transactions greatly reduces the cost to the bank.
3. **Improves Productivity:** Internet banking improves productivity as well. Bank representatives are able to process data more quickly and efficiently; track account activity with automated reports, help customers achieve daily tasks via the Internet and reduce time spent handling service problems. There can be a dramatic reduction in the number of customer service calls, as some banks that are providing this service has proven.
4. **Marketing and Competitive Tools:** Internet banking also offers to the banks an exceptional marketing and competitive tool. Large banking such as Nations Banks and Wells Fargo, in the United States, have already capitalized on the Internet as a mechanism to attract new customers. The majority of people using the Internet are middle to high income and polls indicate that 50% of the people are also the ones who want to have the convenience of online banking for home or business use. This is an excellent opportunity for the community bank to keep their hometown customers from looking to national institutions for an online product.

20.2.2 Disadvantages of Electronic Funds Transfer (EFT)

Electronic Funds Transfer (EFT) suffers from the following limitations:

1. Poorly delivered Electronic Funds Transfer (EFT) services can be slow and time consuming.
2. Some identity authentication requirements can be annoying and overwhelming for clients.

3. Might require lots of paperwork and procedures for registration and set-up, such as documentation and power of attorney to spouses beyond what is required for traditional paper-based dealings.
4. It can be difficult for clients to get familiarized with the bank's website and e-banking channel as each bank has its own unique website and methods.
5. Frequent changes and adjustments to the bank's website and delivery channels that require re-familiarization and in some cases re-registration and documentation.
6. Distrust by some clients in some countries with the primitive legal systems and unreliable technological infrastructure might face security and legal challenges.

20.3 CHALLENGES FOR E-BANKING

The challenges that Indian banks are facing in adopting Electronic Funds Transfer (EFT) are as follows:

1. **Manage Multiple Distribution Channels:** Electronic Funds Transfer (EFT) is bound to become the most important channel in next few years. Even the traditional banking would move towards internet technology with open standards and low cost. Although all traditional channels would not die down in a day and success would depend on how the banks generate synergy in these two vastly different channels. The services provided in all types of distribution channel must be in tandem with each other and must be in synergy.

2. **Issue of Internationalization and Electronic Funds Transfer (EFT):** The real challenges for internet banking is to penetrate the customer base of banks. Maximum usage of Internet banking is for accessing account balances and making bill payments. For most customers, there's nothing more reassuring than watching their cheques getting credit on a paper ledger. The biggest of all concerns for Electronic Funds Transfer (EFT) customers is the security issue. People still aren't comfortable having information about their life's hard-earned money saved on a server they don't know about so that a physical pass-book is still preferred. Another problem is on-line service that merely minimize an off-line which doesn't give customers an adequate inducement to move a significant portion of their banking on-line. As a result, most customers tend to treat on-line banking as no more than an extra channel to check their balances and transactions histories and they continue to do the rest of their business at the ATM or the teller window. There is no more security and customer loyalty. With the internet, the gateway to low cost international expansion around, tackling the virtual competition would be a key. Customers would be loyal as long as the rates offered are competitive. At the same time, banks would have to manage different product portfolios, at different yet competitive prices to different corporate across the world. The issue of offering services

in multiple geographies/customers due to increased global access and competition may ask for new virtual alliances between small local banks and the global players.

3. **Emergences of Value-Focused Specialist Competitors:** The real trouble is that Internet bank doesn't really need to be a bank. It can even be a group of innovative persons with no bank branch at all, just working through alliances and leading the field because of their superior capabilities through focus and innovation advantage. The entry of multiple non-financial institutions and other non-traditional players would just fasten this whole process.

20.4 MEASURES TO IMPROVE ELECTRONIC FUNDS TRANSFER (EFT)

The bank should take the following measures to improve Electronic Funds Transfer (EFT):

1. **Customer Relationship:** Banks and other financial institutions cannot go completely virtual they need physical branches after all. This is probably one area where internet banking in India scores over the 'stand-alone' Internet banks of the West. Several Internet banks like e-trade have acquired ATM networks like Card Capture Services to offer consumers a way to deposit and access their money through ATMs. Physical branches help forge a 'relationship' with customer that a virtual banks cannot. Most online consumers utilize account tracking, bill pay and e-shopping, they would prefer direct, personal contact with their banker when shopping for financial products.

2. **Personalization:** Banking solution become truly personalized when they are able to respond to the changing customer needs and this is possible by using strong data mining and target marketing capabilities.

3. **Integration:** Another important aspect is integrating customer service interfaces and channels, so that the customer deals with a single channel that caters to diverse needs such as Kiosks, ATMs, Web TV, mobile phones, pagers and branches counters. Banks have to get their acts together. If the online banking, ATM's and the branches don't work together, there's no real benefits in having the electronic tools.

4. **Innovation:** Today's value-added product could easily be tomorrow's commodity. That is why banks would need to depend more on product innovation, expending the range of their products and service offerings. Apart from just online accounts, e-banks would need to tailor specific products for the internet, like online bill presentment or credit cards with instant online approval.

5. **Migrate Old Customers and Go After New Ones:** In building an on-line business, a bank's offline customer base is a huge assets for it. It will be harder for competitors to pick off the bank's current customers than for the banks to get them on-line. But to do so, banks must make one-time offers and then constantly provide incentives such as free services (for example, bill payment and online trade) to increase balance.

6. **Account Aggregation:** A new wave called 'Account Aggregation' is slowly sweeping through the online banking/brokerage industry. Account aggregation or account consolidation provides consumers with the ability to access the information about all of their financial transactions sourced from different websites, at a single website.

20.5 TYPES OF ELECTRONIC FUNDS TRANSFER (EFT)

Electronic Funds Transfer (EFT) has following types:

1. **ATM (Automatic Teller Machine):** An ATM is basically a machine that can deliver cash to customers on demand after authentication. An ATM does the basic function of a bank's branch, i.e., delivering money on demand. Hence setting of branches is not required thereby significantly lowering infrastructure costs. These machines also hold the keys to future operational efficiency. Automated Teller Machine is seen everywhere. These machines brought innovation in the banking sector all over the world. The advent of the ATM has made the concept of the clock banking a reality. The ATM has been helpful to both the bankers and customers. The load crowd of customers in the banking hall of a branch waiting for their turn to collect cash is disappearing. The ATM is the device used by the bank customers to process account transaction. This system is known as "anytime money" because with services the person having the ATM card can withdraw cash any time where he wants. Since the ATM machine can be built anywhere like near markets and railway stations etc, so one can easily withdraw money from it.

Advantages of ATM:

To Banks

(*a*) Less space required

(*b*) Capital expenditure is lower as compare to branch

(*c*) Bank's staff gets more time to do marketing

(*d*) Lower transaction cost

(*e*) One more means for advertising bank's products

To Customer

(*a*) Convenience of shopping no need to carry cash

(*b*) No need to visit bank for transaction

(*c*) Banking anytime and anywhere

(*d*) Fast and efficient service

(*e*) Good currency notes

Disadvantages of ATM:

(*a*) Flexible to efficiency's expense, at present, for any one application it is usually possible to find a more optimized technology.

(*b*) Cost, although it will decrease with time.

(*c*) New customer premises hardware and software are required competition from other technologies – 100 Mbps Ethernet and fast Ethernet.

(*d*) Presently the application that can benefit from ATM such as multimedia are rare.

(*e*) The wait, with all the promise of ATM's capabilities many details are still in the standards process.

2. **Tele Banking or Phone Banking:** This means carrying out banking transactions through the telephone. A customer can call up the banks helpline or phone banking number to conduct transaction like transfer of funds, making payments, checking of account balance, ordering cheques, etc. This also, eliminate the customer of the need to visit the bank's branch.

The customer interacts with the bank for various services over phone. There will be no charge for dialing to the toll free number provided by banks Tele-banking, also known as "voice over phone" is consider under anywhere banking. The customer identifies himself to the system by entering his pin number and is guided by a voice response for each banking services namely:

- Balance in the account
- Transaction status, e.g. whether cheque deposited is cleared or not
- Request for issue of cheque book is registered
- Request for issue of bank statement is registered

In normal course all above activities would have involved customer visit a branch and this Tele-banking has improved banking services and enabled remote banking.

Advantages of Tele-banking:

(*a*) You may not have time to visit your bank every week and if your business is located out of town, getting to a branch can be time consuming and expensive. With telephone banking, your bank is on the another end of the line whenever you need it.

(*b*) You can manage your business account at any time, which is ideal if you are busy during the day with running your business.

(*c*) Making payment by phone can simplify your banking – you don't need to confirm the payments in writing and you can check all your transactions against your statement when it arrives.

Disadvantages of Tele-banking:

The most common one would have to be the fact that not all banks and building societies offer 24-hour telephone banking. Also telephone banking is not active usually over bank holidays such as Christmas day or New Year day.

3. **Mobile Banking:** Mobile banking comes in as a part of the bank initiative to offer multiple channels banking providing convenience to its customers. A versatile multi-functional, free service that is accessible and viewable on the monitor of mobile phone. Mobile phones are playing great role in banking and other channels.

Mobile banking can be divided into two broad categories of facilities:

- **Alert facility:** Mobile banking alert facility keeps you informed about the significant transaction in your account. It keeps you update whereever you go.
- **Request facility:** Mobile banking request facility enables you to query for your account balance.

Advantages of Mobile Banking

Mobile banking through cell phone offers many advantages for customers as well as banks. Some of them are as follows:-

(*a*) Mobile banking has an edge over internet banking. In the case of online banking you must have an internet connection and computer. This is a problem in developing countries. However, with mobile banking, connectivity is not a problem. You can find connectivity in the remotest of places also where having an internet connection is a problem.

(*b*) You can make a transaction or pay bills anytime. It saves a lot of time. Mobile banking through cell phone is user friendly. It also saves the record of any transaction made.

(*c*) Cell phone banking is cost-effective. Various banks provide the facility at a lower cost as compared to banking by self.

(*d*) Banking through mobile reduces the risk of fraud. You will get an SMS whenever there is an activity in your account. This includes deposits, cash withdrawals, funds transfer etc. You will get a notice as soon as any amount is deducted or deposited in your account.

(*e*) Banking through cell phone benefits the banks too. It cuts down and the cost of Tele-banking and is more economical.

(*f*) Mobile banking through cell phone is very advantageous to the banks as it serves as guide in order to help the banks improve their customer care service.

(*g*) Banks can be in touch with their clients with mobile banking.

(*h*) Banks can also promote and sell their products and services like Credit Cards, Loans etc. to a specific group of customers.

(*i*) Various banking services like account balance enquiry, Credit/Debit alerts, bill payment alerts, transaction history, fund transfer facilities and minimum balance alerts, etc. can be accessed from your mobile.

(*j*) You can transfer money instantly to another account in the same bank using mobile banking.

4. **PC Banking:** Personal Computer (PC) banking allows the customer to access the information regarding to their bank accounts through a dial up connection. They can also download the information and process it in their own manners. It is different from the internet banking in the sense that internet banking is done over a highly accessible public networks, whereas PC banking is accessible just to bank's customers.

Advantages of PC Banking:

- PC Banking enables you round-the-clock access.
- You usually do not think to stand in queue as a way to perform important banking transaction. The PC banking enables you to do just that suitable from the ultimate comfort and privacy of your homes.
- In comparison to the online banking program, the PC banking provide you increased security.
- Since the level of security is very much greater in PC banking, you can access very much more services that you can use by online banking.
- In case you are using individual economic management computer software and want the inputs from your checking, savings and cash marketplace accounts, PC banking makes it possible for you to download the related information suitable into the computer software program.

Disadvantages of PC banking:

- There is no personal interaction between yourself and the bank (employee/advisor).
- You can access your account from the PC in which you originally installed the software.
- You cannot deposit physical cash using internet banking i.e. cheques, cash-in-hand. This would require a personal visit to the bank.

5. **Internet Banking:** Internet banking means, handle many banking transactions via your personal computer. For instance, you may use your computer to view your account balance, request between accounts and pay bills electronically. Internet banking system and method in which a personal computer is connected by a network service provider directly to a host computer system of a bank such that customer service requests can be processed automatically. The advent of the internet and the popularity of personal computer presented both an opportunity and a challenge for the banking industry. Financial institutions have used powerful computer network to automate million of

daily transactions. Now that their customers are connected to the internet and banks envision similar advantages by adopting that same internet electronic processes to home use. Bank view online banking as a powerful "value added" tool to attract and retain new customers while helping to competitive banking environment. It generally implies a service that allows customers to use some form of computer to access account-specific information and possibly conduct transaction from a remote location – such as at home or the workplace. The obvious advantage to the consumer is convince one bank recently used the advertising motto "bank naked' to emphasize the customer's freedom to conduct routine banking transaction from the comfort and security of his/her home 24x7.

Advantages of Internet Banking:

(*a*) An internet banking account is simple to open and use. You just enter a few answers to question in a form while sitting comfortably in your own home or office. To access your account, you establish security measures such as usernames and passwords. To complete the setup of your account, you just print, sign and send a form.

(*b*) Internet banking cost is less. Because there are fewer building to maintain and less involvement by salaried employees, there is a much lower overhead. These saving allow them to offer higher interest rates on saving accounts and lower lending rates and service charges. Even traditional brick and mortar banks offer better deals such as free bill paying services to encourage their customers to do their banking online.

(*c*) Comparing internet banking to get the best deal is easy. In a short time, you can visit several online banks to compare what they offer resaving and checking account deals as well as their interest rates. Other things you can easily research on what credits cards are available, credit cards interest rates, loan term and the banks own rating with the FDIC.

(*d*) Bouncing a cheque (accidentally) should be a thing of the past because you can monitor your account online any time, day or night. You can track your balance daily, you can see that cheque have cleared and know when automatic deposit and payments are made.

(*e*) Internet banking offers a great deal more convenience that you could get from a conventional bank.

Disadvantages of Internet Banking:

(*a*) **Identity Confirmation:** Federal regulations require that financial institutions confirm each customer's identity. This may present a logistical the issue, as copying and faxing documents is sometimes necessary.

(*b*) **Security Concerns:** With hacking and identity theft on the rise, internet banking customer have to place a certain amount of trust in the bank that their account information and personal information is safe.

(*c*) **Customer Service:** If your bank is a traditional bank, you can go to the bank and speak to someone face to face about your problem but, with an internet bank, you will be likely to spend a lot of time on the phone being passed around and placed on hold.

(*d*) **Accessibility:** If the internet goes down in your area or your banking office area, you will be unable to access your accounts. This includes being unable to withdraw money from ATM's or to use your debit card.

(*e*) **Fees:** Many internet banks don't have ATMs, which means you will have to pay ATM fees. Due to this cost, you have to pay more money that may be monthly or yearly.

6. **Wireless or PDA (Personal Digital Assistant) Banking:** With a phone number and a special PIN number a customer can access to his account balance from his cellular device. It offers following benefits:

- Allows user to pay bills, transfer funds between accounts and check accounts from anywhere.
- Offers wireless banking.

Other Types of Electronic Funds Transfer (EFT)

The most common types of EFTs include:

Basic services that are protected under the EFTA include those made via

- **ATM:** EFTA authorizes 24-hour access to ATMs. If the ATM is owned or operated by an institution other than your bank, you may be charged a fee.
- **Direct Deposit:** Most banks offer direct deposit, which allows you to preauthorize deposits (such as payroll checks or government benefits) or recurring bill payments (such as mortgages, insurance payments or utility bills). You have the right to stop preauthorized transfers at any time, regardless of any opposing contract terms.
- **Pay-by-Phone:** You may authorize your financial institution to make payments or transfer funds via telephone. Banks are required to confirm your identity by asking account-specific questions.
- **Internet:** You may access your accounts via financial institutions' web portals to monitor your accounts, transfer funds and pay bills.
- **Debit Card:** Debit cards issued by financial institutions lets consumers make purchases online or at a retail store or business. This does not include gift cards, stored-value cards, credit cards and prepaid phone cards, which are excluded from the EFTA.
- **Electronic Check Conversion:** This feature enables a business to convert a paper check into an electronic payment by scanning the check and capturing the bank name, address, account number and routing number. After the paper check is scanned into an electronic payment, it becomes null and void.

- **Wire Transfers:** Used for non-regular payments, such as the down payment on a house.
- **Online Banking:** Available via a personal computer, tablet or smart phone. Using online banking, users can access accounts to make payments, transfer funds and check balances.
- **Wallet Banking:** Making payment through wallet as like phone pay, paytm, google pay, airtel wallet, etc.

20.6 ELECTRONIC FUND TRANSFER ACT (EFTA)

1. In 1995, the Reserve Bank had set up the committee for proposing legislation on Electronic Funds Transfer and other electronic payments (Chairperson : Smt. K.S. Shere). The Shere Committee had recommended a set of EFT (Electronic Funds Transfer) Regulations by the Reserve Bank under the Reserve Bank of India Act,1934 and amendment to the Bankers' Books Evidence Act,1881 as short term measures and promotion of a few Acts like the Electronic Funds Transfer Act, the computer misuse and Data Protection Act etc. as long term measures. The Reserve Bank has already initiated steps for the framing of EFT Regulations. The Government of India has also initiated steps for promoting Information and Technology Act, 1999 and consequential amendments to the Reserve Bank of India Act, 1934, the Bankers' Books Evidence Act, 1881, etc.

2. The proposed Information Technology Bill, 1999 and Electronic Commerce Bill, 1999 are intended to be general purpose legislation covering mainly issues like secure electronic records and signatures, acceptance of digital signatures, duties of certification authority, the liability of network service providers, computer crime and data protection. Both the bills deal with electronic contracts and they are being promoted by the Government of India primarily to facilitate the introduction of Electronic Data Interchange in the commercial sector. However, they are equally applicable for electronic funds transfer already launched by the Reserve Bank and is going to be increasingly resorted to by the user banks of the VSAT based network, the INFINET. However, there is still a need for separate Act for Electronic Funds Transfer because certain transactional issues like payments finality, rights and obligations of the parties involved in Electronic Funds Transfer etc. cannot be covered in general purpose bills like the proposed Information Technology Bill or the proposed Electronic Commerce Bill. The EFT Regulations being framed by the Reserve Bank would address only the specific type of EFT system that the Reserve Bank would be involved with as a service provider as also a regulator. The EFT Regulations would, moreover, cover only credit transfer related transactions and not Debit Clearing transactions. A separate legislation on the lines of Electronic Funds Transfer Act of USA is, therefore, required which would be consumer protection oriented and would at the same time address transactional issues like the execution of payment order, settlement finality, etc.

3. The Reserve Bank has taken the help of a consultant in drafting new legislation on Electronic Funds Transfer System and proposing amendment to the Reserve Bank of India Act 1934. The Committee, after a careful examination of the issue, has endorsed the view that the proposed Electronic Funds Transfer Act should cover all forms of electronic payments. The Committee supports the view that the Reserve Bank, at an appropriate time, considers operating the inter-bank payment systems through an agency or subsidiary so that its regulatory role is rendered distinct from its supervisory role. Retail payment systems such as the ECS and the EFT Remittance Processing Scheme presently operational may be managed by a group of large banks with country wide branch network and technical capability, with settlement assistance from the Reserve Bank. This would help the RBI to focus its efforts only on large value time critical funds transfers to be settled on an RTGS basis. In the ongoing debate on the role of central bank in payment systems, the trend is towards distinguishing the central bank role as a regulator from that of service providers which could be commercial banks themselves or the entities under the control of commercial banks. The Committee has considered it necessary that the legal framework for payment system takes into account this international trend.

Ombudsman for Digital Payment Transaction

RBI has introduced the scheme under section 18 Payment and Settlement Systems Act, 2007, No cost mechanism to address the digital transaction complaint by the customers of the System Participants with an effect from January 31, 2019. Prepaid Payment Instruments: Non-adherence to the instructions of Reserve Bank by System Participants about Prepaid Payment Instruments, on any of the following:

(*a*) Failure in crediting merchant's account within a reasonable time;

(*b*) Failure to load funds within a reasonable time in wallets/cards;

(*c*) Unauthorized electronic fund transfer;

(*d*) Non-Transfer/Refusal to transfer/failure to transfer within a reasonable time, the balance in the Prepaid Payment Instruments to the holder's 'own' bank account or back to a source at the time of closure, expiry of validity period etc., of the Prepaid Payment Instrument;

(*e*) Failure to refund within reasonable time/refusal to refund in case of unsuccessful/returned/rejected/cancelled/transactions;

(*f*) Non-credit/delay in crediting the account of the Prepaid Payment Instrument holder as per the terms and conditions of the promotions offer(s) from time to time if any;

(*g*) Non-adherence to any other instruction of the Reserve Bank on Prepaid Payment Instruments.

Mobile/Electronic Fund Transfers: Non-adherence to the instructions of the Reserve Bank on Mobile/Electronic fund transfers by System Participants on any of the following.

(*a*) Failure to effect online payment/fund transfer within a reasonable time;

(*b*) Unauthorized electronic fund transfer;

(*c*) Failure to act upon stop-payment instructions within the time frame and under the circumstances notified to the customers within a prescribed timeline;

(*d*) Failure to reverse the amount debited from customer account in cases of failed payment transactions within a prescribed timeline;

(*e*) Non-adherence to any other instruction of the Reserve Bank on Mobile/ Electronic fund transfers.

Non-adherence to instructions of Reserve Bank/respective system provider to system participants, on payment transactions through Unified Payments Interface (UPI)/Bharat Bill Payment System (BBPS)/Bharat QR Code/UPI QR Code on the following grounds:

(*a*) Failure in crediting funds to the beneficiaries' account;

(*b*) Failure to return within a reasonable time the payment to the originating member in case of failure to credit the funds to the beneficiary's account;

(*c*) Failure to / delay in refund of money back to the account in case of transaction failure or declined transactions (i.e. failed transactions);

(*d*) Non-adherence to any other instruction of the Reserve Bank on payment transactions/through Unified Payments Interface (UPI)/Bharat Bill Payment System (BBPS)/ Bharat QR Code / UPI QR Code.

Non-reversal/failure to reverse within a reasonable time, funds wrongly transferred to the beneficiary account due to lapse at the end of system participant. Any other matter relating to the violation of the directives including on fees/charges, if any, issued by the Reserve Bank in relation to digital transactions.

Note: In respect of digital transactions done on third-party platforms, it will be the responsibility of the payment service provider to resolve customer disputes arising out of such transactions.

Procedure for complaint: The individual can file a complaint with the Ombudsman by writing on a plain paper and sending it to the concerned office of the Ombudsman by post/fax/hand delivery. One can also file it by email to the Ombudsman for digital transactions is available on RBI's website.

Territorial Jurisdiction: An individual may lodge a complaint with the Office of the Ombudsman for digital transactions within whose jurisdiction the branch or office of the System Participant complained against, is located. For complaint arising out of services with centralized operations, complaints can be filed with the office of the Ombudsman for digital transactions within whose territorial jurisdiction the billing/declared address of the customer is located. Advocate cant appears on behalf of the complainant.

Fee

No. There is no charge or any fee for filing/resolving customers' complaints.

The complaint will not be considered under the following circumstances:

(*a*) If the System Participant against whom the complaint is registered is not covered under the scheme.

(*b*) If one has not approached the System Participant concerned in the first instance for redressal of the grievance.

(*c*) If the subject matter of a complaint is not pertaining to the grounds of complaint specified under Clause 8 of the Scheme.

(*d*) If one has not made the complaint within one year from the date of receipt of the reply from the System Participant; or if no reply is received, and the complaint to the Ombudsman is made after the lapse of more than one year and one month from the date of complaint to the System Participant. In exceptional circumstances as decided by the Ombudsman, a complaint made after the period mentioned above may be accepted by the Ombudsman, provided the complaint is made before the expiry of the period of limitation prescribed under the Indian Limitation Act, 1963 for such claims.

(*e*) If the subject matter of the complaint is pending for disposal/has already been dealt with at any other a forum like the court of law, consumer court etc.

(*f*) If the complaint is for the same the subject matter that was settled through the office of the Ombudsman in any previous proceedings.

(*g*) If the complaint is frivolous or vexatious.

(*h*) The complaint falls under the disputes covered under Section 24 of the Payment and Settlement Systems Act, 2007.

(*i*) The complaint pertains to the dispute arising from a transaction between customers.

Offences and Penalties

1. Where a person contravenes the provisions of Penalties Section 4 or fail to comply with the terms and conditions subject to which the authorisation has been issued Under Section 7, he shall be punishable with imprisonment for a term which shall not be less than one month but which may extend to ten years or with fine which may extend to one crore rupees or with both and with a further fine which may extend to one lakh rupees for every day, after the first during which the contravention or failure to comply continues.

2. Whoever in any application for authorisation or in any return or other document or on any information required to be furnished by or under, or for the purpose of, any provision of this Act wilfully makes the statement which is false in any material particular, knowing it to be false or wilfully omits to make a material statement, shall be punishable with imprisonment for a term which may extend to three years and

shall also be liable to fine which shall not be less than ten lakh rupees and which may extend to fifty Lakh rupees.

3. If any person fails to produce any statement, information, returns or other documents, or to furnish any statement, information, returns or other documents, which Under Section 12 or Under Section 13, it is his duty to furnish or to answer any question relating to the operation of a payment system which is required by an officer making an inspection Under Section 14, he shall be punishable with fine which may extend to ten lakh rupees in respect of each offence and if he persists in such refusal, to a further fine which may extend to twenty-five thousand rupees for every day for which the offence continues.

4. If any a person discloses any information, the disclosure of which is prohibited Under Section 22, he shall be punishable with imprisonment for a term which may extend to six months, or with fine which may extend to five lakh rupees or an amount equal to twice the amount of the damages incurred by the act of such disclosure, whichever is higher or with both.

5. Where a direction issued under this Act has not complied with within the period stipulated by the Reserve Bank or where no such the period is stipulated, within a reasonable time or where the penalty imposed by the Reserve Bank Under Section 30 is not paid within a period of thirty days from the date of the order, the system provider or the system participant which has failed to comply with the direction or to pay the penalty shall be punishable with imprisonment for a term which shall not be less than one month but which offences by companies cognizance of offences may extend to ten years, or with fine which may extend to one crore rupees or with both and where the failure to comply with the direction continues, with a further fine which may extend to one lakh rupees for every day, after the first during which the contravention continues.

6. If any provision of this Act is contravened, or if any default is made in complying with any other requirement of this Act, or of any regulation, order or direction made or given or condition imposed there under and in respect of which no penalty has been specified, then, the person guilty of such contravention or default, as the case may be, shall be punishable with fine which may extend to ten lakh rupees and where a contravention or default is a continuing one, with a further fine which may extend to twenty-five thousand rupees for every day, after the first during which the contravention or default continues

Understanding the Electronic Fund Transfer Act

The Electronic Fund Transfer Act (EFTA) is a federal law that protects consumers when they transfer funds electronically; including the use of debit cards, Automated Teller Machines (ATMs) and automatic withdrawals from a bank account. Among other protections, the EFTA provides a way to correct transaction errors and limits the liability resulting from a lost or stolen card.

The EFTA established rules to protect consumers and defined the rights and responsibilities of all participants involved in transferring funds electronically.

Electronic Fund Transfers are transactions that use computers, phones or magnetic strips to authorize a financial institution to credit or debit a customer's account. Electronic transfers include the use of ATMs, debit cards, direct deposits, Point-of-Sale (POS) transactions; transfers initiated by phone, Automated Clearing House (ACH) systems, and pre-authorized withdrawals from checking or savings accounts.

The Electronic Fund Transfer Act outlines requirements for banking institutions and consumers to follow when errors occur. Under the EFTA, consumers may challenge errors and have them corrected within a 45-day period and receive limited financial penalties. The EFTA also requires banks to provide certain information to consumers and defines how consumers can limit their liability in the case of a lost or stolen card.

The Electronic Fund Transfer Act at Work

The use of paper checks has steadily declined since the Electronic Fund Transfer Act was passed, but checks continue to serve as hard evidence of payment. The explosion of electronic financial transactions created a need for new rules that would give consumers the same level of confidence as they have in the checking system.

Key Takeaways

- The Electronic Fund Transfer Act protects consumers when transferring funds electronically.
- The EFTA was effected in 1978 as a result of the increased use of ATMs.
- Protection under the EFTA includes transfers made via ATMs, debit cards, direct deposits, Point-of-Sale and phone.

Requirements for Service Providers under the EFTA

The EFTA requires financial institutions and any third party involved in Electronic Fund Transfer services to disclose the following specific pieces of information to consumers:

- A summary of liability regarding unauthorized transactions and transfers.
- Contact information for the person(s) who should be notified in the event of an unauthorized transaction, along with the procedure to report and file a claim.
- The types of transfers you can make, any fees associated with them and any limitations that might exist.
- A summary of your rights, including the right to receive periodic statements and Point-of-Sale purchase receipts.
- A summary of the institution's liability to you if it fails to make or stop certain transactions.
- The circumstances under which an institution will share information with a third party concerning your account and account activities.
- A notice describing how to report an error, request more information and the amount of time within which you must file your report.

Electronic Funds Transfers Initiated By Third Parties

You may authorize a third party to initiate Electronic Funds Transfers between your account and the third party's account. These transfers to make or receive payment may be one-time occurrences or may recur as directed by you. These transfers may use the Automated Clearing House (ACH) or other payments network. Your authorization to the third party to make these transfers can occur in a number of ways. In some cases, your authorization can occur when the merchant posts a sign informing you of their policy. In all cases, the transaction will require you to provide the third party with your account number and bank information. This information can be found on your check as well as on a deposit or withdrawal slip. Thus, you should only provide your bank and account information (whether over the phone, the Internet or via some other method) to trusted third parties whom you have authorized to initiate these Electronic Funds Transfers. Examples of these transfers include, but are not limited to:

- **Preauthorized Credits:** You may make arrangements for certain direct deposits to be accepted into your checking or savings account(s).
- **Preauthorized Payments:** You may make arrangements to pay certain recurring bills from your checking account(s).
- **Electronic Check Conversion:** You may provide your check to a merchant or service provider who will scan the check for the encoded bank and account information. The merchant or service provider will then use this information to convert the transaction into an Electronic Funds Transfer. This may occur at the point of purchase or when you provide your check by other means such as by mail or drop box.
- **Electronic Returned Check Charge:** Some merchants or service providers will initiate an Electronic Funds Transfer to collect a charge in the event a cheque is returned for insufficient funds. Limitations on frequency of transfers section regarding limitations that applies to savings accounts.

ATM Transfers – types of transfers and dollar limitations – you may access your account(s) by ATM using your Master Money Card and Personal Identification Number to:

- make deposits to checking account(s) with a check card
- get cash withdrawals from checking with a check card
- transfer funds from checking to money market account(s) with a check card.
- get information about the account balance of your checking account(s) with a check card.

Some of these services may not be available at all terminals.

Currency Conversion:

If you effect a transaction with your Master Money Card in a currency other than US Dollars. Master-Card International Incorporated will convert the charge into a US Dollar amount. Master-Card International will use its currency conversion procedure, which is disclosed to institutions that issue Master-Card cards. Currently, the conversion rate used by Master-Card International to determine the transaction amount in US dollars for such transactions is generally either a government mandated rate or a wholesale rate determined by Master-Card International for the processing cycle in which the transaction is processed, increased by an adjustment factor established from time to time by Master-Card International. The currency conversion rate used by Master-Card International on the processing date may differ from the rate that would have been used on the purchase date or card-holder statement posting date.

Advisory against Illegal Use:

You agree not to use your card(s) for illegal gambling or other illegal purpose. Display of a payment card logo by, for example an online merchant does not necessarily meant that transactions are lawful in all jurisdictions in which the card-holder may be located.

Computer Transfer, Types of Transfers:

You may access your account(s) by computer through the internet by logging onto and using your user identification number, your password and a secure web browser, to:

- transfer funds from checking to checking.
- transfer funds from checking to money market.
- transfer funds from money market to checking.
- transfer funds from money market to money market.
- transfer funds from line of credit to checking transfer funds from line of credit to money market.
- make payments from checking to third parties.
- make payments from checking or money market to loan account(s) with us.
- get information about:
- the account balance of checking account(s)
- the account balance of money market account(s)

Limitations on Frequency of Transfers

In addition to those limitations on transfers elsewhere described, if any, the following limitations apply:

- Transfers from a money market account to another account or to third parties by preauthorized, automatic, telephone or computer transfer are limited to six per month with no more than three by check, draft or similar order to third parties.
- For security reasons, there are other limits on the number of transfers and dollar amount you can make by check card.

Financial Institution's Liability

Liability for failure to make transfers. If we do not complete a transfer to or from your account on time or in the correct amount according to our agreement with you, we will be liable for your losses or damages. However, there are some exceptions. We will not be liable, for instance:

1. If, through no fault of ours, you do not have enough money in your account to make the transfer.
2. If you have an overdraft line and the transfer would go over the credit limit.
3. If the Automated Teller Machine where you are making the transfer does not have enough cash.
4. If the terminal or system was not working properly and you knew about the breakdown when you started the transfer.
5. If circumstances beyond our control (such as fire or flood) prevent the transfer, despite reasonable precautions that we have taken.
6. There may be other exceptions stated in our agreement with you.

Confidentiality

We will disclose information to third parties about your account or the transfers you make:

1. Where it is necessary for completing transfers; or
2. In order to verify the existence and condition of your account for a third party, such as credit bureau or merchant; or
3. In order to comply with government agency or court orders; or
4. As explained in the separate privacy disclosure.

Channels of e-payments

In their effort to enable customers to make payments the electronic way banks have developed many channels of payments viz. the internet, mobiles, ATM's (Automated Teller Machines) and drop boxes.

The internet as a channel of payment is one of the most popular especially among the youth. Debit and credit payments are made by customers on various bank's websites for small purchases,(retail payments) and retail transfers (ATM transfers).

ATM's serve many other purposes, apart from functioning as terminals for withdrawals and balance inquiries, such as payment of bills through ATM's, applications for cheque books and loans can also be made via ATM's.

Banks also provide telephone and mobile banking facilities. Through call agents payments can be made and as the number of telephone and mobile subscribers are expected to rise, so is this channel of payment expected to gain popularity.

Drop boxes provide a solution to those who have no access to the internet or to a telephone or mobile. These drop-boxes are kept in the premises of banks and the customers can drop their bills along with the bill payment slips in these boxes to be collected by third party agents.

Role of the RBI in Encouraging e-payments

As the Apex Financial and Regulatory Institution in the country it is compulsory for the RBI to ensure that the payments system in the country is as technologically advanced as possible and in view of this aim, the RBI has taken several initiatives to strengthen the e-payments system in India and encourage people to adopt it.

Raghuram Rajan, Ex-Governor, RBI, and Nandan Nilekani, Ex-Chairman, UIDAI and Advisor, NPCI, and at the launch of Unified Payments Interface (UPI) in Mumbai.

Imagine paying for everyday purchases directly from your bank, without the need for carrying cash. The RBI's new interface helps you do just that. Reserve Bank of India Governor Raghuram Rajan launched the Unified Payments Interface (UPI) system, as its latest offering in boosting digital money transfers.

The interface has been developed by National Payments Corporation of India (NPCI), the umbrella organisation for all retail payments in the country. The UPI seeks to make money transfers easy, quick and hassle free.

- The Payment and Settlement Systems Act, 2007 was a major step in this direction. It enables the RBI to "regulate, supervise and lay down policies involving payment and settlement space in India." Apart from some basic instructions to banks as to the personal and confidential nature of customer payments, supervising the timely payment and settlement of all transactions, the RBI has actively encouraged all banks and consumers to embrace e-payments.

In pursuit of the above-mentioned goal the RBI has granted NBFC's (Non-Banking Financial Companies) the permission to issue co branded credit cards forming partnerships with commercial banks.

The Kisan Credit Card Scheme was launched by NABARD in order to meet the credit needs of farmers, so that they can be free of paper money hassles and use only plastic money.

A domestic card scheme known as RuPay has recently been started by the National Payments Corporation of India (NPCI), promoted by RBI and Indian Banks Association (IBA), inspired by Unionpay in China, which will be promoting the use of cards i.e. "plastic money". Initially functioning as an NPO, Rupay will focus on potential customers from rural and semi-urban areas of India. Rupay will have a much wider coverage than Visa, Master-Card or American Express cards which have always been used for card-based settlements.

The NREGA (National Rural Employment Guarantee Scheme) introduced by the Government will ensure rural employment in turn ensuring that the employees get wages. Each employee will have a smart card functioning as his personal identification card, driver's license, credit card which will also function as an electronic pass book, thus familiarising the rural populations with e-payments.

However, the Indian banking system suffers from some defects due to certain socio-cultural factors which hampers the spread of the e-payments culture even though there are many effective electronic payment channels and systems in place. Despite the infrastructure being there nearly 63% of all payments are still made in cash. A relatively small percentage of the population pays their bills electronically and most of that population is from urban India-the metropolitans. Also in some cases the transaction is done partially online and partially "offline". The main reason for this apathy to switch to e-payments comes from lack of awareness of the customer despite various efforts by the Government.

REVIEW QUESTIONS

1. Explain the concept of Electronic Fund Transfer (EFT).
2. What are the advantages or limitations of Electronic fund transfer?
3. Discuss the challenges for e-banking.
4. Discuss the methods to improve Electronic Funds Transfer.
5. What are the types of EFT?

ECS – Electronic Clearing Services

21

21.1 INTRODUCTION

ECS is an acronym of Electronic Clearing Services. ECS is a mode of Electronic Fund Transfer from one bank account to another bank account using the services of a clearing-house. This service is used for the bulk money transfer from one account to many accounts or vice-versa. This can be used for payment as well as collection purposes. In other words ECS Credit and ECS Debit.

Example, where ECS can be used, are dividend distribution, salary, pension, EMI payment or utility bill collection, house tax, water tax, etc.

Image-based Clearing System (ICS) or Cheque Truncation System (CTS) is a project started by the Reserve Bank of India (RBI) in 2010, to speed up the processing of cheques in banks. CTS is based on an image-based clearing system where **Magnetic Ink Character Recognition** (MICR) data and cheque images are transmitted by the collecting bank to the drawee bank. The CTS stops the flow of physical cheques between the collecting branch and the drawee branch. At some point end route to the drawee branch, an image of the cheque and the MICR data are captured and transmitted to the drawee branch, this has eliminated the need to move physical instruments between branches, thereby, reducing the time taken to process cheques and the costs associated with physically moving instruments between branches.

The Cheque Truncation System (CTS) was first implemented by the Reserve Bank of India in New Delhi on 1 February, 2008 with 10 pilot banks with a deadline of 30 April, 2008 for all banks. CTS were launched in Chennai on 24 September, 2011. After the migration from MICR to CTS, the MICR system was discontinued in NCR and Chennai. Staring 1 August, 2013 only CTS–2010 compliant cheques could be submitted for clearing. But on July 17th, 2013 the deadline was reset to 31 December, 2013.

21.1.1 Purpose of Cheque Truncation System

The Cheque Truncation System (CTS) was introduced to reduce the time taken to collect cheques and clear them, thereby, improving customer service. The system also reduces the scope of clearing related frauds, reduces reconciliation errors, reduces the cost of collection, and almost eliminates logistics-related problems. Even though there are other products on offer, such as the Real-time Gross Settlement (RTGS) and the National Electronic Fund Transfer (NEFT) to make payments, many people prefer using cheques, keeping this in mind, the **Reserve Bank of India (RBI)** decided to increase the efficiency of the cheque clearing system. The CTS is a more secure system than the exchange of physical documents which requires the document to move from one point to another, 'causing an increase in the processing time of cheques and there is a risk of the documents getting misplaced during transit, mutilated during transit or manipulated during transit.

21.1.2 Process of Cheque Truncation

As the CTS is an image-based truncation system the process for clearing a cheque under CTS is different from clearing a non-CTS 2010 cheque. The step-by-step process of clearing a CTS 2010 cheque has been listed below:

1. The presenting bank captures images and data about the cheque on a capturing system.
2. The presenting bank will then transmit the captured data duly signed and encrypted to the clearing housing for further transmission to the paying bank. To provide a secure line of communication the presenting bank and the paying bank are provided with an interface called the Clearing House Interface (CHI), this interface allows both banks to transmit data to the Clearing House in a secure manner.
3. To arrive at a settlement figure the Clearing House processes the data it has received and routes the data and images to the paying bank. This process is Presentation Clearing. Through the CHI the paying bank receives the data from the Clearing House to initiate the processing of the payment. The paying bank's CHI also generates the return file for unpaid instruments.

21.1.3 Electronic Clearing Service (ECS Credit)

Known as a 'Credit-push' facility or one-to-many facility this method is used mainly for large-value or bulk payments where the receiver's account is credited with the payment from the institution making the payment. Such payments are made on a timely-basis like a year, half a year, etc. and used to pay salaries, dividends or commissions. Over time it has become one of the most convenient methods of making large payments.

21.1.4 Electronic Clearing Services (ECS Debit)

Known as many-to-one or 'debit-pull' facility this method is used mainly for small value payments from consumers/individuals to big organizations or companies. It eliminates the need for paper and instead makes the payment through banks/corporates or government departments. It facilitates individual payments like telephone bills, electricity bills, online and card payments, and insurance payments. Though easy this method lacks popularity because of lack of consumer awareness is important.

ECS Debit transaction can be initiated by any institution (called ECS Debit User) which has to receive/collect amounts towards telephone/electricity/water dues, cess / tax collections, loan installment repayments, periodic investments in mutual funds, insurance premium, etc. It is a scheme under which an account holder with a bank branch can authorize an ECS User to recover an amount at a prescribed frequency by raising a debit to his/her bank account.

As mentioned above India is one of the fastest growing countries in the plastic money segment. Already there are 130 million cards in circulation, which is likely to increase at a very fast pace due to rampant consumerism. India's card market has been recording a growth rate of 30% in the last five years. Card payments form an integral part of e-payments in India because customers make many payments on their card-paying their bills, transferring funds and shopping.

Ever since debit cards entered India in 1998 they have been growing in number and today they consist of nearly 3/4 of the total number of cards in circulation.

Credit cards have shown a relatively slower growth even though they entered the market one decade before debit cards. Only in the last five years has there been an impressive growth in the number of credit cards, by 74.3% between 2004 and 2008. It is expected to grow at a rate of about 60% considering levels of employment and disposable income. Most credit card purchases come from expenses on jewelry, dining, and shopping.

Another recent innovation in the field of plastic money is co-branded credit cards, which combine many services into one card-where bank and other retail stores, airlines, telecom companies enter into business partnerships. This increases the utility of these cards and hence they are used not only in ATMs but also at a Point of Sale (POS) terminals and while making payments on the net.

In ECS debit system, the bank customers give an authority(standing instruction) to paying bankers to debit their account towards the electric bill, telephone bill, etc. as and when they receive ECS debit notes received through clearing. This augurs well for consumers of utility services as they need not wait for the monthly bill and take time to remit the bill amount before the due date. Paying bank of ECS debits, should be careful while debiting customer's account. Similarly, domestic and foreign banks take standing instruction from their customers who have availed consumer loans etc., to recover the EMI from their account in another bank under ECS. Paying bankers will verify their records in respect of the name of the account holder, account no., operation instruction in the account, a signature of the account holder etc., when they receive ECS mandate. If they notice any discrepancy they may not approve the ECS debit mandate given by their customer. The account holders must ensure that all the details provided by them in ECS mandate are correct, before making it operational.

21.1.5 ECS Debit Transaction

ECS Debit transaction can be initiated by any institution (called ECS Debit User) which has to receive/collect amounts towards telephone/electricity/water dues, cess/ tax collections, loan installment repayments, periodic investments in mutual funds, insurance premium, etc. It is a scheme under which an account holder with a bank branch can authorize an ECS User to recover an amount at a prescribed frequency by raising a debit to his/her bank account.

The User institution has to first register with an ECS Centre. The User institution has to also obtain the authorization (mandate) from its customers for debiting their account along with their bank account particulars before participation in the ECS Debit scheme. The mandate has to be duly verified by the beneficiary's bank. A copy of the mandate should be available on record with the destination bank where the customer has a bank account.

21.1.6 Working of ECS Debit Scheme

The ECS Debit User intending to collect receivables through ECS Debit has to submit details of the customers (like name, bank/branch/account number of the customer, MICR code of the destination bank branch, etc.), the date on which the customer's account is to be debited, etc., in a specified format (called the input file) through its sponsor bank to the ECS Centre.

The bank managing the ECS Centre then passes on the debits to the destination banks for onward debit to the customer's account with the destination bank branch and credits the sponsor bank's account for onward credit to the User institution. Destination bank branches will treat the electronic instructions received from the ECS Centre on par with the physical cheques and accordingly debit the customer accounts maintained with them. All the unsuccessful debits are returned to the sponsor bank through the ECS Centre (for onward return to the User Institution) within the specified time frame.

For further details about the ECS Debit Scheme, the ECS Debit Procedural Guidelines – available on the website of Reserve Bank of India at *http://www.rbi.org.in/Scripts/ECSUserView.aspx?Id=25* may be referred to.

Any mandate in ECS Debit is on par with a cheque issued by a customer. The customer has to maintain adequate funds in his/her account with the destination bank branch to ensure the ECS Debit instructions are honored when presented. In case of any need to withdraw or stop a mandate, the customer has to give prior notice to the ECS user institution well in time, to ensure that the input files submitted by the user do not continue to include the ECS Debit details in respect of the mandates withdrawn or stopped by customers. The process flow to be followed for withdrawing/stopping mandates is detailed in ECS Debit Procedural Guidelines.

21.1.7 Processing / Service Charges Levied Under ECS Debit

The Reserve Bank of India has deregulated the charges to be levied by sponsor banks from user institutions. The sponsor banks are, however, required to disclose the charges transparently. With effect from 1st July 2011, originating banks are required to pay a nominal charge of 25 paise and 50 paise per transaction to the clearing house and destination bank respectively. Bank branches do not generally levy processing/service charges for debiting the accounts of customers maintained with them.

Benefits

Customers: ECS Debit mandates will take care of automatic debit to customer accounts on the due dates without visiting bank branches/collection centres of utility service providers, etc.

- Customers need not keep track of the due date for payments.
- The debits to customer accounts would be monitored by the ECS Users, and the customers alerted accordingly.
- Cost effective.

User Institutions

- Savings on administrative machinery and costs of collecting the cheques from customers, presenting in the clearing, monitoring their realisation and reconciliation.
- Better cash management because of realisation/recovery of dues on due dates promptly and efficiently.
- Avoids chances of loss/theft of instruments in transit, the likelihood of fraudulent access to the paper instruments, and encashment thereof.
- Realisation of payments on a uniform date instead of fragmented receipts spread over many days.

ECS Credit: ECS Credit payments can be initiated by any institution (called ECS Credit User) which needs to make bulk or repetitive payments to several beneficiaries. The institutional User has to first register with an ECS Centre. The User has to also obtain the consent of beneficiaries (i.e. the recipients of salary, pension, dividend, interest, etc.) and get their bank account particulars before participation in the ECS Credit Scheme. The beneficiary account holders are required to give mandates to the user institutions to enable them to afford credit to their bank accounts through the ECS Credit mechanism. ECS can be used to transfer funds to NRE and NRO accounts in the country subject to FEMA and Wire Transfer guidelines.

Electronic Clearing Service (ECS) in bank transactions is a simple, faster, and cost effective solution for repetitive bulk transactions. The system was first introduced by Reserve Bank of India in April 1995 to facilitate speedier bulk inter-bank transactions. It is most useful to facilitate repetitive payment transactions, such as salary, pension, interest, commission, dividend, etc. ECS is also useful to big corporate, Multinational Companies, Government departments who are required to make payments to a large number of beneficiaries. ECS also facilitates domestic and foreign banks who have obtained standing instructions from the borrowers to recover their monthly loan installments through ECS debit.

21.1.8 ECS Credit to a Large Number of Beneficiaries

In ECS credit system, paper instruments such as cheques, drafts, warrants, etc. are substituted by electronic instructions. Under the system, magnetic media files are provided to clearing houses for bulk and repetitive payment instructions. These magnetic media files are used by clearing houses for effecting credits or debits to the bank accounts of the respective account holders.

21.1.9 ECS Debits towards EMI and Utility Services

Eligible for ECS Credit Transaction

ECS Credit payments can be initiated by any institution (called ECS Credit User) which needs to make bulk or repetitive payments to several beneficiaries. The institutional User has to first register with an ECS Centre. The User has to also obtain the consent of beneficiaries (i.e. the recipients of salary, pension, dividend, interest, etc.) and get their bank account particulars before participation in the ECS Credit Scheme.

ECS Credit payments can be put through by the ECS User only through his/her bank (known as the Sponsor bank). ECS Credits are afforded to the beneficiary account holders (known as destination account holders) through the beneficiary account holders' bank (known as the destination bank). The beneficiary account holders are required to give mandates to the user institutions to enable them to afford credit to their bank accounts through the ECS Credit mechanism.

21.1.10 Working of ECS Credit Scheme

The User intending to effect payments through ECS Credit has to submit details of the beneficiaries (like name, bank/branch/account number of the beneficiary, MICR code of the destination bank branch, etc.), the date on which credit is to be afforded to the beneficiaries, etc. in a specified format (called the input file) through its sponsor bank to one of the ECS Centres where it is registered as a User.

The bank managing the ECS Centre then debits the account of the sponsor bank on the scheduled settlement day and credits the accounts of the destination banks, for onward credit to the accounts of the ultimate beneficiaries with the destination bank branches.

Further details about the ECS Credit Scheme are contained in the Procedural Guidelines and available on the website of Reserve Bank of India at *http://www.rbi.org.in/Scripts/ECSUserView.aspx?Id=1*

Beneficiary

- The beneficiary need not visit his/her bank for depositing the paper instruments which he would have otherwise received had he not opted for ECS Credit.
- The beneficiary need not be apprehensive of loss/theft of physical instruments or the likelihood of fraudulent encashment thereof.
- Cost effective.
- The beneficiary receives the funds right on the due date.

User Institution

- Savings on administrative machinery and costs of printing, dispatch and reconciliation of paper/ instruments that would have been used had beneficiaries not opted for ECS Credit.
- Avoid chances of loss / theft of instruments in transit, the likelihood of fraudulent encashment of paper instruments, etc. and subsequent correspondence/ litigation.
- Efficient payment mode ensuring that the beneficiaries get credit on a designated date.
- Cost effective.

21.1.11 Participation of Beneficiary in ECS Credit Scheme

The beneficiary has to furnish a mandate to the user institution giving consent to avail the ECS Credit facility. The mandate contains details of his/her bank branch, account particulars, and authorizes the user institution to afford credit to his/her account with the destination bank branch. The mandate also provides important information related to bank account details etc. which are useful for the user institution to transfer funds to the right accounts. A model mandate form has been prescribed for the purpose and is available in the ECS Credit Procedural Guidelines. The beneficiary has to notify the changes to the User Institution so that the correct information can be incorporated in its records. This will ensure that transactions do not get rejected at the beneficiary's bank branch due to inconsistencies/mismatch in the data sent by the user institution.

ECS can be used to transfer funds to Non Resident External (NRE) and Non Resident Ordinary (NRO) accounts in the country. This, however, is subject to the adherence to the provisions of the Foreign Exchange Management Act, 2000 (FEMA) and Wire Transfer Guidelines.

If a destination bank is not in a position to credit the beneficiary account due to any reason, the same would be returned to the ECS Centre to enable the ECS Centre to pass on the uncredited items to the User Institution through the Sponsor Bank. The User Institution can then initiate payment through alternate modes to the beneficiary.

In case of delayed credit by the destination bank, the destination bank would be liable to pay penal interest (at the prevailing RBI LAF Repo rate plus two per cent) from the due date of credit till the date of actual credit. Such penal interest should be credited to the destination account holder's account even if no claim is lodged to the effect by the destination account holder.

21.1.12 Processing/Service Charges Levied under ECS Credit

The Reserve Bank of India has deregulated the charges to be levied by sponsor banks from user institutions. The sponsor banks are, however, required to disclose the charges transparently. With effect from 1st July 2011, originating banks are required to pay a nominal charge of 25 paise per transaction to the clearing house and destination bank respectively. Destination bank branches have been directed to afford ECS Credit free of charge to the beneficiary account holders.

ECS Scheme in Country: Based on the geographical location of branches covered, there are three broad categories of ECS Schemes – Local ECS, Regional ECS, and National ECS. These schemes are either operated by RBI or by the designated commercial banks. NACH is also one of the forms of ECS system operated by NPCI and further details about NACH are available at NPCI website under the link *http://www.npci.org.in/clearing_faq.aspx.*

Local ECS: Local ECS is operating at 81 centers/locations across the country. At each of these ECS centers, the branch coverage is restricted to the geographical coverage of the clearing house, generally covering one city and/or satellite towns and suburbs adjoining the city.

Regional ECS: Regional ECS is operating at 9 centers/locations at various parts of the country. RECS facilitates the coverage all core-banking-enabled branches in a state or group of states and can be used by institutions desirous of reaching beneficiaries within the state/group of states. The system takes advantage of the core banking system in banks. Accordingly, even though the inter-bank settlement takes place centrally at one location in the state, the actual customers under the scheme may have their accounts at various bank branches across the length and breadth of the state/group of states.

National ECS: National ECS is the centralized version of ECS Credit which was launched in October 2008. The Scheme is operated at Mumbai and facilitates the coverage of all core-banking enabled branches located anywhere in the country. This system too takes advantage of the core banking system in banks. Accordingly, even though the inter-bank settlement takes place centrally at one location at Mumbai, the actual customers under the scheme may have their accounts at various bank branches across the length and breadth of the country. Banks are free to add any of their core-banking-enabled branches in NECS irrespective of their location. Details of NECS Scheme are available on the website of Reserve Bank of India at *http://www.rbi.org.in/scripts/bs_viewcontent.aspx?Id=2345*

The list of centers where the ECS facility is available has been placed on the website of Reserve Bank of India at *http://www.rbi.org.in/Scripts/ECSUserView.aspx?Id=26.* Similarly, the centre-wise list of bank branches participating at each location is available on the website of Reserve Bank of India at *http://www.rbi.org.in/scripts/ECSUserView.aspx?Id=27*

MICR Code

MICR is an acronym for Magnetic Ink Character Recognition. The MICR Code is a numeric code that uniquely identifies a bank-branch participating in the ECS Credit Scheme. This is a 9 digit code to identify the location of the bank branch; the first 3 characters represent the city, the next 3 the bank, and the last 3 the branch. The MICR Code allotted to a bank branch is printed on the MICR band of cheques issued by bank branches.

Advantages of ECS to the Banking System

Ans: The banking system has many benefits from ECS Debit such as:

- Freedom from paper handling and the resultant disadvantages of handling, receiving, and monitoring paper instruments presented in the clearing.
- Ease of processing and return for the destination bank branches. Destination bank branches can debit the customers' accounts after matching the account number of the customer in their database and the due verification of existence of valid mandate and its particulars. With core banking systems in place and straight-through-processing, this process can be completed with minimal manual intervention.
- Smooth process of reconciliation for the sponsor banks.
- Cost effective.

REVIEW QUESTIONS

1. Explain the concept of Electronic Clearing Services.
2. Discuss the purpose of Cheque Truncation System.
3. What is RTGS?
4. What is NEFT?
5. What is NRE and NRO?

Immediate Payment Services (IMPS) 22

22.1 INTRODUCTION

IMPS is an acronym of Immediate Payment Services. IMPS is the mode of fund transfer by mobile phone services. Under IMPS, the customer uses mobile phones as a medium of fund transfer. All applications used for mobile fund transfer use IMPS. This facility is given by NPCI (National Payments Corporation of India).

MICR..... Cheque/ Drafts

IMPS: Mobile phone banking is a new revolution in the banking system around the world. Mobile banking has several advantages; such as you can do internet banking, online shopping, and bills payment or transfer of the amount to another account in a secure manner. With the advent of mobile phone banking, mobile phones are gradually replacing your wallets, credit cards, debit cards, etc. at any place using your mobile phone buttons.

22.1.1 Process of Mobile Phone Banking

The customers having registered for mobile phone banking will enjoy facilities of balance inquiry, last few transactions, the cheque paid status, intra-bank fund transfers, (channelized through NEFT), book air tickets, movie tickets, etc. using their mobile phone just like internet banking. The greatest advantage of mobile phone banking is that it allows the sender to send money to the mobile number of the beneficiary just with the mobile number and MMID (Mobile Money Identifier) of the beneficiary. Here, the beneficiary does not disclose his/her account number and other financial critical details to the sender. The account details of the beneficiary will, therefore, remain confidential and out of reach of the remitter.

The latest development in Great Britain is that even money can be withdrawn from ATM, with the aid of their mobile phones. The Royal Bank of Scotland has introduced a new system, which facilitates their customers to withdraw cash up to GBP 100 from ATM, using their mobile phones. However, the said facility of cash withdrawal from ATM through mobile phone is yet to be introduced in India.

22.1.2 Parties to Mobile Banking System

For mobile phone banking transactions involves the following parties:

1. Remitter (Sender)
2. Beneficiary (Receiver)
3. Remitting Bank
4. Receiving Bank
5. NPCI-National Financial Switch (The facilitator)

The National Payments Corporation of India (NPCI) is the facilitator of Inter-bank Mobile Payment Service (IMPS).

Requirements to become registered remitter under mobile banking

1. KYC and AML formalities, as in the case of account opening, to be complied with.
2. Remitter shall have GPRs enabled mobile phones.
3. The remitter is required to register the mobile number for a mobile banking facility with his/her bank. Upon registration, he/she should generate the Mobile Money Identifier (MMID), which is a 7 digit number.
4. Bank would provide MPIN (Mobile Banking PIN) to the remitter (its customer), which is a secret-password of 4 digit number, to make payment.

The Beneficiary also needs to register at his bank:

1. No need to register for mobile banking.
2. The mobile number (of a beneficiary) should be linked to the account in the beneficiary's bank.
3. He/she has to collect Mobile Money Identifier (MMID) from his/her bank.

22.1.3 Procedure to send money

The procedure is similar to internet banking. Customer logs into his/her bank and select option for Funds Transfer-'IMPS', enters his/her account number to be debited, beneficiary's nickname, amount, creditors detail, etc. (depending upon the software of the remitting bank) and executes the transaction. The remitter gets the confirmation of the transaction done by way of SMS from his bank. The beneficiary gets the confirmation of credit to the account through SMS from his/her bank.

22.1.4 Limit for Transferring Money under Mobile Banking

The customer has to do the transaction through mobile banking only to the extent of the daily cap and the monthly cap fixed by the bank. Timing to transfer the funds.

22.1.5 Immediate Payment Service (IMPS)

Immediate Payment Service (IMPS) is an initiative of the National Payments Corporation of India (NPCI). It is a service through which money can be transferred immediately from one account to the other account, within the same bank or accounts across other banks. Upon registration, both the individuals are issued an MMID (Mobile Money Identifier) code from their respective banks. This is a 7 digit numeric code. To initiate the transaction, the sender in his mobile banking application needs to enter the registered mobile number of the receiver, MMID of the receiver, and amount to be transferred. Upon a successful transaction, the money gets credited in the account of the receiver instantly. This facility is available 24 × 7 and can be used through the mobile banking application. Some banks have also started providing this service through the internet banking profile of their customers. Though most banks offer this facility free of cost to encourage paperless payment system, ICICI bank, and Axis bank charge for it as per their respective NEFT charges.

Nowadays, money through this service can be transferred directly also by using the receiver's bank account number and IFSC code. In such a case, neither the receiver of the money needs to be registered for the mobile banking service of his bank, nor does he need MMID code. IMPS facility differs from NEFT and RTGS as there is no time limit to carry out the transaction. This facility can be availed 24 × 7 and on all public and bank holidays including RBI holidays.

22.1.6 Unified Payments Interface

Unified Payments Interface (UPI) is an instant real-time payment system developed by the National Payments Corporation of India facilitating inter-bank transactions. The interface is regulated by the Reserve Bank of India and works by instantly transferring funds between two bank accounts on a mobile platform. The Unified Payment Interface (UPI) can be thought of as an email ID for your money. It will be a unique identifier that your bank uses to transfer money and make payments using the IMPS (Immediate Payments Service). IMPS is faster than NEFT and lets you transfer money immediately and unlike NEFT, it works 24×7. This means that online payments will become much easier without requiring a digital wallet or credit or debit card.

22.1.7 Bharat Bill Payment System

Bharat Bill Payment System (BBPS) is an integrated bill payment system in India offering interoperable and accessible bill payment service to customers through a network of agents, enabling multiple payment modes and providing instant confirmation of payment. This is still in the implementation stage. Guidelines for implementation of this system were issued on November 28, 2014.

Comparison

The key difference between RTGS and NEFT is that while RTGS is on a gross settlement basis, NEFT is on a net settlement basis. Besides, RTGS facilitates real-time ("push") transfer, while NEFT involves twelve settlements from 8 am to 7 pm on weekdays and six settlements from 8 am to 1 pm on Saturdays. Customers can access the RTGS facility between 9 am to 4:30 pm on weekdays and 9 am to 1:30 pm on Saturday. Thus if a customer has given instruction to its bank to transfer money through NEFT to another bank in the morning hours, money would be transferred the same day, but if the instruction is given much later during the day, money may be transferred the next day.

RTGS facility is available in over 1,13,000 branches across India, while NEFT is available in little over 1,15,000 branches of 100 banks.

The facility of interbank mobile payment service (IMPS) is the round the clock payment system (24 hours payment system) available in almost all the public sectors and private sector banks. The following banks are having IMPS facilities.

All banks have mobile banking facilities in the present era excluding cooperative banks in India.

REVIEW QUESTIONS

1. Explain the concept of IMPS.
2. What is MICR cheques and drafts?
3. What is the process of Mobile Phone Banking?
4. What is Unified Payments Interface?
5. What is MMID?

National Electronic Funds Transfer (NEFT)

23

23.1 INTRODUCTION

National Electronic Funds Transfer (NEFT) is an electronic funds transfer system maintained by the Reserve Bank of India (RBI). Started in November 2005, the setup was established and maintained by the Institute for Development and Research in Banking Technology (IDRBT). NEFT enables bank customers in India to transfer funds between any two NEFT-enabled bank accounts on a one-to-one basis. It is done via electronic messages. Unlike real-time gross settlement (RTGS), fund transfers through the NEFT system do not occur in real-time basis. NEFT settles fund transfers in half-hourly batches with 23 settlements occurring between 8:00 am and 7:00 pm on weekdays and the first, third and fifth Saturday of the calendar month. Transfers initiated outside this time period are settled at the next available window. No settlements are made on the second and fourth Saturday of the month, or on Sundays, or on public holidays. From 2019 RBI provides the facility 24×7.

As of January 2011, NEFT facilities were available at 74,680 branches offices of 101 banks across the country (out of around 82,400 bank branches), and online through the website of NEFT-enabled banks. NEFT has gained popularity due to the ease and efficiency with which the transactions can be concluded. This is reflected by the fact that 42% of all electronic transactions in the 2008 financial year were NEFT transactions. This transaction is done when an account is less than 2 lakh. And it can be done 2-3 times a day.

23.2 NATIONAL ELECTRONIC FUNDS TRANSFER (NEFT)

NEFT Started in November 2005, the National Electronic Fund Transfer (NEFT) system is a nationwide system that facilitates individuals, firms and corporates to electronically transfer funds from any bank branch to any individual, firm or corporate having an account with any other bank branch in the country. It is done via electronic messages. Even though it is not on real-time basis like RTGS (Real-time Gross Settlement), hourly batches are run in order to speed up the transactions.

For being part of the NEFT funds transfer network, a bank branch has to be NEFT-enabled. NEFT has gained popularity due to its saving on time and the ease with which the transactions can be concluded. As of 31 January 2011, 74,680 branches or offices of 101 banks in the country (out of around 82,400 bank branches) were NEFT-enabled. Steps are being taken to further widen the coverage both in terms of banks and branch offices. As of 30 December 2017 total number of NEFT enabled branches was increased to 139682 of 188 banks.

23.2.1 Meaning of RTGS Transactions

RTGS stands an acronym for 'Real-time Gross Settlement'. The 'Real-time' means the processing of instructions takes place instantly at the time they are received. 'Gross Settlement' means the settlement of funds transfer instructions takes place separately for each instruction. Under the RTGS Scheme, individuals, firms, and corporate can electronically transfer large value funds to accounts of individuals, firms, or corporates having accounts with any other bank branch in the country participating in the Scheme. Funds transfer operation takes place on instruction by instruction basis continuously during the RTGS business hours.

The RTGS system is primarily meant for large value financial transactions. The minimum amount to be remitted under RTGS system is Rupees two lakh and no upper ceiling for an amount that could be transferred. In normal circumstances, the beneficiary branches have to credit the beneficiary's account within two hours of receiving the funds transfer message. If the money cannot be credited for any reason such as the name of the beneficiary or account number mentioned in the RTGS message is different, the receiving bank will return the money to the remitting bank within 2 hours. Once the money is received back by the remitting bank, the original debit entry in the customer's account is reversed. Considering that the funds settlement takes place in the books of the Reserve Bank of India, the payments are final and irrevocable. The RTGS service window for customer's transactions is available from 9.00 hours to 16.30 hours including working Saturdays. The cut-off for interbank transaction (Final cut-off) at 19.45 hours. IDL reversal takes place between 19.45 hours to 20 hours. The day ends for RTGS at 20.00 hours. However, the timings that the banks follow may vary depending on the customer timings of the bank branches. The Future Value dated Transaction of RTGS would enable the customers/participants to initiate RTGS transactions 3 working days in advance for settling in RTGS on the value date

23.2.2 Indo-Nepal Remittance Facility Scheme

Indo-Nepal Remittance Facility is a cross-border remittance scheme to transfer funds from India to Nepal, enabled under the NEFT Scheme. The scheme was launched to provide a safe and cost-efficient avenue to migrant Nepalese workers in India to remit money back to their families in Nepal. A remitter can transfer funds up to ₹50,000 (maximum permissible amount) from any of the NEFT-enabled branches in India. The beneficiary would receive funds in Nepalese Rupees.

23.2.3 Process of RTGS and NEFT

RTGS and NEFT transactions are the fastest electronic funds transfer systems available in India. Under the above systems, funds can be transferred from a bank by its customer to their own account or third parties having their account with another bank across the country. The RTGS and NEFT transactions are distinguished by the processing time taken by them. In RTGS, the processing of instructions takes place instantly at the time they are received rather than at some later time. NEFT operates in batches on an hourly basis.

Detailed process of NEFT is as follows:

1. The customer fills an application form providing details of the beneficiary (like name, bank, branch name, IFSC, account type and account number) and the amount to be remitted. The remitter authorizes his/her bank branch to debit his account and remit the specified amount to the beneficiary. This facility is also available through online banking, and some banks also offer the NEFT facility through ATMs.
2. The originating bank branch prepares a message and sends the message to its pooling centre (also called the NEFT Service Centre).
3. The pooling centre forwards the message to the NEFT Clearing Centre (operated by National Clearing Cell, Reserve Bank of India, Mumbai) to be included for the next available batch.
4. The Clearing Centre sorts the funds transfer transactions destination bank-wise and prepares accounting entries to receive funds from the originating banks (debit) and give the funds to the destination banks (credit). Thereafter, bank-wise remittance messages are forwarded to the destination banks through their pooling centre (NEFT Service Centre).
5. The destination banks receive the inward remittance messages from the Clearing Centre and pass on the credit to the beneficiary customers' accounts.

Settlement Timings

NEFT transfers are settled in half-hourly batches between 8 AM and 7 PM from Monday to Saturday (except the second and fourth Saturday of each month). No transactions are settled on Sundays and bank holidays. The second and fourth Saturdays of each month are declared as bank holidays for the entire calendar year. Any transaction initiated after a designated settlement time would be completed at the next available settlement time.

NEFT originally settled fund transfers in hourly batches. The RBI reduced clearance times to half-hourly batches in April 2016. In August 2019, the RBI announced that it would enable round-the-clock settlements from December 2019.

23.2.4 Service Charges for NEFT Transactions

The structure of charges is as follows:

Inward transactions at destination bank branches (for credit to beneficiary accounts):

- Free, no charges to be collected from beneficiaries

Outward transactions at originating bank branches (charges for the remitter):

- For transactions up to 10,000 (not exceeding) : 2.50 (+ GST)
- For transactions above 10,000 up to 1 lakh (not exceeding) : 5.00 (+ GST)
- For transactions above 1 lakh and up to 2 lakhs (not exceeding) : 15.00 (+ GST)
- For transactions above 2 lakhs : 25.00 (+ GST)

Charges Waived

The RBI announced on 11 June 2019 that all charges for via NEFT and RTGS collected from banks would be waived from 1 July 2019, and asked banks to pass on the benefits to customers.

23.2.5 The Pros and Cons of Electronic Check Conversions

Disclaimer

Today, many businesses are processing check payments as electronic check conversions. Typically, this allows businesses faster access to the funds in your checking account. Many consumers may be unaware that an ordinary paper check that is processed as an electronic check creates has different implications for them. This article will highlight some of the pros and cons of electronic check conversion payment methods for the consumer.

Pros

- If you have a dispute with a merchant and you paid via electronic check conversion then you have the right to have your financial institution investigate any transfers which you believe were unauthorized or incorrect. However, you only have 60 calendar days from the time the bank statement was sent to you to notify the bank of the problem. So, it is important for you to carefully review every statement that you receive.
- Merchants typically cite several benefits to the electronic check conversion payment system. They claim that it reduces their bank fees, reduces the time that their employees spend on deposits and reduces fraud. While these benefits directly benefit the merchants, they may also benefit consumers by preventing price increases.
- If you do not have a debit or credit card, many businesses will accept an electronic check conversion as a form of payment while they may not accept

traditional checks. This may allow you to purchase things that you would not otherwise be able to do absent a credit or debit card and you can do so with the risk of credit card debt since the money is withdrawn directly from your bank account.

Cons

Some of the drawbacks of this payment method for the consumer include:

- Funds are typically released from your bank account much faster than when you pay by ordinary check. Therefore, you must make sure that you have enough money in your account to immediately cover the payment.
- You will not receive any copies of the cancelled checks from your bank, even if you provided a paper check for payment.

The Electronic Funds Transfer Act requires that you be provided prior notice if your payment may be processed as an electronic check conversion. The notice may be included with your paper bill for items that you pay through the mail or posted by the cash register in a retail shop. Notice, in the form of a detailed receipt must also be provided to you after the transaction. The receipt should include the merchant's name, the date the transaction was processed and the amount of the transaction.

The Federal Trade Commission recommends that you carefully review your statement each month to make sure that all transactions were processed correctly and that you be vigilant in protecting your checking account number and other personal information since the information could be used to conduct an unauthorized electronic check conversion. If you believe that your rights have not been honored in an electronic check conversion transaction then you have the right to file a complaint with the Federal Trade Commission (FTC) by calling 1-877-FTC-HELP.

23.2.6 Speak to an Experienced Banking and Finance Attorney Today

This article is intended to be helpful and informative. But even common legal matters can become complex and stressful. A qualified banking and finance lawyer can address your particular legal needs, explain the law, and represent you in court. Take the first step now and contact a local banking and finance attorney to discuss your specific legal situation.

23.2.7 Meaning of IFSC

IFSC stands for a short form of for Indian Financial System Code is an alpha-numeric code that uniquely identifies a bank-branch participating in the Electronic Funds Transfer (NEFT/RTGS) systems. Alpha-numeric code is an 11 digit code with the first 4 alpha characters representing the bank, and the last 6 characters representing the branch. The 5th character is 0 (zero). IFSC is used by the NEFT & RTGS systems to identify the originating/destination banks/branches and also to route the messages appropriately to the concerned banks/branches.

23.3 ADVANTAGES AND DISADVANTAGES OF USING INTERNET BANKING AND NEFT

Internet banking marked the beginning of a new era in the banking sector as it has revolutionized the way banks operate. With Internet banking and money transfer methods like NEFT, banks have given their customers the right to manage their funds in a simplified manner. You are even able to get complete control over your credit card and bank account, using the online banking facility. A NEFT transaction, or National Electronic Funds Transfer, allows you to carry out a one-to-one money transfer in the quickest possible time. For such a transfer, you're just required to enter the bank details of the beneficiary and the IFSC code of your bank branch. One of the major reasons behind the popularity of Internet banking and NEFT transfer is that reputed institutions like ICICI and HDFC too are offering such facilities to customers. For making a transaction, you first need to create a user id on the official website of your banking institution. Once you've created an account, you need to add the respective ICICI IFSC code or HDFC IFSC code, depending upon your requirements. After you've added the beneficiary, you're ready to make or receive payments through NEFT and Internet banking. Benefits of NEFT and Internet Banking:

1. **Safe and Effective:** For a seamless movement of funds on the Internet, you could opt for NEFT as it helps you transfer any amount of money quickly.
2. **Low Processing Charges:** Internet banking and NEFT are flexible payment options which are very economical. For getting this facility, you don't have to reimburse a huge sum of money to your bank. The processing charges are quite low and you can transfer any amount of money without any difficulty.
3. **Highly Dependable:** NEFT, an integral aspect of Internet banking, is a highly dependable method of making payments and receiving funds online. Most of the banks in India are regulated under the norms set by RBI and, hence, the Internet banking facility too is quite safe in nature.
4. **Rapid Settlement:** Unlike the regular banking methods of fund transfer, NEFT transfer is really quick and you can enjoy rapid settlement of accounts, thereby improving the overall functionality of your business.
5. The remitter need not send the physical cheque or Demand Draft to the beneficiary.
6. The beneficiary need not visit his/her bank for depositing the paper instruments.
7. The beneficiary need not be apprehensive of loss/theft of physical instruments or the likelihood of fraudulent encashment thereof.
8. Cost effective.

9. Credit confirmation of the remittances sent by SMS or email.
10. Remitter can initiate the remittances from his home/place of work using internet banking also.
11. Near real-time transfer of the funds to the beneficiary account in a secure manner.

Disadvantages of NEFT and Internet Banking:

1. **Highly technical:** One of the major drawbacks of Internet banking and NEFT transfer in India is that this is a highly technical method of funds transfer which is not easy to operate for everyone. An individual with little knowledge of computers or the Internet might not be able to operate an Internet banking account easily.
2. **The risk involved with online payments:** Even though most of the banks in India take proper steps to secure an NEFT transaction, it is quite possible that your information might get passed on to a hacker if you're using an unsecured browser. This is one of the reasons why a lot of people across the country don't believe in this facility.

Even though Internet banking comes along with certain disadvantages, this is one of the best and the easiest methods of carrying out financial transactions in the country. As a customer, you should definitely give this online payment method a try.

REVIEW QUESTIONS

1. What is National Electronic Funds Transfer (NEFT)?
2. What is RTGS?
3. What are the pros and cons of Electronic cheque conversions?
4. What is the risk in SIP?
5. What is IFSC code? What does it identify?

Real-Time Gross Settlement (RTGS) 24

24.1 INTRODUCTION

Real-time Gross Settlement (RTGS) systems are specialist funds transfer systems where the transfer of money or securities takes place from one bank to any other bank on a "real-time" and on a "gross" basis. Settlement in "real-time" means a payment transaction is not subjected to any waiting period, with transactions being settled as soon as they are processed. "Gross settlement" means the transaction is settled one-to-one basis without bundling or netting with any other transaction. "Settlement" means that once processed, payments are final and irrevocable.

RTGS systems are typically used for high-value transactions that require and receive immediate clearing. In some countries, the RTGS systems may be the only way to get same-day cleared funds and so may be used when payments need to be settled urgently. However, most regular payments would not use an RTGS system, but instead would use a national payment system or automated clearing house that allows participants to batch and net payments. RTGS payments typically incur higher transaction costs and usually operated by a country's central bank.

24.2 REAL-TIME GROSS SETTLEMENT

The acronym 'RTGS' stands for real-time gross settlement. The Reserve Bank of India (India's Central Bank) maintains this payment network. Real-time Gross Settlement is a funds transfer mechanism where transfer of money takes place from one bank to another on a 'real-time' and on a 'gross' basis. This is the fastest possible money transfer system through the banking channel. Settlement in 'real-time' means payment transaction is not subjected to any waiting period. The transactions are settled as soon as they are processed. 'Gross settlement' means the transaction is settled on one to one basis without bunching with any other transaction. Considering that money transfer takes place in the books of the Reserve Bank of India, the payment is taken as final and irrevocable.

Fees for RTGS vary from bank to bank. RBI has prescribed the upper limit for the fees which can be charged by all banks both for NEFT and RTGS. Both the remitting and receiving must have core banking in place to enter into RTGS transactions. Core Banking enabled banks and branches are assigned an Indian Financial System Code

(IFSC) for RTGS and NEFT purposes. This is an eleven digit alphanumeric code and unique to each branch of the bank. The first four letters indicate the identity of the bank and the remaining seven numerals indicate a single branch. This code is provided on the cheque books, which are required for transactions along with the recipient's account number.

RTGS is a large value (minimum value of transaction should be ₹ 2,00,000) funds transfer system whereby financial intermediaries can settle interbank transfers for their own account as well as for their customers. The system effects the final settlement of interbank funds transfer on a continuous, transaction-by-transaction basis throughout the processing day. Customers can access the RTGS facility between 9 am to 4:30 pm (Interbank up to 6:30 pm) on weekdays and 9 am to 2:00 pm (Interbank up to 3:00 pm) on Saturdays. However, the timings that the banks follow may vary depending on the bank branch. Time-Varying Charges has been introduced w.e.f. 1 October 2011 by RBI. The basic purpose of RTGS is to facilitate the transactions which need immediate access for the completion of the transaction.

Banks could use balances maintained under the cash reserve ratio (CRR) and the intra-day liquidity (IDL) to be supplied by the central bank, for meeting any eventuality arising out of the real-time gross settlement (RTGS). The RBI fixed the IDL limit for banks to three times their net owned fund (NOF).

Since 26 August 2019, the RTGS service window for customers' transactions is available from 7:00 AM to 6:00 PM from Monday to Saturday (except the second and fourth Saturday of each month). No transactions are settled on Sundays and bank holidays.

The RBI announced on 11 June 2019 that all charges for payments via RTGS and National Electronic Funds Transfer (NEFT) collected from banks would be waived from 1 July 2019, and asked banks to pass on the benefits to customers.

24.2.1 History of RTGS

As of 1985, three central banks had implemented RTGS systems, while by the end of 2005, RTGS systems had been implemented by 90 central banks. The first system that had the attributes of an RTGS system was the US Fedwire system which was launched in 1970. This was based on a previous method of transferring funds electronically between US Federal Reserve banks via telegraph. The United Kingdom and France both independently developed RTGS type systems in 1984. The UK system was developed by the Bankers Clearing House in February 1984 and was called CHAPS. The French system was called SAGITTAIRE. Several other developed countries launched systems over the next few years. These systems were diverse in operation and technology, being country-specific as they were usually based upon previous processes and procedures used in each country.

In the 1990s international finance organizations emphasized the importance of large-value funds transfer systems which banks use to settle interbank transfers for their own account as well as for their customers as a key part of a country's financial infrastructure. By 1997 several countries, inside as well as outside the Group of Ten, had introduced real-time gross settlement systems for large-value funds transfers. Nearly all G-10 countries had plans to have RTGS systems in operation in the course of 1997 and many other countries were also considering introducing such systems.

24.2.2 RTGS Timings

Open for Business	7:00 AM
Initial Cut-off (Customer Transaction)	6:00 PM
Final Cut-off (Inter Bank Transaction)	7:45 PM
Intra-day liquidity (IDL) Reversal	7:45 PM to 8:00 PM
End of the Day	8:00 PM

24.2.3 Service Charge for RTGS

(*a*) Inward transaction– no charge to be levied.

(*b*) Outward transactions- For transactions of ₹ 2 lakhs to ₹ 5 lakhs -up to ₹ 25 per transaction plus applicable Time Varying Charges (₹ 1/- to ₹ 5/-); total not exceeding ₹ 30 per transaction, (+ GST). Above ₹ 5 lakhs - ₹ 50 per transaction plus applicable Time-Varying Charges (₹ 1/- to ₹ 5/-); total charges not exceeding ₹ 55 per transaction, (+ GST). No time-varying charges are applicable for RTGS transactions settled up to 1300 hrs. On 6 June 2019.

To push digital transactions RBI has removed charges for payments via NEFT and RTGS and asked banks to pass on the benefits to customers. This means that payments via NEFT and RTGS would become either free or charges would be drastically reduced.

24.2.4 Transactions Limit of RTGS

The minimum amount that can be transferred by RTGS is ₹ 2 lakh and there is no upper limit. There are no processing charges for inward transactions in RTGS. However, but for outward the RTGS charges are given below: For ₹ 2 - 5 lakh – not exceeding ₹ 30 per transaction. Above ₹ 5 lakh not exceeding ₹ 55 per transaction.

24.2.5 Timings for RTGS

The RTGS service window for customers is available from 9.00 hours to 16.30 hours on weekdays and from 9.00 hours to 13.30 hours on Saturdays for settlement at the RBI end. However, the timings that the banks follow may vary depending on the customer timings of the bank branches.

24.2.6 Transactions Supported through RTGS

The following are the transactions supported through RTGS system:

- Inter-bank Payments
- Customer Payments

- Own Account Transfers
- Net Clearing
- NDS / CCIL

24.2.7 Information Required for Remittance

The required information that the remitting customer would have to furnish to a bank for the remittance are as follows:

- Amount to be remitted
- Account number which is to be debited
- Name of the beneficiary bank
- Name of the beneficiary customer
- Account number of the beneficiary customer
- Sender to receiver information, if any
- The IFSC Number of the receiving branch.

24.2.8 Transaction Process involved in RTGS

The transaction process involved in RTGS is explained below in step by step procedure.

Step 1: The customer has to submit the outward Instruction slip.

Step 2: The verification of Instruction slip (Clear funds, name, and a/c no. of the customer, IFSC code, and signature) take place.

Step 3: The branch scans the Instruction slip and sends it to the RTGS Central Team.

Step 4: The branch will file the slip to maintain records.

Step 5: The RTGS Central Team executes the transaction in Finacle and Participant Interface (PI) of RTGS.

Step 6: Then the message moves to the Reserve Bank of India (RBI) Server.

Step 7: The bank's RTGS Settlement Account is debited, and the Beneficiary Bank's RTGS Settlement Account is credited.

Step 8: The beneficiary Bank passes the credit to the beneficiary customer's account.

Processing Charges

The processing charges or service charges for RTGS transactions are tabulated below:

Type	Amount	Service Charge
RTGS	From ₹ 2 lakh up to ₹ 5 lakh	Not exceeding ₹ 30/-
	From ₹ 5 lakh and above	Not exceeding ₹ 55/-

Volume and Value of Transactions

On a typical day, RTGS handles transactions a day. The approximate value of turnover ₹ 1,50,000 crores per day. Around 33000 branches at more than 3,000 cities/ towns and taluka places are covered under the RTGS system.

Track the Remittance Transaction

The tracking system depends on the arrangements made between the remitting customer and the remitting bank. Some banks with internet banking facility will offer this service.

Once the funds are credited to the beneficiary bank account, the remitting customer gets intimation from his bank either by a registered e-mail or by a message on the mobile.

Delay or Non-credit

If the amount transacted by the customer is not credited to the payee account in such cases, the customer can contact the bank or branch to resolve their issue.

If the issue is not solved satisfactorily, the Customer Service Department of RBI may be contacted.

Other Related Guides

Cheque truncation system: Cheque Truncation System Cheque truncation is a system for cheque clearing and settlement between banks that are based on electronic data/ images.

24.3 DIFFERENCE BETWEEN NEFT, RTGS & IMPS

24.3.1 NEFT, RTGS and IMPS

Most individuals use one or the other method of online money transfer in their lifetime. The convenience of transferring money online helps an individual in making most out of the modern technology-based banking services. When it comes to transferring money from one account to another, most banks provide multiple options based on various factors and customer's requirements. Currently, banks provide multiple transfer methods such as National Electronic Funds Transfer (NEFT), Real-time Gross Settlement (RTGS), Immediate Payment Service (IMPS), etc. Based on the value of the transaction, the speed of transfer, service availability, and other factors, each of the transfer will provide different kinds of features and flexibility. Though each of them has its own advantages and disadvantages, they provide flexibility and convenience to the customers. Moreover, many banks have their own digital wallets to facilitate additional methods of fund transfers online.

24.3.2 Basic Difference between NEFT, RTGS and IMPS

The following table illustrates the basic difference between the fund transfer methods:

	NEFT	RTGS	IMPS
Minimum transfer value	₹ 1	₹ 2 lakh	₹ 1
Maximum transfer value	No limit	No upper limit	₹ 2 lakh
Type of settlement	Batches	One-on-one settlement	One-on-one settlement
Speed of settlement	2 hours (subject to cut-off timings and batches)	Immediately	Immediately
Service availability	Weekdays: 12 batches between 8:00 a.m. - 6:30 p.m. Saturday: 6 batches between 8:00 a.m. 1:00 p.m. Sunday and bank holidays: Unavailable	Working Days: 7:00 a.m. - 6:00 p.m.	24/7
Trans-action fee	Up to ₹ 10,000 - ₹ 2.50 From ₹ 10,000 up to ₹ 1 lakh - ₹ 5 From ₹ 1 lakh up to ₹ 2 lakh - ₹ 15 From ₹ 2 lakh up to ₹ 5 lakh - ₹ 25 From ₹ 5 lakh up to ₹ 10 lakh - ₹ 50	Between ₹ 2 lakh up to ₹ 5 lakh - ₹ 30 From ₹ 5 lakh up to ₹ 10 lakh - ₹ 55 Time Varying Charge per Outward Transaction: 8:00 a.m. - 11:00 a.m. - Nil 11:00 a.m. - 1:00 p.m. - ₹ 2 1:00 p.m. - 6:00 p.m. - ₹ 5 Post 6:00 p.m. - ₹ 10	Up to ₹ 10,000 - ₹ 2.5 From ₹ 10,000 up to ₹ 1,00,000 - ₹ 5 From ₹ 1,00,000 up to ₹ 2,00,000 - ₹ 15
Online/ Offline	Both	Both	Online

24.3.3 Key Differences between NEFT, RTGS, and IMPS

Online transfer methods are subject to availability based on the customer's eligibility and level of access granted by the bank. Additionally, the limits on fund value, timings, settlement speed, and other factors are a part of the **online fund transfer** method to provide a positive experience to the customer when they choose one transfer method over the other. Currently, NEFT, RTGS, and IMPS are the most popular methods of fund transfer in India, few of the notable differences between these methods are listed as follows.

NEFT: The funds transferred under this method are settled in batches (based on Deferred Net Settlement (DNS) and at a specific time of the day. If the transfer is initiative beyond the cut-off time specified by RBI, the funds are typically settled on the next working day. At present, the fund transfer requests under NEFT are processed in twelve batches between 8 a.m. to 7 p.m. on weekdays and six batches between 8 a.m. to 1 p.m. on Saturdays. Unfortunately, NEFT is not available on Sundays and bank holidays. One of the biggest advantages of NEFT is the cost-effectiveness; an individual can carry out smaller value transfers without worrying about the transaction fee and service charges. A smaller fee on the transfer enables the individual to carry out more payments which make NEFT the most popular and extensively used method for online fund transfers.

Under NEFT, the transactions can be initiated and settled from the bank account of one particular bank to another bank's account throughout India at no additional cost apart from the standard charges, provided both the banks are a part of the NEFT transfer network (NEFT-enabled). Though some banks might have their own policies concerning the NEFT service provided by them, such as restrictions on transferring funds immediately to a newly added beneficiary, fund value limits restricting the value of transfer beyond a specified limit, etc., these protocols are proven to be effective for safeguarding the customer's financials.

RTGS: This type of transfer methods are applicable and available for fund transfers of a minimum of ₹ 2 lakh and there is no upper limit, however, the biggest advantage for RTGS is the fastest/real-time settlement factor. As soon as the transfer instructions are sent, the fund gets settled almost immediately. However, in order to take advantage of the RTGS facility, both the originator's and the beneficiary's account has to be RTGS-enabled. Even though most banks are a part of the vast and popular RTGS transfer network facilitated by RBI, individuals are recommended to either get in touch with their bank directly or refer to their online banking section to discover their eligibility concerning access to RTGS payment system. The transaction fee under RTGS is higher than the other methods due to the faster settlement speed performed on an instruction by instruction basis.

RTGS comes with limits on the minimum; however, there's no maximum fund value and it is efficiently used in situations where individuals and businesses require immediate settlement of high-value funds that are well within the specified limits. Efficiency, speed, and reliability factors are few among the many factors that make RTGS as one the most-sought medium of online fund transfers.

IMPS: Also known for being one of the popular and fastest methods of fund transfer, IMPS is used widely across most banks. Unlike other methods of fund transfer that become unavailable on bank holidays and during off working hours, IMPS functions 24/7 allowing a fund transfer at any time of the day. Similar to NEFT, IMPS also allows transfer of low value-funds but what makes it unique is, it immediately settles the funds. NEFT functions as more or less the combined version of NEFT and RTGS, where remitters are neither worried about the size of the fund and service availability nor do they have to be concerned about the settlement speed.

IMPS facility is provided only on the internet and online banking services. Few banks may offer SMS-based IMPS service to mobile banking users. Many of the digital wallets in India utilize IMPS services to credit the money from an individual's wallet to his/her bank account. Though IMPS provides an immediate fund settlement facility, the transaction fees are as low as NEFT.

Things to consider before initiating a fund transfer:

1. **Timings:** The timings for each type of fund transfer methods are specific to the bank. Since NEFT and RTGS are largely based on the bank's hours of operation, depending on the location and specific working hours, the service availability may differ for either of the party involved in the fund transfer.
2. **GST:** GST is applicable on the transaction fee as per the latest norms which are subject to change.
3. **Transaction fee:** A fee is charged for initiating the transfer and not for receiving the funds.
4. **Transfer network:** The remitter needs to check whether the beneficiary's account is eligible to receive funds or not since the bank might not be a part of the transfer network.

REVIEW QUESTIONS

1. What is NEFT?
2. What is RTGS? Explain the transaction Process involved in RTGS.
3. What is IMPS?
4. What is the difference NEFT, RTGS and IMPS?
5. Give the gist of the RTGS timings.

Systematic Investment Plan (SIPS) 25

25.1 INTRODUCTION

A Systematic Investment Plan or SIP is a smart and hassle-free mode for investing money in mutual funds. SIP allows you to invest a certain pre-determined amount at a regular interval (weekly, monthly, quarterly, etc.). A SIP is a planned approach towards investments and helps you increase the habit of saving and building wealth for the future.

25.1.1 Working of SIP

A SIP is a flexible and easy investment plan. Your money is auto-debited from your bank account and invested into a specific mutual fund scheme. You are allocated a certain number of units based on the ongoing market rate (called NAV or net asset value) for the day. Every time you invest money, additional units of the scheme are purchased at the market rate and added to your account. Hence, units are bought at different rates and investors benefit from Rupee-Cost Averaging and the Power of Compounding.

Rupee-Cost Averaging

With volatile markets, most investors remain speculative about the best time to invest and try to best 'time' for their entry into the market. Rupee-cost averaging allows you to opt-out of the guessing game. Since you are a regular investor, **your money fetches/purchases more units when the price level is low and lesser units in comparison to when the price is high.** During a volatile period, it may allow you to achieve a lower average cost per unit.

Power of Compounding

Albert Einstein once said, "Compound interest is the eighth wonder of the world. He who understands it, earns it... he who doesn't... pays it." The rule for compounding is simple - the sooner you start investing, your money grow very high in short time. Example; If you started investing ₹ 10000 a month on your 40th birthday, in 20 years (up to 60th birthday) you would have put aside ₹ 24 lakhs. If that investment grew by an average of 7% yearly, it would be worth ₹ 52.4 lakhs when you reach 60. However, if you started investing 10 years earlier, your ₹ 10000 each month would add up to ₹ 36 lakh over 30 years. Assuming the same average annual growth of 7%, you would have ₹ 1.22 Cr on your 60th birthday; more than double the amount you would have received if you had started ten years later!

25.1.2 Other Benefits of Systematic Investment Plans

Disciplined Saving: Discipline is the key to successful investments. When you invest through SIP, you commit yourself to save regularly. Every investment is a step towards attaining your financial objectives.

Flexibility: While it is advisable to continue SIP investments with a long-term perspective, there is no compulsion. Investors can discontinue the plan at any time. One can also increase/ decrease the amount being invested.

Long-Term Gains: Due to rupee-cost averaging and the power of compounding SIPs have the potential to deliver attractive returns over a long investment horizon.

Convenience: SIP is a hassle-free mode of investment. You can issue a standing instruction to your bank to facilitate auto-debits from your bank account. SIPs have proved to be an ideal mode of investment for retail investors who do not have the resources to pursue active investments.

Automated investment: SIP is a systematic investment plan which lets you invest a fixed amount periodically in a mutual fund. For example, if you start a monthly SIP of ₹ 100 in a mutual fund, that amount will automatically be deducted from your bank account and invested in that mutual fund every month on the pre-decided date. SIP is essentially an automated investing plan.

25.1.3 Benefits of Investing in SIP

Investing in SIP is always a good idea. It keeps you disciplined, is easy to monitor, takes advantage of rupee cost averaging, can be increased, or reduced anytime. SIP is considered the best investment habit because of the following reasons:

Flexibility: Increase or decrease the investment amount according to your convenience.

Liquidity: Withdraw the investment amount when you need it.

Simplicity: Simple and disciplined way to create wealth.

Inflation-Proof: Regular interval investment reduces the impact of inflation on savings.

Investing one-time

Try our Lump sum Calculator for Mutual Funds here-Lump sum.

25.1.4 Working of SIP Calculator

SIP returns are calculated according to compound interest. You can enter the amount you wish to invest every month, choose the number of years you wish to continue the investment for and our calculator will automatically calculate the amount of return. It will also show you a comparative your SIP return vs Fixed Deposits. You can also enter the target amount you would like to achieve and can revere calculate the SIP amount required to achieve it. You can set a return rate (Equity 15 %, Debt 8 % Balanced 10.5 %) or choose a mutual fund and calculate the SIP Returns.

25.1.5 Duration of Investment in SIP

There is no fixed rule for this but a SIP for five years and above, especially in equity or Equity Linked Saving Scheme (ELSS) mutual funds have a low risk for loss. Short-term investments in these funds can have higher returns but also come with a high risk of loss.

25.1.6 Lump Sum Investments in SIP

Lump sum investments are much safer. Since the markets go up and down (volatility) your investments in a SIP carry much lower risk as the investment points are spread out over a long tenure. When the markets are high, you buy fewer units of the fund and when the markets are low, you buy more units for the same amount.

25.1.7 Best Fund Schemes to Invest in SIP

Equity Mutual Funds, ELSS, and Balanced Mutual Funds are one of the best fund schemes to invest in SIP. All of these are meant for the long-term and hence a SIP allows you to stay invested in them without worrying too much.

25.1.8 Investment Process in SIP Upwardly

Once you have opted for a SIP through any platform, upwardly would send you an email with the procedure to add Bombay Stock exchange (BSE) as a biller on your bank website. This is just like adding utility payments like Electricity/Water/Phone on your banking website. Please remember to add BSE as the biller and not the Mutual Fund that you have invested in. It's a 2-minute process at your end and you can easily do that on your own. Typically it takes 3-5 business days for the SIP mandate to be approved by the bank. Once that is approved, your monthly investments would start. This is a completely paperless process.

Just in case you're Bank or the Mutual Fund (that you have opted for) do not have this option, we would like to do this NACH mandate form through email. This NACH mandate form needs to be signed by you. Please ensure that you do not make any other modifications to the NACH mandate else your Bank would reject your NACH mandate. Once you have signed the NACH mandate, the logistics partner would contact you and pick up the NACH mandate and that would be sent to your Bank for registration. Once your Bank has registered this NACH mandate, the amount of your investment would be debited every month from your account and sent to the Asset Management Company (AMC) for investment. Typically, the banks take 15–20 business days to approve this mandate. You would have the option of stopping or pausing this SIP through the upwardly platform as per your choice. You can also directly stop this SIP with the AMC.

25.1.9 Mutual Fund

A mutual fund is a professionally managed investment scheme. It is run by an asset management company (AMC) which acts as a mediator for the retail investors. The AMC pools in money from a large number of investors and invests it in equity shares, bonds, money market instruments, and other types of securities. Each investor, in return, is assigned a specific number of units proportionate to his invested amount in the fund. The investor is known as the unit holder. The unit holder shares the gains, losses, income, and expenses of the fund in proportion to his investment in the fund.

Working of Mutual Funds

The fund manager manages your mutual fund plan. He frames the investment strategies based on the investment objectives of the fund. The fund manager tracks the fund portfolio daily and decides when to buy/sell the shares of the underlying asset class. As a mutual fund investor, your mutual fund units depict your part of holdings in a specific scheme. These units are valued at Net Asset Value (NAV) which is determined at the end of every day. The NAV keeps fluctuating according to changes in the prices of fund's holdings. A unit holder can purchase or redeem the units as per the prevailing NAV. He participates proportionally in the gain or loss of the fund. SEBI is the regulator of all the mutual funds in India. It formulates the fund provisions keeping the interests of the investor in mind.

Investment Process in Mutual Funds

There are various avenues from where you can buy mutual fund units:

1. **Direct plans:** You can approach the asset management company (AMC) and invest in the direct plan of your choice. These plans have a low expense ratio because they don't charge distributor commission. Hence, you can earn a better rate of return.

2. **Mutual fund distributor:** You can contact a registered mutual fund distributor. He will help you out to complete the required documentation. You will be investing in a regular plan which will charge a distributor's commission.

3. **Online:** There are several third-party portals available online. You can visit one of them and invest in a variety of mutual funds by paying a nominal fee.

Nature of Investment (SIP/Lump sum)

There are two ways of investing money in your favorite mutual funds. You can either invest through a SIP or invest a lump sum amount.

1. **Lump sum investment:** Here, you spend a considerable portion of your disposable funds in a mutual fund scheme of your choice. It generally happens when you receive a massive corpus from the sale of an asset or retirement benefits. However, investing a lump sum involves higher risk. That's why it is always recommended to go via the SIP route.

2. Systematic Investment Plan (SIP): Under a SIP, you instruct the bank to deduct a fixed sum from your savings account every month and invest it in the said mutual fund scheme. In this way, you can buy units continuously without worrying about the right time to enter the market. You can also get the benefit of rupee cost averaging and enjoy the power of compounding.

Working of Mutual Fund Calculator

Your mutual fund scheme is generating returns in line with your expectation. You're wondering the amount of SIP would help you in personal goal accomplishment. The Mutual Fund Calculator will give you the investment value at maturity by calculating fund returns according to your investment horizon. You can adjust the variables of the calculator such as SIP/lump sum, amount of investment, frequency of SIP, the expected rate of returns, and the duration of SIP.

Invest in SIP or a one-time investment (lump sum), choosing one depends on your familiarity with Mutual Funds, the fund you want to invest in and depend on your goals. If you want to invest regularly to accumulate sufficient capital for a goal, invest in a suitable equity scheme through SIP. If you want to save from your monthly income and put it in an option where you can grow your money significantly so that in the long run it'll be sufficient fund for your child's higher education, SIP is the best option for this. You can take help from a fund adviser if needed.

If you have surplus cash now, like a – bonus, proceeds from property sale or retirement corpus, but you want to make optimum use of your fund, for this go for lump sum investment in a debt or liquid fund.

25.1.10 Invest In Mutual Funds through a SIP Investment

Among the many mantras of investing, market timing is the most commonly used one, where investors look to invest, book profits, and exit quite often. There are also diehard followers of the "invest and hold" strategy. At the same time, there are many people who believe that portfolio rebalancing across asset classes, such as equity and debt is a must.

There are several theories of investing, retail investors are better off by simply investing consistently. As it is believed that since no one can time the markets consistently, there is no point in chasing this strategy. One should look for the cost averaging theory, popularly known a systematic investment plan (SIP).

Systematic Investment Plan (SIP) is a smart financial planning tool that helps you build wealth, step by step, over a period of time. You can start a SIP for ₹ 2500 per month and benefit from the power of compounding and rupee-cost averaging. This disciplined approach helps you to hedge the investment against inflation.

1. Disciplined Investing Approach: Some of you may opt for stock options by timing the market to accrue wealth. However, timing the market calls for market knowledge, research, technical analysis, and a lot of time from your end. Further, it could also be risky. But through disciplined, regular investments you can stop worrying about when and how much to invest. In a way, it eliminates the need to actively tracking the market and SIP helps you to achieve just that.

2. Takes Advantage of Rupee Cost Averaging: Rupee Cost Averaging is an effective investment strategy that eliminates the need to time the market. All one has to do is to invest a fixed pre-decided amount of money on a regular basis for a long period of time. Since the amount invested is constant one buys more units when the price is low and fewer units when the price is high which may mean a lower average cost.

3. Simple, Convenient, and easy to Monitor: You do not have to take time from your schedule to make your investments. With a completed application form, one can just submit post-dated cheques or avail the Magnum Easy Pay (auto-debit) facility and relax. You can monitor your progress of investment through the periodic statement of accounts.

4. Benefits of Compounding: The key to building wealth is to start investing early and to keep investing regularly. A small amount of money invested regularly can grow to a large sum. This helps in creating a substantial amount of wealth which includes your own contribution, plus returns compounded over the years. For example, the following graph demonstrates the effect of returns on monthly investments of ₹1000 per month for a period of 30 years.

5. Power of starting early Helps create Wealth: The earlier one starts regular savings, the easier it is for wealth creation. ₹ 1000 were invested on a monthly basis until the retirement age of 60 years. The rate of return on investment was assumed at 10% p.a. It can be seen that even a five-year delay can make a significant reduction in the overall creation of wealth.

Secrets of Wealth Creation

Plan your SIP Investments. Frequent Intervals i.e. monthly, quarterly or semi-annually increase chances of buying units when prices are low.

Chart out a Long-term Investment Plan: SIP works best for long-term investment periods and helps the long-term investor reap good returns over a period of time. Long-term investors tend to profit from the appreciation markets tend to show in the long-term.

Diversify Your Investments: Since, Mutual Fund investments are diversified; it not only reduces risk but also helps in optimizing returns.

25.2 ADVANTAGES AND DISADVANTAGES OF INVESTING IN SIP

25.2.1 Advantages of Investing in SIP

The main advantage of SIP can be realized when the market is bearish. When the market is falling continuously then you can more units (NAV's) in SIP, over the long period of time-based on the principle of the power of compounding. Here your money goes on averaging in the downtrend market hence your loss also gets drastically reduced. For example, suppose NAV of a particular fund is 50 when you started investment and after 2 years if the NAV is again 45 due to bearish market you are in a loss of 5 rupees per unit if you are a lump sum investor but in case you SIP your loss would have negative.

You don't know when the market is going up and you don't know when the market is going down. But you know for sure you are employed and get pay cheque. SIP Investing is about putting money in the right places at right times and hoping. Money can grow on trees, you just need to plant the right seeds.

1. It's called 8th wonder of the world due to the power of compounding and building steady wealth.
2. MF or SIP beats inflation.
3. It can be started with a small amount of ₹ 500 and later increased in the same multiples.
4. It's awesome since it averages ups and downs of the market.
5. Even if you miss one SIP on a particular date the SIP doesn't penalize you.
6. It would make you defiantly wealthy after 7 years of regular investment.

25.2.2 Disadvantages of Investing in SIP

When you invest slowly into the market, the market goes up too quickly for you to catch the full swing of the rally. You wish you had invested everything back in April 14, so that you will be in super profit by Jan. 15, and in moderate profit by now.

Here you will have to take chance.

It's like scoring singles and twos in cricket and let the other batsman go for big shots, and decide to stay till the end.

Pros of Investment in SIP

Minimum Amount: A big benefit of SIPs is that it allows one to participate in the share market at very low amounts. The minimum investment amount in a systematic investment plan can be as low as 500 rupees.

Helps in Tax Saving: The SIP investments are liable for deductions under Section 80C of the Income Tax Act. By investing in a SIP, one can save somewhere between INR ₹ 15,000 to INR ₹ 45,000 in taxes per year.

Power of Compounding: One of the best benefits of SIP investment is to see the increased value and growth of your invested wealth. And, investors realizes this over the long term when his/her investment period is maturing. With the invested amount increasing over time, the accumulated amount keeps on increasing and this being invested in the market would be subject to market growth and returns (refer to the figure as follows).

Growth of Money Over Time

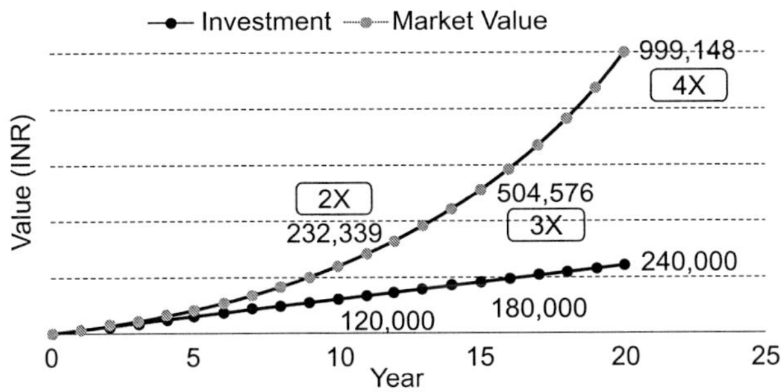

INR 1,000 invested per month for 20 years

Assists in Retirement Planning: SIP invests your money in growth assets and helps you create a powerful corpus for your retirement. For instance, let's suppose you earn INR 30,000 per month at the age of 25 and invest INR 2500 per month in a SIP, increasing it by 10% every year, your savings would be the following- At the age of 60, with the balanced return of 12% per annum, you will earn INR 4.12 crores. Therefore, when deciding how to save money for your retirement, make sure you invest in SIP.

Habit of Saving: Another important benefit of SIPs is that prospective investors see it as a tool that inculcates the habit of saving. With a low investment amount, systematic nature and one-time registration it becomes a method of forced saving.

Cons of Investment in SIP

These are a few major risks in a SIP, some of these are discussed below:

Price Risk: Sometimes your investment in a SIP can go down and you can end up with a value lower than what you invested depending on how the market behaves. The risk in SIP is however related to holding period and usually, the longer the holding period, the lower the risk. With higher holding period the probability of making profit increases.

Credit Risk: When the bond of a particular entity or company undergoes a downgrade by a credit rating agency, its price falls. If the price falls, this impacts the overall value of the portfolio. This is called credit risk.

Liquidity Risk: Usually with mutual funds, liquidity is not an issue, however, there have been periods, when there was an issue in selling securities (like bonds) and that certain mutual funds had to limit withdrawals from some schemes. The equity market is fairly liquid. However, if the sale quantity exceeds the numbers of buyers by a large amount, then this will result in an issue, hence making subsequent payouts a problem and hence liquidity risk.

Fund Management Risk: Another risk in SIP is that the chosen scheme may not deliver up to expectations and performance may be much lower than expected. The Fund Manager may under-deliver on performance, and this will lead to low returns on the SIP investments.

25.3 RISK IN SIP

Assessment of Risk in SIP Investment Updated on November 27, 2019, the risk in SIP varies for different Types of Mutual Funds. Investing in Mutual Funds via SIP (Systematic Investment Plan) involves market-linked risks that are certainly higher for Equity Funds than debt and balanced Mutual Funds. The risk in SIP depends on the investment option that is chosen considering the risk profile, risk appetite and liquidity. However, the risk in SIP can be managed and reduced by the fund managers and the fund house. Risk-in-sip to calculate the risk in SIP there are various tools available like sip calculator (also known as SIP return calculator).

25.3.1 Assessment of SIP Risks

Risk 1: The risk of SIP getting a negative return or price risk Mutual fund investments are subject to market risks, is a commonly heard term. What this means is that your investment in a SIP can go down and you can end up with a value lower than what you invested depending on how the market behaves. The risk in SIP is however related to the holding period and usually, the longer the holding period, the lower the risk. With higher holding period the probability of making profit increases. For e.g. have a look below for equity, a longer holding period for equity results in a lowering chance of loss. (This analysis done on the BSE Sensex from 1979 to 2016).

Risk 2: The risk being able to get your money back quickly or liquidity risk the ability to get your money back quickly depends on the underlying investments. Usually with mutual funds, this is not an issue, however, there have been periods (such in 2008), when there was an issue in selling securities (Bonds) and that certain mutual funds had to limit withdrawals from some schemes. The equity market is fairly liquid (meaning that buying and selling do not pose an issue). However, if the sale quantity exceeds the numbers of buyers by a large amount, then this will result in an issue, hence making subsequent payouts a problem and hence liquidity risk.

Risk 3: The risk of downgrade of a security or credit risk when the bond of a particular company/entity undergoes a downgrade by a credit rating agency, its price falls. If the price falls, this impacts the overall value of the portfolio. This is called credit risk.

Risk 4: The risk of the company not paying the owners of the bond their due or default risk when a company defaults on its payments to the bond holders, it's called default risk. Default-Risk-in-sip with the investor not getting their money back, this will impact their portfolio, negatively.

Risk 5: The risk of processing your transaction correctly or technology risk today, all transactions take place in the electronic mode. With the various touch-points, there is a possibility of a technological failure at various places, at the R & T Agent, the bank to debit funds etc. The non-processing of a transaction is also a risk in SIP.

Risk 6: The risk of scheme performance by the portfolio manager or fund management risk.

Another risk in SIP is that the chosen scheme may not deliver upto expectations, and performance may be much lower than expected. The Fund Manager may under-deliver on performance, and this will lead to low returns on the SIP investment. These are the major risks in a SIP, while we can go on and elaborate further risks in SIP like economy risk etc., most of these risks would fall under one or more of the categories above. Though there is definitely a risk in SIP, one should always remember that SIP or lump sum, this is just an investment route and NOT the underlying investment. One needs to look at the underlying investment, its risks, and then make a final decision.

REVIEW QUESTIONS

1. What is the concept of Systematic Investment Plans (SIPS)?
2. Discuss the Assessment of SIP Risks.
3. What is Liquidity Risk?
4. What is Fund Management Risk?
5. What are the advantages and disadvantages of investing in SIP?

MICR (Magnetic Ink Character Recognition Code)

26

26.1 INTRODUCTION

Magnetic Ink Character Recognition Code, known in short as **MICR code**, is a character-recognition technology used mainly by the banking industry to streamline the processing and clearance of cheques and other documents. MICR encoding, called the MICR line, is at the bottom of cheques and other vouchers and typically includes the document-type indicator, bank code, bank account number, cheque number, cheque amount (usually added after a cheque is presented for payment), and a control indicator. The format for the bank code and the bank account number is country-specific.

The technology allows MICR readers to scan and read the information directly into a data-collection device. Unlike barcode and similar technologies, MICR characters can be read easily by humans. MICR encoded documents can be processed much faster and more accurately than conventional Optical Character Reader (OCR) encoded documents.

The MICRs are used to read the characters inscribed on documents with ink and containing magnetized particles. MICR is used in banks to process large volumes of cheques being handled every day. Banks which employ MICR technology use a special type of cheques.

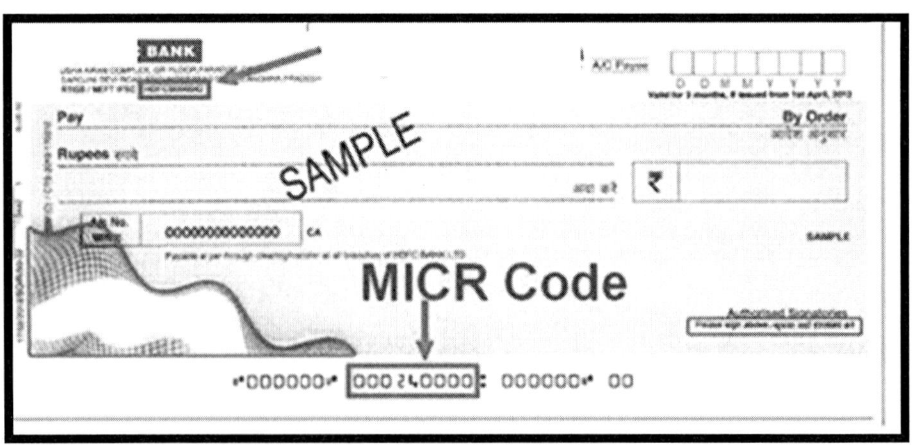

Fig. 26.1

The bank's identification code (viz. name, branch, etc.), account number and cheque number are pre-printed using characters from aspecial character set on all these cheques with special ink which contains magnetizable particles of iron oxide before cheques are given to the customer for use. The sample cheque which uses MICR technology is depicted in the figure. The information on the cheque is processed using MICR reader which updates accounts and performs various other processes.

Magnetic Ink Character Recognition (MICR) is a character-recognition technology used mainly by the banking industry to ease the processing and clearance of cheques and other documents. The MICR encoding called the MICR line, is at the bottom of cheques and other vouchers and typically includes the document-type indicator, bank code, bank account number, cheque number, cheque amount, and a control indicator. The technology allows MICR readers to scan and read the information directly into a data-collection device. Unlike barcodes and similar technologies, MICR characters can be read easily by humans. This MICR code is used By RBI in clearing process to identify the branch and bank for clearing processes.

Magnetic Ink Character Recognition (MICR) Line Updated Nov 21, 2019

Magnetic Ink Character Recognition (MICR) Line: Magnetic ink character recognition (MICR) is the line of numbers that appears at the bottom of a check. The MICR line is a group of three numbers, which are the check number, account number, and bank routing number. The MICR number includes the magnetic ink character recognition line that's printed using technology that allows certain computers to read and process the printed information.

Key Takeaways

Magnetic ink character recognition is the line on the bottom of a personal check that includes the account, routing, and check numbers.

MICR numbers are readable by individuals and computers, where its special font helps limit check fraud.

MICR benefits include quickly facilitating routing information and making it difficult to alter checks.

Working of Magnetic Ink Character Recognition (MICR) Line

The MICR number is used mainly by the banking industry. A benefit of MICR over other computer-readable information such as bar codes is that humans are able to read MICR numbers. The two MICR fonts that are used worldwide are E-13B and CMC-7. These unique fonts are used to help computers recognize the characters and limit check fraud.

The MICR number allows computers to rapidly internalize a check number, routing number, account number and other numbers or information from printed documents, such as a personal check. The MICR number, which is sometimes confused with just the account number, is printed with magnetic ink or toner on a check, usually in one of two major MICR fonts. The magnetic ink allows the computer to read the characters on a check even if they have been covered with signatures, cancellation marks, or other marks.

Benefits of MICR Line

One of the benefits of the magnetic ink character recognition line is its ability to quickly facilitate the use of routing numbers. A routing number (or routing transit number) is a specific nine-digit numerical code, which banking and other financial institutions use for the purpose of clearing funds and/or processing checks in the U.S. As it appears on the front of a cheque, the routing number represents the bank that holds the account from which funds are to be drawn. Wire transfers and direct deposits often rely on routing numbers.

Unfortunately, fraud happens throughout the financial services industry. The definition of fraud is an intentionally deceptive action, designed to provide the perpetrator with an unlawful gain. A range of fraud types exists, including tax fraud, credit card fraud, wire fraud, securities fraud and bankruptcy fraud.

The magnetic ink character recognition line can help prevent financial fraud through the use of its special magnetic ink and unique fonts. For example, MICR makes it challenging to alter checks. An altered check is when someone intentionally and materially changes the name of the payee or the amount of the check.

The Uniform Commercial Code (UCC) Section 3-407 breaks down the term alteration even further. The UCC is a set of business laws that regulate financial contracts. Articles Nine deal with separate aspects of banking and loans.

International Spread

There are two major MICR fonts in use: E-13B and CMC-7. There is no particular international agreement on which countries use which font. In practice, this does not create particular problems as cheques and other vouchers do not usually flow out of a particular jurisdiction.

The MICR E-13B font has been adopted as the international standard in ISO 1004:1995, and is the standard in Australia, Canada, the United Kingdom, the United States, as well as Central America and much of Asia, besides other countries. The CMC-7 font is widely used in Europe, including France and Italy, and South America, including Argentina, Brazil, Mexico, besides other countries.

Israel is the only country that can use both fonts simultaneously, though the practice makes the system significantly less efficient. This situation is the product of the Israelis adopting CMC-7, while the Palestinians opted for E-13B.

Fonts

E-13B

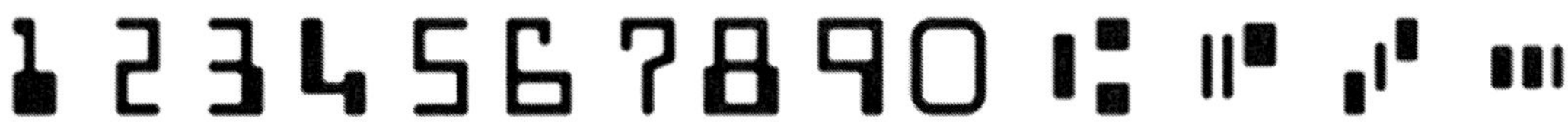

MICR E-13B font of 14 characters. The control characters bracketing each numeral block are (from left to right) transit, on-us, amount and dash.

E-13B has a 14 character set, comprising the 10 decimal digits and the following symbols:

- (Transit: used to delimit a bank code),
- (On-us: used to delimit a customer account number),
- (Amount: used to delimit a transaction amount),
- (Dash: used to delimit parts of numbers e.g., routing numbers or account numbers).

The E-13B repertoire can be represented in Unicode (see below). Prior to Unicode, it could be encoded according to ISO 2033:1983.

CMC-7

MICR CMC-7 font of 15 characters. The control characters after the numerals are (from left to right) internal, terminator, amount, routing, and an unused character.

CMC-7 has a 15 character set, comprising the 10 numeric digits and 5 control characters, internal, terminator, amount, routing, and an unused character. CMC-7 has a barcode format, with every character having two distinct large gaps in different places, as well as distinct patterns in between, to minimize any chance for character confusion while reading.

MICR Reader

MICR characters are printed on documents in one of the two MICR fonts, using magnetizable (commonly known as magnetic) ink or toner, usually containing iron oxide. In scanning, the document is passed through a MICR reader, which performs two functions, the magnetization of the ink and the detection of the characters. The characters are read by a MICR reader head, a device similar to the playback head of a tape recorder. As each character passes over the head, it produces a unique waveform that can be easily identified by the system.

The use of MICR allows the characters to be read reliably even if they have been overprinted or obscured by other marks, such as cancellation stamps and the signature. The error rate for the magnetic scanning of a typical cheque is smaller than with optical character recognition systems. For well printed MICR documents, the "can't read" rate is usually less than 1%, while the substitution rate (misread rate) is in the order of 1 per 100,000 characters Rejected items are hand processed.

MICR readers are the primary tool for cheque sorting and are utilized across the cheque distribution network at multiple stages. For example, a merchant will use a MICR reader to sort cheques by the bank and send the sorted cheques to a clearing house for redistribution to those banks. Upon receipt, the banks perform another MICR sort to determine which customer's account is charged and to which branch the cheque should be sent on its way back to the customer. However, many banks no longer offer this last step of returning the cheque to the customer. Instead, cheques are scanned and stored digitally. Sorting of cheques is done as per the geographical coverage of banks in a nation.

Unicode

MICR characters were added to the Unicode Standard in June 1993 with the release of version 1.1.

The Unicode block that includes MICR characters is called Optical Character Recognition and covers U+2440–U+245F:

26.2 HISTORY OF MICR

Before the mid-1940s, cheques were processed manually using the Sort-A-Matic or Top Tab Key method. The processing and clearance of cheques were very time consuming and was a significant cost in cheque clearance and bank operations. As the number of cheques increased, ways were sought to automating the process. Standards were developed to ensure uniformity in financial institutions. By the mid-1950s, the Stanford Research Institute and General Electric Computer Laboratory had developed the first automated system to process cheques using MICR. The same team also developed the E13B MICR font. "E" refers to the font being the fifth considered and "B" to the fact that it was the second version. The "13" refers to the 0.013- inch character grid.

The trial of MICR E13B font was shown to the American Bankers Association (ABA) in July 1956, which adopted it in 1958 as the MICR standard for negotiable documents in the United States. ABA adopted MICR as its standard because machines could read MICR accurately and MICR could be printed using existing technology. Also, MICR remained machine-readable, even though over stamping, marking, mutilation, and more. The first cheques using MICR were printed by the end of 1959. Although compliance with MICR standards was voluntary in the United States, it had been almost universally adopted in the United States by 1963. In 1963, ANSI adopted the ABA's E13B font as the American standard for MICR printing and E13B was also standardized as ISO 1004:1995.

Other countries set their own standards, though the MICR readers and most other equipment were US manufactured. MICR technology has been adopted in many countries, with some variations. The E13B font was adopted as the standard in the United States, Canada, United Kingdom, Australia, and many other countries. In Australia, the system is managed by the Australian Payments Network.

The CMC-7 font was developed in France by Groupe Bull in 1957. It was adopted as the MICR standard in Argentina, France, Italy, and some other European countries.

In the 1960s, the MICR fonts became a symbol of modernity or futurism, leading to the creation of lookalike "computer" typefaces that imitated the appearance of the MICR fonts, which unlike real MICR fonts, had a full character set.

MICR E-13B is also used to encode information in other applications, such as sales promotions, coupons, credit cards, airline tickets, insurance premium receipts, deposit tickets, and more. E13B is the version specifically developed for offset litho printing. There was a subtly different version for letterpress, called E13A. Also, there was a rival system named 'Fred' (Figure Reading Electronic Device) which used figures that looked more conventional.

MICR characters are printed on documents in one of the two MICR fonts, using magnetizable (commonly known as magnetic) ink or toner, usually containing iron oxide. In scanning, the document is passed through a MICR reader, which performs two functions, the magnetization of the ink and the detection of the characters. The characters are read by a MICR reader head, a device similar to the playback head of a tape recorder. As each character passes over the head, it produces a unique waveform that can be easily identified by the system.

The use of MICR allows the characters to be read reliably even if they have been overprinted or obscured by other marks, such as cancellation stamps and the signature. The error rate for the magnetic scanning of a typical cheque is smaller than with optical character recognition systems. For well printed MICR documents, the "can't read" rate is usually less than 1%, while the substitution rate (misread rate) is in the order of 1 per 100,000 characters. Rejected items are hand processed.

MICR readers are the primary tool for cheque sorting and are utilised across the cheque distribution network at multiple stages. For example, a merchant will use a MICR reader to sort cheques by the bank and send the sorted cheques to a clearing house for redistribution to those banks. Upon receipt, the banks perform another MICR sort to determine which customer's account is charged and to which branch the cheque should be sent on its way back to the customer. However, many banks no longer offer this last step of returning the cheque to the customer. Instead, cheques are scanned and stored digitally. Sorting of cheques is done as per the geographical coverage of banks in a nation.

26.3 ADVANTAGES AND DISADVANTAGES OF MAGNETIC INK CHARACTER RECOGNITION

The last line on all checks in the United States and many other countries is printed using a special character font family and technology known as magnetic ink character recognition. Banks use the technique to verify the validity and enhance the security of signed checks, while some airlines use MICR to validate flight tickets. However, the technology is expensive and often impractical when used in small businesses. MICR characters are printed with a magnetic toner or ink made of iron oxide. A MICR reader or scanner magnetizes the characters before it decodes the complete text. The characters are then run through a MICR read head a device that converts the characters to waveform, which are then identified by the system. Someone is signing a blank check.

Benefits or Advantages of MICR

Following are the benefits or advantages of MICR:

1. In spite of rough handling, one can read the MICR information with high degree of accuracy. The processing of MICR information is fast.
2. It offers greater security compared to Optical Character Recognition (OCR) technology as printed characters cannot be altered.
3. There is no manual input and hence errors are reduced.
4. The characters can be read even if somebody writes on them. This is due to the fact that special ink containing iron particles is used to print the characters.
5. The document is not easy to forge.

Drawbacks or Disadvantages of MICR

Following are the drawbacks or disadvantages of MICR:

1. **Time Consuming Standards:** The printing of MICR is demanding, setting precise but difficult-to-achieve standards, which is a distinct disadvantage in terms of time consumption. The American National Standards Institute (ANSI) implements and manages all MICR printing standards. It sets precise requirements for MICR character fonts, MICR registration, paper-moisture content, and grain and toner adhesion. All MICR character fonts must meet ANSI requirements. Standard X9.27-1995 lays down font standards while ANSI standard X9.7-1990 specifies line positioning of MICR characters. Additionally, the two published standards currently used for MICR includes the American Bankers Association (ABA) standards 092200 and ABA 092700, which stipulate how and where the MICR characters are printed on the check. ABA 092200 specifies the printing requirements for MICR and ABA 092700 stipulates printing locations and placement. MICR fonts that do not adhere to these standards will lead to rejected checks at banks and processing errors at other institutions.

2. **Expensive Equipment:** MICR readers are expensive and capable of recognizing only MICR fonts written in a specific format. MICR printers run on cartridges that cost far more than plain ink toner cartridges. As of March 2010, a single HP 05A MICR toner cartridge costs $110 and an HP 42X MICR toner cartridge costs $248, as opposed to the price of a single HP 60XL inkjet toner cartridge that costs $33.

REVIEW QUESTIONS

1. What is MICR code? Discuss briefly.
2. Discuss the history of MICR.
3. What is the significance of Nov 21, 2019, regarding MICR code?
4. What do you mean by MICR Reader?
5. What are the advantages and disadvantages of MICR?

ANNEXURE

QUESTION PAPERS

End Term Examination

First Semester BBA (B&I) February 2023

Principles of Banking Code: BBA (B&I) 103

Time: 3 hours **Max Marks: 75**

Note: Attempt any five questions. All questions carry equal marks.

Q1. What is money? Discuss its evolution. What are the functions which are performed by it?

Q2. What is a banking system? What are the different types of banking systems? Which banking system is being followed in India? Also mention the importance of banking system for an economy.

Q3. Explain the policy of the Reserve Bank of India on detection and impounding of counterfeit currency. How does counterfeit currency pose threat for the banking system and economy?

Q4. What is credit control? What are the different methods of credit control used by Reserve Bank of India?

Q5. Define commercial banking. What are the important functions of a commercial bank? Explain how the role of a commercial bank has changed in the age of digitalisation.

Q6. What is the importance of customer relationship in context of a bank? Explain the measures taken by banks in India for better customer management and retention.

Q7. What is e-banking? What is its significance? Explain the different types of electronic fund transfer system in detail.

Q8. What is money laundering? Why is it a threat to the economic sovereignty? What are the different measures taken by the Indian government to control it?

End Term Examination
First Semester (BBA B&I) September-2014
Principles of Banking Paper code 18111

Note: Attempt all questions. Internal choice is indicated.

Q1. Write short notes on the following: (3×5=15)

(*a*) Money and near Money.

(*b*) Deflation.

(*c*) Credit creation.

(*d*) Call money market.

(*e*) Banking ombudsman.

Q2. What are the functions of money in Indian Economy? Examine the significance of money in capitalist economy and socialist system. 15)

Or

What are the controlling measures of price inflation? Distinguish between demand pull, and cost push inflation.

Q3. Compare the merits & demerits of unit banking & branch banking. Which system would you recommend to India. (15)

Or

Explain briefly the functions of RBI. What are the instruments of monetary policy available to RBI?

Q4. Explain briefly the structure and functions of Indian Financial System. (15)

Or

Write critical notes on: (3×5=15)

(*a*) Mutual Fund.

(*b*) Venture Capital.

(*c*) Merchant Banking.

Q5. Explain the main features of innovative banking in India. (15)

Or

Write short notes on: (3×5=15)

(*a*) Consumer credit.

(*b*) Education and housing loan.

(*c*) Social Banking.

End Term Examination
First Semester (BBA B&I) December 2013/ Jan 2014
Principles of Banking Paper code 18111

Note: Attempt all questions. Internal choice is indicated.

Q1. Write short notes on any three of the following: (3x5=15)

(*f*) Quantity theory of Money.

(*g*) Bank Credit & Bank Deposit.

(*h*) C.R.R & S.L.R.

(*i*) Merchant Banking Vs E-Banking.

Q2. What are the primary & dynamic functions of money? Explain the role of Money in Mixed economy. (15)

Or

Distinguish clearly between demand pull, cost push & sectorial inflation.

Q3. Compare the merits & demerits of unit banking & branch banking. Which system would you recommend to India? (15)

Or

What are the main objectives of monetary policy pursued by RBI?

Q4. Explain the nature of Indian Money Market. What are its functions? (15)

Or

Explain briefly the role of SEBI in controlling the Indian Capital Market?

Q5. What are the source & uses of funds in Commercial Banks?

Or

Write critical notes on: (3x5=15)

(*a*) Mutual Fund.

(*b*) Venture Capital Companies.

(*c*) E-Banking.

End Term Examination
First Semester (BBA B&I) December 2012
Principles of Banking Paper code 18111

Note: Attempt five questions including Q.No.1 which is compulsory.

Q1. Write short notes on the following: (3×5=15)

(*a*) Credit card trends.

(*b*) Merchant Banking.

(*c*) Structure of banks.

(*d*) Banking ombudsman scheme.

(*e*) Emerging trends in banking.

Q2. (*a*) Define money and explain the role of money in the functioning of the modern economy. (7)

(*b*) Critically examine the quantity theory of money. (8)

Q3. What is Inflation? Discuss the causes of Inflation and suggest the monetary measure to control the inflation. (3+5+7)

Q4. (*a*) Discuss the role of Reserve Bank of India as (5×2=10)

(*i*) Banker's Bank.

(*ii*) Banker's of the Government.

(*b*) Discuss the forms of Money Supply. (5)

Q5. "Banks are not only Purveyors of money but are also in an important sense manufactures of Money". Explain the statement by focusing on the process of credit creation by commercial banks. (15)

Q6. The Indian Financial Market is composed of two elements. The money market and the capital market explain the statement. (15)

Q7. (*a*) Evaluate the effectiveness of the monetary policy in developing economy. (7)

(*b*) "RBI uses its monetary policy for controlling deflationary situation in the economy by using one or more of the tools of monetary control" explain. (8)

Q8. (*a*) "Universal banking has resulted in the blessing of distinctive financial boundaries". Explain the statement with the help of an example of a universal bank. (10)

(*b*) What is venture capital? (5)

Q9. Write short notes on the following: (3×5=15)

(*a*) E-Banking.

(*b*) Value Chain analysis in banking industry.

(*c*) Project financing.

End Term Examination
First Semester (BBA B&I) December 2011
Principles of Banking Paper code 18111

Note: Attempt any five questions selecting at least one from each unit.

Q1. Write short notes on any three of the following: (3×5=15)

(*a*) Quantity theory of Money.

(*b*) Bank Credit & Bank Deposit.

(*c*) C.R.R & S.L.R.

(*d*) Merchant Banking Vs E-Banking.

Q2. What are the primary & dynamic functions of money? Explain the role of Money in Mixed economy. (15)

Or

Distinguish clearly between demand pull, cost push & sectorial inflation.

Q3. Compare the merits & demerits of unit banking & branch banking. Which system would you recommend to India? (15)

Or

What are the main objectives of monetary policy pursued by RBI?

Q4. Explain the nature of Indian Money Market. What are its functions? (15)

Or

Explain briefly the role of SEBI in controlling the Indian Capital Market.

Q5. What are the source & uses of funds in Commercial Banks?

Or

Write critical notes on: (3×5=15)

(*a*) Mutual Fund.

(*b*) Venture Capital Companies.

(*c*) E-Banking.

End Term Examination
First Semester (BBA B&I) December 2010
Principles of Banking Paper code 18111

Note: Attempt any five questions selecting at least one from each unit.

Q1. Write short notes on any three of the following: (3×5=15)

(*a*) Qualities of good money.

(*b*) Repo Rate as tool of Inflation control.

(*c*) Certificate of deposits.

(*d*) Banking ombudsman scheme.

Q2. What is demand for money? Explain the various motives due to which money is demanded. (15)

Or

What are the concepts of money supply? Describe the four measures of money supply adopted by RBI.

Q3. Explain the various methods of credit control which are adopted by RBI. (15)

Or

Draw a typical Balance Sheet of a commercial bank and explain its various components.

Q4. What do you mean by Money Market? What are the distinctive features of Indian Money Market? (15)

Or

How NBFCs are different from banks? Describe their role in the development of Indian Capital Market?

Q5. What do you mean by monetary policy of a country? What are the objectives of a monetary policy.

Or

Write short notes on any three of the following: (3×5=15)

(*a*) Venture Capital.

(*b*) E-Banking.

(*c*) Project Financing.

(*d*) Micro Financing.

End Term Examination
First Semester (BBA B&I) December 2009
Principles of Banking Paper code 18111

Note: Attempt all questions. Internal choice is indicated.

Q1. Write short notes on any three of the following: (3×5=15)

(*a*) Measures of money supply.

(*b*) Commercial paper.

(*c*) Group banking.

(*d*) Merchant Banking.

Q2. What is speculative demand for money? Explain the relationship between the rates of interest prevailing in the economy and bond prices with the help of an example. (15)

Or

What is Quantity Theory of Money? Explain cash transactions approach of quantity theory of money.

Q3. What different banking systems have evolved all over the world? Which banking system or mixture of systems is best suited to the Indian environment? (15)

Or

What are the various constituents of Indian Banking System? Explain the role of development banks in this system.

Q4. Discuss the various reforms that have been initiated by RBI to develop the Indian Money Market. (15)

Or

What is the composition of Indian Capital Market? What are the different steps taken by SEBI to improve practices and transparency in the Indian Capital Market?

Q5. What are the different types of deposits available to a customer in a bank? How the bank uses these deposits to comply with the various legal requirements and also earns profit?

Or

Write short notes on any three of the following: (3×5=15)

(*a*) Private placement.

(*b*) Prime lending rate.

(*c*) Priority sector advances.

(*d*) Value chain analysis.

End Term Examination
First Semester (BBA B&I) December 2008
Principles of Banking Paper code 18111

Note: Attempt all questions. Internal choice is indicated.

Q1. Write short notes on the following: (3×5=15)

(*a*) Role of SBI in the development of Agricultural Sector.

(*b*) The velocity of money.

(*c*) Value chain analysis in banking industry.

(*d*) Venture capital.

Q2. Explain the primary functions of money and describe the role played by money in the mechanism of a modern capitalist economy. (15)

Or

What is Quantity Theory of Money? Explain its significance in the context of understanding the factors determining the value of money?

Q3. Distinguish between cost push and demand pull inflation. Examine the view that there is nothing as cost push inflation and that every inflation is a demand pull inflation. (15)

Or

Why should inflation be controlled? To what extent has the price policy of the government been successful in checking inflation?

Q4. Discuss various methods by which the RBI seeks to contract and expand the total volume of bank credit in the country from time to time. (15)

Or

Write the characteristics of Indian Money Market. Outline the measures to improve the functioning of Indian Money Market.

Q5. Distinguish between branch banking and unit banking. Discuss the merits and limitations of branch banking. (15)

Or

What is Universal Banking? Explain the importance of credit cards and E-Banking in the present global context.